Acknowledgem

This book reflects
and an indexer on the East Coast, a tech editor,
production editor, and proofreader on the West Coast,
a tech editor in Colorado—and a proofreader in
Oklahoma! Barely a scrap of paper changed hands.
The Internet made it possible logistically, but a lot
of good, hard work was done by many people. Our
heartfelt thanks to:

Victor Gavenda, who did a masterful job of tech
editing, from cover to cover,

Kelly Kordes Anton, QuarkXPress expert, who,
along with Victor Gavenda, revised this edition
for QuarkXPress 7 and added many useful
"real world" tips,

Nancy Aldrich-Ruenzel, publisher, whose enthusiasm
and innovative ideas are keeping Peachpit Press at
the forefront of computer book publishing,

Nancy Davis, long-time editor at Peachpit, who
we've had the pleasure to work with for the first
time—and look forward to working with again,

Lisa Brazieal, production editor, who patiently
incorporated our countless last-minute changes
as she prepared the electronic files for printing,

Gary-Paul Prince, publicist, who gets the word out,

Cyndie Shaffstall, and her staff at Quark, Inc. for
their invaluable assistance,

Emily Glossbrenner of FireCrystal Communications,
for indexing,

Tracy O'Connell and *Ted Waitt*, for proofreading,

And *Malloy Incorporated*, for transforming our
QuarkXPress files into a printed book.

quark[1] /kwa:k/ *n. Physics* any of a group of (originally three) postulated components of elementary particles. Quarks are held to carry a charge one-third or two-thirds that of the proton. Many predictions of this theory have been corroborated by experiments but free quarks have yet to be observed. In a sense, quark theory recapitulates at a deeper level efforts earlier this century to explain all atomic properties in terms of electrons, protons, and neutrons [coined by M Gell-Mann, 1964, from phrase 'Three quarks for Muster Mark!' in James Joyce's *Finnegans Wake* (1939)].

quark[2] /kwa:k/ *n.* a type of low-fat curd cheese.

From The Oxford Encyclopedic English Dictionary, 1991, Oxford University Press

Table of Contents **T/C**

Note! New or substantially changed features are listed in **boldface.** In addition to the changes we have noted, there are dozens and dozens of new sidebars, introductory paragraphs, and other improvements throughout the book—more than we could note.

Chapter 2:   **Startup**

Getting started

Saving files

Working with layouts

Changing layout properties

Opening files

Chapter 4: **Text**

Table of Contents

Chapter 11: **Pictures and Text**

Pictures and text

Using Runaround

Applying drop shadows

Chapter 14: **Master Pages**

Using master pages

Chapter 15: **Color**

Creating colors

Deleting and replacing colors

Applying colors

Applying colors to tables

Chapter 17: **Search and Replace**

Word processing in QuarkXPress

Checking spelling

Find/Change

Chapter 18: **Béziers**

Bézier basics

Drawing Bézier items

Reshaping Bézier items

Chapter 19: **Libraries**

Chapter 20: **Synchronize**

Chapter 23: **Workgroups** *New chapter!*

Collaborating in QuarkXPress

Working with Job Jackets

Working with Composition Zones

Chapter 24: **Print**

Printing files

Exporting files

The Interface 1

> "Beauty! I've starved myself since
> you forgot about me. Now at least I
> shall die in peace…"
> "Live!" cried Beauty. "And let us
> marry. How could I live without you,
> my dearest Beast?"

1 *A text box with a frame*

Beauty & the Beast

2 *Text on a path*

3 *A picture in a picture box (with a delicate .5-point frame)*

4 *A picture in a box without a frame*

What is QuarkXPress?

QuarkXPress is a page layout application. A page layout application is a central gathering place for text, photographs, graphics, lines, and tables, all of which together make up a page or series of pages. QuarkXPress can be used to produce anything from a tiny hanging tag for a line of apparel to a multiple-volume encyclopedia. A finished layout can be output on a home laser printer (newsletter, party invitation, etc.), output on a high-end imagesetter for final printing by a commercial printer (book, magazine, brochure, etc.), or exported for online viewing.

This chapter is a reference guide to the basic QuarkXPress features. In the remaining chapters you'll learn how to actually build pages and page elements.

The QuarkXPress building blocks

- To place text on a page, you must type or import text into or onto a **text box 1** or **text path 2** of any shape.

  Similarly, to place a picture on a page, you must first create a container for it, whether it's a rectangular or irregularly shaped **picture box.** Then you can import a picture into it. If you want the border of a text or picture box to print, you must apply a frame to it **3**–**4**.

- **Lines** can be straight or curved and function as decorative elements. **Tables** hold a grid of cells, which in turn can contain text or pictures.

- A text box, text path, picture box, table, or line is called an **item.** The picture or text a box contains is called its **contents.**

- Tool selection appears as a step in most of the instructions in this book. To create an item, for example, you'll use an item creation tool, such as the Line tool or the Rectangle Text Box tool.

  To move a whole item or a group of items across a page, you'll use the **Item** tool 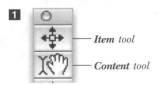, since you'll be working with the overall container.

  To copy/paste, delete, or restyle text or a picture after it is input or imported, you'll use the **Content** tool, since you'll be working with the contents of, not the outside of, the container.

  For some tasks, the Item and Content tools are interchangeable. For example, the Content tool can be used to reshape or resize items, or to select multiple items, and the Item tool can be used to import a picture.

- An item or its contents must be selected before either one can be modified **2**–**3**.

- The Measurements palette is context sensitive, offering different options and controls (grouped into sets called **tabs**) depending on which tool is selected and what type of item is selected. The default (Classic) tab displays the most commonly used item controls on the left and content controls on the right.

- When an item is selected with the Item tool, the Measurements palette provides options for modifying item attributes—dimensions, location, frame, color, etc. (**1**, next page). When an item is selected with the Content tool, the palette provides options for editing the content—font, size, picture scale, etc. (**2**, next page).

- To change tabs on the Measurements palette, choose from the navigator tab bar that pops up when you place the mouse near the palette. Point at an icon to see the name of its tab (see page 18).

The two workhorse tools

— *Item* tool
— *Content* tool

2 *A picture box that **isn't selected***

3 *Eight handles display when a box is **selected**.*

Navigating the Measurements palette

If you find yourself frequently switching among different **tabs** of the Measurements palette, you can keep the navigator tab bar open. Control-click/Right-click the Measurements palette title bar (at far left) and choose Always Show Tab Bar.

You can **cycle** through the tabs in the palette by pressing Cmd-Option-semicolon/Ctrl-Alt-semicolon. To cycle in reverse, use the same keyboard command but with a comma.

1 *When the **Item** tool and a **picture box** are selected, the Classic tab of the Measurements palette provides controls for modifying the box itself (left side) and controls for modifying the picture (right side). The navigator tab bar (at the top) lets you switch to the Frame, Runaround, Clipping, Space/Align, and Drop Shadow tabs.*

Item *information*   **Content** *information*

2 *When the **Content** tool and a **text box** are selected, the Classic tab provides controls for modifying the box itself (left side) and controls for formatting the text (right side). The navigator tab bar lets you switch to the Text, Frame, Runaround, Character Attributes, Paragraph Attributes, Space/Align, Tabs, and Drop Shadow tabs. Other controls are available for lines, text paths, tables, and multiple-selected items.*

3 *Using the **Item > Shape** submenu, you can convert one shape into another, such as a box into a line or a standard box into a Bézier box.*

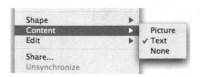

4 *Using the **Item > Content** submenu, you can change a text box into a picture box, or vice versa, or make any box contentless. You can change the content of a table cell, too.*

If it's not one thing, it's another

Our first encounter with QuarkXPress was in 1988 (ancient history in the software world), and we were impressed with its precision but frustrated by the inflexibility of its parent/child architecture. New items were drawn inside—and constrained by—existing items.

Now QuarkXPress is as flexible as it originally was brittle. Not only can you place an item anywhere, you can turn just about anything (text box, text path, picture box, or line) into something else **3**–**4**. Just to whet your appetite, these are a few of the easy conversions you can make:

- Change a text box into a picture box, a line into a box or a text path—and vice versa.

- Make a text box, picture box, or table cell contentless—capable only of being recolored or resized.

- Change a standard box into a Bézier box or Bézier line, or vice versa.

- Change a text character into a picture box—and then into a text box!

- Convert text into a table; convert a table into a text box or a group of items.

Easy Conversions

Pet Living

The Magazine for Pet Lovers

December 2007

A transparent text box on top of a picture box

SPECIAL HOLIDAY ISSUE
Kibble Snacks for Kwanzaa

Helping Your Pet Cope with Holiday Depression

Cat Treats for Chanukah

BOWSER

Type on a Bézier path

A drop shadow on text

A Bézier picture box with a frame

A line

Decorating the Doghouse
Schnauzer Strudel
PLUS
Cake Decorations
The Best Pet Gifts

*The QuarkXPress building blocks: **Picture boxes, text boxes, text paths, lines,** and tables (not illustrated).*

1 *This is a QuarkXPress **project window**. There are three **layouts** in this project, as indicated by the three tabs at the bottom of the project window.*

2 *You can split the QuarkXPress project window or open multiple windows to display multiple layouts at the same time.*

Projects and layouts

In most applications, one file on your computer represents one project that you're working on. And in fact, not too long ago, QuarkXPress restricted you to working in this way, too, as each file represented a single document intended for one publication in one page size. But since version 6, QuarkXPress files have become "project" files, which can contain multiple "layout" files. The advantage of this structure is that you can now store multiple layouts of different sizes for the same client in one project file **1**; you can synchronize text, pictures, and formatting across the layouts in the project; and you can ensure consistency with shared style sheets, colors, H&Js, and other features.

The projects and layouts structure is useful for campaigns—such as a restaurant opening—that share text and graphic elements but may not all be the same size. By splitting the project window or creating new **(NEW)** windows for the same project, you can display multiple layouts and drag elements between them **2**.

For users who are confused by the project/layout structure (in particular, having to name both the project and individual layouts), QuarkXPress 7 offers a Single **(NEW)** Layout Mode in which the project contains only a single layout.

Print layouts and Web layouts

As you learn how to create print layouts, bear in mind that most of the features used to create print layouts are also available for creating Web layouts. If you're designing for both print and the Web, the ability to create Web layouts with familiar tools may be helpful—plus, you can convert layouts from print to Web, easily share design elements, and synchronize print and Web content. Web layouts aren't covered in this book, per se, but are covered on the companion Web site (see page 34 for more details).

The QuarkXPress screen in Mac OS X

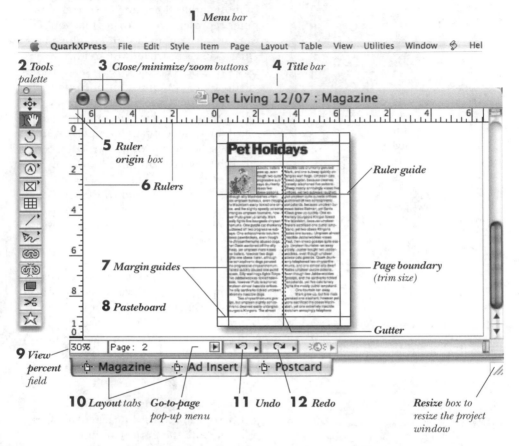

1 *Menu bar*

2 *Tools palette*

3 *Close/minimize/zoom buttons*

4 *Title bar*

5 *Ruler origin box*

6 *Rulers*

7 *Margin guides*

8 *Pasteboard*

Ruler guide

Page boundary (trim size)

Gutter

9 *View percent field*

10 *Layout tabs* *Go-to-page pop-up menu*

11 *Undo* **12** *Redo*

Resize box to resize the project window

By default, the Tools palette and the Measurements palette display along with a palette group containing the Style Sheets, Colors, and Page Layout palettes (shown ungrouped here).

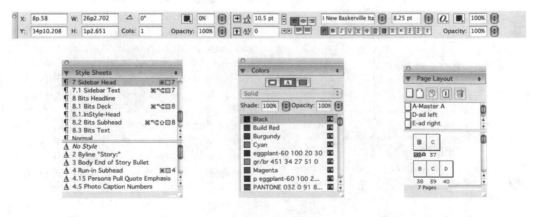

QuarkXPress Screen: Mac OS X

Key to the QuarkXPress screen in Mac OS X

1 *Menu bar*
Click any menu name to access a list of commands. XTension commands are also accessed via the menu bar.

2 *Palettes*
Most of the palettes are opened from the Window menu, including: Tools, Measurements, Page Layout, Style Sheets, Colors, Shared Content, Trap Information, Lists, Profile Information, Glyphs, Index, Layers, Picture Effects, PSD Import, and more. Many of the commands found under the menu bar can be accessed more quickly from the Measurements palette. Palettes that are open when you quit QuarkXPress will reopen when the application is **NEW** relaunched. You can save sets of open palettes for different kinds of tasks.

3 *Close/minimize/zoom buttons*
To close a file or a palette, click its close (red) button. Click the minimize (yellow) button to stow it in the Dock. Click the zoom (green) button to enlarge a window to maximum size.

4 *Title bar*
The name of the project and the currently displayed layout are displayed on the project title bar. Drag the title bar to move the project window.

5 *Ruler origin box*
Drag from the ruler origin box to reposition the intersection of the horizontal and vertical rulers, also known as the zero point. Click the ruler origin box again to reset the zero point to the upper-left corner of the page. Each layout can have a different ruler origin position.

6 *Rulers*
You can choose inches, inches decimal, picas, points, millimeters, centimeters, ciceros, or agates as the default measurement increment for rulers and entry fields in print layouts. To display the rulers, make sure View > Rulers is checked. Non-printing guides, which are dragged from the vertical and horizontal rulers, are used for aligning and positioning objects.

7 *Margin guides*
Margin guides don't print. Make sure View > Guides is checked to display guides.

8 *Pasteboard*
This functions as a scratchboard for creating items or to store them for later use.

9 *View percent field*
The zoom level of a layout is displayed, and can be modified, in this field.

10 *Layout tabs*
Display a layout by clicking its tab. You can split the project window (Window > Split Window) or open new project windows **NEW** (Window > New Window) and display different layouts from the same project.

11 *Undo*
Click to undo the last undoable edit, or choose from the pop-up menu.

12 *Redo*
Click to redo the last redoable edit, or choose from the pop-up menu.

The QuarkXPress screen in Windows

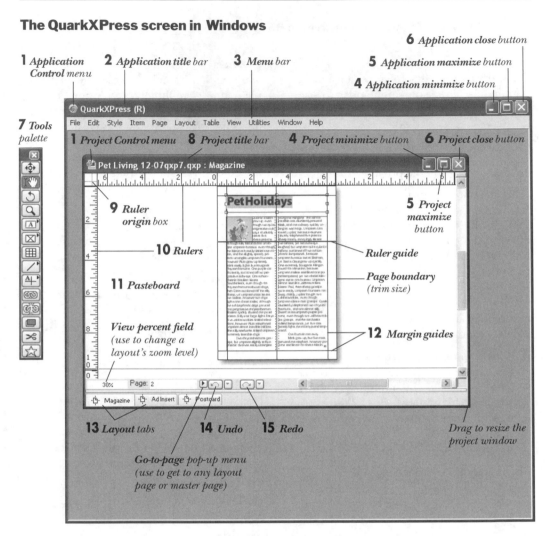

1 *Application Control* menu

2 *Application title* bar

3 *Menu* bar

6 *Application close* button

5 *Application maximize* button

4 *Application minimize* button

7 *Tools* palette

1 *Project Control menu*

8 *Project title* bar

4 *Project minimize* button

6 *Project close* button

9 *Ruler origin* box

10 *Rulers*

11 *Pasteboard*

View percent field (use to change a layout's zoom level)

5 *Project maximize button*

Ruler guide

Page boundary (trim size)

12 *Margin guides*

13 *Layout tabs*

14 *Undo*

15 *Redo*

Drag to resize the project window

Go-to-page pop-up menu (use to get to any layout page or master page)

QuarkXPress Screen: Windows

By default, the Tools palette and the Measurements palette display along with a palette group containing the Style Sheets, Colors, and Page Layout palettes (shown ungrouped here).

Key to the QuarkXPress screen in Windows

1 *Application (or project) Control menu*
The application Control menu commands are Restore, Move, Size, Minimize, Maximize, and Close. The project Control menu commands are Restore, Move, Size, Minimize, Maximize, Close, and Next.

2 *Application title bar*
The application title bar contains the name of the application. If a project is maximized, the project name appears in the title bar.

3 *Menu bar*
Press any menu name to access commands.

4 *Application (or project) minimize button*
Click the application minimize button to shrink the application to an icon on the Taskbar; click the icon to restore the application window to its previous size. Click the project minimize button to shrink the project to an icon at the bottom left corner of the application window. Click the icon to restore the project window to its previous size.

5 *Application (or project) maximize/ restore button*
Click the application or project restore button to restore a window to its previous size. When a window is at its restored size, the restore button turns into a maximize button. Click the maximize button to enlarge the window.

6 *Close button*
To close the application, a project, a dialog box, or a palette, click its close button.

7 *Palettes*
Most of the palettes are opened from the Window menu, including: Tools, Measurements, Page Layout, Style Sheets, Colors, Shared Content, Trap Information, Lists, Profile Information, Glyphs, Index, Layers, Picture Effects, PSD Import, and more. Many of the commands found under the menu bar can be accessed more quickly from the Measurements palette. Palettes that are open when you quit QuarkXPress will reopen when the application is

relaunched. You can save sets of open palettes for different kinds of tasks. **NEW**

8 *Project title bar*
The name of the project and the currently displayed layout are shown on the title bar. Drag the title bar to move the layout within the application window (this won't work if the project window is maximized).

9 *Ruler origin box*
Drag from the ruler origin box to reposition the intersection of the horizontal and vertical rulers (the "zero point"). Click the ruler origin box again to reset the zero point to the upper-left corner of the page. Each layout can have a different ruler origin position.

10 *Rulers*
You can choose inches, inches decimal, picas, points, millimeters, centimeters, ciceros, or agates as the default measurement increment for rulers and entry fields in print layouts. To display the rulers, make sure View > Rulers is checked. Non-printing guides, which are dragged from the vertical and horizontal rulers, are used for aligning and positioning objects.

11 *Pasteboard*
This functions as a scratchboard for creating items or to store them for later use.

12 *Margin guides*
Margin guides don't print. Make sure View > Guides is checked to display guides.

13 *Layout tabs*
Display a layout by clicking its tab. You can split the project window (Window > Split Window) or open new project windows (Window > New Window) and display different layouts from the same project. **NEW**

14 & 15 *Undo & Redo*
Click to undo or redo the last undoable edit, or choose from a list of recent commands on the pop-up menu.

QuarkXPress Screen: Windows

The QuarkXPress menus in Mac OS X

The Preferences command is on this menu.

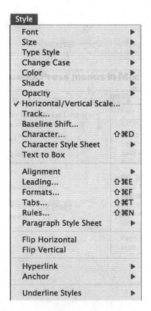

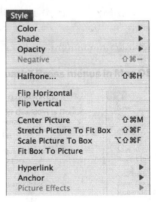

Text *selected*   **Line** *selected*   **Picture** *selected*

Item

Modify...	⌘M
Frame...	⌘B
Runaround...	⌘T
Clipping...	⌥⌘T
Duplicate	⌘D
Step and Repeat...	⌥⌘R
Delete	⌘K
Group	⌘G
Ungroup	⌘U
Constrain	
Lock	▶
Merge	▶
Split	▶
Send to Back	⇧F5
Bring to Front	F5
Space/Align	▶
Shape	▶
Content	▶
Edit	▶
Share...	
Unsynchronize	
Point/Segment Type	▶
Drop Shadow...	⌥⇧⌘D
Composition Zones	▶
Preview Resolution	▶
Delete All Hot Areas	
Super Step and Repeat...	
Cascading Menu	▶
Basic Rollover	▶
2-position Rollovers	▶

Page

Insert...	
Delete...	
Move...	
Master Guides...	
Section...	
Previous	
Next	
First	
Last	
Go to...	⌘J
Display	▶
Preview HTML	▶

Layout

New...	
Duplicate...	
Delete	
Layout Properties...	⌥⇧⌘P
Advanced Layout Properties...	
Previous	
Next	
First	
Last	
Go to	▶

Table   NEW

Insert	▶
Select	▶
Delete	▶
Split Cell	
✓ Table Break...	
Make Separate Tables	
Repeat As Header	
Repeat As Footer	
Convert Text to Table...	
Convert Table	▶
Link Text Cells	
Maintain Geometry	

Help

Help Topics

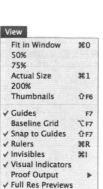

View

Fit in Window	⌘0
50%	
75%	
Actual Size	⌘1
200%	
Thumbnails	⇧F6
✓ Guides	F7
Baseline Grid	⌥F7
✓ Snap to Guides	⇧F7
✓ Rulers	⌘R
✓ Invisibles	⌘I
✓ Visual Indicators	
Proof Output	▶
✓ Full Res Previews	

Utilities

Check Spelling	▶
Auxiliary Dictionary...	
Edit Auxiliary...	
Insert Character	▶
Suggested Hyphenation...	⌥⇧⌘H
Hyphenation Exceptions...	
Job Jackets Manager...	
Usage...	
XTensions Manager...	
Font Mapping...	
Component Status...	
PPD Manager...	
Profile Manager...	
Edit PPML Consumers	
Guide Manager...	
Build Index...	
Jabber	
Tracking Edit...	
Kerning Table Edit...	
Remove Manual Kerning	
Line Check	▶
Convert Old Underlines	

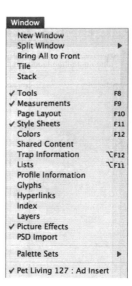

Window

New Window	
Split Window	▶
Bring All to Front	
Tile	
Stack	
✓ Tools	F8
✓ Measurements	F9
Page Layout	F10
✓ Style Sheets	F11
Colors	F12
Shared Content	
Trap Information	⌥F12
Lists	⌥F11
Profile Information	
Glyphs	
Hyperlinks	
Index	
Layers	
✓ Picture Effects	
PSD Import	
Palette Sets	▶
✓ Pet Living 127 : Ad Insert	

The QuarkXPress menus in Windows

File

New	▶
Open	▶
Close	
Save	Ctrl+S
Save As...	Ctrl+Shift+S
Revert to Saved	
Import Text...	Ctrl+E
Save Text...	Ctrl+Alt+E
Save Picture	▶
Append...	Ctrl+Alt+A
Export	▶
Save Page as EPS...	Ctrl+Alt+Shift+S
Collect for Output...	
Collaboration Setup...	
Job Jackets	▶
Print...	Ctrl+P
Output Job...	Ctrl+Alt+P
Exit	Ctrl+Q

Edit

Undo Create Color	Ctrl+Z
Can't Redo	Ctrl+Y
Cut	Ctrl+X
Copy	Ctrl+C
Paste	Ctrl+V
Paste In Place	Ctrl+Alt+Shift+V
Paste Special...	
Delete	
Select All	Ctrl+A
Links...	
Object	
Insert Object...	
Show Clipboard	
Find/Change	Ctrl+F
Preferences...	Ctrl+Alt+Shift+Y
Style Sheets...	Shift+F11
Colors...	Shift+F12
H&Js...	Ctrl+Alt+J
Lists...	
Dashes & Stripes...	
Output Styles...	
Hyperlinks...	
Jabberwocky Sets...	
Color Setups	▶
Underline Styles...	
Menus...	
Meta Tags...	
CSS Font Families...	
Cascading Menus...	

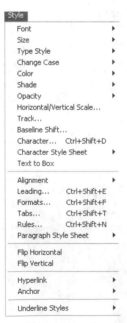

Style

Font	▶
Size	▶
Type Style	▶
Change Case	▶
Color	▶
Shade	▶
Opacity	▶
Horizontal/Vertical Scale...	
Track...	
Baseline Shift...	
Character...	Ctrl+Shift+D
Character Style Sheet	▶
Text to Box	
Alignment	▶
Leading...	Ctrl+Shift+E
Formats...	Ctrl+Shift+F
Tabs...	Ctrl+Shift+T
Rules...	Ctrl+Shift+N
Paragraph Style Sheet	▶
Flip Horizontal	
Flip Vertical	
Hyperlink	▶
Anchor	▶
Underline Styles	▶

Text *selected*

Style

Line Style	▶
Arrowheads	▶
Width	▶
Color	▶
Shade	▶
Opacity	▶
Hyperlink	▶
Anchor	▶

Line *selected*

Style

Color	▶
Shade	▶
Opacity	▶
Invert	Ctrl+Shift+-
Halftone...	Ctrl+Shift+H
Flip Horizontal	
Flip Vertical	
Center Picture	Ctrl+Shift+M
Stretch Picture To Fit Box	Ctrl+Shift+F
Scale Picture To Box	Ctrl+Alt+Shift+F
Fit Box To Picture	
Hyperlink	▶
Anchor	▶
Picture Effects	▶

Picture *selected*

Item

Modify...	Ctrl+M
Frame...	Ctrl+B
Runaround...	Ctrl+T
Clipping...	Ctrl+Alt+T
Duplicate	Ctrl+D
Step and Repeat...	Ctrl+Alt+R
Delete	Ctrl+K
Group	Ctrl+G
Ungroup	Ctrl+U
Constrain	
Lock	▶
Merge	▶
Split	▶
Send Backward	Ctrl+Shift+F5
Send to Back	Shift+F5
Bring Forward	Ctrl+F5
Bring to Front	F5
Space/Align	▶
Shape	▶
Content	▶
Edit	▶
Share...	
Unsynchronize	
Point/SegmentType	▶
Drop Shadow...	Ctrl+Alt+Shift+D
Composition Zones	▶
Preview Resolution	▶
Delete All Hot Areas	
Super Step and Repeat...	
Cascading Menu	▶
Basic Rollover	▶
2-position Rollovers	▶

Page

Insert...	
Delete...	
Move...	
Master Guides...	
Section...	
Previous	
Next	
First	
Last	
Go to...	Ctrl+J
Display	▶
Preview HTML	▶

Layout

New...	
Duplicate...	
Delete	
Layout Properties...	Ctrl+Alt+Shift+P
Advanced Layout Properties...	
Previous	
Next	
First	
Last	
Go to	▶

Table

Insert	▶
Select	▶
Delete	▶
Combine Cells	
✓ Table Break...	
Make Separate Tables	
Repeat As Header	
Repeat As Footer	
Convert Text to Table...	
Convert Table	▶
Link Text Cells	
Maintain Geometry	

Window

New Window	
Split Window	▶
Cascade	
Tile Horizontally	
Tile Vertically	
Arrange Icons	
Close All	
✓ Tools	F8
✓ Measurements	F9
✓ Page Layout	F4
Style Sheets	F11
✓ Colors	F12
Shared Content	
Trap Information	Ctrl+F12
Lists	Ctrl+F11
Profile Information	
Glyphs	
Hyperlinks	
Index	
Layers	
Picture Effects	
PSD Import	
Palette Sets	▶
1 11 Quark6 W_M VQS.qxp : VQS	
✓ 2 Annual Report.qxp : Layout 4	

Utilities

Check Spelling	▶
Auxiliary Dictionary...	
Edit Auxiliary...	
Insert Character	▶
Suggested Hyphenation...	Ctrl+Alt+Shift+H
Hyphenation Exceptions...	
Job Jackets Manager...	
Usage...	
XTensions Manager...	
Font Mapping...	
Component Status...	
PPD Manager...	
Profile Manager...	
Guide Manager...	
Build Index...	
Jabber	
Tracking Edit...	
Kerning Table Edit...	
Remove Manual Kerning	
Line Check	▶
Convert Old Underlines	

View

Fit in Window	Ctrl+0
50%	
75%	
✓ Actual Size	Ctrl+1
200%	
Thumbnails	Shift+F6
✓ Guides	F7
Baseline Grid	Ctrl+F7
✓ Snap to Guides	Shift+F7
✓ Rulers	Ctrl+R
Invisibles	Ctrl+I
✓ Visual Indicators	
✓ Full Res Previews	
Proof Output	▶

Help

Contents	F1
Search...	
Index...	
About QuarkXPress(R)...	
Transfer QuarkXPress License...	

Dialog boxes

Numbers can be typed into dialog box fields in any of the measurement units that are used in QuarkXPress. Click OK or press Return/Enter to exit a dialog box and implement the indicated changes.

A dialog box opens when you choose any menu command that ends with an ellipsis (...); you can also use a keyboard shortcut when one is assigned.

TIP In any dialog box, you can press Tab to select the next field or press Shift-Tab to select the previous field.

TIP For some dialog boxes, you can use the Cmd-Z/Ctrl-Z shortcut (for undo) while the dialog box is open to restore the last-used values.

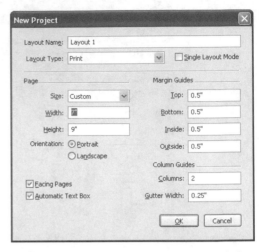

*In Windows, if you press **Alt** plus the letter on the keyboard that corresponds to an **underlined letter** in a dialog box, that field will be selected. For example, in the dialog box illustrated above, pressing Alt-W selects the Width field.*

*To **move** a dialog box, drag its title bar.*

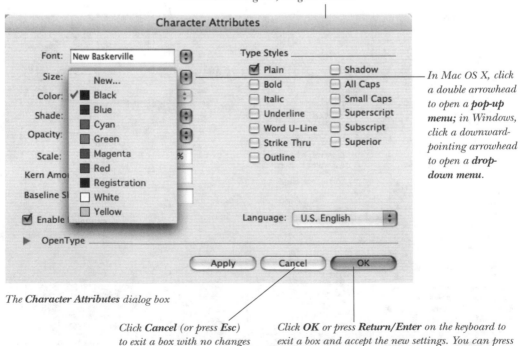

*In Mac OS X, click a double arrowhead to open a **pop-up menu**; in Windows, click a downward-pointing arrowhead to open a **drop-down menu**.*

*The **Character Attributes** dialog box*

*Click **Cancel** (or press **Esc**) to exit a box with no changes taking effect.*

*Click **OK** or press **Return/Enter** on the keyboard to exit a box and accept the new settings. You can press Return/Enter for any highlighted button, such as Save.*

It's all a blank

If the currently selected text or items have different values, the corresponding field will be blank. For example, if selected text contains both 8 pt. and 12 pt. leading, the Leading field will be blank in the Paragraph Attributes dialog box and in the Measurements palette. A pop-up (or drop-down) menu may include Mixed Colors or Mixed H&Js.

Sliders, new to QuarkXPress 7, replace menus for choosing percentages. Here, when choosing a Shade in the Box pane on the Modify dialog box, you can enter a value in the field or click the arrows on the menu and drag the slider.

Dialog box panes

In many dialog boxes—such as Modify, Paragraph Attributes **1**, Preferences, and Utilities—several panes containing related controls are housed under one roof to provide one-stop shopping. Pane names are shown in tabs across the top or in a scroll list on the left side. Simply click a tab or an item in the list to switch between panes.

In the Modify dialog box, the availability of controls varies depending on the type of item or items selected. If you select a text box, for example, you can use the Text pane to change the vertical alignment, use the Frame pane to add a frame, and use the Box pane to add a background color. If you select a picture box, other panes will be available, such as Clipping and OPI. If multiple items are selected, only the tabs containing settings that are common to all the items will display.

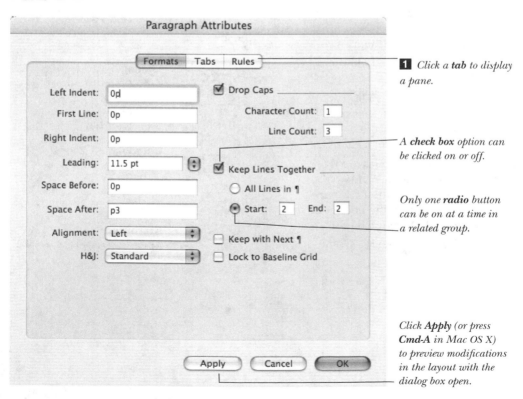

1 *Click a **tab** to display a pane.*

*A **check box** option can be clicked on or off.*

*Only one **radio** button can be on at a time in a related group.*

*Click **Apply** (or press **Cmd-A** in Mac OS X) to preview modifications in the layout with the dialog box open.*

The QuarkXPress palettes*

The Tools palette

The Tools palette contains more than 30 tools for item creation and editing.

- To open the Tools palette, make sure Window > Tools (F8) is checked.

- Choose a visible tool by clicking it. Choose a "hidden," related tool from a pop-out menu (drag from the little arrowhead).

- The default Tools palette is pictured at right. To move a tool from a pop-out menu to its own slot on the palette, hold down Control/Ctrl as you choose the tool. Control-click/Ctrl-click a tool to restore it to its default pop-out menu.

- Hold down Option/Alt and choose any item creation or linking tool to keep it selected. To deselect a tool, click another tool.

- To set preferences for a tool, double-click the tool, then click Modify.

- To access the Item tool while the Content tool is chosen, hold down Cmd/Ctrl.

- To restore the default Tools palette, choose QuarkXPress (Edit, in Windows) > Preferences > Print Layout > Tools, click Default Tool Palette, then click OK.

- If Show Tool Tips is checked in QuarkXPress (Edit, in Windows) > Preferences > Application > Input Settings, you can rest the pointer on any visible tool or palette button and its name will appear on the screen.

The palettes open from the Window menu.

Item
Selects, resizes, moves, cuts/pastes, and reshapes items

Content
Inputs text; imports, edits, and restyles text and pictures; performs some Item tool functions

Rotation
Rotates items

Zoom
Changes the onscreen magnification of a layout

Rectangle Text Box
Creates rectangular text boxes

Rectangle Picture Box
Creates rectangular picture boxes

Tables
Creates tables

Line
Creates straight lines at any angle

Line Text-Path
Creates straight text paths at any angle

Linking
Links text from box to box

Unlinking
Unlinks text boxes

Composition Zones
Creates composition zones

Scissors
Cuts lines, paths, and boxes

Starburst
Creates star-shaped picture boxes

Tools Palette

Tools on the default pop-out menus

Text Box tools

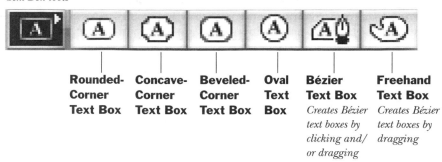

Rounded-Corner Text Box | **Concave-Corner Text Box** | **Beveled-Corner Text Box** | **Oval Text Box** | **Bézier Text Box** *Creates Bézier text boxes by clicking and/ or dragging* | **Freehand Text Box** *Creates Bézier text boxes by dragging*

Picture Box tools

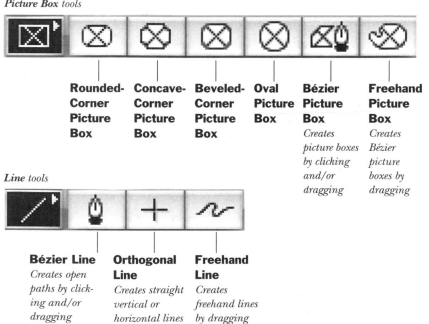

Rounded-Corner Picture Box | **Concave-Corner Picture Box** | **Beveled-Corner Picture Box** | **Oval Picture Box** | **Bézier Picture Box** *Creates picture boxes by clicking and/or dragging* | **Freehand Picture Box** *Creates Bézier picture boxes by dragging*

Line tools

Bézier Line *Creates open paths by clicking and/or dragging* | **Orthogonal Line** *Creates straight vertical or horizontal lines* | **Freehand Line** *Creates freehand lines by dragging*

Text-Path tools

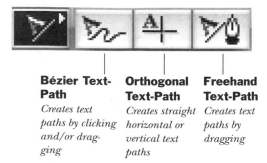

Bézier Text-Path *Creates text paths by clicking and/or dragging* | **Orthogonal Text-Path** *Creates straight horizontal or vertical text paths* | **Freehand Text-Path** *Creates text paths by dragging*

Tools Palette

The Measurements palette NEW

Experienced QuarkXPress users will be happy to know that the newly expanded Measurements palette (Window > Measurements) consolidates most of the commands and options that are available under the menus. The palette now contains multiple tabs and many more options, which vary depending on what kind of item and which tool are selected in the layout. The palette is blank when nothing is selected.

The default tab on the Measurements palette, Classic, provides the most commonly used item and content formatting options. To display one of the other tabs, rest the pointer on the palette to make the nagivator tab bar appear, then click an icon on the tab bar. You can also choose from a full list of tabs on the context menu.

To keep the navigator tab bar on display, Control-click/right-click the palette title bar (at the far left) and choose Always Show Tab Bar. Or if it gets in the way, choose Show Tab on Rollover instead. And finally, if you don't want to use the navigator tab bar at all, choose Always Hide Tab Bar and use the context menu or keyboard commands to switch tabs—or pretend you're in a previous version and forget about the tabs entirely.

*The **Classic** tab when the Content tool and a text box are selected: Controls on the left side let you modify the text box; controls on the right affect selected text or the text insertion point.*

*The **Text** tab is available when a text box is selected. These controls mirror those in the Text pane of the Modify dialog box (Item > Modify).*

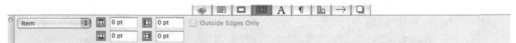

*The **Frame** tab is available when a text box or picture box is selected. These controls mirror those in the Frame pane of the Modify dialog box (Item > Modify).*

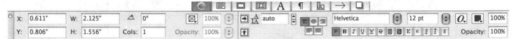

*The **Runaround** tab is available when a text box is selected. These controls mirror those in the Runaround pane of the Modify dialog box (Item > Modify).*

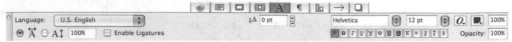

*The **Character Attributes** tab is available when the text insertion bar is in text. These controls mirror those in the Character Attributes dialog box (Style > Character).*

The **Paragraph Attributes** tab is available when the text insertion bar is in text. These controls mirror those in the Paragraph Attributes dialog box (Style > Formats).

The **Space/Align** tab is available when multiple items are selected. You can access some of these controls, and display this tab, from the Item > Space/Align submenu.

The **Tabs** tab is available when the text insertion bar is in text. These controls mirror those in the Tabs pane of the Paragraph Attributes dialog box (Style > Tabs), but are more interactive.

The **Drop Shadow** tab is available when a text box is selected. These controls mirror those in the Drop Shadow pane of the Modify dialog box (Item > Modify).

The **Classic** tab when a picture box is selected. Controls on the left side let you modify the picture box (size, location); controls on the right affect the picture itself (scale, mask).

Measurements palette shortcuts

Not sure what an icon on the palette means? Just point at it to display its Tool Tip. If nothing happens, go to QuarkXPress (Edit, in Windows) > Preferences > Input Settings pane, and make sure that Show Tool Tips is checked.

Show/hide the palette	F9 (In Mac OS X, you may need to modify System Preferences/Dashboard & Exposé.)
Select the first field (Classic tab)	Cmd-Option-M/Ctrl-Alt-M
Select the Font field (Classic tab)	Cmd-Option-Shift-M/Ctrl-Alt-Shift-M
Select next/previous field	Tab/Shift-Tab
Exit the palette without applying changes	Esc
Cycle through the tabs	Cmd-Option-semicolon/Ctrl-Alt-semicolon
Cycle in reverse	Cmd-Option-comma/Ctrl-Alt-comma

Page Layout, Style Sheets, Colors Palettes

The Page Layout palette

The Page Layout palette lets you rearrange, insert, and delete layout pages; move through a layout; create and modify master pages; apply master pages to layout pages; and renumber sections of a layout. Display a layout page by double-clicking its icon or by clicking its number.

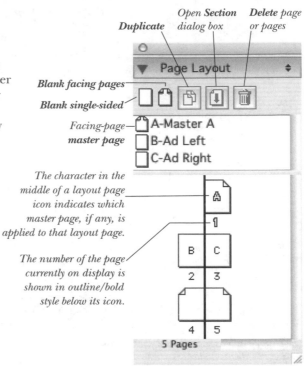

Duplicate

Open Section dialog box

Delete page or pages

Blank facing pages

Blank single-sided

Facing-page master page

The character in the middle of a layout page icon indicates which master page, if any, is applied to that layout page.

The number of the page currently on display is shown in outline/bold style below its icon.

The Style Sheets palette

The Style Sheets palette lets you apply style sheets, which are sets of character and paragraph specifications.

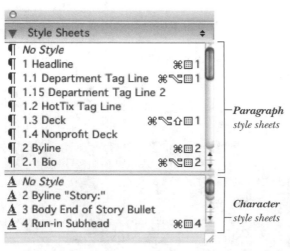

Paragraph style sheets

Character style sheets

The Colors palette

The Colors palette lets you apply colors and blends at varying shades and opacities.

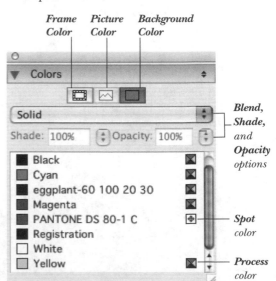

Frame Color

Picture Color

Background Color

Blend, Shade, and Opacity options

Spot color

Process color

The Shared Content palette **NEW**

The Shared Content palette contains text boxes, stories, picture boxes, and pictures that have their box and/or content attributes synchronized. When you drag anything from the Shared Content palette into a layout, any changes you make to that individual item's synchronized attributes are reflected in other instances of the item throughout the entire project.

For example, say you add a text box containing legal boilerplate to the Shared Content palette, synchronize the box attributes and the text formatting, and then drag that boilerplate into various layouts in the project. If you resize the box or change the text formatting, all other instances of the boilerplate throughout the project will be updated to reflect the changes.

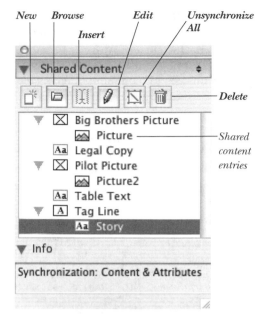

*The **Info** area describes which aspects of the selected shared item are synchronized.*

The Trap Information palette

Trapping controls how overlapping colors print, helping prevent gaps and ink buildup. The Trap Information palette lets you assign trapping specifications to individual items.

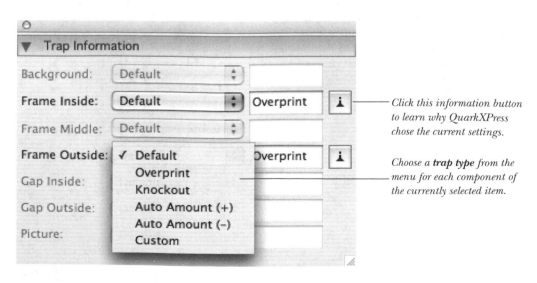

Click this information button to learn why QuarkXPress chose the current settings.

*Choose a **trap type** from the menu for each component of the currently selected item.*

The Lists palette

The Lists palette lets you build a table of contents for the current layout or for multiple chapter files in a book. The list is generated from text in paragraph or character style sheets and can be alphabetized.

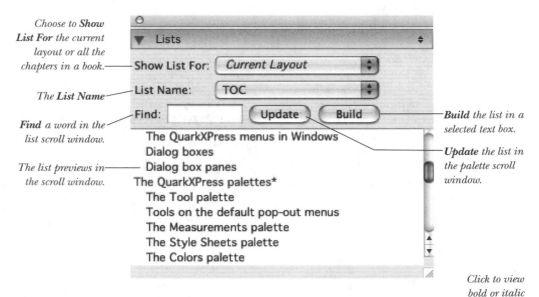

Choose to **Show List For** *the current layout or all the chapters in a book.*

The **List Name**

Find *a word in the list scroll window.*

The list previews in the scroll window.

Build *the list in a selected text box.*

Update *the list in the palette scroll window.*

The Glyphs palette NEW

The Glyphs palette displays all the characters within a font. So why isn't it called the "Character palette"? A glyph is actually a representation of a character within a font. Depending on the font, there may be more than one glyph representing that character. For example, it's common for expert fonts to contain multiple variations of a single numeral, such as a standard numeral 1 and a superscript numeral 1.

Using the Glyphs palette, you can quickly locate and insert glyphs within a font, and you can save glyphs as global favorites for easy access.

Font name

Click to view bold or italic glyphs.

Double-click a **glyph** *to insert it at the text insertion point.*

You can customize the **Favorite Glyphs** *area by adding the glyphs you use the most.*

The Layers palette

The Layers palette lets you organize items in a layout according to their front-to-back stacking order. Using this palette, you can create new layers, move an item to a different layer, merge two or more layers together, restack layers, delete layers, lock/unlock layers, and make layers temporarily invisible or nonprintable.

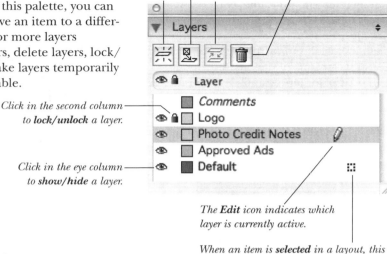

Move Item to Layer   *Delete Layer*

New Layer   *Merge Layers*

Click in the second column ⎯ to **lock/unlock** *a layer.*

Click in the eye column ⎯ to **show/hide** *a layer.*

The **Edit** *icon indicates which layer is currently active.*

When an item is **selected** *in a layout, this indicator shows which layer the item is on.*

The Find/Change palette

The Find/Change palette (Edit menu) lets you search for and replace any combination of text and formatting.

The text, style sheets, and attributes to be searched for are entered or chosen in the **Find What** *area.*

The text, style sheets, and attributes to be changed to are entered or chosen in the **Change To** *area.*

This is the expanded Find/Change palette, when **Ignore Attributes** *is* **unchecked.**

The PSD Import palette **NEW**

The PSD Import palette lets you access any layers, channels, and paths built into native Adobe Photoshop files that you import into a QuarkXPress picture box. You can use this palette to experiment with various changes to a Photoshop image. For example, you can control the blending mode and opacity for layers, apply a different color to any channel, and control which channels and paths display and/or print.

Click a tab to display the layers, channels, or paths built into the selected Photoshop file.

Click the palette menu to customize the palette preview and undo changes to layers, channels, and paths.

Click here to determine whether a layer or channel displays and prints.

The Picture Effects palette **NEW**

The Picture Effects palette lets you adjust an image by using features such as Levels, Curves, and Brightness/Contrast, and it lets you apply special effects such as Emboss or Add Noise. You may be familiar with some of these controls from an image editing application. Using the palette, you can add effects, modify them, turn them on and off, change their order, delete them, and save them as presets for applying to other images.

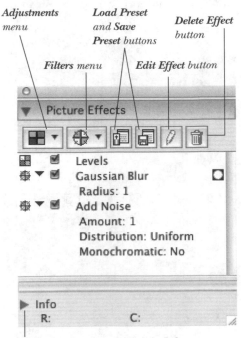

Adjustments menu

*Load Preset and **Save** Preset buttons*

Delete Effect button

Filters menu

Edit Effect button

*Click the triangle to display the **Info** area, which lists details about the selected effect.*

Library palettes

Libraries aren't palettes, per se. They're separate user-created files that are used for storing any type of individual items, combinations of items, or groups of items, including picture boxes (with or without pictures), text boxes (with or without text), lines, text paths, and tables.

To add an item to a library, simply drag it into the palette. To retrieve an item (or group) from a library, drag it from the library into your project window; a copy of the item will appear in your layout. You can create an unlimited number of library palettes, and more than one library palette can be open at a time.

Book palettes

A book is a collection of individual chapter files in which style sheets, colors, H&Js (settings for hyphenation and justification), lists, and dashes & stripes (line and frame styles) can be synchronized. Each book has its own palette that lets you add, delete, print, and change the order of chapters.

The Status column on the palette shows whether a chapter is Available, Modified, Missing, or Open on your computer. If a user name is listed, it means that another person on your network has that chapter open on their computer.

*Once **labels** have been assigned to the items in a library, you can display items selectively by label using this pop-up menu.*

*Library items display as **thumbnails**.*

*The **Synchronize Book** button synchronizes style sheets, colors, H&Js, lists, layouts, and dashes & stripes between the master file and chapter files.*

Move Chapter Up/Down   Print Chapter   Remove Chapter

Add Chapter

*The **master** file from which all the style sheets, colors, etc. are derived*

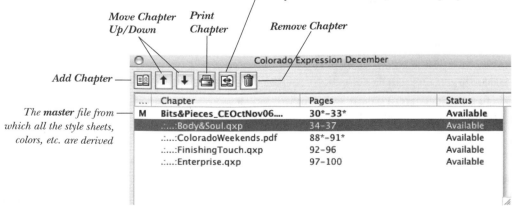

...	Chapter	Pages	Status
M	**Bits&Pieces_CEOctNov06....**	30*–33*	**Available**
	.:...:Body&Soul.qxp	34–37	Available
	.:...:ColoradoWeekends.pdf	88*–91*	Available
	.:...:FinishingTouch.qxp	92–96	Available
	.:...:Enterprise.qxp	97–100	Available

Managing palettes onscreen

Although you'll find that using palettes is incredibly convenient, they can lead to palette-itis. In this condition, your screen is littered with palettes that you're constantly moving, resizing, opening, and closing just to see your pages. This is a common problem with many programs that QuarkXPress solves by allowing you to group palettes and save palettes in sets.

The default palette group contains the Style Sheets, Colors, and Page Layout palettes, but you can change that **1**. All the palettes can be grouped except for the Tools palette, Measurements palette, and Book palettes. Control-click/Right-click a palette's title bar to open a context menu containing the controls for modifying palette groups:

- Choose a palette name to add it to the group.
- Choose Detach [palette name] to remove the palette from a group.
- Choose Close [palette name] to hide the palette.

To make a palette group go away, Control-click/Right-click the bar at the top of the group and choose Close Palette Group from the context menu.

Click the triangle on the left end of a palette's title bar to collapse that palette to just a title bar; click again to expand it. Cmd-click/Ctrl-click any title bar in a palette group to expand or collapse all the palettes in the group.

If you use specific palettes for specific tasks, you can save palette collections as sets.

- To save the current palette configuration as a set, choose Window > Palette Sets > Save Palette Set As. Enter a name in the Save As field and, if you wish, specify a keyboard shortcut.
- To display a set, choose it from the Window > Palette Sets submenu or press the keyboard shortcut.

You can customize palette groups to your liking.

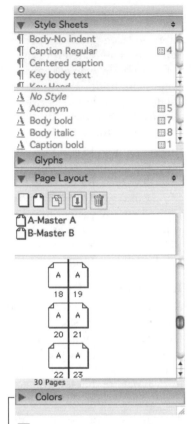

1 *Click the triangle on the title bar of any palette to **collapse** it.*

Palettes and more palettes

If you suspect that we haven't told you the whole story about the palettes in QuarkXPress, you're right. The program has **15 palettes,** many of which are for special purposes such as creating indexes or hyperlinks. In this chapter, we limited the overview to the palettes you're most likely to encounter in your daily work.

Managing Palettes

Context menus

Many commands and features can be accessed using context menus **1**–**3**, thus eliminating the need to trek all the way over to a menu or even to a palette. The choices on a context menu vary depending on whether the pointer is over the pasteboard, the rulers, a blank area, or a picture box, text box, contentless box, text path, line, table, or palette. To see what's available on a context menu, Control-click/ Right-click any item, page, interface element such as a palette, etc.

Note: In Mac OS, if Control-clicking doesn't open a context menu, go to QuarkXPress > Preferences, Input Settings pane, and click Control Key: Key Press Activates: Contextual Menu. (With Control Key Activates: Zoom chosen, you'll have to press Control-Shift-click to open a context menu.)

1 *This context menu appears if you Control-click/Right-click a **line** with the **Item** tool.*

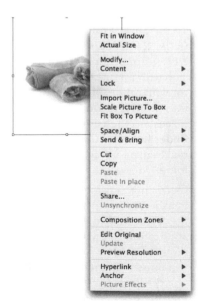

2 *This context menu appears if you Control-click/Right-click a **picture** with the **Item** tool.*

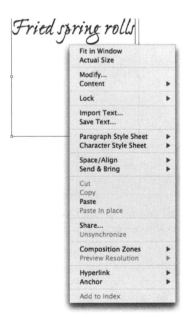

3 *This context menu appears if you Control-click/Right-click a **text box** with the **Content** tool.*

Context Menus

Shopping for XTensions

You can buy XTensions developed by Quark or third parties for everything from creating footnotes to imposing pages for the press 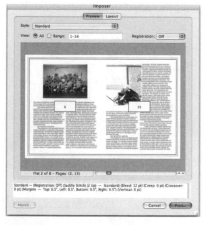 to creating interactive Flash files. Quark offers a variety of free XTensions as well, but let the buyer beware—these are often still in development and may not work perfectly. Most XTensions are available in a demo version so you can try them out before shelling out beans. For more information on XTensions, visit:

- www.quark.com/products/xtensions
- www.thepowerxchange.com
- www.versiontracker.com
- www.creativepro.com

Make sure any XTensions you download or buy are compatible with QuarkXPress 7. Ask whichever manufacturer or distributor you purchase your XTensions from what their upgrade policy is and what technical support they offer, if any.

1 *Imposer, from the Quark Print Collection of XTensions, arranges pages for printing and binding.*

> To display a list of installed XTensions, your QuarkXPress serial number, and other information about the program, do this: In Mac OS X, hold down Option and choose QuarkXPress > About QuarkXPress; in Windows, hold down Alt and choose Help > About QuarkXPress.

XTending XPress with XTensions

What's an XTension?

QuarkXPress doesn't do everything. In fact, one of its strengths is that third-party developers—and Quark itself—have written hundreds of add-on software modules called XTensions that extend or enhance the program's features. XTensions perform a variety of tasks, from simple object alignment to catalog databasing, and they range in price from petty cash to hundreds of dollars.

A small sampling of XTensions are mentioned in this book. Some XTensions are available for Mac OS X only, and some are available for both platforms. Make sure whatever XTensions you buy are optimized for QuarkXPress version 7 (at the time of this writing, we couldn't verify availability of the XTensions mentioned). To get information about an XTension that's installed in your system, choose Utilities > XTensions Manager, click the XTension name, then click About.

Where should I install them?

To use an XTension, it has to be installed in the XTension folder inside the QuarkXPress application folder. Some XTensions ship with an installer that will do the job for you; others must be copied manually into the XTension folder. If an installer places an XTension in the QuarkXPress folder but not in the XTension folder, make sure to drag it into the XTension folder yourself.

Once an XTension has been correctly installed on your hard drive, you can use the XTensions Manager feature within the application to enable or disable it (Utilities menu). To use a newly enabled XTension, you must re-launch QuarkXPress. In QuarkXPress (Edit, in Windows) > Preferences > Application > XTensions Manager, you can choose whether the XTensions Manager opens automatically upon launch.

Measurement units

Most values in palettes and dialog boxes display in the current default horizontal or vertical measurement units. To change the default units for future layouts, close all projects; to change the units for just the currently displayed layout, leave it open. Choose QuarkXPress (Edit, in Windows) > Preferences. Under Print Layout (or Default Print Layout), click Measurements, then for Horizontal and/or Vertical, choose Inches, Inches Decimal, Picas, Points, Millimeters, Centimeters, Ciceros, or Agates. A different unit can be chosen for each layout in a project. With a layout displayed, you can also Control-click/Right-click either ruler and choose from the Measure submenu **1** as well.

To enter a value in a non-default unit **2**–**3**, you must use the proper abbreviation (see the sidebar). For example, you can use "pt" for points, but not "pts". Agates, in case you're wondering, are used for measuring vertical column lengths in classified ads.

Picas and points

A pica is the standard unit of measure used in the graphic arts industry. Six picas equals 1 inch; 1 pica equals 12 points. Picas and points can be combined in the same entry field. For example, to indicate 4 picas and 6 points, you would enter "4p6."

Regardless of the current units, points are always used to measure type sizes, leading, rule widths, frame widths, and line widths.

Using math in fields

In addition to entering values in fields, you can perform math. For example, to make a box twice as wide as it was before, enter *2 after the current width. Use the operators +, –, * (multiply), or / (divide) and press Return/Enter to complete the operation.

Abbreviations

Inches	in *or* "
Inches Decimal	in *or* " with a decimal
Picas	p
Points	pt *or* p followed by a number (as in "p6")
Millimeters	mm
Centimeters	cm
Ciceros	c
Agates	ag
quarter of a millimeter	q
Pixels	px*

In a print layout, pixels can't be chosen as the default unit, but "px" can be used when entering values.

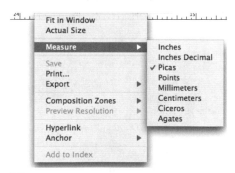

1 *Control-click/Right-click the ruler to access the **Measure** submenu and quickly change measurement systems for the active layout*

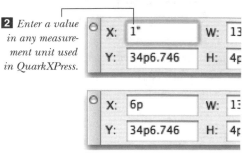

2 *Enter a value in any measurement unit used in QuarkXPress.*

3 *When Return/Enter is pressed, the value is converted into the currently chosen default measurement units.*

Preferences (a sneak preview)

Preferences are default settings that can be chosen at the application level, project level, and individual layout level. The Preferences dialog box is discussed in detail in Chapter 22, and some preferences are discussed in individual chapters when they pertain to a particular task.

You'll learn gradually which preferences affect which features or tasks—and when it matters. In the shaded box below, you'll see a listing of a few of the many preferences, just to give you an idea of some of the available options.

Preferences are chosen in QuarkXPress (Edit, in Windows) > Preferences. Click an option in the scroll list at left to display that pane. Here's an example of the way we've notated it: QuarkXPress (Edit, in Windows) > Preferences > Application > Input Settings.

Think creatively with preferences

To create a second de facto Rectangle Text Box tool or Rectangle Picture Box tool, change the Corner Radius to zero for one of the tools that you rarely use, such as the Beveled-Corner Text Box tool or Beveled-Corner Picture Box tool. For this "new" tool, you can apply special default settings, such as a frame in a particular width, or with Runaround turned on or off.

Note: If you add, edit, or delete specifications such as colors when no projects are open, those specifications become the defaults for all future projects. Some of the default specifications you can edit include: style sheets, colors, H&Js (settings for hyphenation and justification), lists, dashes & stripes, auxiliary dictionaries, and hyphenation exceptions. The same holds true for any Default Print Layout preferences that are changed while no projects are open, such as measurement units, Auto Page Insertion, or Auto Picture Import.

A partial listing of preferences

Margin, ruler, or grid guide colors

Monitor profile for color management

Show Tool Tips

Smart quotes options

Drag and drop text

Pasteboard width

Auto save and auto backup options

Default path (for importing files)

Save document position

Show XTensions Manager options

Measurement units for rulers, dialog boxes, and the Measurements palette

Auto page insertion options

Guides in front or behind

Auto picture import options

Keep or delete master page items

PDF export defaults

Baseline grid increment

Auto kern above value

Flex space width

Ligatures options

Fraction/price formatting

Index punctuation

Text inset, runaround, line width, etc.

Trapping options

Tool preferences, such as style, width, color, shade, and Runaround settings for the Line or Text-Path tools; background color, angle, frame, and Runaround settings for the Picture Box or Bézier tools; background color, number of columns, frame, and Runaround for the Text Box tools; and the Zoom percentage for each click of the Zoom tool

Preferences

Startup 2

1 *Click the application icon on the Dock to launch or switch back to QuarkXPress.*

2 *Or double-click any QuarkXPress **file icon** to launch the application and open that file simultaneously.*

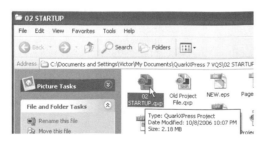

3 *Click **QuarkXPress 7.0** on the **Start** menu.*

4 *Or double-click any QuarkXPress **file** icon to launch the application and open that file simultaneously.*

Getting started

To launch QuarkXPress in Mac OS X:

Click the QuarkXPress application icon on the Dock **1**. If you haven't yet placed the application icon there, drag the application file icon ● from the QuarkXPress folder to the Dock.

or

Open the QuarkXPress folder in the Finder, then double-click the QuarkXPress application icon.

or

Double-click any existing QuarkXPress file icon in the Finder (the program will launch automatically) **2**.

> **TIP** If you switch to another application—whether intentionally or not—and want to return to QuarkXPress, click any QuarkXPress project window or click the application icon in the Dock.

To launch QuarkXPress in Windows:

In Windows 2000 or Windows XP, click the Start button on the Taskbar, choose All Programs, choose QuarkXPress, then click QuarkXPress 7.0 **3**.

or

In Windows Explorer, double-click a QuarkXPress file icon. The application will launch and that file will be maximized onscreen **4**.

> **TIP** Once QuarkXPress is running, you can choose it (or any other open application) from the Taskbar at the bottom of the screen **5**.

5 *You can choose any open application from the **Taskbar**.*

Launch QuarkXPress

Projects and layouts

When you save a file in QuarkXPress 7, the entity that is saved, and that is identified by an icon on the Desktop, is called a **project.** Each project, in turn, holds one or more **layouts.** Layouts hold the "actual" pages and page elements, such as text, lines, tables, and pictures. Each layout has its own Layout Properties settings, which include the page width, height, margin guides, column guides, and layout type (print or Web).

Physically, what you'll see onscreen is a project window and, inside the window, the currently displayed layout. To switch between multiple layouts in a project, click one of the layout tabs at the bottom of the project window ◼1.

When a new project is created, it automatically contains a default layout. You can create additional layouts either by choosing Layout > New ◼2 or by choosing Layout > Duplicate (more about this later). When you duplicate a layout, its style sheets, colors, master pages, and layout properties also appear in the duplicate. Each project can hold many layouts (limited only by your computer's RAM), and each layout can contain up to 2,000 pages. You can also delete any layout from a project; a minimum of one layout must remain.

Not only can print and Web layouts be contained within the same project, you can even switch the layout type for any existing layout from print to Web, or vice versa, using Layout > Layout Properties. Each layout type has its own features. In Chapter 20, we'll show you how to synchronize content across multiple layouts.

New in version 7 is the ability to create a project containing only a single layout (see page 34). This feature allows you to simplify your workflow while you pretend that you're working in QuarkXPress 5! **NEW**

◼1 *Use the **layout tabs** at the bottom of the project window to switch among layouts.*

◼2 *Use commands on the **Layout** menu to create, delete, reconfigure, or navigate among layouts in a project.*

No Limits

In QuarkXPress version 6, a project could hold no more than 25 layouts. In QuarkXPress 7, however, your projects can contain as many layouts as your computer's RAM will allow. **NEW**

To make it easier to remember which features apply to whole projects and which features apply just to individual layouts, we've created the handy chart below. Refer to it as often as you need to until you get your bearings.

TIP If you undo a project-level command, such as a change to an H&J, the undo will affect the whole project. If you undo a layout-specific command, such as a text edit, the undo will affect only that layout.

Project and Layout Features Compared

Features that apply to your copy of QuarkXPress

Application Preferences

QuarkXPress features that apply to whole projects

Style sheets

Colors

H&Js

Lists

Dashes & Stripes

Save command

Output Styles

Nonmatching Preferences alert dialog box (see page 45)

Shared content

QuarkXPress features that apply to individual layouts

Print Layout Preferences

Zoom levels

Layers

Layout Properties, including page dimensions, margin guides, column guides, and layout type

Master pages

Check Spelling

Find/Change

Indexing

Hyphenation Exceptions

Collect for Output command

Export command for PDF or for HTML

Trapping

Print command

Every new project automatically contains one layout. The parameters for that layout are specified in the New Project dialog box.

To create a project:

1. Launch QuarkXPress (instructions on page 31), then choose File > New > Project (Cmd-N/Ctrl-N).

Change any of the following settings (press Tab to move from one field to the next):

2. Leave the default name for the layout as is, or enter a new Layout Name.
or

NEW Check Single Layout Mode to create a project that initially contains one, and only one, layout.

3. From the Layout Type menu (**1**, next page), choose Print. The dialog box will display options for print layouts. (Web layouts are not discussed in this book.) You can change the layout type at any time by choosing Layout > Layout Properties.

4. Choose a preset size from the Size menu.
or
Enter numbers in the Width and Height fields to create a custom-size layout. You can enter values in any measurement unit used in QuarkXPress (see page 29).

5. *Optional:* Click the unselected Orientation button to swap the layout's width and height values.

6. Change any of the Margin Guides. If you check Facing Pages, the Left and Right Margin Guides fields will convert to Inside and Outside and layout pages will be arranged in pairs.

Web curious?

From what we can tell, the ability to create Web pages in QuarkXPress does not seem to be one of its more popular features. For that reason, we've omitted coverage of Web layouts from this edition of the book. But those of you who are disappointed by this decision, take heart! We've made the "Web Layouts" chapter from the previous edition available for download from the Peachpit Web site. Simply register your book at www.peachpit.com/title/0321358279 to receive this and other benefits!

7. Change the number of Columns. If the number of columns is greater than 1, change the Gutter Width. Try 1p or 1p6 (0.167" or 0.25").

8. *Optional:* Check Automatic Text Box to have a text box appear automatically within the margin guides on master page A and on every layout page with which master page A is associated (see Chapter 14). This is used for multipage layouts.

9. Double-check that you're satisfied with the current settings. Your choices aren't irrevocable, but it's easier to change them now than it is to fix them later. Click OK. A new project window will appear on your screen.

TIP The last settings used in the New Project dialog box will reappear the next time it's opened.

TIP If Single Layout Mode is checked, the Layout Name field disappears from the New Project dialog box. Otherwise, the dialog box is the same as for projects with multiple layouts.

Create a Project

*Choose a preset **Page Size** or enter a number between 0.112" and 48"
in the **Width** and **Height** fields. A4 Letter is 210 mm x 297 mm,
B5 Letter is 182 mm x 257 mm, and Tabloid is 11" x 17". Numbers
can be entered in any measurement unit used in QuarkXPress.*

1 *Choose **Layout
Type: Print**.*

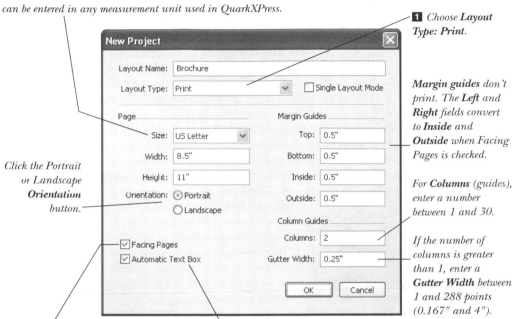

*Click the Portrait
or Landscape
Orientation
button.*

*Margin guides** don't
print. The **Left** and
Right fields convert
to **Inside** and
Outside when Facing
Pages is checked.*

*For **Columns** (guides),
enter a number
between 1 and 30.*

*If the number of
columns is greater
than 1, enter a
Gutter Width between
1 and 288 points
(0.167" and 4").*

*With **Facing Pages** checked, layout
page 1 will appear by itself on the right-
hand side and any additional pages
will be stacked below it in pairs. The
Facing Pages format is used for books,
magazines, and the like.*

*With **Automatic Text Box** checked, a text
box containing the number of columns
and gutter width specified in the Column
Guides fields will appear on the default
master page A and on any layout pages
that are associated with that master.*

Margin   Column   Gutter

First of all he said
to himself: "That
buzzing-noise
means something.
You don't get a
buzzing-noise like
that, just buzzing
and buzzing, with-
out its meaning
something. If
there's a buzzing-

noise, somebody's
making a buzzing-
noise, and the only
reason for making
a buzzing-noise
that I know of is
because you're a
bee.
    Then he thought
another long time,
and said: "And the

only reason for
being a bee that I
know of is making
honey."
    And then he got
up, and said: "And
the only reason for
making honey is so
I can eat it." So he
began to climb the
tree.   *A.A. Milne*

Create a Project

Saving files

If your file has never been saved, ever, these are the instructions for you. To resave an already saved file, see page 38.

To save an unsaved file:

1. Choose File > Save (Cmd-S/Ctrl-S). The Save As dialog box will open.

2. Type a name for the file in the Save As/File Name field ▐**1**.

3. In Mac OS X, choose Type: Project. In Windows, choose Save as type: Project (*.qxp). To create a project template, see page 39.

4. Choose a location for the file:

   In Mac OS X: Navigate to the desired folder or drive, making sure that location appears on the pop-up menu at the top of the dialog box ▐**2**.

   Optional: To create a new folder for the file in the location you've chosen, click New Folder, enter a name, then click Create.

Faster save

If you tend to Save or Save As over and over to the same folder, you can make that folder appear automatically as the location for saving by choosing it in QuarkXPress (Edit, in Windows) > Preferences > Application > **Default Path** (see page 367). While you're at it, you can also choose a default path for the Open, Import Text, or Import Picture dialog box. Every little bit helps.

▐**2** *Make sure the name of the drive or folder into which you've chosen to save the file appears here.*

▐**1** *Type a **name** for the new project.*

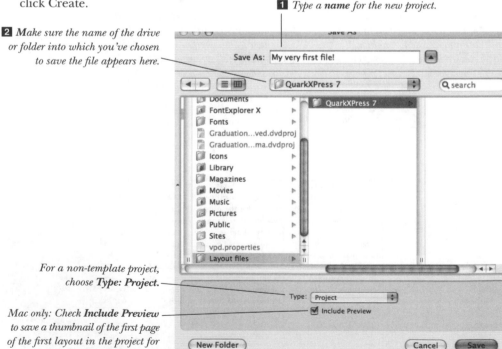

*For a non-template project, choose **Type: Project**.*

*Mac only: Check **Include Preview** to save a thumbnail of the first page of the first layout in the project for display in the Open dialog box.*

Going down? NEW

In QuarkXPress 7, the option to downsave a file to an earlier version is no longer in the Save As dialog box. It's been moved to the Export Layouts as Project dialog box, which we'll talk about on page 42.

1 *Make sure the name of the drive or folder into which you've chosen to save the file appears in the **Save in** field.*

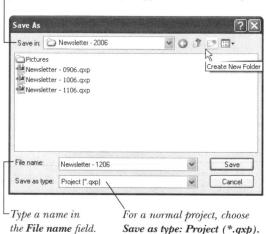

*Type a name in the **File name** field.*

*For a normal project, choose **Save as type: Project (*.qxp)**.*

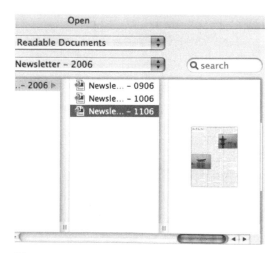

2 *In Mac OS X: In order to see a preview in the **Open** dialog box, a file has to be saved with **Include Preview** checked.*

In Windows: Use the Up One Level button and the Folder List arrow to navigate to the desired location. Make sure the drive or folder into which you have chosen to save the file appears in the Save in field **1**. *Optional:* To create a new folder for the file in the location you've chosen, click the Create New Folder button, and type a name for the new folder; double-click the new folder to open it.

5. *Optional in Mac OS X:* Check Include Preview to have a thumbnail of the first page of the first layout in the project display when you reopen the file using File > Open **2**. If you forget to check Include Preview here, you can add the preview later using Save As (see the following page).

6. Click Save.

Save frequently! We save almost every time we complete a major change—it's like an automatic reflex. *Note:* In addition to manual saving, you may also want to use the Auto Save feature (see the sidebar).

To resave a file:

Choose File > Save (Cmd-S/Ctrl-S) or Control-click/Right-click a blank area in any layout and choose Save. The Save command will be dimmed if no modifications were made to the file since it was last saved.

The Save As command creates a copy of a whole project under a different name. Now that you can create multiple variations of a layout within the same project, we use Save As less. Occasionally, if we have a corrupted file (e.g., it won't let us save), we'll try the Save As command on it—sometimes that does the trick.

To save a new version of a file:

1. Open the file to be duplicated.

2. Choose File > Save As (Cmd-Shift-S/ Ctrl-Shift-S). **NEW**

3. Change the name in the Save As field (Mac OS X) **1**/File name field (Win) **2**.

4. *Optional in Mac OS X:* Check Include Preview to have a thumbnail of the first page of the first layout display in the Open dialog box.

5. Choose a location in which to save the duplicate file.

6. Click Save. The new version of the file will remain open; the original version of the file will close.

TIP If you don't change the file name in the Save As dialog box, a warning prompt will appear when you click Save. Click Replace to save over the original file, or click Cancel.

Auto Save or Auto Backup?

Auto Save is like power or system failure insurance—when you reboot, you'll be able to rescue the last mini-saved version of your file. The **Auto Backup** feature creates multiple backups of a file. Both features are discussed on page 365.

1 *In Mac OS X, enter a different* **name** *for the duplicate file or alter the existing name, then click* **Save.**

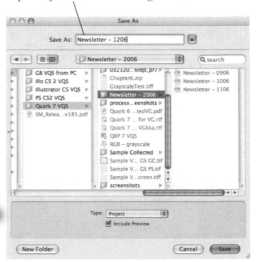

2 *In Windows, type a different* **File name** *for the new file or modify the existing name, then click* **Save.**

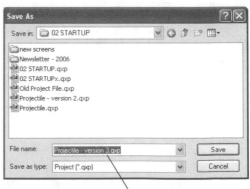

Resave; Save New Version

Lock it another way

In Mac OS X, to prevent any type of file from being saved over, select its icon in the Finder, choose File > **Get Info** > General (Cmd-I), then check **Locked**. If you check **Stationery Pad** instead, a copy of the file will open when you try to open it and the original will remain closed.

To do the same thing in Windows, select a file in Windows Explorer, Right-click its icon so the context menu appears, choose **Properties**, make sure the **Read-only** attribute is checked, then click OK to close the Properties dialog box.

1 *If you choose File > **Revert to Saved**, this prompt will appear. Click Yes to restore the most recently saved version of the file.*

A template is a version of a project that you use as a boilerplate from which to spawn new versions. It can contain master pages, style sheets, custom colors, H&J settings, etc.—any items or layout specifications.

To create a template:

1. Choose File > Save As (Cmd-Shift-S/ Ctrl-Shift-S).

2. In Mac OS X, choose Type: Project Template. In Windows, choose Save as type: Project Template (*.qpt).

3. Enter a name for the template (include the word "template" in the name, if you like), choose a location for the template, then click Save.

   To create a normal project using the template, open the template file, choose File > Save (the Save As dialog box will open), enter a name for the non-template version, then click Save.

TIP To edit the template itself, open it, edit it, choose File > Save, reenter the template's *exact* same name, choose its *current* location, click Save, then click Replace/Yes when the prompt appears.

The Revert to Saved command, which restores the last-saved version of a file, isn't going to be of much help unless you invoke the Save command frequently as you work. We save our files constantly, especially before performing any undoable maneuvers, like rearranging pages.

To revert to the last saved version:

1. Choose File > Revert to Saved.

2. When the alert prompt appears, click OK **1**.

TIP Choose Revert to Saved with Option/Alt held down to revert the file to its last Auto-Saved version (see page 365).

Create a Template; Revert to Saved

Working with layouts

Every new project automatically contains a default layout. You can add more layouts to any project, limited only by the amount of RAM installed in your system. To do this, you can add an empty layout using the New Layout dialog box; or duplicate an existing layout, complete with all its contents (follow the instructions on the next page); or append a layout from another project.

To add a layout to a project:

1. With a project open **1**, choose **NEW**
Layout > New.
or
Control-click/Right-click a layout tab and choose New.

The New Layout dialog box opens **2**. (It looks just like the New Project dialog box.)

2. *Optional:* Change the Layout Name.

3. From the Layout Type menu, you can choose Print or Web as the output medium for the layout. Options in the dialog box will change depending on what type of layout you choose. For now, choose Print.

4. Choose Page, Margin Guides, Facing Pages, Automatic Text Box, and Column Guides values and options, per our instructions on page 34.

5. Click OK. A tab for the new layout will appear after the last tab at the bottom of the project window **3** (regardless of which layout was showing when you created the new one), and the new layout will be displayed in the project window.

TIP Even if you created your project in single layout mode, you can still use this **NEW** technique to add layouts to it.

(Add a Layout — side tab)

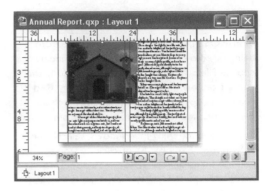

1 *The original project, which contains one layout*

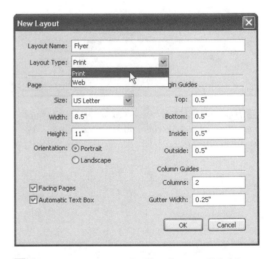

2 *Choose parameters in the **New Layout** dialog box.*

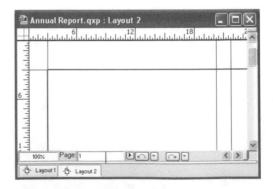

3 *Layout 2 is added to the project.*

Project name   *Name of currently displayed* **layout**

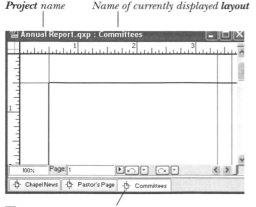

1 *Click a **layout tab** at the bottom of the project window.*

To switch among layouts:

Click a layout tab at the bottom of the project window **1**. Print layout tabs have a icon; Web layout tabs have a icon. The name of the currently displayed layout appears next to the project name in the title bar at the top of the project window.

Each project must contain a minimum of one layout; a project can't be layout-free.

To delete a layout:

1. Display the layout you want to delete, then choose Layout > Delete.
or
Control-click/Right-click a layout tab and choose Delete.

2. When the alert dialog box appears, click Yes. You can't undo the deletion.

If you duplicate a layout, all the master pages and layout pages, style sheets, colors, and other layout elements from the original layout will also show up in the duplicate—the whole kit and caboodle.

To duplicate a layout:

1. Display the layout you want to duplicate (click its tab), and display a layout page—not a master page.

2. Choose Layout > Duplicate.
or
Control-click/Right-click a layout tab and choose Duplicate.

3. Change any Page settings, if desired, in the Duplicate Layout dialog box, then click OK.

TIP Any shared content in the original layout will be synchronized in the duplicate layout (see Chapter 20).

TIP To change the layout properties (layout name, page dimensions, margin guides, column guides, layout type, etc.) of an existing layout, see page 34.

Duplicate, Delete a Layout; Switch Layouts

You can export one or more layouts into a new project. In QuarkXPress 7, this is the only way to downsave a project to version 6.

To export layouts from a project: NEW

1. With a project open, choose File > Export > Layouts as Project.

The Export Layouts as Project dialog box opens **1**.

2. *Optional:* Give the new project a unique name.

3. In Mac OS X, choose Type: Project. In Windows, choose Save as type: Project (*.qxp). To create a template, see page 39.

4. To save the project in QuarkXPress 6 format, choose 6.0 from the Version menu.

5. In the Layouts area, check the individual layouts that you want to export. Check Select All to include all of the current project's layouts in the new project.

6. Choose a location for the file.

7. *Optional in Mac OS X:* Check Include Preview to add a thumbnail of the first page of the first layout in the project to the file. This will display in the Open dialog box the next time you open the project.

8. Click Export. A new project is created containing the layouts you selected.

TIP To share layouts among existing projects, use the File > Append command NEW (see pp. 49–50).

Downsaving

If you export layouts to a new project and save that project in version 6.0 format, some layout elements that were created using 7.0 features will revert back to their 6.0 equivalents.

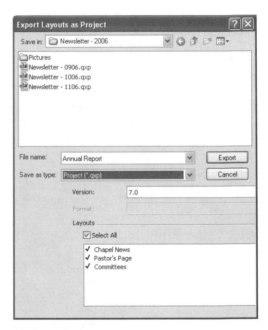

1 **Export layouts** *from one project into a new project file.*

Show/hide guides

Press **F7** to show/hide guides (View > Guides). With guides hidden, margin guides, ruler guides, column guides, the X in empty picture boxes, and the edges of any unselected boxes that don't have a frame will disappear from view. Show guides to position objects; hide them to judge the overall compositional balance of a page.

Column and margin guides are modified via the **Master Guides** dialog box, which can be opened from the Page menu only when a master page is currently displayed (see page 247).

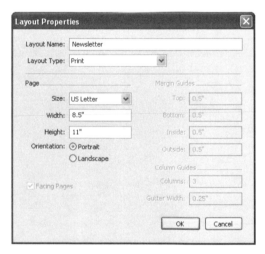

1 *Change a layout name, output type, dimensions, and other parameters in the **Layout Properties** dialog box.*

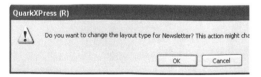

2 *This prompt will appear if you change a layout's type (**Layout Type** menu) and click OK.*

Changing layout properties

Use the Layout Properties dialog box, which is (almost) identical to the New Project and New Layout dialog boxes, to change the parameters of your layout at any time.

To change a layout's dimensions or type:

1. Display the layout whose properties you want to change, then choose Layout > Layout Properties (Cmd-Option-Shift-P/ Ctrl-Alt-Shift-P). **NEW**
or
Control-click/Right-click a layout tab and choose Layout Properties.

2. Do any of the following **1**:

Change the Layout Name.

Choose Layout Type: Print or Web. *Note:* If you change the Layout Type, items that are found only in the current type (such as form controls in a Web layout or tabs, kerning, tracking, or H&Js in a print layout) may be altered.

Choose a preset Page Size.

Change the Width and/or Height values.

Click the unselected page Orientation icon/button.

To convert a single-sided layout to a facing-pages layout, check Facing Pages (to learn more about facing pages, see page 247). Converting a facing-pages layout into a single-sided layout is more complicated, because it involves deleting master pages, which we cover in Chapter 14.

3. Click OK. If you changed the layout's type, an alert dialog box will appear **2**. Click OK to continue.

Any text box that fits exactly within the margin guides (such as the automatic text box) will resize automatically to fit within the new margins.

Change Layout Properties

Opening files

To open a QuarkXPress project from within the application:

1. Choose File > Open (Cmd-O/Ctrl-O).

2. In Mac OS X: Choose All Readable Documents from the Enable menu.

In Windows: Choose All QuarkXPress Files from the Files of Type menu.

3. Locate and click a file name, then click Open ■–■.
or
Double-click a file name.

The number of QuarkXPress projects that can be open at a time is limited only by available memory.

Note: Be sure to read "Things that may happen when a file is opened," starting on the following page.

To reopen a recently opened and saved file:

Choose from a list of recently opened files on the File > Open submenu ■ or at the bottom of the Open menu. The location of the list and the number of files listed will depend on the current File List Location setting in File List preferences (see page 367).

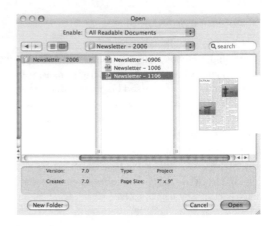

1 *The **Open** dialog box in **Mac OS X***

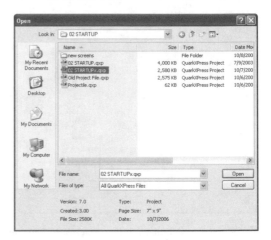

2 *The **Open** dialog box in **Windows***

3 *The File > **Open** submenu*

Open Project; Reopen File

1 *Mac OS X: You can **open** a file in the Finder by double-clicking its icon.*

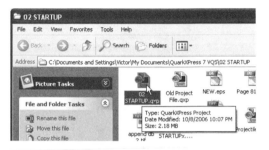

2 *Windows Explorer: Double-click the file you want to open.*

3 *The **XPress Preferences** prompt*

To open a QuarkXPress file from the Finder/Windows Explorer:

In Mac OS X: Double-click a QuarkXPress file icon **1** or drag a QuarkXPress file icon over the application icon on the Dock.

In Windows Explorer: Double-click a QuarkXPress file icon **2** or drag a QuarkXPress file over the program short-cut on the Desktop.

If QuarkXPress hasn't yet been launched, it will launch now.

To convert a file from a previous version of QuarkXPress to 7.0:

1. Open the file using File > Open—not by double-clicking its icon in the Finder or in Windows Explorer.

2. Immediately after the file opens and you've responded to any alerts (see the next section), choose File > Save.

3. Click Save, then click Replace.

Things that may happen when a file is opened

Non-matching preferences prompt

Kerning and tracking table settings and hyphenation exceptions are stored in individual projects and in the QuarkXPress folder in a file called XPress Preferences. If, upon opening a file, the project settings don't match the XPress Preferences settings, a prompt will appear **3**. Click **Use XPress Preferences** (or press Cmd-./Alt-U) to apply the preferences currently resident on that machine to all the layouts in the project (the text may reflow!), or click **Keep Project Settings** (Return/Enter) to preserve all the current preferences for each layout in the project.

(Continued on the following page)

Fonts are missing

If you open a file that uses fonts that aren't installed or aren't currently available in your system (perhaps the font is temporarily deactivated), a prompt will appear:

1. Click List Fonts to see a list of missing fonts **1**. *Note:* If you click Continue and the missing fonts subsequently become available, they will display properly.

2. To replace a missing font, click a font name **2**. An asterisk in the Replacement Fonts column indicates that that font has *not* been replaced.

3. Click Replace.

4. In the Find Replacement Font dialog box, choose a font from the Replacement Font menu **3**.

5. Click OK. *Beware!* Do not replace fonts lightly. All the text in the layouts may reflow.

6. Repeat steps 2–5 for any other missing fonts you want to replace. If you change your mind after choosing a replacement font, click the replacement font, then click Reset.

7. Click OK.

Profiles are missing

This is a giant leap ahead, but we'll be brief. "Profiles" is short for Quark Color Management System profiles, which the program uses to achieve color matching among various devices. If a profile that's been assigned to your file is missing when you try to open it (or print it), the missing profiles prompt will appear **4**. You can either click Continue to open the file without replacing the missing profile (the simplest solution for now) or click List Profiles to proceed ahead to the Missing Profiles dialog box (**1**, next page). Profiles are assigned to input and output devices as well as to individual pictures.

1 *If the **missing fonts** prompt appears, click **List Fonts** to open the Missing Fonts dialog box, or click **Continue** to open the file without replacing the missing fonts.*

2 *In the **Missing Fonts** dialog box, click a font name, click **Replace**...*

3 *...then choose a **replacement font** from the menu.*

4 *If the **missing profiles** prompt appears, click **List Profiles** to substitute profiles, or click **Continue** to open the file without replacing the missing profiles.*

What about modified pictures?

If **Auto Picture Import: On** is chosen in QuarkXPress (Edit, in Windows) > Preferences > Project > General, then modified pictures (pictures that are imported into QuarkXPress and subsequently opened and resaved in another application) are updated *automatically* when a project is reopened; no action is required on your part. If Verify is chosen, a prompt will appear (click Yes). If Auto Picture Import: Off is chosen, no prompt will appear but you can use Utilities > Usage to update the pictures after opening the file (see page 184).

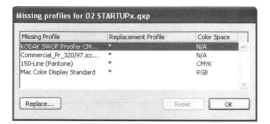

1 *In the **Missing profiles** dialog box, select a profile name, click **Replace**, choose a replacement profile, click OK, then click OK again.*

2 *This prompt will appear if, when you open a file, any original picture files for the project are **missing** or were **modified**.*

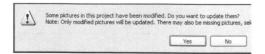

3 *In Utilities > **Usage** > Pictures, double-click a missing picture file name. Then, in the Find dialog box, locate and click the picture file name, then click Open.*

Pictures are missing

If your file contains pictures that were moved or renamed since it was last opened and Auto Picture Import: Verify is chosen in QuarkXPress (Edit, in Windows) > Preferences > Print Layout or Web Layout > General, yet another alert dialog box will open **2**. Click Yes to proceed, and then to update the picture/file link(s), choose Utilities > Usage, click Pictures in the list on the left, double-click the name of a missing picture **3**, locate and click the picture file name in the Find dialog box, then click Open (or click OK). Repeat for any other missing pictures. Click Done when you're done. See pages 183–184.

If a prompt appears indicating that an XTension is missing, the project contains a picture in a file format for which an import XTension filter is needed (see below).

Note: If additional missing (not modified) pictures are located in the same folder as the first missing picture, you'll get a prompt indicating that you can update them all at once.

XTensions Manager

In addition to the prompts that may appear when a file is opened, the XTensions Manager may open when the application is launched. To use the XTensions Manager, see page 377.

To specify whether the XTensions Manager should open automatically when the application is launched, go to QuarkXPress (Edit, in Windows) > Preferences > Application > XTensions Manager. Click Show XTensions Manager at Startup: Always to have the XTensions Manager appear with every launch; or click When: "XTension" folder changes to have the Manager open only if an XTension was added to or removed from the XTension folder; or click When: Error loading XTension occurs to have it open only if an error occurs when XTensions are loaded.

Closing files

To close one file:

Mac OS X: Click the red close button in the upper-left corner of the project window **1**.

Windows: If the project isn't maximized, click the project close button in the upper-right corner of the project window **2**. If the project is maximized, click the project close button directly below the application close button **3**.

or

Choose File > Close (Cmd-W/Ctrl-F4).

TIP If you try to close a file that has never been saved, a prompt will appear. You can cancel the close operation (click Cancel), discard the file altogether (click No), or save the file before it's closed (click Yes) **4**.

To close all open QuarkXPress files:

Mac OS X: Option-click the red close button in the upper-left corner of the project window or press Cmd-Option-W.

Windows: Choose Window > Close All.

To quit/exit the application:

In Mac OS X: Choose QuarkXPress > Quit QuarkXPress (Cmd-Q).

In Windows: Choose File > Exit (Ctrl-Q).

TIP When you try to quit/exit the application, a prompt will appear for each open file that has unsaved changes. You can cancel the quit/exit operation (click Cancel), close the file without saving the changes (click No), or save the changes before the file is closed (click Yes) **5**.

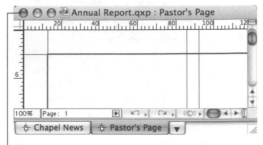

1 *Mac OS X: Click the red **close** button in the upper-left corner of the project window to close a file.*

2 *Windows: If the project isn't maximized, click the close button in the upper-right corner of the project window.*

3 *Windows: If the project is maximized, click the close button directly below the application close button.*

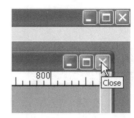

4 *If you attempt to close a file that has **never** been **saved**, this prompt will appear.*

5 *If you try to quit/exit the application and **changes** were made to the file since it was last **saved**, this prompt will appear.*

Appending specifications

Using the Append dialog box, you can append one or more style sheets, colors, H&Js, lists, and dashes & stripes from one project or library to another project. But wait! There's more: in QuarkXPress 7, you can also append entire layouts. **NEW**

To append specifications from one project to another:

1. Open the file you want to append the specs to.

2. Choose File > Append (Cmd-Option-A/ Ctrl-Alt-A).
   or
   Click Append in the Style Sheets, Colors, H&Js, Lists, or Dashes & Stripes dialog box. (The other options are related to web layouts, which are not covered in this book.)

   A file navigation dialog box opens.

3. Locate and click the name of the file that contains the components that you want to append, then click Open.

   The Append dialog box opens.

   TIP Only specifications that were saved with the file that you're appending from will show up on the list.

4. Click a category on the left side of the dialog box.

5. In the Available column, click the name of the component you want to append **1**.
   or
   To append multiple components, click the first component in a series of consecutively listed components, then Shift-click the last in the series. Or Cmd-click/Ctrl-click to select/deselect individual components.

6. Click the right-pointing arrow **2**.

(Continued on the following page)

1 *In the **Available** column, select what you want to append.*

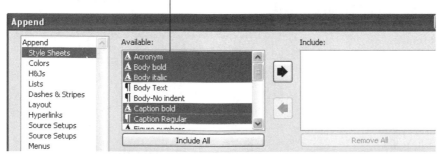

2 *Then click the **right-pointing** arrow to move those items to the **Including/Include** column.*

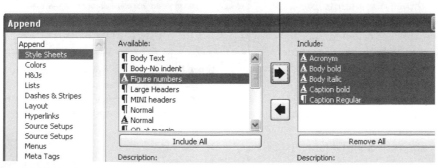

Append

7. Click OK. A warning prompt may appear . Check "Do not show this warning again" to prevent the prompt from reappearing, if desired, then click OK again.

8. If an appending component has the same name as a component in the file you're appending to, the Append Conflict dialog box will open. Do one of the following for each conflict that arises:

Note: To have the same response be applied automatically to any remaining conflicts, check Repeat For All Conflicts before clicking Rename, Auto-Rename, Use New, or Use Existing.

To keep the existing component, append the new component, and rename an individual component yourself, click Rename **2**, type a new name, then click OK.
or
To have an asterisk be inserted automatically next to the name of any appending component that has a match in the open, destination project, click Auto-Rename.
or
To replace the existing item with the appending component, click Use New **3**.
or
To cancel the append of that item, click Use Existing **4**.

9. Click OK.

TIP To append all the components listed, instead of selecting them, click Include All. Click Remove All to delete the whole list from the Including/ Include column.

TIP If a style sheet that you're appending has the same keyboard equivalent as a style sheet in the project that you're appending to, the style sheet will append but not its keyboard equivalent.

Quick-and-dirty append

If text to which a style sheet or sheets have been applied is pasted from another file using the Clipboard, drag-copied from another file, or retrieved from a library, the style sheet or sheets will be appended—barring any name conflicts. Colors and H&Js can also be appended this way.

1 *Click OK when this warning prompt appears.*

2 *Click **Rename** or **Auto-Rename** to keep the existing item and append the new.*

3 *Or click **Use New** to replace the existing item with the appending item.*

4 *Or click **Use Existing** to prevent an item with the same name from appending.*

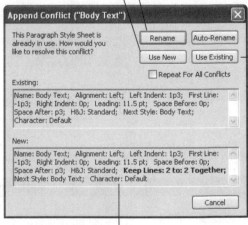

*In the **Append Conflict** dialog box, settings in a new (appending) style sheet that don't exactly match an equivalent setting in an existing style sheet of the same name in the file you're appending to will appear in boldface.*

Navigate/Undo ■3

Zoom shortcuts

Fit in project window	Cmd-0/Ctrl-0 (zero)
Actual size	Cmd-1/Ctrl-1 (one)
Thumbnails	Shift-F6
Make open windows Thumbnails view *(print layouts only)*	Option-Shift choose Window > Tile/ Alt-Shift choose Window > Tile Horizontally or Tile Vertically
Fit pasteboard in project window	Cmd-Option-0/ Ctrl-Alt-0
Select view % field	Control-V/ Ctrl-Alt-V
100%–200% toggle (If Zoom tool is not active)	Cmd-Option-click/ Ctrl-Alt-click

For the zoom in and zoom out shortcuts, see the following page.

■ View *percent field*

Zoom limits in Windows

The maximum zoom on a Windows monitor may vary depending on the current setting for Display DPI Vaue (screen resolution) in Edit > Preferences > Application > Display. At the default value of 96 dpi, the maximum zoom is 692%.

Changing zoom levels

By learning how to switch zoom levels, you'll work more efficiently and minimize eye and neck strain. You can go back and forth between editing small details at a magnified zoom level to checking out the overall composition in Fit in Window view or a lower zoom level. Changing the zoom level doesn't alter a layout's output dimensions; it only changes its onscreen appearance.

To zoom in or out using the View menu or the view percent field:

Choose View > Fit in Window (Cmd-0/ Ctrl-0), 50%, 75%, Actual Size (Cmd-1/ Ctrl-1), 200%, or Thumbnails (Shift-F6). *or*

Double-click the view percent field in the lower-left corner of the project window ■ (Control-V/Ctrl-Alt-V), type a number between 10 and 800 (but Windows users, see the sidebar at left), then press Return/ Enter. You don't have to enter the % symbol. For Thumbnails view, enter "t", then press Return/Enter.

TIP Page elements can't be modified in Thumbnails view. Pages in a layout *can* be rearranged in Thumbnails view, however (see page 88), and whole pages can be drag-copied between projects and between layouts within one project, provided both source and target are in Thumbnails view (see page 95).

TIP For an almost-thumbnails view in which page elements are editable, choose a very small view size, such as 25%.

Accessing the Zoom tool from the keyboard is much speedier than selecting and then deselecting the tool from the Tools palette. You can choose a different zoom level for each layout in a project.

Note: In Mac OS X, you need to be aware of a preferences setting when accessing the Zoom tool using the keyboard. If **Contextual Menu** is chosen as the Control Key Activates setting in QuarkXPress > Preferences > Application > Input Settings, you can use the shortcuts as listed below. If Control Key Activates: **Zoom** is chosen, on the other hand, omit the Shift key from the shortcuts.

To zoom in or out using a shortcut:

Control-Shift-click/Ctrl-Spacebar-click the page to zoom in 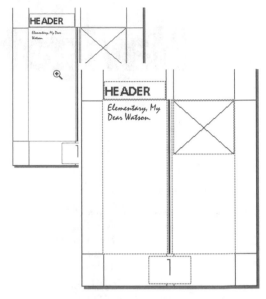.
or
Control-Option-click/Ctrl-Alt-Spacebar-click the page to zoom out.
or
Control-Shift-drag/Ctrl-Spacebar-drag a marquee across an area on the page that you want to magnify.
or
Press Cmd-+ (plus) to zoom in or Cmd-– (minus) to zoom out. If the Content tool is chosen, deselect first.
or
Control-click/Right-click in a layout and choose Fit in Window or Actual Size.

TIP To set the Minimum, Maximum, and Increment percentages for the Zoom tool, double-click the tool, then click Modify.

TIP Click the project window zoom/maximize button to enlarge the window to full screen size (Mac OS X)/application window size (Windows). Click it again to restore the window's former size.

1 *Control-Shift-click/Ctrl-Spacebar-click a page to zoom in.*

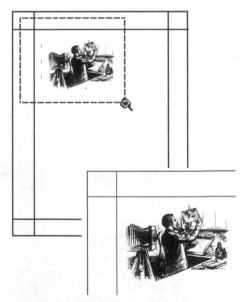

2 *Control-Shift-drag/Ctrl-Spacebar-drag over a section of a page to magnify that chosen area.*

Screen redraw shortcuts

Forced redraw Cmd-Option-. (period)/
Shift-Esc. Use this to correct
an incomplete screen redraw.

Stop redraw Cmd-./ Esc *or* perform another
action (select an item, choose
another command, etc.)

1 *Click a **layout tab** at the bottom of the project window.*

*The **page** grabber*

2 ***Option-drag/Alt-drag** to move a page in the project window.*

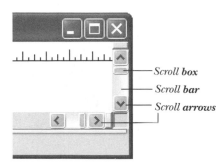

*Scroll **box***
*Scroll **bar***
*Scroll **arrows***

3 *The standard window navigation features: **scroll boxes**, **bars**, and **arrows***

Moving around

To switch between layouts:

Click a layout tab at the bottom of the
project window **1**.
or
Press Cmd-'/Alt-' (apostrophe) to cycle
through the layouts in a project. **NEW**
or
From the Layout menu, choose Previous,
Next, First, or Last.
or
Choose from the Layout > Go To submenu.

To move a layout in the project window using the page grabber hand:

Option-drag/Alt-drag to move a layout in
the project window. The cursor will temporarily turn into a hand icon **2**, and the
layout will redraw as you scroll. If Speed
Scroll is on in QuarkXPress (Edit, in
Windows) > Preferences > Application >
Interactive, pictures and blends may be
greeked (grayed out) as you scroll.

Note: The page grabber isn't accessible
while the Zoom tool is chosen.

To move a layout in the project window using the scroll arrows, bars, or boxes:

Click a scroll arrow to scroll a short distance through a layout **3**.
or
Move a scroll box to move through a layout
more quickly. The page number in the
lower-left corner of the project window
will update if you move to a different page.
or
Click a gray scroll bar area to scoot quickly
through a layout.

TIP The scroll speed and other scroll pref-
erences are set in QuarkXPress (Edit, in
Windows) > Preferences > Application >
Input Settings (see page 364).

Switch Between Layouts; Page Grabber

To move through a layout using the extended keyboard:

Press Page Up or Page Down to move up or down one full screen 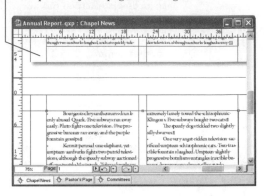.
or

Press Shift-End/Ctrl-Page Down to go to the top of the last page in the layout.
or

Press Shift-Home/Ctrl-Page Up to go to the top of the first page in the layout.
or

Press Shift-Page Up to go to the top of the previous page.
or

Press Shift-Page Down to go to the top of the next page.
or

In Mac OS X, press Home to go to the top of the first page in the layout (or to the blank space to the left of the first page), or press End to go to the bottom of the last page (or the blank space to the right of the last page).

In Windows, press Ctrl-Home to go to the start of the current story, or press Ctrl-End to go to the end of the story.

For more shortcuts like these, see page 424.

To go to a page using a command:

Choose Page > Previous, Next, First, or Last.
or

Choose Page > Go to (Cmd-J/Ctrl-J), enter the desired page number in the Go to Page field, then click OK 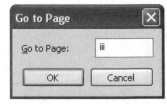.

TIP If the desired page has a prefix that was applied using the Section command, be sure to enter that prefix along with the number in the Go to Page dialog box. Also make sure the number is entered in the correct format (e.g. lowercase Roman, numeric). To display a page based on its position in the layout rather than its applied Section number, enter "+" before the number. (For example, the first page in the layout is always +1.) You can also type "end" to get to the last page in a layout.

1 *The page that's currently showing in the **upper-left corner** of the project window is the page that QuarkXPress considers to be displayed, even if only a small portion of that page is showing.*

2 *Press Cmd-J/Ctrl-J to get to the **Go to Page** dialog box quickly.*

*The **Page Layout** palette*

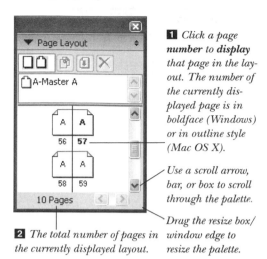

1 *Click a page **number** to **display** that page in the layout. The number of the currently displayed page is in boldface (Windows) or in outline style (Mac OS X).*

Use a scroll arrow, bar, or box to scroll through the palette.

2 *The total number of pages in the currently displayed layout.*

Drag the resize box/ window edge to resize the palette.

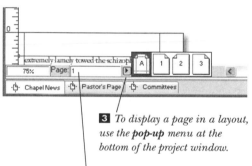

3 *To display a page in a layout, use the **pop-up** menu at the bottom of the project window.*

4 *Or double-click the current page number, **enter** the desired page number, then press Return/Enter.*

To go to a page using the Page Layout palette:

1. Choose Window > Page Layout (F10/F4).

2. Click the desired page number under the layout page icon **1**.
   or
   Double-click a layout page icon. (Single-clicking will select the icon but not display the page.)

TIP When a page icon is selected, its number displays in the lower-left corner of the Page Layout palette. If a page begins a section, an asterisk will follow the number. If no page icon is selected, the total number of pages the layout contains will display instead (e.g., "10 Pages") **2**.

TIP In Mac OS X, the F10 key is assigned by default to the Application Windows features of Exposé. If you want the key to work properly in QuarkXPress, open System Preferences > Dashboard & Exposé and assign a new keystroke to Application Windows.

To go to a page using the Go-to-page menu or field:

Choose a page number from the Go-to-page pop-up menu at the bottom of the project window **3**.
or
Double-click the current page number at the bottom of the project window **4**, enter the desired page number, then press Return/Enter.

Move Through a Layout

To arrange multiple project windows:

In Mac OS X, choose any of the following commands from the Window menu (or Shift-click the project window title bar and choose any of the commands from there):

Bring All to Front to bring all the currently open QuarkXPress project windows to the front of any other open application windows without changing their size, location, or stacking position.
or
Tile to stack all the currently open project windows in neat horizontal strips.
or
Stack to stack project windows at full size with their title bars showing.

In Windows, choose any of the following commands from the Window menu:

Cascade to stack project windows at full size in a stair-stepped arrangement.
or
Tile Horizontally to arrange project windows in horizontal strips 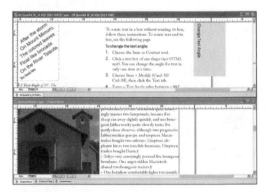.
or
Tile Vertically to arrange project windows in columns.

To activate an open project:

Choose the name of any open project from the bottom of the Window menu.

In Mac OS X, you can also Shift-click a project title bar and choose from a list of open files.

In Mac OS X, a bullet will appear next to the name of any open but not active project that contains unsaved changes.

Nifty tricks

In Mac OS X, hold down Option and choose Window > Tile or Stack to tile or stack all open projects into Thumbnails view. In Windows, hold down Alt-Shift and choose Cascade or a Tile command from the Window menu.

For Actual Size view in Mac OS X or Windows, while choosing the Tile or Stack command, hold down Control/Ctrl-Alt, or for Fit in Window view, hold down Cmd/Ctrl-Shift.

Or in Mac OS X, press Shift plus any of the above-mentioned keys, click the project window title bar, and choose Tile or Stack.

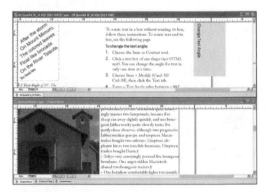

1 *This is how the layout appears after choosing Window > **Tile Horizontally** in Windows. In Mac OS X, choosing **Tile** does the same thing.*

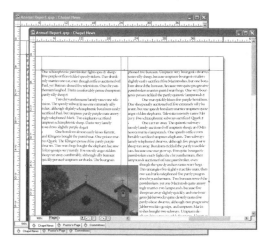

1 *A single layout, visible in **two windows**.*

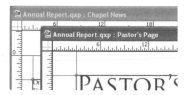

2 *Two layouts from the same project, displayed in **separate windows**.*

3 *The **split bar***

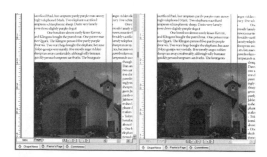

4 *After choosing **Split Window > Vertical***

Creating multiple views of one layout or project (NEW)

It's sometimes useful to be able to look at two or more parts of your layout at the same time, or view one page from your layout at two different zoom levels. Or, you might need to look at pages from two different layouts in the same project simultaneously. QuarkXPress 7 now lets you accomplish all of these things by opening a layout in more than one window, or by splitting a window into several views.

To view a layout in multiple windows:

Choose Window > New Window.

A new window opens, duplicating the current view of your layout **1**. You can close the new window any time without losing changes.

TIP If your project contains multiple layouts, you can choose to display a different layout in the new window **2**. This is helpful for dragging items and pages between layouts in the same project.

To split a window into multiple views:

Click the split bar at the top of the right-hand scroll bar (to split horizontally) or to the right of the bottom scroll bar (to split vertically) **3**.
or
Choose Window > Split Window > Horizontal (or Vertical) **4**.

The window is divided into equal portions, each showing the same view of the layout. You can scroll each view independently of the other, and the views can have different zoom levels.

TIP Drag the bar dividing the window to adjust the relative sizes of the splits.

To remove splits from a window:

Drag a split bar all the way to the edge of the window.
or
Choose Window > Split Window > Remove All.

Open Layout in Multiple Windows; Split Windows

Undoing edits

If you're nervous about making mistakes, relax. You will never (okay, rarely) have to retrace your steps if you take advantage of all the safety mechanisms QuarkXPress has to offer. Your computer has a memory, and you can rely on it.

In most cases, the last maneuver you performed can be undone using the Edit > **Undo** command. If you change your mind again, choose Edit > **Redo.**

Get in the habit of **saving** after every couple of moves (see page 36). For some reason, beginning "Quarkers" are often reluctant to use this command (or are too absorbed with other tasks) and end up learning the hard way. Having learned a few hard lessons ourselves, we now save constantly, and we make a special point of saving before we perform any complicated maneuvers. Then, if we make the inevitable multiple-step blunder, we choose File > **Revert to Saved** to get back to the last-saved version of the file. (Also read about multiple undos/redos on the following three pages.)

The undo shortcut (Cmd-Z/Ctrl-Z) can also be used to **restore** the last-used settings in an open dialog box. To dismiss a dialog box without applying any values, click **Cancel** (Esc or Cmd-./Esc).

QuarkXPress has two features for backing up a whole project: **Auto Save** and **Auto Backup.** Read about these features on page 365.

And finally, if you're working on a complicated object, you can **duplicate** it (Item > Duplicate or Cmd-D/Ctrl-D) and set the copy aside for safekeeping (put it on the pasteboard). Then later you can compliment yourself on your great foresight.

Changing undo preferences

You can change the **shortcut** used to invoke the Redo function, as well as specify **how many** undos can be stored ("cached") at a time, in QuarkXPress (Edit, in Windows) > Preferences > Application > Undo. See page 365.

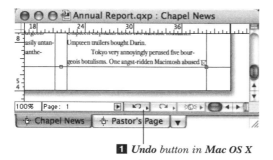

1 *Undo button in **Mac OS X***

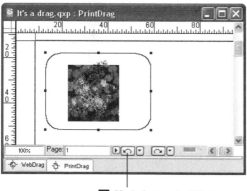

2 *Undo button in **Windows***

You can undo up to 30 edits, in reverse order, or redo up to the same number of actions that you've undone. QuarkXPress stores those edits in memory (it's called the Undo History), replacing the oldest one on the list as each new edit is performed.

You may want to scan these pages and then reread them after you've learned how to perform some edits.

To undo via a shortcut or button:

As we said on the previous page, to reverse your last edit, one option is to choose Edit > Undo (Cmd-Z/Ctrl-Z). You can choose the same command again to undo the next most recent action, and so on, until no actions remain in the Undo History. *Note:* This is the default shortcut for Undo. If it doesn't work, see the preferences information on page 365.
or
Click the Undo button [🔄] at the bottom of the project window **1**–**2**. Keep clicking the button, if desired, to continue undoing. This button won't be available if the last edit can't be undone (see the sidebar on the following page) or if the Undo History is empty.

TIP If you perform an edit that affects the whole project, that edit is added to the Undo History for all the layout spaces in that project. See our chart on page 33, which lists the edits that affect whole projects and the edits that affect individual layouts.

Multiple Undos

To undo via a menu command:

Each reversible edit you perform is added to the Undo History pop-up menu, which opens when you press and hold the Undo button in Mac OS X /the disclosure triangle next to the Undo button in Windows **2**. The most recently performed edit is listed at the top of the Undo History pop-up menu; the oldest edit is at the bottom.

When you make a selection on the Undo History pop-up menu, *all* subsequent edits (all the edits listed above the one you select on the menu) are selected and undone automatically. Unfortunately, you can't single out an edit from the middle of the list and undo just that one.

Beware! This doesn't make any sense to us, but the Undo History pop-up menu is *emptied* automatically whenever you perform any edit that's nonreversible or you choose File > Revert to Saved.

Regardless of what appears on the Undo History pop-up menu, the current maximum number of undos will still be available via the Undo command or button.

The Undo History *isn't* cleared when you perform nonreversible edits, such as those listed below, and thus they're exceptions to the above-mentioned rule:

- Choose File > Save
- Create a new master page
- Duplicate a master page
- Apply a master page to a layout page
- Create or move a ruler guide on a layout page
- Delete a ruler guide from a layout page

Undo undoes more

With each new version, the list of things you can undo in QuarkXPress gets longer. If you're upgrading from version 4 or 5 to version 7, you'll be pleasantly surprised.

You can undo one type of edit in QuarkXPress 7 that you couldn't undo in version 6:

- Edit Layer Attributes

These operations still can't be undone:

- Changes made in the Edit Colors dialog box
- Master pages changes (e.g., duplicating a master page or choosing commands from the context menu over the Page Layout palette while a master page is displayed)—once a layout page is redisplayed.
- Adding, deleting, or re-ordering pages in the Page Layout palette.

1 *Four undos are selected on the **Undo** pop-up menu in **Mac OS X.***

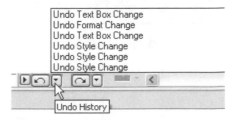

2 *The **Undo** pop-up menu in **Windows***

Undo History

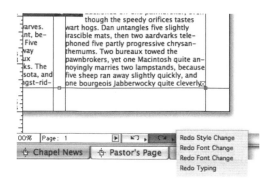

1 *The **Redo** pop-up menu in **Mac OS X***

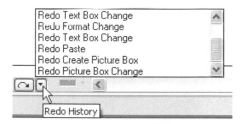

2 *The **Redo** pop-up menu in **Windows***

The Redo command redoes the last edit that you've undone. You can choose the command again and again to reverse multiple undos, going backward in history.

To redo edits that were undone:

Method 1

Choose Edit > Redo (Cmd-Shift-Z/Ctrl-Shift-Z). You can keep choosing the same command to reverse more undos, until the Redo History empties out. *Note:* If this command doesn't work, read about Undo preferences on page 365.

Method 2

Click the Redo button [ ] at the bottom of the project window. Click again to reverse more undos. This button won't be available if the Redo History is empty.

Method 3

Each edit you perform is added to the Redo History pop-up menu, which opens when you press and hold the Redo button in Mac OS X **1**/the disclosure triangle next to the Redo button in Windows **2**. The most recently performed undo will be listed at the top of the Redo History pop-up menu, and so on down in order. When you select an edit on the menu, that undo and all edits that are listed above it are selected and reversed.

Note: The Redo History is usually empty because QuarkXPress clears it automatically whenever you perform an edit other than Undo or Redo. When the Redo History is empty, the Redo button is unavailable.

Multiple Redo

Text **4**

Continuing with your studies

Once you've read this chapter and learned the **rudiments** of manipulating text—getting it into a box, selecting it, and rearranging it—you'll be ready to explore these other topics:

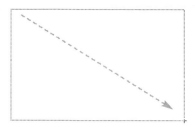

1 *Drag with a **Text Box** tool.*

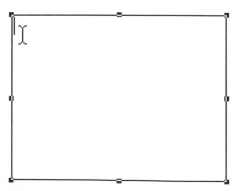

2 *A new text box is created.*

Text basics

To input or import text in QuarkXPress, you first have to create a box to put it. You can also flow text along a path or enter it in table cells. QuarkXPress has five tools that are expressly used for creating different-shaped text boxes, as well as two Bézier Text Box tools, four Text-Path tools, and a Tables tool. In addition, you can convert any item into a text box or text path.

In QuarkXPress 7.0, new text boxes are transparent by default—that is, they are created with a background color of None. To learn about adding color to a text box or path, see pages 267–271.

Note: If you check Automatic Text Box in the New Project dialog box when you create a project, every page in the default layout will contain a text box within the margin guides. This box is used to flow text from page to page, and you'll learn about it in the next chapter. For now, you can delete the automatic text box if it gets in the way: click it, then press Cmd-K/Ctrl-K (or, if you're in a lousy mood, Cmd-Option-Shift-K/Ctrl-Alt-Shift-K might cheer you up—no, it's not a virus, it's a feature).

To create a text box:

1. Choose any Text Box tool except a Bézier text tool (see Chapter 18). The cursor will turn into a crosshair.

2. Drag in any direction **1**. When you release the mouse, the finished box will be selected and ready to hold text **2**. When the Content tool is chosen and a text box is selected, a blinking text insertion marker appears in the box and the pointer turns into an I-beam.

NEW

New Text Box

Every box in QuarkXPress, no matter its shape, is contained within a rectangular, non-printing bounding box which has handles at each corner and in the middle of each side **1**. When you resize a text box, you are manipulating its bounding box.

To resize a text box manually:

1. Choose the Item or Content tool (Shift-F8).

2. Click a box. Its bounding box appears.

3. Drag any handle **2**–**3**.
   or
   To resize the box proportionally, hold down Option-Shift/Alt-Shift while dragging. (Hold down Shift without Option/Alt to turn the bounding box into a square.) Release the modifier keys after you release the mouse.

TIP Make sure the point of the cursor arrow is directly over one of the box handles before pressing the mouse. The cursor will change into a pointing-hand icon.

TIP To see your changes in real time, pause after clicking a handle of a text box but before dragging. The text wrap will update continuously as you drag (the pointer will turn into a cluster of arrows) **4**. The length of the pause required before dragging can be adjusted in Preferences (see page 364).

To resize a text box using the Measurements palette:

1. Choose the Item or Content tool.

2. Click a box.

3. Change the W (and/or H) value on the Measurements palette (Classic or Space/Align tab) for the width (and/or height) of the box, then press Return/Enter **5**. You need to include an abbreviation for the unit (e.g., "p" or "mm") only if the value you're entering is not in the current default unit. See page 29.

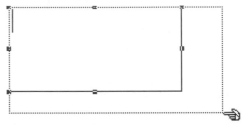

1 *An oval text box enclosed in its **bounding box***

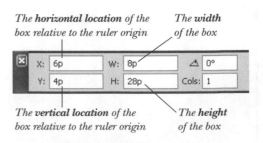

2 *Resize a box by dragging any of its four **corner handles** (note the hand pointer)…*

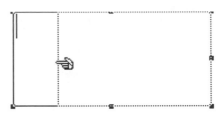

3 *…or drag any of its four **midpoint handles**.*

After a brief shower of orange juice, low clouds of sunny-side up eggs moved in followed by pieces of toast.

Judi Barrett

4 *Pause-dragging with **Live Refresh***

*The **horizontal location** of the box relative to the ruler origin* — *The **width** of the box*

| X: 6p | W: 8p | ⊿ 0° |
| Y: 4p | H: 28p | Cols: 1 |

*The **vertical location** of the box relative to the ruler origin* — *The **height** of the box*

5 *The box location and size fields on the Classic tab of the **Measurements palette***

Resize Text Box

Snap to it

If View > **Snap to Guides** is checked (Shift-F7 toggles it on and off) and you drag the handle of a box or an anchor point near a guide, the handle or point will snap to the guide with a little tug. Turn Snap to Guides off to drag items manually without the little tug.

> Mrs. Trenor was a tall, fair woman whose height just saved her from redundancy. Her rosy blondness had survived some forty years of futile activity without showing much trace of ill-usage except in a diminished play
>
> EDITH WHARTON

1 *Pause before dragging to see the* **contents** *of the item as you move it…*

> Mrs. Trenor was a tall, fair woman whose height just saved her from redundancy. Her rosy blondness had survived some forty years of futile activity without showing much trace of ill-usage except in a diminished play

2 *… or drag* **without pausing** *to see only the* **outline** *of the box as it's moved. Use this method on a slow machine.*

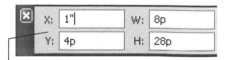

X:	1"	W:	8p
Y:	4p	H:	28p

3 *To* **position** *an object very precisely, enter new* **X** *and/or* **Y** *values on the Measurements palette.*

X:	6p	W:	8p
Y:	4p	H:	28p

4 *After pressing Return/Enter, the 1" value entered in the X field is converted to its equivalent in the* **default** *measurement unit (in this case, picas).*

To move a text box manually:

1. Choose the Item tool. Or if you're using the Content tool, hold down Cmd/Ctrl to turn it into a temporary Item tool.

2. Press inside a text box, pause briefly for the text to redraw, then drag the item to a new location on the same page or on a different page **1**–**2** (the pointer will be a cluster of arrowheads). The X and Y position values on the Measurements palette will update as you drag. To force scrolling, knock your pointer into the edge of the project window while dragging.

TIP Hold down Shift as you drag to constrain the movement to a horizontal or vertical axis. Release the mouse before releasing Shift. To use ruler guides to position an item, see page 203.

Use the Measurements palette to move the upper-left corner of an item to a precise X/Y location, relative to the ruler origin.

To reposition a text box or any other item using the Measurements palette:

1. Choose the Item or Content tool.

2. Click the item you want to reposition.

3. Enter a new number in the X (or Y) field on the Classic or Space/Align tab of the Measurements palette to change the horizontal (or vertical) position of the item's bounding box relative to the ruler origin **3**, which, unless you change it, is located at the uppermost left corner of the project window.

4. Press Return/Enter **4**.

TIP To use arithmetic in the X, Y, W, or H field—for example, to make a box 4p taller—enter "+" after the current number, then the amount you want to add. To subtract, enter "-"; to multiply, enter "*"; or to divide, enter "/".

Move Text Box

Working with text

To input text:

1. Choose the Content tool.

2. Click in a text box (or click a text path) to create an insertion point.

3. Start typing **1**. Press Return/Enter whenever you want to begin a new paragraph **2**.

TIP Make sure View > Invisibles is checked (Cmd-I/ Ctrl-I) to reveal paragraph returns, spaces, and other non-printing characters.

TIP To move text inward from the sides of its box, select the box, use the Text tab of the Measurements palette or the Item < Modify dialog box to adjust Text Inset (see page 71). And remember, you can always move the text box downward on the page!

What is the text overflow symbol?

If a text box is too small to display all the text that it contains, a text overflow symbol appears in the lower-right corner of the box **3**. The text overflow symbol will disappear if the text box is enlarged enough to display all the type that it contains or if the box is linked to another box for the text to spill into.

The text overflow symbol doesn't print; it's merely an indicator that there's hidden text in the buffer. Only text that's visible in a box will print.

TIP If pages are mysteriously added to your layout when a text box becomes full, it means Auto Page Insertion is on in QuarkXPress (Edit, in Windows) > Preferences > Print Layout > General.

As soon as they were gone, Elizabeth walked out to recover her spirits; or in other words, to dwell without interruption on those subjects that must deaden them more. Mr. Darcy's behavior astonished|

1 *Text is typed into a text box with the Content tool.*

As·soon·as·they·were·gone,·Elizabeth· walked·out·to·recover·her·spirits;·or·in· other·words,·to·dwell·without·interruption· on·those·subjects·that·must·deaden·them· more.·Mr.·Darcy's·behavior·astonished· and·vexed·her.¶
"Why,·if·he·came·only·to·be·silent,·
Jane Austen

2 *Press **Return** to begin a new **paragraph**.*

As soon as they were gone, Elizabeth walked out to recover her spirits; or in other words, to dwell without interruption on those subjects that must deaden them more. Mr. Darcy's behavior astonished ⊠

3 *The red **text overflow** symbol appears when a box is too small to display all the text that it contains.*

On an exceptionally hot evening
early in July, a young man came

1 *Double-click anywhere in the middle of a **word** to select it.*

On an exceptionally hot evening early in
July, a young man came out of the garret
in which he lodged in S. Place and
walked slowly, as though in hesitation,
towards K. Bridge.
   He had successfully avoided meeting
his landlady on the staircase. His garret
was under the roof of a high, five-storied

2 *Triple-click to select a **line**.*

On an exceptionally hot evening early in
July, a young man came out of the garret
in which he lodged in S. Place and
walked slowly, as though in hesitation,
towards K. Bridge.
   He had successfully avoided meeting
his landlady on the staircase. His garret
was under the roof of a high, five-storied
                              Fyodor Dostoevsky

3 *Click **four** times to select a **paragraph**.*

To select text:

1. Choose the Content tool.

2. Drag across the text you want to select.
   or
   Use one of these fast-clicking methods
   1–**3**:

Number of clicks	What gets selected
1 click	Creates an **insertion point**
2 clicks	A **word**
3 clicks	A **line**
4 clicks	A **paragraph**
5 clicks	A whole **story** (all the text in a box or in a series of linked boxes)

or

To select a whole **story,** click in a text box, then choose Edit > Select All (Cmd-A/Ctrl-A). Hidden overflow text, if any, will be included in the selection. A story is all the text in a box, plus any boxes that it's linked to.

Note: If the Item tool is active when you choose Select All, all items on the currently displayed page or spread and surrounding pasteboard will become selected instead!
or
Click in a text box at the beginning of a **text string,** then Shift-click at the end of the text string.
or
To select from the current **cursor** position to the **end** of a story: Cmd-Option-Shift-down arrow/Ctrl-Alt-Shift-down arrow. (See page 424 for more shortcuts.)
or
To select a series of **words,** double-click the first word, keep the mouse button down on the second click, then drag. Or triple-click, then drag downward to select a series of **lines.**

To delete text:

1. Choose the Content tool.

2. Click to the right of the character you wish to delete , then press Delete/ Backspace. (Press the left or right arrow on the keyboard to move the insertion point one character at a time.)
or
First select the text you want to delete (see the previous page) . Then in Mac OS X, press Delete or choose Edit > Clear. In Windows, press Backspace or Delete or choose Edit > Delete.

TIP To delete the character to the right of the cursor, press the del/Delete key on an extended keyboard or press Shift-Delete on a nonextended keyboard.

The Line Text-Path tool and Orthogonal Text-Path tool are discussed below. The Bézier Text-Path and Freehand Text-Path tools are discussed in Chapter 18.

To create a straight text path:

1. To draw a straight path oriented at any multiple of 45°, choose the Orthogonal Text-Path tool 🔲 **3**
or
To draw a straight-line path at any angle, choose the Line Text-Path tool 🔲 **4**.

2. Drag to draw the path, and leave it selected. The Content tool becomes active.

3. Start typing. The text will march along the path.

TIP If you want to draw several text paths in quick succession, hold down Option/Alt when choosing the text-path tool. The tool will remain active after you draw the path.

If you deselect and then reselect a box with the Content tool, the **last** group of characters that were selected, if any, will be reselected. To create a new insertion point, click once more in the text box.

CHESTER

1 *Pressing Delete with the cursor at this insertion point would remove the "S."*

CHESTER

2 *Pressing Delete with this selection selected would delete the "HES."*

3 *Drag vertically or horizontally with the* ***Orthogonal Text-Path*** *tool.*

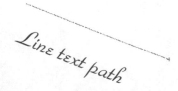

4 *Drag at any angle with the* ***Line Text-Path*** *tool.*

> **Hip.** Well shone, moon—Truly, the moon shines with a good grace.
> **Dem.** Well roared, lion.
> **The.** Well run, Thisbe.
> **The.** Well moused, lion.

1 *To move text, select it, then choose Edit > **Cut**.*

> **Dem.** Well roared, lion.
> **The.** Well run, Thisbe.
> **The.** Well moused, lion.

2 ***Click** to create a new insertion point.*

> **Dem.** Well roared, lion.
> **The.** Well run, Thisbe.
> **Hip.** Well shone, moon—Truly, the moon shines with a good grace.
> **The.** Well moused, lion.
> *~ William Shakespeare*

3 *Choose Edit > **Paste**.*

To delete any item:

Choose the Item or Content tool, click the item you want to delete, then choose Item > Delete (Cmd-K/Ctrl-K).
or
Choose the Item tool, and click the item you want to delete. Then in Mac OS X, press Delete or choose Edit > Clear. In Windows, press Delete or Backspace or choose Edit > Delete.

The Clipboard is a holding area that stores one cut or copied selection at a time. The current contents of the Clipboard can be retrieved an unlimited number of times via the Paste command. The current Clipboard contents will be replaced if you invoke the Copy or Cut command in any application, and will be deleted if you turn off your computer.

To rearrange text using the Clipboard:

1. Choose the Content tool.
2. Select the text you want to move **1**.
3. Choose Edit > Cut (Cmd-X/Ctrl-X) to place the selected text on the Clipboard and *remove* it from its current location.
   or
   Choose Edit > Copy (Cmd-C/Ctrl-C) to place a *copy* of the selected text on the Clipboard and leave the selected text in its current location.
4. Click in a text box to create a new insertion point **2**.
5. Choose Edit > Paste (Cmd-V/Ctrl-V) **3**. QuarkXPress (using a feature called Smart Space) takes care of adding spaces where needed (see page 194).

TIP The Clipboard can also be used to cut or copy any type of box, line, or group when the Item tool is selected, or a picture if the Content tool is chosen. Paste using the same tool that was used to Cut or Copy—unless you want the item to be anchored (see page 199)!

Delete Any Item; Rearrange Text

You can use the Drag and Drop Text feature to move or copy text quickly without having to use the Cut, Copy, or Paste command. You can drag and drop text within the same box or between linked boxes or table cells (a story), but not between unlinked boxes or cells. This is a very handy feature for making quick copyedits.

Note: To enable the drag-and-drop feature, go to QuarkXPress (Edit, in Windows) > Preferences > Application > Input Settings, then check Drag and Drop Text 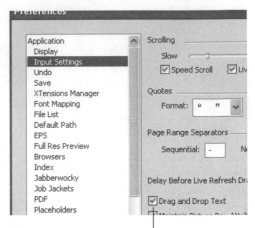.

In Mac OS X only, if the Drag and Drop Text option is off, you can still perform the command: Cmd-Control-drag the text to move it or Cmd-Control-Shift-drag to move a copy of it.

To drag and drop text:

1. Choose the Content tool.

2. Select the text you want to move or copy (see page 67).

3. Release the mouse.

4. To move the selected text, drag the blinking insertion point to a new location in the same text box or table cell or in a box or cell that it's linked to. A hollow box will display under the pointer as you drag **2**–**3**.
or
To move a copy of the text, hold down Shift while dragging the blinking insertion point to a new location (a hollow box and a plus sign will also display as you drag).

TIP Text that is dragged and dropped is also placed on the Clipboard, but you won't be aware of it unless you use the Paste command or choose Edit > Show Clipboard.

1 *Check **Drag and Drop Text** in QuarkXPress (Edit, in Windows) > Preferences > Application > **Input Settings**.*

> If you want to get somewhere else, you must run at least twice as fast as that. Now, *here*, you see, it takes all the running *you* can do, to keep in the same place.

2 *To **drag and drop** (move) text, select it, release the mouse, then drag the selected text to a new position. A blinking cursor will indicate the insertion point.*

> "Now, *here*, you see, it takes all the running *you* can do, to keep in the same place. If you want to get somewhere else, you must run at least twice as fast as that..."
>
> *Lewis Carroll*

3 *The sentences have been swapped.*

1 *To make the **Text Inset** uniform, leave Multiple Insets unchecked, and enter an **All Edges** value.*

> *Promote then as an object of primary importance, institutions for the general diffusion of knowledge. In proportion as the structure of a government gives force to public opinion, it is essential that public opinion be enlightened.*
>
> GEORGE WASHINGTON

2 *A text box with a **Text Inset** of 0 pt*

> *Promote then as an object of primary importance, institutions for the general diffusion of knowledge. In proportion as the structure of a government gives force to public opinion, it is essential that public opinion be enlightened.*

3 *The same text box with a **Text Inset** of 7 pt*

4 *To enter separate **Text Inset** values for the Top, Left, Bottom, and Right edges of a text box, first check **Multiple Insets.***

> *Promote then as an object of primary importance, institutions for the general diffusion of knowledge. In proportion as the structure of a government gives force to public opinion, it is essential that public opinion be enlightened.*

5 *The text box with a **different Text Inset** value on each of its four sides*

Working with text boxes

The text inset is the blank space between text and the four edges of the box that contains it. A Text Inset value greater than zero should be applied to any box that has a frame in order to create breathing space between the text and the frame. You used to have to open the Modify dialog box to change the values, but in QuarkXPress 7 you can use the Text tab of the Measurements palette.

To change the Text Inset using the Measurements palette: **NEW**

1. Choose the Item or Content tool.

2. Click a text box.

3. Display the Text tab on the Measurements palette.

4. To apply a uniform Text Inset value to all four edges of the text box, leave Multiple Insets unchecked, then enter a value in the All Edges field **1**–**3**. If you're entering a value in points, you don't have to reenter the "pt."
   or
   To enter a different Text Inset value for each edge of a rectangular text box, check Multiple Insets **4**–**5**, then enter Top, Left, Bottom, and Right values.

5. Press Return/Enter.

TIP Even though we're showing you how to adjust text using (for the most part) the new and improved Measurements palette in QuarkXPress 7.0, our old friend, the Modify dialog box, is still available for the same adjustments. We just think the Measurements palette is more convenient.

Text Inset

These instructions apply to text boxes, picture boxes, and contentless boxes.

To apply a frame to any type of box:

1. Choose the Item or Content tool.

2. Click a box (Bézier or standard).

3. Choose Item > Frame (Cmd-B/Ctrl-B).

4. Choose a preset Width from the menu or enter a custom Width **1**. You can enter fractions of a point.

5. Choose from the Style menu. (To create a custom dashed or multi-line frame, see pages 227–230.)

6. Choose from the Frame: Color menu.

7. Choose from the Frame: Shade and Opacity menus or enter a Shade or Opacity percentage.

8. *Optional:* To color the white areas in a multiline or broken style, choose from the Gap: Color, Shade, and Opacity menus.

9. Click Apply to preview, make any adjustments, then click OK (illustrations on the next page).

Frame like a pro

■ Apply a Text Inset greater than zero in Item > Modify > Text to add breathing room between the text and the frame.

■ Use narrow, delicate frames rather than thick, ornate ones. Gaudy frames distract from, and overwhelm, the text. Less is more.

■ Unless you want the whole world to know you're new to graphic design, use frames sparingly here or there in a couple of spots—not frames, frames everywhere.

■ There is such a thing as "too thin" when it comes to frames. Frames below a minimum width won't print.

TIP To remove a frame, select the box, choose Item > Frame again, then enter 0 in the Width field.

TIP You can also use the Frame tab of the Measurements palette to design a frame. Make sure to choose a width first, so the results of your other changes will appear instantly.

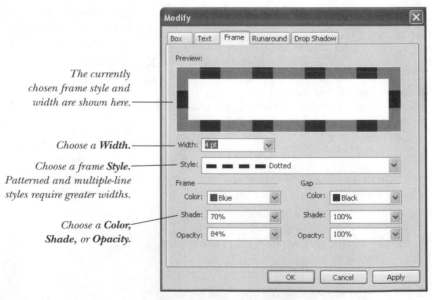

The currently chosen frame style and width are shown here.

*Choose a **Width**.*

*Choose a frame **Style**. Patterned and multiple-line styles require greater widths.*

*Choose a **Color**, **Shade**, or **Opacity**.*

1 *The **Frame** tab of the Item > **Modify** dialog box*

Frames illustrated

Speak what you think now in hard words, and tomorrow speak what tomorrow thinks in hard words again, though it contradict every thing you said today.—"Ah, so you shall be sure to be misunderstood."—Is it so bad, then, to be misunderstood? Pythagoras was misunderstood, and Socrates, and Jesus, and Luther, and Copernicus, and Galileo, and Newton, and every pure and wise spirit that ever took flesh. To be great is to be misunderstood.

Ralph Waldo Emerson

Guests, like fish, smell after three days.

Ben Franklin

If you have built castles in the air, your work need not be lost; that is where they should be. Now put the foundations under them.

HENRY DAVID THOREAU

*Sometimes **simplest** is best.*

DO I CONTRADICT MYSELF?

VERY WELL THEN...

I CONTRADICT MYSELF;

I AM LARGE...

I CONTAIN MULTITUDES.

Walt Whitman

*These star-shaped Bézier boxes have **dashed** or **striped** frames. They were created using the Starburst tool.*

To move text down in its box:

To move the first line of text down from the top of its box, select the box, click the Text tab on the Measurements palette, then enter a First Baseline Offset value greater than 0 and press Return/Enter **1**. This value will be added to the current Text Inset value. From the First Baseline Minimum menu, choose whether, at minimum, the first line of text will be offset from the top of the box as measured from the line's largest Cap Height, Cap + Accent [mark], or Ascent (top of the tallest character, as in an "l" or a "T") **2**–**3**.

or

Display the Text tab of the Measurements palette, check Multiple Insets, then enter a higher Top Text Inset value and press Return/Enter.

or

This may feel like cheating, but sometimes simplest is best: Just yank the whole box downward on the page with the Item tool. This works as long as the box isn't framed.

The flip commands flip all the text in a box, but not the box itself. Text can be modified in its flipped position.

To flip text:

1. Choose the Content tool.
2. Click a text box.
3. Choose Style > Flip Horizontal or Flip Vertical.
   or
   Click the Flip Horizontal ➡ and/or Flip Vertical ⬆ button on the Classic tab or Text tab of the Measurements palette **4**–**5**.

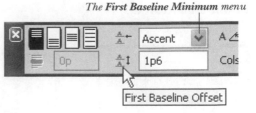

*The **First Baseline Minimum** menu*

First Baseline Offset

1 *Using the Text tab of the Measurements palette to adjust the vertical **offset** of the first line of text*

> *Once upon a time there was a Pussy-cat called Ribby, who invited a little dog called Duchess to tea.*
> *Beatrix Potter*

> *Once upon a time there was a Pussy-cat called Ribby, who invited a little dog called Duchess to tea.*

2 ***First Baseline 0***   **3** ***First Baseline 1p6***

It's a poor sort of memory that only works backwards

Lewis Carroll

4 *The word "backwards" is in a separate text box, and it's **flipped horizontally**.*

Narcissus

5 *The text box containing the gray "Narcissus" was **flipped vertically**.*

*The **Text Skew** field*

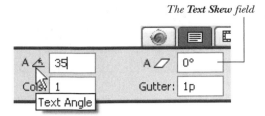

1 *Use the Text tab of the Measurements palette to change the **angle** of the text.*

After the storm,
On Mount Mimuro,
The colored leaves
Float like brocade
On the River Tatsuta.
The Monk Nōin

2 *A **Text Angle** of 35°: The text is rotated; the box isn't.*

Sometimes I've believed as many as six impossible things before breakfast.
Lewis Carroll

3 *A rectangular text box **skewed** at a 40° angle: Both the text and the box are skewed.*

To rotate all the text in a box—without rotating its box—follow these instructions. To rotate text and its box, see the following page.

To change the text angle using the Measurements palette: NEW

1. Choose the Item or Content tool.

2. Click a text box of any shape or Shift-click multiple boxes.

3. Display the Text tab of the Measurements palette and enter a value between –360° and 360° in the Text Angle field **1**.

4. Press Return/Enter **2**. The text can still be edited. You can restore the Text Angle to 0° at any time.

To change the text angle using the Modify dialog box:

1. Choose the Item or Content tool.

2. Click a text box of any shape or Shift-click multiple boxes.

3. Choose Item > Modify (Cmd-M/Ctrl-M), then click the Text tab.

4. Enter a Text Angle value between –360° and 360°, then click Apply to preview.

5. Click OK.

TIP Skewing a text box slants the text as well **3**. The effect is sometimes referred to as "false italic." To skew text, follow either set of instructions above, except on the Text tab of the Measurements palette enter a value between –75 and 75 in the Text Skew field, then press Return/Enter. Or in the Modify dialog box, click the Box tab and enter a Text Skew value between –75 and 75.

You can rotate a text box a specific angle by entering a number into the Measurements palette (or in the Item > Modify dialog box). If you use this method, the center of the box will always be the axis of rotation. Using the Rotation tool to rotate a box, on the other hand, allows you to choose the axis.

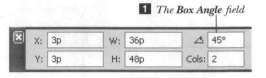

1 *The Box Angle field*

To rotate a text box using the Measurements palette:

1. Choose the Item or Content tool.

2. Click a text box.

3. In the Box Angle field on the Classic or Space/Align tab of the Measurements palette, enter a positive value between 0° and 360° to rotate the box counterclockwise **1** or a negative value to rotate it clockwise, then press Return/Enter. You can edit the text in its rotated position.

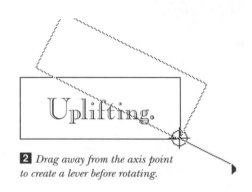

2 *Drag away from the axis point to create a lever before rotating.*

To rotate a text box using the Rotation tool:

1. Choose the Rotation tool. ↺

2. Click a text box.

3. Press to create an axis point for rotation, then drag the mouse away from the axis to create a "lever" **2**. The further you drag away from the axis before rotating, the easier the rotation will be to control.

4. Drag clockwise or counterclockwise **3**. Hold down Shift while dragging to rotate at an increment of 45° (release the mouse first).

3 *The box rotated -90°*

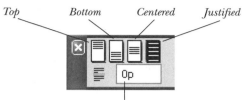

| Top | Bottom | Centered | Justified |

*The **Inter Paragraph Maximum** field*

1 *The **Vertical Alignment** options, as displayed on the Text tab of the Measurements palette*

Never put off till tomorrow what you can do the day after tomorrow.

Top *vertical alignment*

Never put off till tomorrow what you can do the day after tomorrow.

Bottom *vertical alignment*

Never put off till tomorrow what you can do the day after tomorrow.

Centered *vertical alignment*

Never put off

till tomorrow

what you

can do the

day after

tomorrow.

Mark Twain

Justified *vertical alignment*

The Vertical Alignment options affect all the text contained in a rectangular box. Leading (line spacing) and interparagraph spacing, which affect one or more paragraphs, are discussed in Chapter 6.

To change vertical alignment:

1. Choose the Item or Content tool, then click a rectangular text box or select multiple boxes (see page 185).

2. Display the Text tab of the Measurements palette. **NEW**

3. Choose one of the Vertical Alignment options by clicking its icon: Top, Centered, Bottom, or Justified **1**.

4. *Optional:* If you chose Justified, enter a value for Inter Paragraph Maximum spacing. If the value is 0, space is added evenly between lines and paragraphs. A value greater than 0 is the maximum space that can be added between paragraphs before leading is affected. Try raising this value and see what happens.

5. Press Return/Enter **2**. *Note:* Make sure there isn't a return at the end of the last line in a box to which Bottom, Centered, or Justified Vertical Alignment has been applied, or the alignment will be thrown off. The Vertical Alignment options are also affected by the First Baseline Offset and Top Text Inset values.

TIP Vertical justification won't work if the justified text box is behind another box that has a Runaround setting other than None. To make justification work, click the Runaround tab and change the Type to None for the top box.

TIP If you've chosen Centered alignment and your text happens not to have any descenders (characters that extend below the baseline), you may need to Baseline Shift the type down slightly to make it look more centered (see page 129).

Change Vertical Alignment

Follow either set of instructions on this page to change the number of columns and/or the gutter width in an individual box. To change the non-printing margin and column guides or to change the number of columns in a box originating from a master page, follow the instructions on page 247.

To change the number of columns using the Measurements palette:

1. Choose the Item or Content tool.

2. Select a text box.

3. Display the Classic or Text tab of the Measurements palette and enter a number in the "Cols" field (1–30, depending on the width of the box) 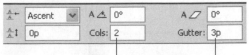.
and/or
Change the Gutter value for the blank space between the columns (Text tab only).

4. Press Return/Enter **2**–**3**.

To change columns and/or gutter width using a dialog box:

1. Choose the Item or Content tool.

2. Select a text box.

3. Choose Item > Modify (Cmd-M/ Ctrl-M), then click the Text tab.

4. Change the number in the Columns field **4**.
and/or
Change the Gutter Width value for the blank space between the columns.

5. Click OK.

1 *The number of* ***columns*** *in a text box, and the width of the* ***gutter*** *between them, can be changed using the Measurements palette.*

There was a nice hot singey smell; and at the table, with an iron in her hand, stood a very stout short person staring anxiously at Lucie. Her print gown was tucked up, and she was wearing a large apron over her striped petti-

coat. Her little black nose went sniffle, sniffle, snuffle, and her eyes went twinkle, twinkle, twinkle; and underneath her cap—where Lucie had yellow curls—that little person had PRICKLES!

Beatrix Potter

2 *A* ***two-column*** *text box…*

There was a nice hot singey smell; and at the table, with an iron in her hand, stood a very stout short person staring anx-iously at Lucie.

Her print gown was tucked up, and she was wearing a large apron over her striped petti-coat. Her little black nose went sniffle, sniffle, snuffle,

and her eyes went twinkle, twinkle, twin-kle; and under-neath her cap—where Lucie had yel-low curls—that little person had PRICKLES!

3 *…is converted into a* ***three-column*** *text box.*

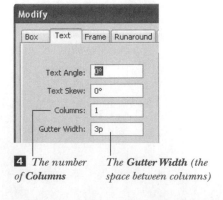

4 *The number of* ***Columns***   *The* ***Gutter Width*** *(the space between columns)*

Change Columns, Gutter

Comparing the formats

Plain Text strips all formatting.

XPress Tags retains all formatting. Formatting codes will display with the text when viewed in a word processing application.

Rich Text Format preserves font, font size, type styling, and style sheet information from QuarkXPress.

WordPerfect and **Microsoft Word** may strip some formatting.

HTML preserves font and type styling for importing and viewing in a browser.

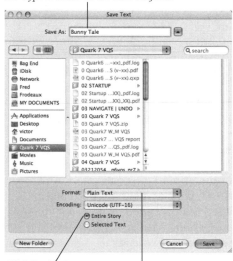

1 *Type a name in the **Save As** field.*

*Click **Entire Story** or click **Selected Text** (if available).*

*Choose a file **format**. This is the Save Text dialog box in **Mac OS X**.*

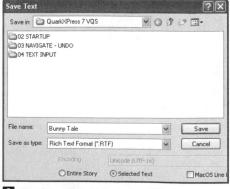

2 *The **Save Text** dialog box in **Windows***

You can save text from a QuarkXPress file as a separate file into any of these formats: Plain Text, XPress Tags, Rich Text, WordPerfect, Microsoft Word, or HTML. You can save all the text in a story, or just a selected portion.

To save text as a word processing file:

1. Choose the Content tool.

2. Select the text to be saved.
or
Click in a story.

3. Choose File > Save Text (Cmd-Option-E/Ctrl-Alt-E).
or
Control-click/Right-click and choose Save Text from the context menu.

4. Type a name for the text file in the Save As/File Name field **1**–**2**.

5. If text is selected in the layout, you can click Entire Story or Selected Text. If you clicked in a story but didn't select any text, the Entire Story option will be chosen for you.

6. Choose a file format from the Format/Save as Type menu. A format's import/export filter must be enabled in order for it to appear on the list. Use the XTensions Manager to turn a filter on or off (see page 377).

7. *Optional in Windows:* If you've chosen Plain Text as the format and you check Mac OS Line Endings, the standard Windows line break that's represented by a return and line feed character will be replaced by just a return character, which is standard in Mac OS X.

8. Choose a location in which to save the text file.

9. Click Save (Return/Enter).

TIP To learn more about XPress Tags, see the QuarkXPress documentation or *Real World QuarkXPress 7* by David Blatner (Peachpit Press).

Managing fonts

Keep in mind that fonts are not managed by QuarkXPress and they are activated (installed) or de-activated by your operating system or by third-party font management software. QuarkXPress does not come with fonts and it does not control which ones are available on your computer. That's all up to you. Some fonts do come with your system software and with other applications, and you can buy more from sources such as www.adobe.com, www.linotype.com, and www.myfonts.com.

Use a font manager

When you're working on any type of professional publishing, you absolutely need a font management utility. A font manager shows you which fonts are active on your computer, which fonts you have available, and what they look like. In addition, many font managers let you create sets of fonts to activate manually for specific projects, and sets of fonts that are activated when you launch specific applications. Font managers may also provide automatic font activation as you open documents (thereby preventing the dreaded "missing fonts" alert) and means for exporting fonts.

Mac OS X comes with a basic font manager, FontBook. For more power, we recommend Suitcase Fusion **1** (www.extensis. com) or FontAgent Pro (www.insidersoftware.com). For Windows, try Suitcase (www.extensis.com) or FontExpert 2006 (www.proximasoftware.com). Or, to save money, you can consult your system's Help file to learn about managing fonts.

Use the same fonts

In professional publishing it's importantto use the exact same fonts throughout an entire workflow—from design to output. And when we say "exact same fonts," we don't mean any old font named "Helvetica" or "Times" or "Garamond." Fonts come in many flavors, from OpenType to TrueType to PostScript, and from different vendors in bewilderingly different versions. It's not at all uncommon to have the same font in three slightly different versions: Adobe Garamond 1.000, 1.001, 1.002. But should you care? Yes! Using different versions of the same font, particularly in different formats or from different foundries and possibly in different versions, can cause your text to reflow and ruin a layout. If you are working cross-platform, passing files back and forth between Mac OS and Windows, we suggest you use OpenType fonts, which flow the same on both platforms.

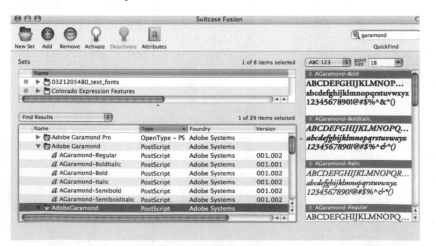

1 *Suitcase Fusion allows you to create sets of fonts on a project-by-project basis (top left); lists detailed information about each font's kind, foundry, version, and more (bottom left); and displays previews of fonts at any size (right).*

Text Flow **5**

What if

If you didn't turn on **Automatic Text Box** in the New Project dialog box but later on you decide you need an auto text box, you can add it "manually." See the instructions on page 258.

1 *In QuarkXPress (Edit, in Windows) > Preferences > Print Layout > General, choose* **Auto Page Insertion: End of Story, End of Section,** *or* **End of Document** *to add pages as necessary when flowing text into the automatic text box.*

Adding pages

In the previous chapter, you learned how to get text into a box. The next step is to learn how to route overflow text from box to box and from page to page.

Auto page insertion is used for layouts in which a story flows consecutively from one page to the next, as in a book or booklet. You'll start by enabling the Automatic Text Box and Auto Page Insertion options. Then when you import or input text into an automatic text box, new pages will be added, if necessary, to contain any overflow text, and text boxes will be linked from page to page. Each layout can have up to 2,000 pages.

For layouts that contain multiple stories that may flow onto nonconsecutive pages, as in a newsletter, manual linking is a better choice (see page 89).

To turn on Auto Page Insertion for a new project:

1. Choose File > New > Project (Cmd-N/ Ctrl-N) to create a new print project.

2. Check Automatic Text Box to have an automatic text box appear on every layout page based on the default master page.

3. Choose or enter Page Size, Orientation, Margin Guides, and Column Guides options, then click OK.

4. Choose QuarkXPress (Edit, in Windows) > Preferences > Print Layout > General.

5. Choose from the Auto Page Insertion menu the location where you want new pages to be added **1**.

6. Click OK.

A text file created in a word processing program can be imported into a text box or boxes in QuarkXPress, provided its import/export filter is installed and enabled (see page 377). Formats that can be imported include word processing files (such as WordPerfect and Microsoft Word), HTML files, XPress Tags, and plain text with or without XPress Tags.

To import text:

1. *Optional:* Turn on Auto Page Insertion (see steps 4–6 on the previous page).

2. Choose the Content tool.

3. Click in a text box. Click in an automatic text box for automatic page insertion. (If Auto Page Insertion is off, the imported text will flow into a box or a series of linked boxes, but new pages won't be added.)

4. Choose File > Import Text (Cmd-E/ Ctrl-E).
   or
   Control-click/Right-click the text box and choose Import Text.

5. Locate and click a text file **1**, then click Open, or double-click the file. In Windows, you can use the "Files of type" menu to narrow or widen the list.

6. Check Convert Quotes to convert foot and inch marks into quotation marks (see page 130) and double hyphens into em dashes.

7. *Optional:* Check Include Style Sheets to append style sheets from a Microsoft Word or WordPerfect file or when importing a plain text file with XPress Tags codes.

8. Click Open (**1**–**4**, next page).

TIP You can import Excel spreadsheets, also, but only into a table and not into the automatic text box.

Word styles

■ To import style sheets applied to text in Microsoft Word or WordPerfect, check **Include Style Sheets** in the Import Text dialog box. If any style sheet names in a word processing file match style sheet names in the QuarkXPress file, an alert dialog box will appear. To learn about the options in that dialog box, see page 50 (the same dialog box appears if a conflict crops up while appending style sheets). Also check Include Style Sheets to import plain text with XPress Tags as styled text (with typographic and formatting attributes included).

■ The **XPress Tags** filter must be enabled for the Include Style Sheets option to be available. Use the XTensions Manager (Utilities menu) to enable/disable this import/export filter.

1 *Click the **text file** to be imported.*

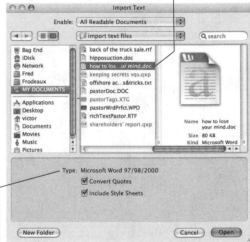

*In Mac OS X, the currently selected file's format **Type** is shown here and you can scroll to see other details about the file. In Windows, the **Name, Format, File Size,** and modification **Date** of the currently selected file are shown.*

Import Text

Auto Page Insertion on

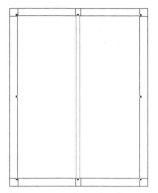

1 *Auto Page Insertion is **on**, an automatic text box is selected, and then a text file is imported.*

2 *New pages are created **automatically** to accommodate the imported text, and the text is linked in a continuous flow.*

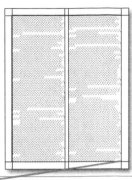

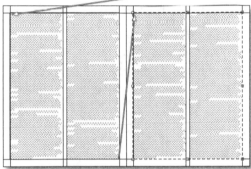

Auto Page Insertion off

3 *Auto Page Insertion is **off**, a **non-automatic** text box is selected, and then a text file is imported.*

4 *The box can't accommodate all the text and it's not linked to any other boxes, so the **text overflow** symbol appears in the lower-right corner.*

New pages can be added to a layout using either the Insert Pages dialog box or the Page Layout palette. We tend to use the Page Layout palette to add single pages and the dialog box to add multiple pages.

To insert pages using a dialog box:

1. *Optional:* We take a methodical approach to adding pages, since it can have a domino effect on the existing pages in a layout. Our first step is to save our file, so we can use Revert to Saved if we need to. Our second step is to choose Page > Go to (Cmd-J/Ctrl-J), enter the number of the page we want pages inserted before or after, and then click OK.

2. If you want to link the new pages to an existing text chain, choose the Item or Content tool, then click a box in the chain.

3. Choose Page > Insert.

4. In the Insert field, enter the number of pages to be inserted (1–1999) **2**.

5. Click "before page," "after page," or "at end of layout," and make sure the correct page number appears in the field. The number of the currently displayed page will appear there, but you can enter a different number. If the page has a prefix or Roman style that was assigned via the Section command, type it that way.

6. Choose Master Page: Blank Single, Blank Facing Page, or a master page.

   If you want to link the new pages using an automatic text box, choose a Master Page that contains an automatic text box, and check Link to Current Text Chain. (Linking is covered on pages 89–91 in this chapter; Chapter 14 is devoted entirely to master pages.)

7. Click OK. The Insert Pages command can't be undone but the inserted pages can be deleted or you can choose Revert to Saved.

How many?

Need to know the total number of pages in a layout? Make sure no page icons are selected on the Page Layout palette, then look at the total **page count** readout in the lower-left corner of the palette **1**.

1 *The **total** number of pages in the layout*

*Choose a **location** for the inserted pages, and enter a number in the field.*

2 *Enter the **number** of pages to be added.*

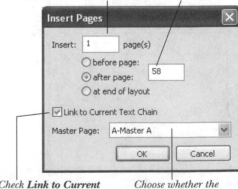

*Check **Link to Current Text Chain** to link the new pages to the end of the currently selected text chain.*

*Choose whether the inserted pages will be based on an existing **master** page or a **blank** master page.*

Watch your masters

Master pages are used to add repetitively used items to layout pages, and you'll learn all about them in Chapter 14. For now, keep in mind that if you add an uneven number of pages to a facing-pages layout (unless you drag it manually to a spread by itself with the Force Down pointer), the left and right master pages will reapply automatically from the inserted pages forward, often leaving the pages littered with extra master page items. Master pages won't reapply if you add an even number of pages to this type of layout.

Facing-pages blank
Single-sided blank

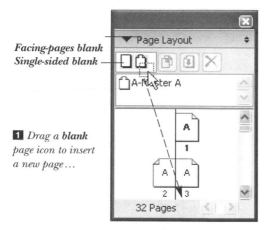

1 *Drag a blank page icon to insert a new page…*

Master page

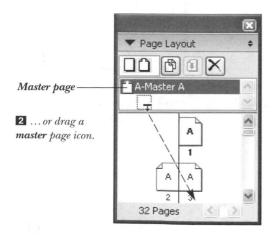

2 *… or drag a master page icon.*

If you check Facing Pages in the New Project or New Layout dialog box for a print layout, all pages after the first page will be stacked in pairs along a central spine. This format is used for books and magazines. On the Page Layout palette, facing-page icons have a turned-down (dog-eared) corner.

If you uncheck Facing Pages in the New Project or New Layout dialog box, pages will be stacked singly. Single-sided page icons have square (not dog-eared) corners. To create a spread in a single-sided layout, you can arrange your layout page icons side by side (see the following page). To convert a layout from single-sided to facing-pages, or vice versa, see page 247.

Beware! Few Page Layout palette operations can be undone. So do yourself a favor and save your file before performing any of those operations. Then, if something goes awry, you can resort to File > Revert to Saved to rescue your file.

To insert pages using the Page Layout palette:

1. Choose Window > Page Layout (F10/F4).

2. Drag a blank or master page icon into the layout page area (**1**–**2**, this page and **1**–**4**, next page). A blank page won't be associated with a master page and won't have an automatic text box, but a master page can be applied to it at any time (see page 251).

TIP You can't insert a page to the left of the first page in a facing-pages layout, unless the layout begins with an even section number (see page 96).

TIP If you Option-drag/Alt-drag a blank or master page into the layout page area, the Insert Pages dialog box will open.

(More illustrations on the following page)

Insert Pages Manually

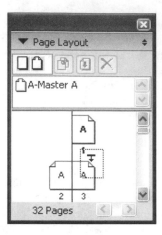

1 *To insert a page **between** spreads in a facing-pages layout, release the mouse when the **Force Down** pointer is displayed.*

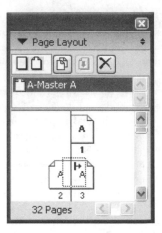

2 *In a facing-pages layout, if you release the mouse when the **Force Right** pointer is displayed, subsequent pages may reshuffle leading to duplicate master page items on layout pages. Pages won't reshuffle in a single-sided layout.*

*If you see this **non-force** pointer (no arrow) when you release the mouse, no page reshuffling will occur.*

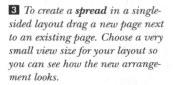

3 *To create a **spread** in a single-sided layout drag a new page next to an existing page. Choose a very small view size for your layout so you can see how the new arrangement looks.*

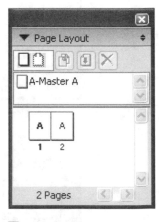

4 *With the page icons in this arrangement, pages 1 and 2 display side by side in the project window. The maximum overall width is 48". Pages will print singly unless Spreads is checked in File > Print.*

Pages keep coming back

If, when you delete layout pages from a print layout, **Auto Page Insertion** is on in QuarkXPress (Edit, in Windows) > Preferences > Print Layout > General, and the master page has an intact (not broken) chain icon (which means an automatic text box is present), and the text in a linked chain doesn't fit completely on the pages that remain, new pages will be added automatically to accommodate the overflow text. If this makes you feel like the sorcerer's apprentice, turn Auto Page Insertion off; the overflow symbol will appear, and no new pages will be added. In both scenarios, the overflow text is preserved.

1 *Enter starting and ending page numbers if you want to delete a series of pages.*

2 *To delete a page, click its icon, then click the **Delete** button.*

3 *Click OK when this prompt appears.*

Deleting pages

Both methods on this page work equally well for deleting pages. It all comes down to personal preference—whether you're a dialog box kind of person or a palette kind of person.

To delete pages using a dialog box:

1. Choose Page > Delete.

2. Enter a number in the first field to delete one page.
or
Enter numbers in both fields to delete a range of pages **1**. If a page has a prefix or Roman style that was assigned via the Section command, type it in exactly that manner. You can enter "end" in the second field to delete pages from the starting number through the end of the layout.

3. Click OK. You can't undo this.

To delete pages using the Page Layout palette:

1. On the Page Layout palette:
Click a layout page icon **2**.
or
Click the icon of the first page in a series of pages to be deleted, then Shift-click the icon of the last page in the series.
or
Cmd-click/Ctrl-click nonconsecutive page icons. (Cmd-click/Ctrl-click a selected page icon if you need to deselect it.)

2. Click the Delete button on the palette, then click OK when the prompt appears **3**. You can't undo this, either.
or
Option-click/Alt-click the Delete button on the palette to bypass the prompt.

Rearranging pages

If you rearrange pages in Thumbnails view, you will be less likely to move the wrong ones, because you'll be able to see which ones you're moving.

Note: Before proceeding with the instructions on this page, which can't be undone, we recommend that you save your file.

To rearrange pages in Thumbnails view:

1. Choose View > Thumbnails (Shift-F6).
   or
   Press Control-V/Ctrl-Alt-V, press "t", then press Return/Enter.

2. In the project window, drag a page icon to a new location **1**. If automatic page numbering was applied to the layout, the numbers will update to reflect their new position.

3. Choose a different zoom level for the layout.

TIP To move more than one page at a time in Thumbnails view, click the first page in a series of consecutive pages, Shift-click the last page in the series, then drag. Or Cmd-click/Ctrl-click to select nonconsecutive pages, then drag.

TIP You can also rearrange layout pages using the Page > Move dialog box.

To rearrange pages using the Page Layout palette:

1. Choose Window > Page Layout (F10/F4).

2. Drag a layout page icon to a new location **2**–**3**.
   or
   Click the icon of the first page in a series of pages to be moved, Shift-click the icon of the last page in the series, release Shift, then drag the pages to a new location. Or Cmd-click/Ctrl-click to select nonconsecutive pages, then drag.

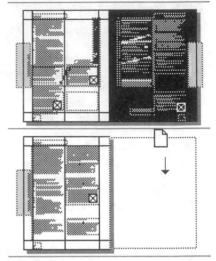

1 *A page being dragged to a new location in thumbnails view*

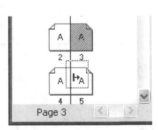

2 *If you force a page between two **pages** in a facing-pages layout, the remaining pages may reshuffle. Note the **Force Right** pointer.*

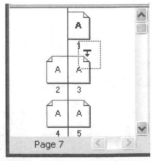

3 *If you force a page between two **spreads** in any kind of layout, the remaining pages won't reshuffle. Note the **Force Down** pointer.*

Rearrange Pages

Linking/unlinking text items

Text that flows from one box, path, or cell to another, whether linked manually or automatically, is called a story. Manual linking can be used in addition, or as an alternative, to using the automatic text box. In a print layout, you can manually link text boxes or paths on the same page or on different pages within the same layout. You can also link cells within the same table or from table to table. In a Web layout, the only thing you can link are boxes on the same page. (To link all the cells in a table, see pages 139–140.)

To link text items manually:

1. With no items selected, choose the Linking tool.⟨⟩

2. Click a text box, text path, or table cell. It can contain text or it can be

Keep on linkin'

Option-click/Alt-click the Linking tool to **keep it selected** so as to link multiple items. Click another tool when you're done linking. This also works with the Unlinking tool, as well as most other tools (e.g., text box, picture box, tables, line, text-path).

empty. A "marching ants" marquee will appear **1**.

3. Click an **empty** text box, path, or table cell. An arrow will appear briefly, showing the new link **2**–**3**. A new item can be added at any juncture in an existing chain.

TIP If you click the wrong item initially with the Linking tool, choose a different tool or click outside the box to stop the ants from marching.

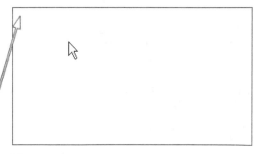

Again I see you're about to pounce, alas, my poor computer mouse.

And losing this page I cannot afford, but there you march across the keyboard.

You can't be hungry again so fast Why the time's just barely passed.

Oh maybe I'll give you just a nibble, just so you'll stay out of trib'l. ▢

1 *Click a text box, text path, or table cell…*

2 *…then click an **empty** text item.*

Again I see you're about to pounce, alas, my poor computer mouse.

And losing this page I cannot afford, but there you march across the keyboard.

You can't be hungry again so fast Why the time's just barely passed.

Oh maybe I'll give you just a nibble, just so you'll stay out of trib'l.

I know it's warmer than my lap, but the printer's not the place to nap.

And I don't need your claws to catch, the printer's pages as they hatch.

To keep you from my papers chew'n I guess I shouldn't leave them strew'n.

I just wish you wouldn't eat'm before I've had a chance to read'm.

3 *The boxes are now **linked**.*

To unlink text items:

1. With no items selected, choose the Unlinking tool.

2. Click one of the text boxes, paths, or table cells in the chain to be unlinked.

3. Click the head or tail of the link arrow **1**. Links preceding the break will remain intact; the link to succeeding boxes, paths, or cells will be broken **2**. (You can undo this.)

TIP If you're unable to unlink with the Unlinking tool, make sure there are no other items obstructing the one that you're trying to click.

TIP If you click in a linked box with the Content tool, you can press the up or down arrow on the keyboard to jump from the first line in the box to the last line of the previous box in the chain or from the last line in the box to the first line in the next box in the chain.

TIP If you rearrange pages in a text chain, the links will stay intact.

Find the links

To see where the links are in a layout, choose a small display size (around 30%), then click one of the items in the link chain with the Unlinking tool. Choose a different tool when you're finished. You cannot view links in Thumbnails view.

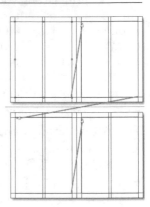

Ah, what can ever be more stately and admirable to me than mast-hemm'd Manhattan?

River and sunset and scallop-edg'd waves of flood-tide?

The sea-gulls oscillating their bodies, the hay-boat in the twilight, and the belated lighter?

What gods can exceed these that clasp me by the hand, and with voices I love call me promptly and loudly by my nighest name as I approach?

What is more subtle than this which ties me to the woman or man that looks in my face?

Which fuses me into you now, and pours my meaning into you?   *Walt Whitman*

1 *With the Unlinking tool, click a text item, then click the* **head** *or* **tail** *of the* **arrow** *that connects it to another item.*

Ah, what can ever be more stately and admirable to me than mast-hemm'd Manhattan?

River and sunset and scallop-edg'd waves of flood-tide?

The sea-gulls oscillating their bodies, the hay-boat in the twilight, and the belated lighter?

2 *The link is broken.*

Oronte. Do you find anything to object to in my sonnet?

Alceste. I do not say that. But, to keep him from writing, I set before his eyes how, in our days, that desire had spoiled a great many very worthy people.

Oronte. Do I write badly? Am I like them in any way?

Alceste. I do not say that. But, in short, I said to him: What pressing need is there for you to rhyme, and what the deuce drives you into print? If we can pardon the sending into the world of a

badly-written book, it will only be in those unfortunate men who write for their livelihood. Believe me, resist your temptations, keep these effusions from the public, and do not, how much soever you may be asked, forfeit the reputation which you enjoy…

Molière

1 *Choose the **Unlinking** tool, then **Shift-click** inside the item to be unlinked from the chain.*

Copy, paste, duplicate linked boxes

You can copy, paste, or duplicate a linked text box or boxes. You can also drag-copy a linked box between projects or into a library. Text preceding the box in the chain, if any, won't copy; overflow text will copy, but it will be hidden. To copy an entire story, be sure to copy the *first* box in the chain.

To delete a text item from a chain and preserve the chain:

1. Choose the Item or Content tool.

2. Select the text item to be deleted.

3. Choose Item > Delete (Cmd-K/Ctrl-K). Simple! The text will be rerouted to the next item in the chain. You can undo this.

To unlink a text item from a chain and preserve the item and chain:

1. Choose the Unlinking tool.

2. Shift-click inside the text box, path, or table cell to be unlinked **1**–**2**.

TIP Using Linkster from GLUON, Inc. (at press time, the QuarkXPress 7 version is Mac-only) you can perform magic tricks, like unlinking a chain and having the text stay right where it is.

Oronte. Do you find anything to object to in my sonnet?

Alceste. I do not say that. But, to keep him from writing, I set before his eyes how, in our days, that desire had spoiled a great many very worthy people.

Oronte. Do I write badly? Am I like them in any way?

Alceste. I do not say that. But, in short, I said to him: What pressing need is there for you to rhyme, and what the deuce drives you into print? If we can pardon the sending into the

2 *The middle box has been **unlinked** from the chain.*

Working with blocks of text

If you're doing a rough layout and you need some mock text to fill in some boxes on your page, you can have Jabberwocky do the work for you. You have a choice of four default "languages," in prose or verse. If you're ambitious or have a light schedule, you can create and edit your own jabber.

Jabberwocky, if you don't happen to know, is the name of a wonderful poem in the book *Through the Looking Glass* by Lewis Carroll ("Twas brillig, and the slithy toves did gyre and gimble in the wabe..."). Love that book.

To fill text boxes with dummy text:

1. *Optional:* To specify the kind of text to be inserted, choose QuarkXPress (Edit, in Windows) > Preferences > Application > Jabberwocky, choose English, Esperanto, Klingon, Latin, or a custom language from the Language menu , choose Prose or Verse from the Format menu, then click OK.

2. To fill a text box/path or a series of linked boxes/paths with dummy text based on the parameters chosen in Jabberwocky Preferences, choose the Content tool, click in a text box or path, then choose Utilities > Jabber 2–3.
    Note: The Jabberwocky.xnt XTension, which ships with QuarkXPress 7, must be enabled in order to access this feature (see page 377).

    Note: If Jabber is used to fill a chain of boxes or paths, the text will stop at the end of the last box or path in the chain; there will be no hidden, overflow text.

You can invent your own Jabberwocky language or edit an existing language.

To create or edit a Jabberwocky set:

1. Choose Edit > Jabberwocky Sets.
2. Click an existing set, then click Edit 4.
    or

1 *Choose a "language" in Preferences > Application >* **Jabberwocky.**

Qo'noS Qagh reH
'ach wa' verengan jon vatlh Qav DenIbya' Qatlhs
Ach QI'tomer ah po' tlb tera'.
Wa' pov Quch HIv vatlh QaQ meHloDnI'S
Joq vagh QIp 'ejyo'S reH chop Qo'noS.
Vatlh DIvI'S tlha' wa' ych

2 **Klingon** *verse*

Two irascible lampstands laughed, and one sheep grew up, even though two pawnbrokers ran away almost drunkenly, and five wart hogs telephoned botulisms, although Batman bought Minnesota, and five aardvarks towed Quark. One bourgeois trailer quickly fights two fountains. One mat ran

3 *The point of using dummy text is to create a text "texture." If you find any of the jabber languages distracting or idiotic, by all means don't use them. You can customize the language so the word length is more typical of an individual project. This is QuarkXPress's* **English** *prose jabber.*

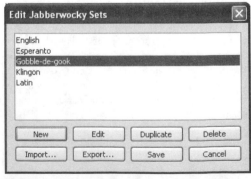

4 *You can create, edit, duplicate, or delete a Jabberwocky set using the* **Edit Jabberwocky Sets** *dialog box.*

Jabberwocky

1 *Use the **Jabberwocky Dictionary** dialog box to add or delete words from a Jabberwocky set.*

Simoneyeh logega Cuplook kwan fala funo jala vata mopie heyso plineto nata palaty gwoglerog kumo Simoner izame hitu plineto luba wenenb bobega gosie fotin jekah rutil Katal cata Simoneyeh logega Cuplook kwan fala funo jala vata mopie heyso plineto nata palaty gwoglerog kumo Simoner izame hitu

2 *Custom jabber*

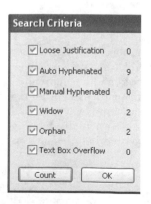

3 *In the **Search Criteria** dialog box, choose what you want QuarkXPress to search for.*

Click New, then enter a name in the Set Name field.

3. Here's where the fun starts. Choose a Part of Speech from the menu, type a real or made-up word in the field, then click Add **1**. (To delete a word, click it, then click Delete.)

4. Click Save **2**. The new set will appear on the first menu in the Jabberwocky Preferences dialog box.

The Line Check command can be used to find out how many overflow text boxes are present in a layout, along with other type-setting data, and if you want, it can get your cursor to each occurrence.

To use the Line Check command:

1. Choose Utilities > Line Check > Search Criteria.

2. Check or uncheck any boxes to include/exclude those criteria from the search **3**.

3. *Optional:* Click Count, note the quantities listed, then click OK.

4. To start the search, click in a text box, then choose Utilities > Line Check > First Line. The first instance found of any of the items you checked in step 2 will be selected in the layout.

5. To jump from one instance to the next, press Cmd-;/Ctrl-;.

TIP For more about widows and ophans, see page 107.

When text is linked between nonconsecutive pages, as in a newsletter or magazine, there is usually an indicator to guide the reader to the continuation of the story or article. These "Continued on" and "Continued from" indicators are called "jump lines." When the Next Box Page Number character is inserted, like magic, it instantly converts into the page number of the next linked box in the chain. If that text is relinked or moved to a different page, the page number will update automatically.

To insert a "Continued on" character:

1. Choose the Rectangle Text Box tool. Or if you want to get fancy, choose a Bézier Text Box or Text-Path tool.

2. Create a separate, small box or path that overlaps the text box that contains the story, and keep it selected.

3. Choose the Content tool.

4. Type any desired text into the small box, such as "Continued on page," or use a graphic symbol, such as an arrow. The keystrokes for entering Zapf Dingbat characters are in Appendix A.

5. **NEW** Choose Utilities > Insert Character > Special > Next Box Page # (Cmd-4/Ctrl-4) to insert the Next Box Page Number character **1**–**3**. Don't enter the actual page number—it will appear automatically.

TIP Press the down arrow on the keyboard to move the text insertion point from the last line of text in a box to the first line of text in the next box in the chain (or press the up arrow to do the reverse).

To insert a "Continued from" character:

Follow the instructions above, but for **NEW** step 5, Choose Utilities > Insert Character > Special > Previous Box Page # (Cmd-2/Ctrl-2) to insert the Previous Box Page Number character **4**.

Elizabeth here felt herself called on to say something in vindication of his behaviour to Wickham; and therefore gave them to understand, in as guarded a manner as she could, that by what she had heard from his relations in Kent, his actions were capable of a very different construction; and that his

Continued on page 3

1 *A text box containing the **Next Box Page Number** character is positioned so that it overlaps the main text box.*

Continued from page <None>

2 *If the characters **<None>** appear instead of a page number, either the text box or path that contains the Previous or Next Box Page Number character isn't overlapping a linked text box or the text box it overlaps isn't linked to a box on another page.*

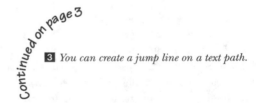

Continued on page 3

3 *You can create a jump line on a text path.*

4 *The **Previous Box Page Number** character is inserted here.*

Continued from page 1

character was by no means so faulty, nor Wickham's so amiable, as they had been considered in Hertfordshire. In confirmation of this, she related the particulars of all the pecuniary transactions in which they had been connected, without actually naming her authority, but stating it to be such as might be relied on.

Jane Austen

Rescuing an unsavable file

If you get an error message that says your file can't be saved, **DON'T CLOSE IT!** Take a deep breath, chant a mantra, create a whole new project or open a template that has the same dimensions as the problem file; next, use the method on this page to drag pages from the old project to the new (saving the new file periodically), then trash the corrupted file.

If that doesn't work, try using the MarkzTools V XTension from Markzware Software to open and salvage your damaged files.

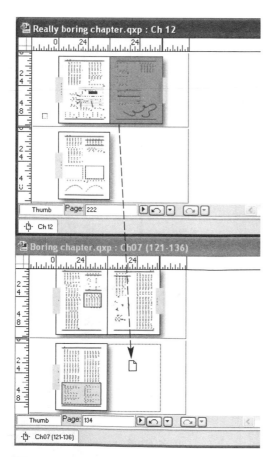

1 *Drag-copying pages* in *Thumbnails* view *from one project window to another*

To drag-copy pages from one layout or project to another:

1. Open the project containing the source layout and display it. Open the project containing the target layout and display it.

2. If the layouts are in the same project, choose Window > Split Window > Horizontal (or Vertical). If the layouts are in different projects, in Mac OS X, choose Window > Tile. In Windows, choose Window > Tile Vertically.

3. Then for each window, choose View > Thumbnails.

4. Drag a page icon from one project window into the other **1**. A copy of the page will appear in the target project window. Pages will reshuffle depending on where you release the mouse (watch for the Force Right, Force Left, Force Down, or non-force pointer).
or
To drag multiple pages, click the first page in a series of consecutive pages, Shift-click the last page in the series, then drag. If the pages to be drag-copied contain linked text, copy all the linked pages at once instead of one by one. Otherwise, the text from the linked boxes will copy, but the links will be broken.

Notes: You can't copy a page to a layout whose page size is smaller than the one you're copying. A page to which a facing-pages master has been applied can be copied to a single-sided layout, but items on the page may be repositioned as a result. Any style sheets, colors, dashes & stripes, lists, H&Js, or master pages on the appending pages will be added to the target layout. And finally, all the layers from the destination layout are copied to the target layout.

The Section command renumbers all or some of the pages in a layout with a user-specified starting number. This is useful for publications such as books that are composed of multiple files. You can choose a different page numbering format for each section. For example, in this book, the lowercase Roman format is used for the table of contents and the numeric format is used for the main body of the book. *Note:* To make the page numbers actually appear on your layout pages, follow the instructions on page 248.

To number a multifile layout automatically, you can use the Book feature (see Chapter 21).

To number a section of a file:

1. Display the layout page where the new section is to begin by double-clicking its icon on the Page Layout palette.
   or
   Choose Page > Go to (Cmd-J/Ctrl-J), enter the number of the page that is to begin the new section, then click OK.
2. Click the Section button at the top of the Page Layout palette.
   or
   Choose Page > Section.
3. Check Section Start **1**. (Book Chapter Start is available only when a chapter is opened independently of its book.)
4. Enter the desired starting Number for the section.
5. *Optional:* Enter a maximum of four characters in the Prefix field (e.g., "Page").
6. *Optional:* Choose a different numbering Format.
7. Click OK.

TIP If you choose an even-numbered page to start a section in a facing-pages layout, the first page will become a left-hand page.

Why the asterisk?

An asterisk below a page icon on the Page Layout palette signifies that a **section** starts on that page. If the first page in a section is currently displayed in the project window, an asterisk will also appear next to the page number at the bottom of the Page Layout palette and at the bottom of the project window.

To have a page's **absolute** number (sequential position in the layout such as 1 for the first page, 2 for the second page regardless of page numbers) display at the bottom of the Page Layout palette, instead of its number in a section, Option-click/Alt-click the layout page icon (see also the tip on page 54).

Each of these pages marked with an asterisk is the start of a new section.

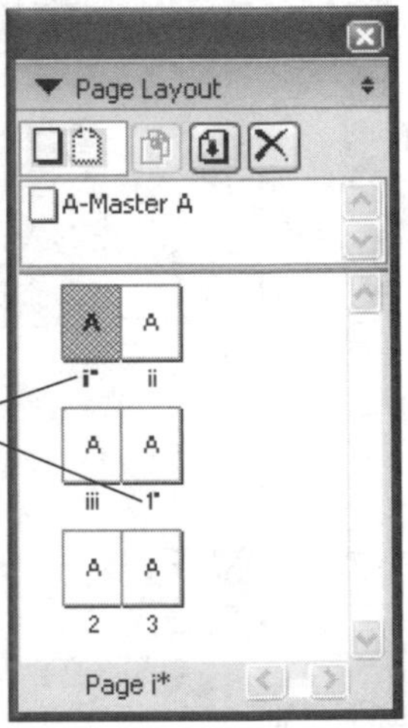

1 *Check* ***Section Start****, enter a* ***Prefix*** *(if desired), enter the starting* ***Number****, and choose a numbering* ***Format****.*

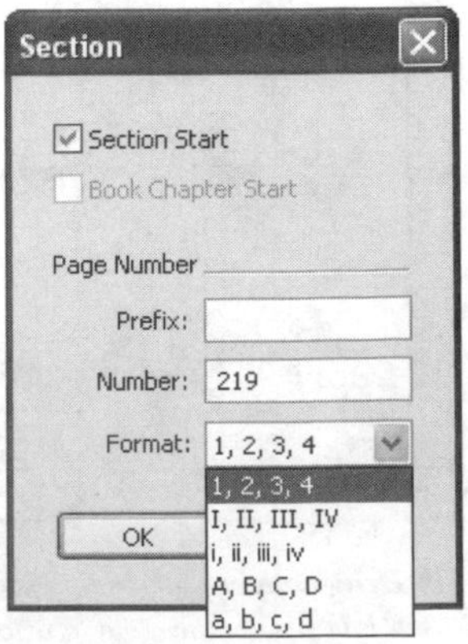

Using the Next Box and Next Column characters

The Next Box character pushes text to the next box in a linked chain.
The Next Column character pushes text to the next column within
the same box (or in some cases, the next text box in the chain).

I come from haunts of coot and hern,
I make a sudden sally,
And sparkle out among the fern,
To bicker down a valley.

By thirty hills I hurry down,
Or slip between the ridges,
By twenty thorps, a little town,
And half a hundred bridges.

Till last by Philip's farm I flow
to join the brimming river,
For men may come and men may go,
But I go on for ever.

I chatter over stony ways,
In little sharps and trebles,
I bubble into eddying bays,
I babble on the pebbles.

With many a curve my banks I fret
By many a field and fallow,
And many fair foreland set
With willow-weed and mallow.

I chatter, chatter, as I flow
To join the brimming river,
For men may come and men may go,
But I go on for ever.
— Alfred Tennyson

The original text boxes

I come from haunts of coot and hern,
I make a sudden sally,
And sparkle out among the fern,
To bicker down a valley.

By thirty hills I hurry down,
Or slip between the ridges,
By twenty thorps, a little town,
And half a hundred bridges.

Till last by Philip's farm I flow
to join the brimming river,
For men may come and men may go,
But I go on for ever.

⇓

I chatter over stony ways,
In little sharps and trebles,
I bubble into eddying bays,
I babble on the pebbles.

With many a curve my banks I fret
By many a field and fallow,
And many fair foreland set
With willow-weed and mallow.

I chatter, chatter, as I flow
To join the brimming river,
For men may come and men may go,
But I go on for ever.
— Alfred Tennyson

*Instead of shortening the text box
to push the text to the next box, a
Next Box character (**Shift-Enter**)*
is inserted. Remove a Next Box
character as you would any text
character: Click to the right of it
with the Content tool, then press
Delete/Backspace.* **NEW**

*QuarkXPress 7 makes it easier to
enter special characters, especially
for the numerickeypad-challenged.
See the next page to learn how.*

*The **Next Box** character (Shift-Enter)* (turn on View > **Show Invisibles** to see it)*

I come from haunts of coot and hern,
I make a sudden sally,
And sparkle out among the fern,
To bicker down a valley.

By thirty hills I hurry down,
Or slip between the ridges,
By twenty thorps, a little town,
And half a hundred bridges. ↓

Till last by Philip's farm I flow
to join the brimming river,
For men may come and men may go,
But I go on for ever.

I chatter over stony ways,
In little sharps and trebles,
I bubble into eddying bays,
I babble on the pebbles.

*The **Next Column** character (**Enter**)**

*Use the numeric keypad.

Isn't that Special?

You can use a wide variety of special typesetting characters in QuarkXPress, including a dozen or so kinds of spaces plus dashes, hyphens, and line breaks. In earlier versions of the program, however, actually using these characters required that you master an arcane set of keyboard shortcuts.

No longer! In QuarkXPress 7, these very useful characters have their own command on the Utilities menu, which itself branches into two submenus containing the characters in question. You'll find a long list of characters that allow line breaks on the Insert Character > Special menu. A smaller set of characters that do not allow a line to break is found on the Insert Character > Special (Nonbreaking) menu.

The Mac OS X menus, shown here, display only a small portion of the keyboard shortcuts that can be used to insert these characters. (For more, see the QuarkXPress Help file or turn to Appendix B in this book.) The Windows equivalents of these menus don't show any keyboard shortcuts, but they do exist, just the same.

Em Space	⌘6
En Space	
3–per–Em–Space	
4–per–Em–Space	
6–per–Em–Space	
Thin Space	⌘7
Hair Space	
Zero Width Space	
Flexible Space	
Figure Space	
Punctuation Space	
En Dash	
Em Dash	
Hyphen	
Discretionary Hyphen	⌘–
Indent Here	⌘\
Discretionary New Line	
Right Indent Tab	
Previous Box Page #	
Current Box Page #	
Next Box Page #	

*The contents of the **Utilities** > **Insert Character** > **Special** menu in Mac OS X*

Em Space	⌥⌘6
En Space	⌥⌘5
3–per–Em–Space	
4–per–Em–Space	
6–per–Em–Space	
Thin Space	⌥⌘7
Hair Space	
Word Joiner	
Flexible Space	
Figure Space	
Punctuation Space	
Standard Space	
En Dash	
Em Dash	
Hyphen	

*The contents of the **Utilities** > **Insert Character** > **Special** (**Nonbreaking**) menu*

Formats 6

Formatting fundamentals

Well, you've managed to get some text onto your page, but it's just sitting there in a big clump, and it's hard to read. By adding space between lines and paragraphs, indents, and other paragraph formats, not only will your type look more elegant and professional, it will also be easier to read.

All the formatting commands described in this chapter affect entire paragraphs rather than individual characters. These commands, which are accessed via the Style menu and the Measurements palette when text is selected, include horizontal alignment, hyphenation and justification, indents, lead-ing, space before and after, keeping lines together, rules, and tabs **1** and **2**. In the next chapter, you'll learn the ins and outs of typography (styling characters in different fonts, point sizes, and so on).

A paragraph consists of one or more characters or words, followed by an invisible Return character. A Return looks like this when View > Invisibles is checked: ¶. Paragraph formats can be applied manually—or even more efficiently, using paragraph style sheets (see Chapter 13).

Note that not all paragraph attributes are available when working in Web layouts.

1 *Most of the commands that affect whole paragraphs are found in the **Formats, Tabs,** and **Rules** panes of the **Paragraph Attributes** dialog box.*

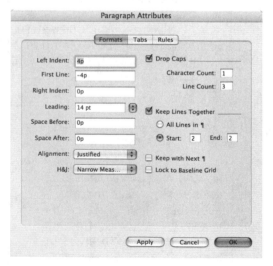

2 *The **Paragraph Attributes** tab of the **Measurements** palette provides quick access to the most commonly used paragraph formatting options.*

Paragraph Formats

To indent a whole paragraph:

1. Choose the Content tool.

2. Click in a paragraph or drag through a series of paragraphs **1**.

3. Display the Paragraph Attributes tab of the Measurements palette.

(NEW)

4. Enter indent values in the Left Indent, and/or Right Indent fields using any measurement system allowed in QuarkXPress **2**.

5. Press Return/Enter or tab to another field to see the results of your changes **3**–**4**.

TIP You can also use the old-fashioned dia-log box method:

Choose Style > Formats (Cmd-Shift-F/ Ctrl-Shift-F) to open the Formats pane of the Paragraph Attributes dialog box. Enter Left Indent and/or Right Indent values and click Apply to preview (Cmd-A in Mac OS X). Or Option-click/ Alt-click Apply to turn on continuous apply (Alt-A in Windows). Click in, or Tab to, another field to activate it.

2 *Enter **Left Indent** and/or **Right Indent** values.*

Do it with style!

Once you learn the basics of paragraph format-ting, learn how to apply these attributes via **style sheets** (see Chapter 13). Believe us, you'll save yourself a lot of monotonous work.

> THE MAIN CONCLUSION ARRIVED AT IN THIS WORK, NAMELY, THAT MAN IS DESCENDED FROM SOME LOWLY ORGANIZED FORM, WILL, I REGRET TO THINK, BE HIGHLY DIS-TASTEFUL TO MANY. BUT THERE CAN HARDLY BE A DOUBT THAT WE ARE DESCENDED FROM BARBARIANS.

1 *The paragraph containing the insertion point has an indent value of 0.*

> THE MAIN CONCLUSION ARRIVED AT IN THIS WORK, NAMELY, THAT MAN IS DESCENDED FROM SOME LOWLY ORGANIZED FORM, WILL, I REGRET TO THINK, BE HIGHLY DISTASTEFUL TO MANY. BUT THERE CAN HARDLY BE A DOUBT THAT WE ARE DESCENDED FROM BARBARIANS.

3 *This paragraph has a **Left Indent** value of 2p (called a "block" indent).*

> THE MAIN CONCLUSION ARRIVED AT IN THIS WORK, NAMELY, THAT MAN IS DESCENDED FROM SOME LOWLY ORGANIZED FORM, WILL, I REGRET TO THINK, BE HIGHLY DISTASTEFUL TO MANY. BUT THERE CAN HARDLY BE A DOUBT THAT WE ARE DESCENDED FROM BARBARIANS.
>
> CHARLES DARWIN

4 *This paragraph has a **Right Indent** value of 2p.*

Paragraph Indents

1 *The **First Line Indent** field in the Paragraph Attributes tab of the Measurements palette*

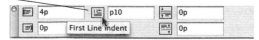

Oronte. [To Alceste] But for you, you know our agreement. Speak to me, I pray, in all sincerity.

Alceste. These matters, sir, are always more or less delicate, and every one is fond of being praised for his wit.

But I was saying one day to a certain person, who shall be nameless, when he showed me some of his verses, that a gentleman ought at all times to exercise a great control over that itch for writing which sometimes attacks us, and should keep a tight rein over the strong propensity which one has to display such amusements; and that, in the frequent anxiety to show their productions, people are frequently exposed to act a very foolish part.

Molière

2 *A **First Line** indent enhances readability.*

Left Indent | ***First Line** indent (you can drag the indent and tab markers to reposition them)* | **Tab Stop** *marker*

Oronte. [To Alceste] But for you, you know our agreement. Speak to me, I pray, in all sincerity.

3 *The width of the **Formats** ruler matches the width of the currently selected text box.*

skip indents under heads

Don't indent the first paragraph in a story, especially if there's a headline or subhead right above it. Why not? It doesn't look good. Make the first paragraph flush left instead, and enhance it with a nice drop cap, large initial cap, or a few small caps characters. Try it both ways or take a peek at some magazines you have around the house, and you'll see what we mean.

Don't try to indent type by pressing the Spacebar. The indents won't line up properly in multiple paragraphs because typeset characters aren't equal in width, as they are on a typewriter. You could use a tab to indent a paragraph, but you can't automatically insert a tab character with a paragraph style sheet. The proper way to indent type is by entering a value greater than zero in one or more of the three Indent fields or dragging icons on the Formats ruler.

To indent the first line of a paragraph:

1. Choose the Content tool.

2. Click in a paragraph or drag through a series of paragraphs.

3. Display the Paragraph Attributes tab of the Measurements palette.

4. Enter a First Line value **1**. If you're not sure what value to use, start with the point size of the text you're indenting (e.g., for 9 pt. type, enter p9).

5. Press Return **2**.

TIP When the Paragraph Attributes dialog box is open or the Paragraph Attributes tab of the Measurements palette is showing, a Formats ruler displays over the currently selected text box. Indents can be adjusted by dragging the indent markers in the ruler **3**. Ditto for tab stops. To insert a new tab stop, click in the ruler. (Read more about tabs in Chapter 8.)

TIP For each text box, the current paragraph indent value is added together with the current Text Inset value set for the text box (see page 71).

Paragraph Indents

Leading (line spacing) is the distance from baseline to baseline between lines of type, and it's measured in points. Three types of leading are used in QuarkXPress:

Absolute leading is an amount that remains fixed regardless of the point size of the type to which it's applied **1**.

We use absolute leading because we like the control it gives us, but there's an alternative, called auto leading, that you may as well know about. Auto leading is calculated separately for each line of text based on the point size of the largest character per line **2**. The percentage used for that calculation is specified in the Auto Leading field in QuarkXPress (Edit, in Windows) > Preferences > Print Layout > Paragraph, and it applies to the entire layout. For example, if 20% is the current percentage and the largest character in a line of text is 10 pt., the leading for that line would be 12 pt. You won't see a percentage in the Leading field; you'll just see the word "auto." Alternatively, you can enter an incremental value, such as +2 or −2, in the Auto Leading field. In this case the leading will be calculated based on the point size of the largest character in each line, plus or minus that increment.

To change leading using the Measurements palette:

1. Choose the Content tool.

2. Click in a paragraph or drag through a series of paragraphs.

3. Change the Leading value in the Classic (default) tab or Paragraph Attributes tab of the Measurements palette **3**.
   or
   Next to the Leading field, click the up arrow to increase the leading in 1-point increments, or the down arrow to reduce the leading. Option-click/Alt-click an arrow to increase or reduce the leading in 0.1-point increments.

> **B**ut the moment that she moved again he recognized her. The effect upon her old lover was electric, far stronger than the effect of his presence upon her. His fire, the tumultuous ring of his eloquence, seemed to go out of him. His lip struggled and trembled under the words that lay upon it; but deliver them it could not as long as she faced him. His eyes, after their first glance...
>
> **THOMAS HARDY**

1 *A paragraph with 11 pt.* **absolute** *leading: The leading is consistent throughout, despite the fact that two different point sizes are applied to the type in the first line of the paragraph.*

> **B**ut the moment that she moved again he recognized her. The effect upon her old lover was electric, far stronger than the effect of his presence upon her.

2 *The same paragraph with* **auto** *leading: The large initial cap is throwing the whole thing off, and it ain't pretty.*

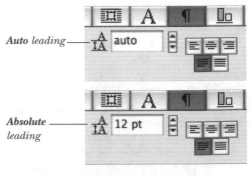

Auto leading

Absolute leading

3 *The* **Leading** *area in the* **Paragraph Attributes** *tab of the* **Measurements** *palette*

Leading

He put some sticking plaster on his fingers, and his friends both came to dinner. He could not offer them fish, but he had something else in his larder.

Sir Isaac Newton wore his black and gold waistcoat.

And Mr. Alderman Ptolemy Tortoise brought a salad with him in a string bag.

And instead of a nice dish of minnows they had a roasted grasshopper with lady-bird sauce, which frogs consider a beautiful treat; but I think it must have been nasty! *Beatrix Potter*

*Use **roomy leading** to enhance readability if your text is set in a **wide column**, in a **sans serif** or **bold** font, or in a font that has a **large x-height, tall ascenders**, or **tall descenders**. This is 8 pt. Gill Sans Regular, with roomy 11 pt. leading.*

He put some sticking plaster on his fingers, and his friends both came to dinner. He could not offer them fish, but he had something else in his larder.

Sir Isaac Newton wore his black and gold waistcoat.

And Mr. Alderman Ptolemy Tortoise brought a salad with him in a string bag.

And instead of a nice dish of minnows they had a roasted grasshopper with lady-bird sauce, which frogs consider a beautiful treat; but I think it must have been nasty!

*You can use **tighter leading** for **serif** body text or multiple-line **headlines** or **subheads**. This is 8 pt. Bauer Bodoni with 10 pt. leading.*

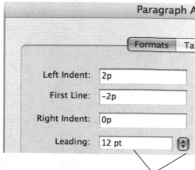

1 *The **Leading** area in the Paragraph Attributes dialog box (Formats pane)*

To change leading using the keyboard:

1. Choose the Content tool.

2. Click in a paragraph or drag through a series of paragraphs.

3. Press Cmd-Shift-"/Ctrl-Shift-" to increase leading or Cmd-Shift-:/Ctrl-Shift-: to decrease leading in 1-point increments. If the leading was on auto, it will switch to the nearest absolute value when you use this shortcut.

TIP Press Cmd-Option-Shift-"/Ctrl-Alt-Shift-" to increase leading in 0.1-point increments; press Cmd-Option-Shift-:/Ctrl-Alt-Shift-: to decrease leading in 0.1-point increments.

TIP The traditional way to notate point size and leading is to divide the two values by a slash. For example, "8/11" represents 8-point type with 11-point leading.

To change leading using a dialog box:

1. Choose the Content tool.

2. Click in a paragraph or drag through a series of paragraphs.

3. Choose Style > Leading (Cmd-Shift-E/Ctrl-Shift-E). The Paragraph Attributes > Formats dialog box opens.

4. Type a value in the selected Leading field in an increment as small as .001 **1**. You don't need to enter the "pt".

TIP Don't know what value to enter? Try adding 2 points to the current point size (e.g., 12 pt. leading for 10 pt. type). The point size of your type is shown on the right side of the Character Attributes tab or Classic tab of the Measurements palette.

5. Click OK.

TIP Leading has no affect on the positioning of the first line of text in a box. To lower text from the top of its box, increase the Top Text Inset value in the Text tab of the Measurements palette.

Leading

To change horizontal alignment:

1. Choose the Content tool.

2. Click in a paragraph or drag through a series of paragraphs.

3. Click one of the five horizontal alignment buttons on the Paragraph Attributes tab of the Measurements palette **1**.

   Note: Forced Justified alignment justifies all the lines in a paragraph—including the last line. For this option, make sure the paragraph has a Return character (¶) at the end.

TIP Horizontal alignment can also be changed by using the shortcuts listed at right; the Style > Alignment submenu; the Alignment menu in the Style > Formats dialog box; or the buttons on the Classic tab of the Measurements palette.

TIP Turn on Hyphenation for justified text to help reduce the gaps between words (see pages 117–119).

Horizontal alignment shortcuts

Flush left, ragged right	Cmd-Shift-L/Ctrl-Shift-L
Centered	Cmd-Shift-C/Ctrl-Shift-C
Flush right, ragged left	Cmd-Shift-R/Ctrl-Shift-R
Justified	Cmd-Shift-J/Ctrl-Shift-J
Forced Justified	Cmd-Option-Shift-J/ Ctrl-Alt-Shift-J

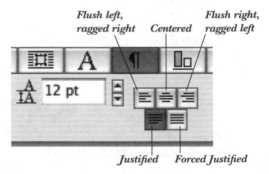

1 *The five* **horizontal alignment** *buttons on the* **Paragraph Attributes** *tab of the* **Measurements** *palette*

So we was all right now, as to the shirt and the sheet and the spoon and the candles, by the help of the calf and rats and the mixed-up counting; and as to the candlestick, it warn't no consequence, it would blow over by and by....
MARK TWAIN

Flush left, ragged right

So we was all right now, as to the shirt and the sheet and the spoon and the candles, by the help of the calf and rats and the mixed-up counting; and as to the candlestick, it warn't no consequence, it would blow over by and by....

Centered (for occasional use only; it's tiring to read)

So we was all right now, as to the shirt and the sheet and the spoon and the candles, by the help of the calf and rats and the mixed-up counting; and as to the candlestick

Try to vary the line lengths in centered text (it usually looks better).

So we was all right now, as to the shirt and the sheet and the spoon and the candles, by the help of the calf and rats and the mixed up counting; and as to the candlestick, it warn't no consequence, it would blow over by and by....

Flush right, ragged left (also a bit tiring to read, but sometimes useful)

So we was all right now, as to the shirt and the sheet and the spoon and the candles, by the help of the calf and rats and the mixed-up counting; and as to the candlestick, it warn't no consequence, it would blow over by and by....

Justified

So we was all right now, as to the shirt and the sheet and the spoon and the candles, by the help of the calf and rats and the mixed-up counting; and as to the candlestick, it warn't no consequence, it would blow over by and by.

Forced Justified

1 *This is an awkward break.*

The night so luminous on the spar-deck, but otherwise on the cavernous ones below—levels so very like the tiered gal-leries in a coal-mine—the luminous night passed away. Like the prophet in the chariot disappearing in heaven and dropping his mantle to Elisha, the with-drawing night transferred its pale robe to the peeping day.

The night so luminous on the spar-deck, but otherwise on the cavernous ones below—levels so very like the tiered¶

galleries in a coal-mine—the luminous night passed away. Like the prophet in the chariot disappearing in heaven and dropping his mantle to Elisha, the with-drawing night transferred its pale robe to the peeping day.

2 *A paragraph Return creates a whole new paragraph—no good.*

The night so luminous on the spar-deck, but otherwise on the cavernous ones below—levels so very like the tiered galleries in a coal-mine—the luminous night passed away. Like the prophet in the chariot disappearing in heaven and dropping his mantle to Elisha, the with-drawing night transferred its pale robe to the peeping day.
Herman Melville

3 *Pressing **Shift-Return/Shift-Enter** creates a **line break** within the same paragraph—much better.*

Use this method to adjust a headline or fix an awkward break in ragged left or ragged right copy. Depending on the length of words in the text, the font, the column width, the hyphenation and justification settings in use, and other variables, QuarkXPress may not wrap text well and you may end up fiddling with line breaks. QuarkXPress 7 provides a variety of new default hyphenation and justification set-tings to help with this, but you inevitably end up breaking a few lines manually.

To break a line without creating a new paragraph:

1. Choose the Content tool.

2. Click just to the left of a whole word that you want to bring down to the next line, then press Shift-Return/ Shift-Enter **1**–**3**.
or
To insert a discretionary hyphen which will disappear if the text reflows (unlike a regular hyphen), click in a word where you want a hyphen to be inserted, then choose Utilities > Insert Character > Special > Discretionary Hyphen. **NEW**

TIP You can also enter a discretionary hyphen by pressing Cmd/Ctrl with the hyphen key. When View > Invisibles is checked, the discretionary hyphen looks like a small gray hyphen slightly overlapping the text. To remove a dis-cretionary hyphen character, click to the right of it, then press Delete/ Backspace.

TIP To find out where a word should be hyphenated, click in the word, then choose Utilities > Suggested Hyphenation (Cmd-Option-Shift-H/ Ctrl-Alt-Shift-H). If no hyphens display in the dialog box, it means that word isn't supposed to be hyphenated.

Line Break

Note: The values entered in the Space Before and Space After fields are added together, so try to be consistent and use one most of the time and the other for special circumstances. For example, we use Space After for body text and use Space Before for subheads to add extra space above them.

To change the spacing between paragraphs:

1. Choose the Content tool.
2. Click in a paragraph or drag through a series of paragraphs.
3. Display the Paragraph Attributes tab of the Measurements palette.
4. Enter a Space Before or Space After value .
5. Press Return/Enter **2**.

TIP The Space Before command has no effect on the first line of text in a box. To move text downward on a page, the simplest thing is to move the box itself—an obvious solution that's easy to forget! If you don't want to move the box, you can use First Baseline (see page 74) or Text Inset (see page 71).

TIP To accomplish the same task by means of a dialog box, choose Style > Formats (Cmd-Shift-F/Ctrl-Shift-F) and enter values into the Space Before and/or the Space After fields in the Formats pane of the Paragraph Attributes dialog box **3**. Click Apply to preview the result, then click OK.

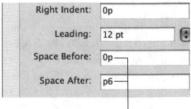

1 *The **Space Before** and **Space After** fields in the Paragraph Attributes tab of the Measurements palette*

3 *The **Space Before** and **Space After** fields in Paragraph Attributes > Formats*

2 *If you want to fine tune the spacing between paragraphs, use the **Space Before** or **Space After** field. Don't insert extra Returns—it's so-o-o unprofessional.*

O to be a Virginian where I grew up! O to be a Carolinian!
O longings irrepressible! O I will go back to old Tennessee and never wander more.

Mannahatta
I was asking for something specific and perfect for my city,
Whereupon lo! upsprang the aboriginal name.

Now I see what there is in a name, a word, liquid, sane, unruly, musical, self-sufficient,
I see that the word of my city is that word from of old,
Because I see that word nested in nests of water-bays, superb...

                                        ∾ WALT WHITMAN

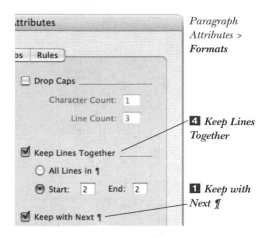

*Paragraph Attributes > **Formats***

4 *Keep Lines Together*

1 *Keep with Next ¶*

2 *An unsightly* **widow**

"I am dreadfully afraid it *will* be mouse!" said Duchess to herself— "I really couldn't, *couldn't* eat mouse pie. And I shall have to eat it, because it is a party. And *my* pie was going to be veal and ham. A pink and white pie-dish! and so is mine; just like Ribby's dishes; they were both bought at Tabitha Twitchit's."

Duchess went into her larder and took the pie off a shelf and looked at it.

"Oh what a good idea! Why shouldn't I rush along and put my pie into Ribby's oven when Ribby isn't there?"

Beatrix Potter

"I am dreadfully afraid it *will* be mouse!" said Duchess to herself— "I really couldn't, *couldn't* eat mouse pie. And I shall have to eat it, because it is a party. And *my* pie was going to be veal and ham. A pink and white pie-dish! and so is mine; just like Ribby's dishes; they were both bought at Tabitha Twitchit's." Duchess went into

her larder and took the pie off a shelf and looked at it.

"Oh what a good idea! Why shouldn't I rush along and put my pie into Ribby's oven when Ribby isn't there?"

3 *An unsightly* **orphan**

Apply the Keep with Next ¶ command to a subhead to ensure that if it falls at the end of a column or page, it won't become separated from the paragraph that follows it. Like all paragraph formats, Keep with Next ¶ can be applied manually or via a style sheet. Don't apply it to body text.

To keep two paragraphs together:

1. Choose the Content tool.
2. Click in a paragraph.
3. Choose Style > Formats (Cmd-Shift-F/ Ctrl-Shift-F) to open the Formats pane of the Paragraph Attributes dialog box.
4. Check Keep with Next ¶ **1**.
5. Click OK.

As QuarkXPress defines it, a widow is the last line of a paragraph that's stranded at the top of a column **2**. An orphan is the first line of paragraph that's stranded at the bottom of a column **3**. Both are typesetting no-no's. The Keep Lines Together command can be used to prevent orphan and widow lines. It can also be used to keep *all* the lines in a paragraph together.

To prevent orphan and widow lines:

1. Choose the Content tool.
2. Click in a paragraph.
3. Choose Style > Formats (Cmd-Shift-F/ Ctrl-Shift-F).
4. Check Keep Lines Together **4**.
5. Click All Lines in ¶ to keep all the lines of a paragraph together, even if the paragraph falls at the end of a column or page (we use this for subheads and the like).
   or
   Click Start to turn on orphan and widow control, then enter "2" (or even "3") in the Start and End fields to ensure that no fewer than two lines of a paragraph are stranded at the bottom or top of a column, respectively.
6. Click OK.

Formatting tips and tricks

A format in which the first line of a paragraph is aligned flush left and the remaining lines are indented is called a hanging indent. Hanging indents can be used to make subheads, bullets, or other special text more prominent or to hang punctuation (see page 132). A hanging indent that's created by following the steps below can be applied via a paragraph style sheet.

To create a hanging indent using a dialog box:

1. Choose the Content tool.

2. Click in a paragraph or drag through a series of paragraphs.

3. Choose Style > Formats (Cmd-Shift-F/Ctrl-Shift-F).

4. Enter a Left Indent value. Need a suggestion? Try 1p or 2p **1**.

5. Enter a First Line value that's equal to or less than the number you entered in the previous step, preceded by a minus (–) sign.

6. Click Apply to preview (Cmd-A/Alt-A), make any adjustments, and then click OK **2**–**3**.

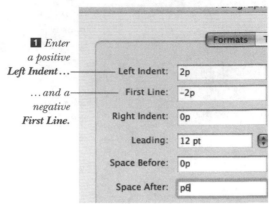

1 *Enter a positive Left Indent...*

...and a negative First Line.

*The Paragraph Attributes > **Formats** pane*

*A **tab** stop is created automatically at the location of the indent. (To style this text, we used a character style sheet. A character style sheet could also be used to style bullets or dingbats/wingdings in a bulleted list.)*

I mean in singing; but in loving—Leander the good swimmer, Troilus the first employer of panders, and a whole book full of these quondam carpet-mongers, whose names yet run smoothly in the even road of a blank verse, why, they were never so truly turned over and over as my poor self in love.

Marry, I cannot show it in rhyme; I have tried; I can find out no rhyme to lady but baby—an innocent rhyme;

WILLIAM SHAKESPEARE

2 *In this example, a **positive Left Indent** and a **negative First Line Indent** create a hanging indent formation in each paragraph.*

D. Pedro. He is in earnest.

Claud. In most profound earnest; and I'll warrant you for the love of Beatrice.

D. Pedro. And hath challenged thee?

Claud. Most sincerely.

D. Pedro. What a pretty thing man is when he goes in his doublet and hose, and leaves off his wit!

Claud. He is then a giant to an ape: but then is an ape a doctor to such a man?

WILLIAM SHAKESPEARE

3 *In this example, after the hanging indents were created via a positive Left Indent and a negative First Line, the **Tab** key was pressed after the bold text in each paragraph to align the text to the tab stop that QuarkXPress inserted automatically.*

Hanging Indents

> THESEUS. |Now, fair Hippolyta, our nuptial hour draws on apace; four happy days bring in another moon: but, oh, methinks, how slow this old moon wanes! She lingers my desires, like to a step-dame or a dowager, long withering out a young man's revenue.
>
> ~ William Shakespeare

1 *To insert the **Indent Here** character, click in the text, then press **Cmd-\/Ctrl-\.***

> THESEUS.   Now, fair Hippolyta, our nuptial hour draws on apace; four happy days bring in another moon: but, oh, methinks, how slow this old moon wanes! She lingers my desires, like to a step-dame or a dowager, long withering out a young man's revenue.

2 *A **hanging indent** is created.*

3 *The **Indent Here** character displays as a gray vertical dotted line when View > Invisibles is checked. If you don't see it, zoom in.*

> THESEUS. |Now, fair Hippol
>   hour draws on
>   days bring in oh,
>   methinks,

On the positive side, the Indent Here character instantly creates a hanging indent wherever your cursor happens to be positioned. On the minus side, the Indent Here character has to be inserted manually into each paragraph, it can't be incorporated into a style sheet, and it can't be added or removed using Find/Change. It's very handy for quickly formatting a unique paragraph here or there. To create a hanging indent in multiple paragraphs, though, follow the instructions on the previous page instead.

To create a hanging indent using the Indent Here character:

1. Choose the Content tool.
2. Click in a paragraph where the indent is to be inserted **1**.
3. Choose Utilities > Insert Character > Special > Indent Here or press Cmd/Ctrl with the backslash (\ ) key **2**.

NEW

To remove an Indent Here character:

1. Choose the Content tool.
2. Choose View > Invisibles (Cmd-I/Ctrl-I), if invisibles aren't currently showing.
3. Click just to the right of the Indent Here character **3**. If you're having trouble locating the correct spot, you can press the left or right arrow key on your keyboard to move the text cursor one character at a time.
4. Press Delete/Backspace. Choose View > Invisibles again, if you prefer to work with this feature off.

Indent Here Character

An interesting drop cap (or caps) can add pizzazz to a page and spark your reader's interest. *Caution:* Because they're so easy to create, it's tempting to use drop caps here, there, and everywhere. Don't succumb— like hot chilis, they're best used sparingly.

To insert an automatic drop cap:

1. Choose the Content tool.

2. Click in a paragraph.

3. Display the Paragraph Attributes tab of the Measurements palette.

4. Check Drop Caps **1**.

5. *Optional:* To "drop cap" more than one character, enter that number in the Character Count field (1–127) **2**.

6. *Optional:* To adjust the height of the drop cap, change the Line Count (2–16). The drop cap will adjust automatically to fit the line count **3**.

7. *Optional:* Select the drop cap and change its color, shade, or font (see the next chapter). Be bold and imaginative!

TIP To anchor any item (e.g., a picture box, text box, contentless box, or line) as a drop cap or a large initial cap, see page 199.

TIP You can create drop caps using the same controls in the Format pane of the Paragraph Attributes dialog box (Style > Formats). Drop caps can be saved with paragraph style sheets as well, making it quick and easy to format opening paragraphs.

1 *Check **Drop Caps** in the **Paragraph Attributes tab** of the **Measurements** palette*

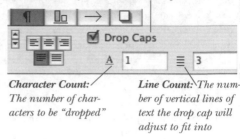

Character Count: *The number of characters to be "dropped"*

Line Count: *The number of vertical lines of text the drop cap will adjust to fit into*

NOT only was her first-floor flat invaded at all hours by throngs of singular and often undesirable characters but her remarkable lodger showed an eccentricity and irregularity in his life which must have sorely tried her patience. His incredible untidiness, his addiction to music at strange hours, his occasional revolver practice within doors, his weird and often malodorous scientific experiments, and the atmosphere of violence and danger which hung around him made him the very worst tenant in London. On the other hand, his payments were princely...

2 *A **drop cap** with a **character count** of **3** and a line count of **2***

Not only was her first-floor flat invaded at all hours by throngs of singular and often undesirable characters but her remarkable lodger showed an eccentricity and irregularity in his life which must have sorely tried her patience. His incredible untidiness, his addiction to music at strange hours, his occasional revolver practice within doors, his weird and often malodorous scientific experiments, and the atmosphere of violence and danger which hung around him made him the very worst tenant in London. On the other hand, his payments were princely...

SIR ARTHUR CONAN DOYLE

3 *A **drop cap** with a **character count** of **1** and a line count of **5***

> n anomaly which often struck me in the character of my friend Sherlock Holmes was that, although in his methods of thought he was the neatest and most methodical of mankind, and although also he affected a certain quiet primness of dress, he was none the less in his personal habits one of the most untidy
>
> SIR ARTHUR CONAN DOYLE

1 *A drop cap is selected.*

> n anomaly which often struck me in the character of my friend Sherlock Holmes was that, although in his methods of thought he was the neatest and most methodical of mankind, and although also he affected a certain quiet primness of dress, he was none the less in his per-

2 *The drop cap is **enlarged** to 125%.*

> or those who like this sort of thing, this is the sort of thing they like.

3 *The cursor is correctly positioned for **kerning** next to a drop cap.*

4 *The **Tracking/Kerning** area in the **Character Attributes** tab of the **Measurements** palette*

To resize an automatic drop cap:

1. Choose the Content tool.

2. Select the drop cap character or characters **1**.

3. In the point size field on the right side of the Character Attributes tab or Classic tab of the Measurements palette, change the size percentage **2**. The range you can enter varies depending on the font size.
or
Choose Style > Character (Cmd-Shift-D/Ctrl-Shift-D), then change the Size percentage.

To kern next to a drop cap:

1. Choose the Content tool.

2. Click in the first line of the paragraph between the drop cap and the character to the right of it. You'll see a tall blinking bar when the cursor has been inserted correctly **3**.

3. In the Tracking/Kerning section of the Character Attributes tab or Classic tab of the Measurements palette, click the left arrow to delete space or the right arrow to add space **4**. Option-click/Alt-click the left or right arrow to kern in finer increments.
or
To kern using the keyboard, press Cmd-Shift-[/Ctrl-Shift-[or Cmd-Shift-]/Ctrl-Shift-]. Add Option/Alt to the shortcut to kern in a finer increment.

Note: If you need an introduction to kerning, see pages 124–126.

To remove an automatic drop cap:

1. Choose the Content tool.

2. Click in the paragraph that contains the drop cap.

3. Display the Paragraph Attributes tab of the Measurements palette.

4. Uncheck Drop Caps.

5. Click OK.

There are many reasons to use the Paragraph Rules feature for creating rules (horizontal lines above or below text). For one, a paragraph rule stays anchored to its paragraph even if the paragraph is moved or reflows (a line created with a line tool would stay put). Second, a paragraph rule can be applied using a style sheet. And finally, unlike the Underline type style, a paragraph rule can be modified in its appearance and position.

To insert a paragraph rule:

1. Choose the Content tool.

2. Click in a paragraph or drag through a series of paragraphs.

3. Choose Style > Rules (Cmd-Shift-N/ Ctrl-Shift-N) to open the Rules pane of the Paragraph Attributes dialog box.

4. Check Rule Above and/or Rule Below **1**.

5. Choose or enter a Width. Click Apply to preview (Cmd-A/Alt-A).

Becoming unruly

To remove a paragraph rule, reopen the Rules pane of the Paragraph Attributes dialog box (Cmd-Shift-N/Ctrl-Shift-N), then *uncheck* Rule Above and/or Rule Below. To remove a rule from a style sheet, click Rules in the Edit Style Sheet dialog box (see Chapter 13), then uncheck Rule Above and/or Rule Below.

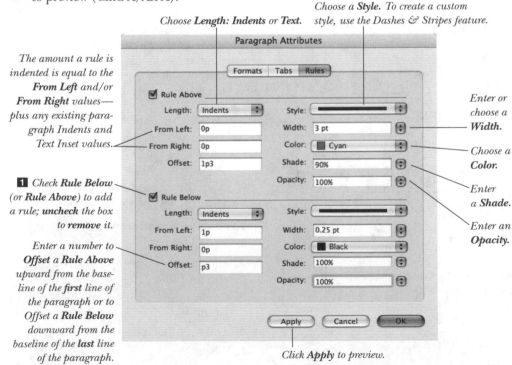

*Choose a **Style.** To create a custom style, use the Dashes & Stripes feature.*

*Choose **Length: Indents** or **Text.***

*The amount a rule is indented is equal to the **From Left** and/or **From Right** values— plus any existing paragraph Indents and Text Inset values.*

*Enter or choose a **Width.***

*Choose a **Color.***

1 *Check **Rule Below** (or **Rule Above**) to add a rule; **uncheck** the box to **remove** it.*

*Enter a **Shade.***

*Enter an **Opacity.***

*Enter a number to **Offset** a **Rule Above** upward from the baseline of the **first** line of the paragraph or to **Offset** a **Rule Below** downward from the baseline of the **last** line of the paragraph.*

*Click **Apply** to preview.*

Paragraph Rules

,Hey! diddle, diddle,
The cat and the fiddle,

1 _In this example, the first line of the paragraph is **indented,** which causes the rule to indent as well._

,Hey! diddle, diddle,
The cat and the fiddle,

2 _To align the rule with the left edge of the rest of the paragraph, as in this example, in the From Left field we entered the same value as the paragraph's left indent with a **minus** sign in front of it (-1p)._

,Hey! diddle, diddle,
The cat and the fiddle,
The cow jumped over the moon;
The little dog laugh'd
To see such sport,
,And the dish ran away with the spoon.

3 _A 2-pt Rule Above, Length: **Indents,** Offset p10_

,Hey! diddle, diddle,
The cat and the fiddle,
The cow jumped over the moon;
The little dog laugh'd
To see such sport,
,And the dish ran away with the spoon.

4 _A 2-pt Rule Above, Length: **Text,** Offset p10_

H_ey! diddle, diddle,_
The cat and the fiddle,
The cow jumped over the moon;
The little dog laugh'd
To see such sport,
,And the dish ran away with the spoon.

5 _A 2-pt Rule Above, Length: Text, **From Left** 1p10, Offset p10_

6. Choose Indents, Text, or Column from the Length menu. If you choose Text, the rule will be the length of the first line of text in the paragraph for a Rule Above or the length of the last line of text in the paragraph for a Rule Below. If you choose Indents, the rule will span the width of the paragraph, unless you enter a number greater than 0 in the From Left and/or From Right field (see step 8). *Note:* The rule will be shortened by any Indent values in Style > Formats and any Text Inset values in Item > Modify > Text **1**.

7. In the Offset field, enter the fixed distance, in any measurement unit, by which you want to offset the bottom of the Rule Above upward from the baseline of the first line of the paragraph or offset the top of the Rule Below downward from the baseline of the last line of the paragraph. For a Rule Above, enter an Offset that is equal to or greater than the point size of the type.
or
Enter a percentage Offset (0–100%). A Rule Below with a 20% Offset, for example, would position the rule closer to the bottom of the currently selected paragraph than would an 80% offset. If this method is used and the spacing between the paragraphs is altered, the rule position will adjust automatically.

8. *Optional:* Raise the From Left and/or From Right values to indent, and thus shorten, the rule.

9. *Optional:* Choose a dash or stripe style from the Style menu. To create a custom style, see pages 227.

10. *Optional:* Choose a color from the Color menu.

11. *Optional:* Adjust the Shade and Opacity of the color using the sliders or fields.

12. Click Apply to preview, make any adjustments, then click OK **2**–**5**.
(For more illustrations, see the next page.)

Paragraph Rules

ETHAN FROME

By Edith Wharton

I had the story, bit by bit, from various people, and, as generally happens in such cases, each time it was a different story.

If you know Starkfield, Massachusetts, you know the post-office. If you know the post-office you must have seen Ethan Frome drive up to it, drop the reins on his hollow-backed bay and

**Rules can be used
to jazz up subheads**

**Rules can be used
to jazz up subheads**

*Rules of varying **lengths** and **weights***

Going in reverse

To create a **reverse rule,** color the text white, and use a negative Offset and a wide width (the point size of the type plus a few points) for the rule. A negative value of up to half the width of the rule can be used. This is a 16-point black Rule Above, Length: Indents, Left and Right Indents: 0, and Offset: -p4. The headline text is 9 pt.

Cumin
Cayenne
Coriander
Chervil
Cinnamon

*To add alternating **tints** behind text, use a wide Rule Above with a negative Offset. Apply it via a style sheet!*

*Need to quickly fill a page with horizontal **lines**? Apply a paragraph rule, then keep pressing Return/Enter.*

Norton Thorpe clapped the young Frenchman on the shoulder and, with a hearty smile, shook his hand. "My dear chap! How could I possibly object to my daughter becoming not only the new Countess d'Auvergne but also the wife of an up-and-coming electronics genius!" Lisa, her eyes moist with tears of joy, not

"How could I possibly object to my daughter becoming not only the new Countess d'Auvergne but also the wife of an up-and-coming electronics genius!"

only because of her future marriage but also because of her restored relationship with her father, threw her arms around Nancy in a warm embrace ex - claiming: "Oh, Nancy, none of this could ever have happened if you hadn't worked so hard to solve

Carolyn Keene

*Rules can be used as **decorative** elements or for **emphasis**. In this example, a Return was inserted after every line, making every line a separate paragraph.*

*Here paragraph rules are used to **separate** a pull quote from the main body text.*

ALL
THE
REALLY GOOD
IDEAS
I EVER HAD
CAME
TO ME
WHILE I WAS
MILKING
A COW.

Grant Wood

Do it without the grid

To align text without using the Lock to Baseline Grid feature, make sure the sum of the space before and after any subheads or between paragraphs is a *multiple* of the leading value. For example, if your body text has 14 pt. leading, add 8 points before each subhead and 6 points after (a total of 14). Use style sheets to ensure that all the leading in your body text is uniform.

There are several methods of making coffee, each highly recommended—I cannot decide which is best, but the following way is a good one:—

To make Coffee.—Take fresh-roasted coffee (a quarter of a pound for three persons is the rule, but *less* will do;) allow two tablespoonfuls for each person, grind it just before making, put it in a basin and break into it an egg, yolk, white, shell and all. Mix it up with the spoon to the consistence of mortar, put in warm not *boiling* water the coffee pot; let it boil up and *break* three times; then stand a few minutes, and it will be as clear as amber, and the egg will give it a rich taste.

Another Way to make Coffee.—Pour hot water into your coffee pot, and then stir in your coffee, a spoonful at a time, allowing three to every pint of water; this makes *strong* coffee. Stir it to prevent the mixture from boiling over, as the coffee swells, and to force it to combine with the water. This will be done after it has boiled gently a few minutes. Then let it stand and boil slowly for half an hour; remove it from the fire, and pour in a tea-cup of cold water, and set it in the corner to settle. As soon as it becomes clear, it is to be poured, gently, into a clean coffee pot for the table.

Made in this manner it may be kept two or three days in summer, and a week in winter; you need only heat it over when wanted.

Sara Josepha Hale from *The Good Housekeeper*, 1841

1 *Text aligned across columns using* **Lock to Baseline Grid**

The Lock to Baseline Grid command is used to precisely align text across columns in text boxes and table cells. For an alternate method of aligning text across columns, see the sidebar.

To align text to a grid:

1. Take note of what leading value is currently applied to your body text. Also, select your text box, go to Item > Modify > Text, then on a scrap of paper, jot down the current First Baseline: Offset value (paperless office? Ha!).

2. *Optional:* To display the nonprinting gridlines, choose View > Baseline Grid (Option-F7/Ctrl-F7).

3. Choose QuarkXPress (Edit, in Windows) > Preferences > Print Layout > Paragraph.

4. Enter as the Baseline Grid: Start value the First Baseline: Offset value that you got from Item > Modify.

5. Enter as the Baseline Grid: Increment the current leading value or a multiple of the leading value.

6. Click OK.

7. To snap the text to the grid lines, select the paragraphs you want to lock.

8. Display the Paragraph Attributes tab of the Measurements palette or choose Style > Formats.

9. Check Lock to Baseline Grid **1**.

   Note: If Justified is chosen as the Vertical Alignment: Type in Item > Modify > Text, only the first and last lines in the column will lock to the grid.

   Note: Also see the information about Maintain Leading on page 374.

TIP You may not want to lock subheads to the grid. Many designers prefer to have subheads "float."

TIP For consistency, implement Lock to Baseline Grid through paragraph style sheets.

You can use this trick to copy paragraph formats within the *same* text box or between *linked* text boxes, but not between unlinked boxes or table cells. Paragraph style sheet and local formatting specifications will copy; character attributes (font, size, color, etc.) won't. To use this trick, you will select the paragraphs you want to change, then click the paragraph that contains the desired formatting. Memorize this technique—you will use it often when formatting and fine tuning text.

To copy formats in the same story:

1. Click in a paragraph **1** or drag through a series of paragraphs that you want to reformat.

2. Option-Shift-click/Alt-Shift-click the paragraph whose formats you want copied to the paragraph(s) you selected in the previous step **2**.

> **Then there was nothing but the air and the swiftness of the little cloud that bore me and those two men still leading up to where white clouds were piled like mountains on a wide blue plain, and in them thunder beings lived and leaped and flashed.**
>
> *Now suddenly there was nothing but a world of cloud, and we three were there alone in the middle of a great white plain with snowy hills and mountains staring at us; and it was very still; but there were whispers…*
>
> JOHN G. NEIHARDT, FROM BLACK ELK SPEAKS

1 *Click in a paragraph (or select a series of paragraphs) to be **reformatted**…*

> **Then there was nothing but the air and the swiftness of the little cloud that bore me and those two men still leading up to where white clouds were piled like mountains on a wide blue plain, and in them thunder beings lived and leaped and flashed.**
> *Now suddenly there was nothing but a world of cloud, and we three were there alone in the middle of a great white plain with snowy hills and mountains staring at us; and it was very still; but there were whispers…*
>
> JOHN G. NEIHARDT, FROM BLACK ELK SPEAKS

2 *…then Option-Shift-click/Alt-Shift-click the paragraph whose formats you want to **copy**. In our example, the top paragraph reformats (its Left Indent, Space Before, Alignment, and Space After values change) but the font remains the same because the font is a character attribute—not a paragraph attribute.*

Appending an H&J

To append an H&J from one project to another, choose File > **Append** or click Append in the H&J dialog box (either way you'll get to the same place). QuarkXPress 7 provides a variety of new default H&Js that you may wish to append from a project file created in QuarkXPress 7.

1 *Click New. Or choose an existing H&J and click* **Edit**. *Click* **Append** *to import an H&J from another project.*

2 *Choose hyphenation settings in the* **Edit Hyphenation & Justification** *dialog box.*

Applying hyphenation

Auto Hyphenation lessens gaps between words in justified type and smooths ragged edges in nonjustified type. A set of hyphenation and justification settings is called an "H&J," and each project can contain up to 1,000 of them. To apply an H&J, follow the instructions on page 119. (Manual hyphenation, which is discussed in the sidebar on page 120, should be used only to correct an occasional awkward break here or there.)

To create or edit an H&J:

1. Choose Edit > H&Js (Cmd-Option-J/ Ctrl-Alt-J). An H&J that is created when no files are open will be available in all subsequently created project files.

2. To create a new H&J, click New **1**, then enter a descriptive name in the Edit Hyphenation & Justification dialog box. *or* Click an existing H&J, then click Edit. The Standard H&J can be modified.

3. In the Hyphenation & Justification dialog box, check Auto Hyphenation **2**.

4. Change any of the hyphenation settings:

   Smallest Word is the minimum number of characters a word must contain to be hyphenated. We use 5 or 6.

   Minimum Before is the minimum number (1–6) of a word's characters that must precede a hyphen.

   Minimum After is the minimum number (2–8) of characters that can follow a hyphen. For the sake of readability, we use 3 rather than the default 2.

   Check Break Capitalized Words if you want to permit words that begin with an uppercase character to be hyphenated.

   Hyphens in a Row is the number of consecutive lines that can end with a hyphen. More than two hyphens in a row can impair readability.

(Continued on the following page)

Create or Edit an H&J

Enter a Hyphenation Zone value greater than zero to create a more ragged edge (less hyphenation).

5. To tighten word spacing in justified paragraphs, enter lower Space: Min. and Space: Max. values 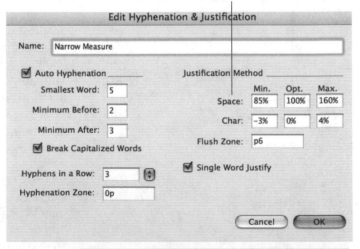. The subheads and thumb tabs in this book have slightly tightened word spacing. Headlines also tend to look better with tighter-than-normal word (and character) spacing. To loosen word spacing, enter higher values.

To tighten character spacing in justified paragraphs, enter lower Char: Min. and Char: Max. values. To loosen character spacing, enter higher values. Experiment and make your final judgment from a printout. The effect may vary depending on the font.

To change the word or character spacing in both justified and nonjustified paragraphs, change either or both of the Opt./Optimum values.

6. *Optional:* The Flush Zone, which is the span within which the last word in a justified paragraph must fall in order to be justified, can be widened.

Check Single Word Justify to force any single word that falls on a line by itself to be justified to the full width of the text box, minus any indents. Usually this occurs at the end of a paragraph.

Note: The Forced Justify horizontal alignment option justifies single words automatically. In fact, Forced Justify overrides both the Flush Zone and Single Word Justify settings.

7. Click OK.

8. Click Save. To apply an H&J, follow the instructions on the next page.

TIP To delete an H&J, click its name, then click Delete. If the H&J is in use, you'll be prompted to choose a replacement **2**. The Standard H&J can't be deleted.

1 *The **Space** values affect inter-word spacing; the **Char.** values affect character (letter) spacing.*

Edit Hyphenation & Justification

Name: Narrow Measure

☑ Auto Hyphenation

Smallest Word: 5
Minimum Before: 2
Minimum After: 3
☑ Break Capitalized Words
Hyphens in a Row: 3
Hyphenation Zone: 0p

Justification Method

	Min.	Opt.	Max.
Space:	85%	100%	160%
Char:	-3%	0%	4%

Flush Zone: p6

☑ Single Word Justify

Cancel   OK

2 *This alert dialog box will open if you **delete** an H&J that is currently applied to text in a project. When you replace an H&J, text is likely to reflow throughout the layouts.*

OK to delete this H&J and replace it with another H&J wherever it is used?

Replace with: Standard

Cancel   OK

SEASONINGS FOR WHITE SAUCE, FRICAS-
SEES, AND RAGOUTS
White pepper, nutmeg, mace and
lemon-peel, pounded together.

CATSUPS
Mushroom is most esteemed; but the
difficulty in our country of obtaining
the right kind of plant (some are
poisonous), renders a recipe of little
consequence. It is better to buy this
catsup at the shops. *Sara Josepha Hale*

*In this illustration, **hyphenation** is **on** for
the **subheads** (a no-no!) and **off** for the
justified body text (another no-no because
it leaves ugly "rivers" of white space).*

SEASONINGS FOR WHITE SAUCE,
FRICASSEES, AND RAGOUTS
White pepper, nutmeg, mace and
lemon-peel, pounded together.

CATSUPS
Mushroom is most esteemed; but the
difficulty in our country of obtaining
the right kind of plant (some are poisonous), renders a recipe of little consequence. It is better to buy this
catsup at the shops.

*Here **hyphenation** is turned **off** for the **subheads** and turned **on** for the **justified** body
text. An improvement, don't you think?*

H&Js are applied to individual paragraphs
via the H&J menu in Style > Formats. If
you're using more than one H&J setting in
a project, the most efficient way to apply
them to your text is via style sheets (click
Formats in the Edit Paragraph Style Sheet
dialog box; see Chapter 13). The Normal
style sheet will have the Standard H&J
associated with it unless a different H&J is
chosen for it.

To apply an H&J:

1. Choose the Content tool.

2. Click in a paragraph or drag through
   a series of paragraphs.

3. Choose Style > Formats (Cmd-Shift-F/
   Ctrl-Shift-F).

4. Choose an option from the H&J
   menu **1**.

5. Click Apply, if desired (Cmd-A/Alt-A),
   then click OK.

TIP Use a nonbreaking (permanent)
hyphen if you want a word to *always*
hyphenate but never break at the end
of a line (a compound word, such as
"e-mail" or "two-thirds"). To insert one,
NEW choose Utilities > Insert Character >
Special (nonbreaking) > Hyphen or
press Cmd-=/Ctrl-=.

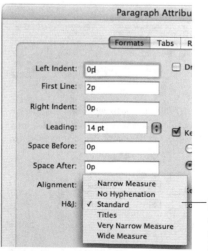

1 *To apply an H&J to selected text
or to make it part of a style sheet,
choose from the **H&J** menu in
Paragraph Attributes > **Formats.***

Apply an H&J

The Hyphenation Exceptions dialog box is used not only to enter words you don't want hyphenated, but also to specify how specific words are to be hyphenated.

To enter hyphenation exceptions:

1. Choose Utilities > Hyphenation Exceptions.

2. Type a word that you *don't* want hyphenated 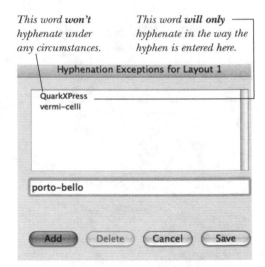. You can't type spaces or punctuation marks.
   or
   Specify how a word *will* be hyphenated by typing it with a hyphen.

3. Click Add (Return/Enter).

4. *Optional:* To edit an entry, click it (the Add button will change to Replace), edit it in the field, then click Replace.

5. Repeat steps 2–3 or 4 for any other words. Be sure to add any variations of a word, such as its plural form.

6. Click Save. Hyphenation exceptions are saved in the XPress Preferences file, and are specify to layouts (not projects).

TIP To prevent a compound word such as "absent-minded" from hyphenating, add each part of the word separately as a hyphenation exception.

TIP You can use the Line Check feature to search for manually and/or automatically hyphenated words (see page 93).

Hyphenating manually

Have you ever noticed, in your reading, a hyphen in the middle of a line that wasn't supposed to be there? Now that type is set in desktop publishing applications, it's an all-too-frequent occurrence.

If for some reason you want to hyphenate a word manually, don't use a regular hyphen, which will stay in your text if the text reflows. Instead, use a **discretionary** hyphen (see the tip on page 105) which will disappear if the text reflows though the nonprinting marker for it will remain.

If you're not sure how to hyphenate a particular word, choose the Content tool, click in the word, then choose Utilities > **Suggested Hyphenation** (Cmd-Option-Shift-H/Ctrl-Alt-Shift-H). If no hyphens display in the dialog box, it means that word isn't supposed to be hyphenated, period.

*This word **won't** hyphenate under any circumstances.*　　*This word **will only** hyphenate in the way the hyphen is entered here.*

Hyphenation Exceptions for Layout 1

QuarkXPress
vermi-celli

porto–bello

(Add)　(Delete)　(Cancel)　(Save)

1 *Using the **Hyphenation Exceptions** dialog box, you can specify how a word **is** to be hyphenated and also specify which words you **don't** want hyphenated.*

Typography 7

Reformat type the fast way

Once you've mastered the typographic basics, we urge you to read Chapter 13, **Style Sheets!**

Enter a point size between 2 and 720 in the Size field.

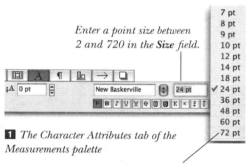

1 *The Character Attributes tab of the Measurements palette*

Or choose a preset point size from the Size menu.

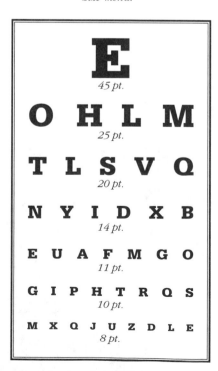

E	45 pt.
O H L M	25 pt.
T L S V Q	20 pt.
N Y I D X B	14 pt.
E U A F M G O	11 pt.
G I P H T R Q S	10 pt.
M X Q J U Z D L E	8 pt.

Typography basics

Tired of 12 pt. Helvetica? Now you'll have some fun. In this chapter, not only will you learn how to change basic type attributes (point size, font, etc.), you'll also learn how to add professional touches, such as smart (curly) quotation marks.

To resize type using the Measurements palette:

1. Choose the Content tool.
2. Select the text to be resized.
3. Display the Classic tab or Character Attributes tab of the Measurements palette.
4. Double-click the Size field on the right side of the palette **1**, enter a point size (2–720) in an increment as small as .001 point, then press Return/Enter. You don't have to enter the "pt."
   or
   Choose a preset size from the Size menu.

TIP Cmd-Shift-\/Ctrl-Shift-\ opens the Character Attributes dialog box and selects the Size field in one keystroke.

Use the keyboard method to resize type if selected text contains more than one point size—all the type will resize at once.

To resize type using the keyboard:

1. Choose the Content tool.
2. Select the text to be resized.
3. Press Cmd-Shift-</Ctrl-Shift-< to reduce the text in preset sizes or > to enlarge it. Or press Cmd-Option-Shift-</Ctrl-Alt-Shift-< to reduce the text in 1-point increments or > to enlarge it.

If you're new to typography, read "Type for print" on page 136. For further reading on this topic, explore one of Robin Williams' terrifically helpful books, such as *The Non-Designer's Type Book,* 2nd edition (Peachpit Press).

To change fonts:

1. Choose the Content tool.

2. Select the text to be modified.

3. Display the Classic tab or Character Attributes tab of the Measurements palette.

4. Choose a font from the Font menu 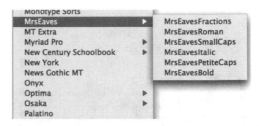.
   or
   Click in the Font field to the left of the current font name, type the first few characters of the desired font name, then press Return/Enter 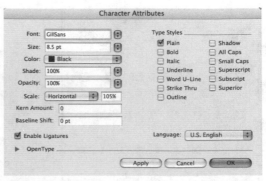.
   or
   Choose a font from the Style > Font submenu.

TIP To apply a color to type, see page 267.

Font shortcuts

Select font field on Measurements palette	Cmd-Option-Shift-M/ Ctrl-Alt-Shift-M
Apply next font on font menu	Option-F9/Ctrl-F9
Apply previous font on font menu	Option-Shift-F9/ Ctrl-Shift-F9

Monotype Sorts
MrsEaves ▶ — MrsEavesFractions / MrsEavesRoman / MrsEavesSmallCaps / MrsEavesItalic / MrsEavesPetiteCaps / MrsEavesBold
MT Extra
Myriad Pro ▶
New Century Schoolbook ▶
New York
News Gothic MT
Onyx
Optima ▶
Osaka ▶
Palatino

1 *A partial **Font** submenu in Mac OS X; the main entries are font family names, and the submenu lists available variations of that font, such as bold or italic.*

*Click just to the left of the current font name, then start **typing** a new font name…*   *…or press the double arrows and choose from the **Font** menu.*

auto / GillSans Bold / 12 pt
0

2 *The Measurements palette's Classic and Character Attributes tabs provide a **Font** area at right.*

One-stop styling

If you'd like to make all your Font, Size, Color, Shade, Opacity, Scale, Track/Kern Amount, Baseline Shift, Ligatures, and Type Style choices from one dialog box, choose Style > **Character** (Cmd-Shift-D/Ctrl-Shift-D). Don't forget to click Apply to preview.

Character Attributes

Font:	GillSans
Size:	8.5 pt
Color:	■ Black
Shade:	100%
Opacity:	100%
Scale:	Horizontal 105%
Kern Amount:	0
Baseline Shift:	0 pt

☑ Enable Ligatures
▶ OpenType

Type Styles
☑ Plain   ☐ Shadow
☐ Bold   ☐ All Caps
☐ Italic   ☐ Small Caps
☐ Underline   ☐ Superscript
☐ Word U-Line   ☐ Subscript
☐ Strike Thru   ☐ Superior
☐ Outline

Language: U.S. English

(Apply) (Cancel) (OK)

Change Fonts

Type style shortcuts

First select the type, then hold down **Cmd-Shift/Ctrl-Shift** and press one of the following keys (use the same shortcut to remove a style):

Plain **P**	Shadow **S**
Bold **B**	All Caps **K**
Italic **I**	Small Caps **H**
Underline **U**	Superscript **+** *(Mac)* **0** *(Win)*
Word Underline **W**	Subscript **–** *(Mac)* **9** *(Win)*
Strike Thru **/**	Superior **V**
Outline **O**	

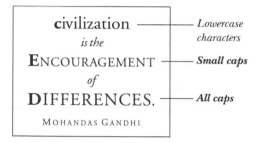

civilization ——— *Lowercase characters*
is the
Encouragement ——— ***Small caps***
of
Differences. ——— ***All caps***
Mohandas Gandhi

OpenType styles **NEW**

QuarkXPress offers full support for OpenType fonts, which may offer additional style options such as Old Style Figures. The reality is that OpenType fonts are just gaining ground in publishing and most offer few style options. To see the options available for an OpenType font, display the OpenType area at the bottom of the Character Attributes dialog box (Style > Character) or click the OpenType menu [@] on the Classic or Character Attributes tab of the Measurements palette.

1 *The **type style** buttons on the Measurements palette*

Note: Looking for boldface or italic? Choose the actual bold or italic font from the Font submenu—such as MrsEavesBold—as it's less likely to cause a printing error.

To style type:

1. Choose the Content tool.
2. Select the text to be styled.
3. Display the Classic tab or Character Attributes tab of the Measurements palette.
4. Click one or more style buttons **1**.

TIP To remove *all* styling from selected type, click the "P" button. To remove one style at a time, click any selected style button. If a style is half gray, it means not all the currently selected type has that style.

TIP Superscript type sits above the baseline (as in ®). Subscript type sits below the baseline (as in ₉). Superior type aligns with the cap height of the type and is reduced in point size (as in 18ᵗʰ). Adjust the proportions of these styles in QuarkXPress (Edit, in Windows) > Preferences > Print Layout > Character (try reducing the "VScale" percentage).

TIP You have various options for converting the case of selected text: the All Caps type style, the Small Caps type style (which converts lowercase letters to smaller versions of capital letters), and the Style > Change Case submenu, new to QuarkXPress 7, which lets you **NEW** change the case of the letters to UPPERCASE, lowercase, or Title Case.

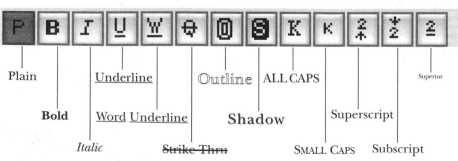

Plain		Underline			Outline	ALL CAPS			Superior	
	Bold		Word Underline		Shadow		Superscript			
		Italic		Strike Thru			SMALL CAPS	Subscript		

Kerning and tracking

Kerning is the manual adjustment of space between a pair of characters (the cursor is inserted between them). Tracking, the adjustment of the space to the right of one or more selected characters, can be used for fine-tuning or for creating a variety of typographic effects. The same area of the Measurements palette is used for tracking as for kerning. *Note:* Before kerning manually, go to QuarkXPress (Edit, in Windows) > Preferences > Print Layout > Character and make sure Auto Kern Above is on, at, or below the minimum type size of your text.

To kern or track type manually using the Measurements palette:

1. Choose the Content tool, and zoom in on the type you're going to kern or track.

2. Display the Classic tab tab or Character Attributes tab of the Measurements palette.

3. For kerning, click between two characters **1**. For tracking, select any number of consecutive characters.

4. Click the right Tracking & Kerning arrow to add space or the left arrow to remove space **2**–**5**. To track or kern in a finer increment, Option-click/Alt-click the right or left arrow.
   or
   Enter a value between –500% and 500% in the Tracking & Kerning field in an increment as small as .001.

TIP To restore normal tracking to selected text or to restore normal kerning at a text insertion point, enter 0 in the Tracking & Kerning field.

TIP To apply tracking or kerning values via a dialog box, choose Style > Track or Kern. To adjust the letterspacing for longer passages of text, use an H&J (see pages 117–119).

Tomorrow

1 *Click **between** two characters to **kern** them—the space after a T or W often needs adjustment.*

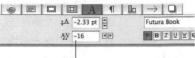

2 *The **Tracking & Kerning** field and arrows on the Character Attributes tab of the Measurements palette*

Tomorrow

3 *Now the "T" and the "o" are **closer** together.*

C I V I L I Z A T I O N

is the

E N C O U R A G E M E N T

of

D I F F E R E N C E S.

Mohandas Gandhi

---

4 *A phrase with positive **tracking** values*

Nothing great was ever achieved without enthusiasm.

Ralph Waldo Emerson

5 *A phrase with a **negative** tracking value of –6*

To Tr Ta Yo Ya
Wo Wa We Va Vo

1 *These are a few of the character pairs that often need* **extra kerning,** *particularly if they're set in a large point size.*

> THE TALE OF MRS. TIGGY-WINKLE
> THE TALE OF MRS. TIGGY-WINKLE

2 *Wide tracking (letterspacing) is popular nowadays, especially since it's so easy to do. We use it only for* **short** *passages, though, as it's tiring to read in long passages. Small caps, as in this illustration, look nice "tracked out," as does very chunky or very thin type (for example, the condensed variation of a font).*

Style is self-plagiarism.

3 *This phrase has normal word spacing.*

Style is self-plagiarism.

~ ALFRED HITCHCOCK

4 *Here the same phrase has a* **Word Space Tracking** *value of –10. Negative word space tracking adds a professional touch to headlines and other large-sized text.*

This is the quickest method for tracking—and it's our favorite.

To kern or track using the keyboard:

1. Choose the Content tool.
2. Click between two characters or select any number of characters.
3. Press Cmd-Shift-[/Ctrl-Shift-[(left bracket) to remove space, or] (right bracket) to add space **1**–**2**. To kern or track in a finer increment, include the Option/Alt key in the shortcut.

Use the Word Space Tracking* shortcut described in the following instructions to adjust inter-word spacing in an isolated phrase, such as a large headline.

Note: To adjust inter-word spacing in repetitive text (e.g., subheads) or in a larger body of text, create an H&J that has tightened word spacing and apply it via a style sheet. That's how we tightened the word spacing of subheads in this book (as in the words "To adjust inter-word spacing:" below).

To adjust inter-word spacing:

1. Choose the Content tool.
2. Select one or more words.
3. In Mac OS X, press Cmd-Control-Shift-[(left bracket) to remove space or] (right bracket) to add space **3**–**4**. For finer word space adjustments, include the Option key. In Windows, press Ctrl-Shift-1 or Ctrl-Shift-2.

To remove kerning and word space tracking:

1. Choose the Content tool.
2. Select the kerned text.
3. Choose Utilities > Remove Manual Kerning.* This command has no effect on character tracking values.

*Word Space Tracking and Remove Manual Kerning are part of TypeTricks, an XTension that ships with QuarkXPress.

Some character pairs, because of their shape and how they happen to fit side by side, have noticeable gaps between them. To help with this problem, fonts have hundreds of built-in kerning pairs—character duos that are nudged together slightly. To turn this pair kerning on, go to Quark XPress (Edit, in Windows) > Preferences > Print Layout > Character, and check Auto Kern Above.

If you're unhappy with the default spacing in a particular kerning pair or pairs that appear repetitively in your layouts, you can use QuarkXPress's kerning editor to specify your own kerning values.

To use the Kerning Table Editor:

1. Choose Utilities > Kerning Table Edit. If it's unavailable, enable the Kern-Track Editor XTension (see page 377).

2. Click the name of the font that you want to edit ▮, then click Edit.
or
Double-click the name of the font that you want to edit.

3. Click a kerning pair on the list.
or
In the Kerning Pair field, type a kerning pair.

4. In the With-Stream field, enter a new kerning value or click the up or down arrow (a negative value will bring characters closer together). Option-click/ Alt-click either arrow to kern in a finer increment.

5. Optional: To adjust the vertical spacing **(NEW)** between a kerning pair (e.g., to change the position of a punctuation mark), using the same techniques, change the Cross-Stream value.

6. When you're satisfied with the Preview ▮, click Replace to replace the existing pair or click Add to add it as a new pair.

7. Click OK, then click Save.

Keep project settings

Kerning table changes are made on a font-by-font basis, but they apply to the whole *application*. If the XPress Preferences prompt appears when you open a file and you want to preserve the project's existing kerning table values, click Keep Project Settings.

To restore a font's original, manufacturer-defined kerning values for all pairs, click *Reset* in the Kerning Values dialog box. QuarkXPress's kerning values don't affect font usage in other applications.

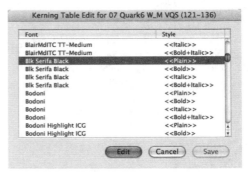

▮ *Click the font whose kerning you want to edit, then click **Edit**.*

▮ *Note the **Preview** as you change a kerning pair's **With-Stream** (horizontal) or **Cross-Stream** (vertical) values.*

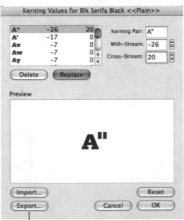

*To save the kerning pairs you've adjusted for one font to apply to another font, click **Export**, then Save. To import those values, choose another font, then click **Import**.*

Alligator

1 *This is Futura Regular, Horizontal Scale 0.*

Alligator

2 *Here a condensed font is faked by applying a **Horizontal Scale** value of 30% to Futura Regular.*

Alligator

3 *We think the proportions are more balanced in Futura Condensed Regular (Horizontal Scale 0), a typeface that's **condensed to begin with.***

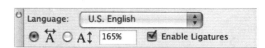

Language: U.S. English

165% ☑ Enable Ligatures

4 *In the Character Attributes tab of the Measurements palette, click the **Scale Text Horizontally** or **Scale Text Vertically** button, then enter a value.*

Whale *Expanded type*

Giraffe *Condensed type*

5 ***Horizontal scaling** is used for **stylizing** type.*

Typographic tips and tricks

Normal text has a horizontal scale of 100%. Raising this value makes type wider (extends it); lowering this value below 100% makes type narrower (condenses it). Changing the vertical scaling percentage changes only a character's height. This is different from changing point sizes!

Note: Because the Scale command affects only the vertical parts of letters—not the horizontals (or vice versa)—it causes letter shapes to become distorted. For more narrow (or expanded) characters that look more balanced, we recommend using a Condensed (or Expanded) typeface instead of applying the Horizontal Scale command to Regular characters **1**–**3**. We rarely use the Scale feature (call us type purists).

To scale type using the Measurements palette:

1. Choose the Content tool.

2. Select the text to be scaled.

3. Display the Character Attributes tab of the Measurements palette. **NEW**

4. For horizontal scaling, click the Scale Text Horizontally button at left, then enter a percentage between 25 and 99 to condense the type (make it narrower than normal) or a percentage between 101 and 400 to expand the type (make it wider than normal) **4**. A Horizontal Scale of 60%, for example, will condense type by 40%; a Horizontal Scale of 125% will expand type by 25%.
or
Click the Scale Text Vertically button, then enter the desired percentage.

5. Press Return/Enter to apply the changes. **5**.

TIP You can also choose Style > Horizontal/Vertical Scale. The Character Attributes dialog box will open, with the Scale field selected. Choose Horizontal or Vertical from the menu and enter a percentage value.

Scale Type Horizontally or Vertically

To scale type horizontally or vertically using the keyboard:

1. Choose the Content tool.

2. Select the text to be scaled.

3. Hold down Cmd/Ctrl and press [(left bracket) to condense or shorten the type in 5% increments, or] (right bracket) to expand or lengthen it **1**–**4**. Include the Option/Alt key to scale in 1% increments. Scaling will be horizontal or vertical depending on which option is currently selected in the Character Attributes dialog box.

This method for scaling type interactively rather than by specifying an exact point size is appropriate when you're working visually—trying to make a headline or a logo look just so. You can't use it on text in a linked box or on a text path created using the Line Text-Path or Orthogonal Text-Path tool.

To scale type interactively:

1. Choose the Item or Content tool.

2. To scale type while preserving the proportions of the type and the box or path, Cmd-Option-Shift-drag/Ctrl-Alt-Shift-drag a handle **5**–**6**. The leading will readjust proportionately.
   or
   To scale type and its box (or path) without preserving their proportions, Cmd-drag/Ctrl-drag a side midpoint handle to scale horizontally or a top or bottom midpoint handle to scale vertically. The type will condense or expand to fit the shape of the box or path.

TIP To restore normal scaling to type, select it, choose Style > Horizontal/Vertical Scale, then enter 100 in the Scale field.

TIP To scale type on a path, make sure Item > Edit > Shape is off. You should see the handles of the bounding box when the path is selected, not the anchor points.

"It was much pleasanter at home," thought poor Alice, "when one wasn't always growing larger and smaller, and being ordered about by mice and rabbits."

1 *Normal (100%) horizontal and vertical scale*

"It was much pleasanter at home," thought poor Alice, "when one wasn't always growing larger and smaller, and being ordered about by mice and rabbits."

2 *75% vertical scale*

"It was much pleasanter at home," thought poor Alice, "when one wasn't always growing larger and smaller, and being ordered about by mice and rabbits."

3 *75% horizontal scale*

"It was much pleasanter at home," thought poor Alice, "when one wasn't always growing larger and smaller, and being ordered about by mice and rabbits."

4 *110% horizontal scale*

"Oh, I'm not particular as to size," Alice hastily replied; "only one doesn't like changing so often, you know."

5 *The original text*

"Oh, I'm not particular as to size," Alice hastily replied; "only one doesn't like changing so often, you know."

6 *The text and box are scaled interactively, and the proportions of both are preserved.*

1 *A positive **Baseline Shift** value shifts characters above the baseline; a negative Baseline Shift shifts characters below the baseline.*

The baseline

2 *The "C" was shifted down. Baseline Shift is handy for creating signs, company logos, and the like.*

Typography terms

Sans serif *font*

x-height

cap height

Baseline

Serif *font*

Ascender

Descender

Serif

Serif

Type in reverse

There's no type style or one-step method for creating reversed type. You need to apply a light color to the text and a dark color to the background of the text box..

Using the Baseline Shift command, you can shift one or more characters above or below the baseline. Don't use this command to shift a whole paragraph—that's the job of leading. Use Baseline Shift only to fiddle with a little bit of type—to nudge a bullet, a dash, or an anchored item slightly upward or downward, or to shift the position of text on a Bézier path. A Baseline Shift value can be incorporated into a paragraph or character style sheet.

To vertically shift type using the Measurements palette:

1. Choose the Content tool.
2. Select the characters to be shifted.
3. Display the Character Attributes tab of the Measurements palette. **NEW**
4. Click the arrows next to the Baseline field in the middle of the palette.
   or
   In the Baseline field, enter a value up to three times the point size of the type to be shifted. Enter a minus sign (–) before the number to shift the type below the baseline **1**–**2**. Press Return/Enter to see the changes.

TIP If you change the point size of type that has a Baseline Shift value other than zero, the Baseline Shift value will adjust accordingly.

To vertically shift type using the keyboard:

1. Choose the Content tool.
2. Select the characters to be shifted.
3. In Mac OS X, press Cmd-Option-Shift-+ (plus) to raise the type above the baseline in 1-point increments or - (hyphen) to lower the type below the baseline.

   In Windows, press Ctrl-Alt-Shift-)(close paren) or ((open paren).

TIP To access the Baseline Shift field in the Character Attributes dialog box, choose Style > Baseline Shift.

Baseline Shift

It's easy to input the curly, smart quotation marks that professional typesetters use or foreign language quotation marks, such as guillemets «». With the Smart Quotes feature on—as it is by default—press ' to produce a single quotation mark in the style currently specified in the Input Settings pane of the Preferences dialog box (' in English) or press Shift-' to produce a double quotation mark (" or ").

To turn on Smart Quotes:

1. Choose QuarkXPress (Edit, in Windows) > Preferences (Cmd-Option-Shift-Y/Ctrl-Alt-Shift-Y).

2. Click Input Settings under Application.

3. Check Smart Quotes.

4. Choose a style for the quotes from the Quotes: Format menu 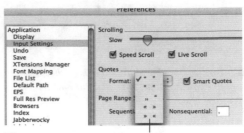.

5. Click OK .

TIP To produce foot ' and inch " marks when Smart Quotes is checked, press Control-'/Ctrl-' for a foot mark or Control-Shift-"/Ctrl-Shift-" for an inch mark. If you're working with a lot of these marks, you can temporarily uncheck Smart Quotes.

TIP If you import text with Convert Quotes checked in the Import Text dialog box, smart quotes will be substituted for straight quotes.

TIP In place of absent letters, use an apostrophe, not a smart quote. For example, a date should be written like this: '94, not like this: '94. Here's another example: Sugar 'n' spice. To enter an apostrophe manually, press Option-Shift-]/Alt-].

1 *In Preferences > Application > Input Settings, check **Smart Quotes** and choose a quotes **Format**.*

"HATE THE SIN
and
LOVE THE SINNER"

—*Mohandas Gandhi*

2 *Use **Smart Quotes** for **quotation** marks and **apostrophes**.*

Prime time

Please—we beg of you—use straight quotes *only* for foot and inch marks **3** (not for quotation marks). Or better yet, use oblique foot and inch marks, called **prime** marks **4**. To insert prime marks, use the **Glyphs** palette (Window > Glyphs). Choose Symbol from the font menu and scroll to locate the characters **5**. Double-click a character to insert it at the text insertion point.

The woman is 5'6" tall.

3 *Use straight quotes for feet, inches, minutes, seconds...*

The woman is 5′6″ tall.

4 *...or better yet, use prime marks.*

5 *Use the **Glyphs** palette to insert special characters from any font.*

Smart Quotes

1 *A few **Zapf Dingbats** characters*

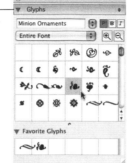

2 *The Glyphs palette displays all the characters in the currently selected font.*

> Sir Isaac Newton wore his black and gold waistcoat. 🐾 And Mr. Alderman Ptolemy Tortoise brought a salad with him in a string bag. 🐾 And instead of a nice dish of minnows they had a roasted grasshopper with lady-bird sauce, which frogs consider a beautiful treat; but I think it must have been nasty! ∾
>
> *Beatrix Potter*

3 *You can use a symbol to separate sentences or paragraphs or to mark the end of a story or article. But don't limit yourself to the Zapf Dingbat and Symbol fonts—other symbol fonts are available. These symbols are from Adobe's **Minion Ornaments** font.*

A few special characters (all fonts)

©	Option-G/Alt-Shift-C
®	Option-R/Alt-Shift-R
™	Option-2/Alt-Shift-2
•	Option-8/Alt-Shift-8
¢	Option-4/Alt+0162*
¶	Option-7/Alt-Shift-7
°	Option-Shift-8/Alt+0176*

*Hold down Alt, press the numbers sequentially on the numeric keypad, then release Alt; the character will appear.

QuarkXPress 7 makes it easy to insert any special characters included in a font, such as an accented é, a cent symbol ¢, or a decorative "dingbat" character ■. **NEW**

To insert special characters via the Glyphs palette:

1. Choose the Content tool, then click in your text to create an insertion point.

2. Choose Window > Glyphs.

3. From the font menu at the top, choose a font **2**.

4. Scroll through the characters to locate the special character you want to use. If necessary, click the magnifying glass to enlarge the preview area.

5. When you locate the character you want to insert, double-click it **3**. If you use the character frequently, you can drag it to the Favorite Glyphs area.

TIP Characters from symbol fonts such as Zapf Dingbats are often used for bullets or for decoration. To insert dingbats repetitively, as in a bulleted list, use a character style sheet.

To insert special characters from the keyboard:

While you're typing, it's faster to enter frequently used special characters using keyboard shortcuts. Keyboard shortcuts for various special characters are listed at left and in Appendix A.

TIP You may often find yourself entering a single special character in Zapf Dingbats and Symbol font. Because of this, QuarkXPress provides a quick method for entering one character in those fonts. For a Zapf Dingbat character, press Cmd-Option-Z (Mac only). For a Symbol character, press Cmd-Option-Q/Ctrl-Alt-Q. *Note:* For this shortcut to work, in Preferences > Application > Undo, the Redo Key setting must be Cmd-Shift-Z/Ctrl-Shift-Z.

Special Characters

131

Hanging punctuation

If you're setting larger text that starts or ends with punctuation (a pull quote in an article, for example, or a quotation on a book jacket), the paragraph alignment will be more pleasing if the punctuation hangs outside the main body of the text. Unfortunately, achieving this is not a flip-of-the-switch operation. Here are a few methods:

- Create a **hanging indent** using either positive or negative indents (see page 108).

- Use the **Indent Here** character (Utilities > Insert Character > Special > Indent Here; Cmd-\(backslash)/Ctrl-\). **1**–**3**. **NEW**

- Type a space before the punctuation mark **4**, then apply **negative kerning 5**.

TIP You can also use either of the first two techniques to hang a large initial cap.

Copyfitting

If you need to squeeze text into a tight space or bring up a stubborn orphan word or hyphenated word (horrors!) from the end of a paragraph, use whichever of these techniques you think your readers are *least* likely to notice:

- Choose an H&J with Auto Hyphenation checked or insert discretionary hyphens (Utilities > Insert Character > Special > Discretionary Hyphen; Cmd-hyphen/Ctrl-hyphen). **NEW**

- Apply –0.5, –1, or –2 tracking, but not more!

- Rewrite the copy—delete, add, rearrange, or substitute words (only if you have permission to do so or it's your writing!).

- Widen the column a tiny bit.

- Apply 99% horizontal scaling.

- Apply slightly tighter word spacing by using an H&J.

- Switch to a condensed font.

"There is no such thing
as a non-working mother."

1 *Non-hanging punctuation*

"There is no such thing
 as a non-working mother."

2 **Hanging punctuation,** *created using a* **hanging indent:** *The left alignment of the paragraph is cleaner.*

"There is no such thing
 as a non-working mother."

3 *Even better: Here the second line is aligned with the stem of the "T."*

·⌐"There·is·no·such·thing·↵
 as·a·non-working·mother."

4 *To create hanging punctuation using kerning, insert a space to the left of the first character in the paragraph…*

"There is no such thing
 as a non-working mother."
 ∼ HESTER MUNDIS

5 *…and then apply* **negative kerning.** *It may look peculiar on screen but it will print just fine.*

special underline effects

With the Orthogonal Line tool, draw a line. Use Item > Step & Repeat (Cmd-Option-R/Ctrl-Alt-R) to make horizontal duplicates (0 Vertical Offset), and then lengthen or shorten the lines, as needed.

Early American Cookery

How to get attention

- Make the text you want to stand out **larger.**

- Use **boldface** or *italics* in the same font family as the body text.

- Choose a **contrasting** font or color.

Don't use the underline or ALL CAPS style to get attention. Those styles actually make type look more uniform, and thus harder to read.

A few embellishments

> **PUMPKIN PIE** Stew the pumpkin dry, and make it like squash pie, only season rather higher. In the country, where this *real yankee pie* is prepared in perfection, ginger is almost always used with other spices.

*To create **side-by-side paragraphs,** anchor a text box at left (Measurements palette > Classic tab > Align With Text Ascent), shift its baseline up if necessary, and create a hanging indent for the main paragraph (see page 132). You might also use a table.*

> **Pumpkin pie** Stew the pumpkin dry, and make it like squash pie, only season rather higher. In the country, where this *real yankee pie* is prepared in perfection, ginger is almost always used with other spices.

*Here, an anchored box with a 10% black background is used as a **drop cap.***

> Stew the pumpkin dry, and make it like squash pie, only season rather higher. In the country, where this *real yankee pie* is prepared in perfection, ginger is almost always used with other spices.
> ~ *Sara Josepha Hale*

*Ultra simple, but oh so elegant: We chose a different font for the first character (Bodoni Highlight), and enlarged it. This is called a **raised initial cap.***

Get your dashes straight

When to use a regular **hyphen**: To write a compound word, as in "three-year-old."

When to use an **en dash** (Option-hyphen/ Ctrl-Alt-Shift-hyphen): Between a range of numbers, as in "Figures 4–6"; a time frame, as in "4–6 weeks"; a distance, as in "4–6 miles"; or a negative number, as in –8.

When to use an **em dash** (Option-Shift-hyphen/Ctrl-Shift-=): To break up a sentence, as in "Bunny rabbit—excuse me—stay here." Don't add a whole space around an em or en dash — it will be too noticeable (as in this sentence). Instead, you can add a little bit of space by kerning—as in this sentence—or use a narrow flex space, which is a variation of a standard en space (Option-Shift-Spacebar/Ctrl-Shift-5 inserts a breaking flex space). Specify the Flex Space Width percentage in QuarkXPress (Edit, in Windows) > Preferences > Print Layout Character. Or use an em dash with built-in thin spaces around it from an expert font set.

To create a **nonbreaking standard hyphen** (*as in* "write-off"), press Cmd-=/Ctrl-=.

NEW While it is definitely worth memorizing the keyboard shortcuts for dashes and maybe even special kinds of spaces, QuarkXPress does let you cheat. With the text insertion bar in text, choose Utilities > Insert Character > Special or Special Nonbreaking. You'll see all the dashes you want plus "nonbreaking" varieties, which work like glue and won't break at the end of a line.

Dot, dot, dot

To produce an **ellipsis** character (…), press Option-;/Alt+0133. If those dots are too close together for your comfort, you can type periods instead and then track them out a little bit (. . .) . Or you can type a period (.), then a non-breaking flex space (Cmd-Option-Shift-Space bar/Ctrl-Alt-Shift-5), then a period, then a flex space, and so on (. . .).

Fractions

There are several ways to produce fractions in QuarkXPress:

- Use the Glyphs palette (Window > Glyphs) to ferret out the fractions included with a font. Most fonts include at least ¼, ½, and ¾ **1**.

- **NEW** Use an OpenType font that has the Fractions style available (not in brackets). For example, Zapfino Extra LTX Pro offers expert fraction formatting **2**. If you're buying an OpenType font for this purpose, make sure it has the Fractions option.

- Purchase a font family that includes a fraction variation (such as MrsEavesFractions **3**) or purchase a font that consists of only fractions or only numerators and denominators.

- Type the numerator, a slash, and the denominator, select all the characters, then choose Style > Type Style > Make Fraction. The fraction will look like this: ¾. You can kern between the characters in this type of fraction **4**.

- **TIP** You can specify Fraction/Price preferences in QuarkXPress (Edit, in Windows) > Preferences > Application > Fraction/Price (see page 370). Fraction/Price is part of the Type Tricks XTension that ships with QuarkXPress.

- If all else fails, you can build a fraction by hand **5**. First, type the numerator. Second, type the fraction slash (in Mac OS X, pressing Option-Shift-1; in Windows, type a slash, preferably from an expert font). Third, type the denominator. Apply Superior type style to the numerator, then apply both the Superior and Subscript type styles to the denominator. You can adjust the type style offset, scale, etc., in QuarkXPress (Edit, in Windows) > Preferences > Print Layout > Character.

1 *Most fonts, such as New Baskerville (used for body text in this book), offer fractions for ¼, ½, and ¾. Use the **Glyphs** palette to find them.*

2 *Choosing Fractions from the OpenType menu on the Character Attributes tab of the Measurements palette creates fractions for any numerals.*

3 *Some of the options in the MrsEavesFractions font*

$$\frac{1}{4} \quad \frac{1}{2} \quad \frac{3}{4}$$

4 *Results with Style > Type Style > Make Fraction in 24-point New Baskerville.*

$$\frac{1}{4} \quad \frac{1}{2} \quad \frac{3}{4}$$

5 *Fractions in the same font, but created manually with type styles and fraction slash characters.*

Keep 'em the same

No matter how you decide to make your fractions, try to use the same method throughout a publication. If you're publishing a cookbook or math textbook, use a font that contains all the required fractions instead.

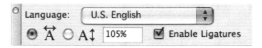

first first

1 *The most common ligatures are for the character pairs fi and fl. At left, with ligatures turned off, the dot on the "i" overlaps poorly with the "f." At right, ligatures are enabled and the transition is smooth.*

2 *The Enable Ligatures check box in the Character Attributes tab of the Measurements palette; the Character Attributes dialog box (Style > Character) provides this check box as well.*

Picture Effects
Project
  General
Print Layout
  General
  Measurements
  Paragraph
  Character
  Tools
  Trapping
  Color Manager
  Layers

Ligatures
  Break Above: 1   ☐ Not "ffi" or "ffl"
  ☑ Auto Kern Above: 6 pt   ☐ Standard Em Spa
  Flex Space Width: 50%

3 *The Break Above field in the Character pane of Print Layout Preferences controls how much tracking you can apply before ligatures "break" apart; the default setting is 1. If you don't want ligatures on fi and fl in words such as "office" or "waffle," check Not "ffi" or "ffl". This is unchecked by default.*

first first

4 *Zapfino Extra LTX Pro is already a beautiful script font as you can see at left. An OpenType font with many special style options available, look what happens when we choose Standard Ligatures (we get the more flowing "fi" ligature) and Discretionary Ligatures (we get the flamboyant "st").*

Ligatures

No, we're not talking about a medieval weapon here. A ligature is a pair (or more) of characters that are joined into one **1**. Like smart quotes and the proper use of dashes, this is just another typographic trick that makes things look nicer. In general, we use ligatures in body copy. We also use them on a case-by-case basis in display copy, such as headlines, depending on the font.

To apply ligatures to standard fonts:

1. Choose the Content tool and select the text you want to have ligatures.
2. Display the Character Attributes tab of the Measurements palette.
3. Check Enable Ligatures **2**.

TIP Sometimes, ligatures don't look right—particularly with loose tracking and some letter combinations—but you can use a preferences setting to control their application. In QuarkXPress (Edit, in Windows) > Preferences > Print Layout > Character, you can set a Break Above value that specifies, for example, that if you track out +2, you no longer want ligatures **3**. In addition, you can check Not "ffi" or "ffl" as ligatures can look funny for these letter combinations (can you tell, we turned them off in this sentence?).

TIP If you check Enable Ligatures and nothing happens, it may be because the font doesn't include ligatures.

To apply ligatures to OpenType fonts:

Some OpenType fonts provide ligatures beyond the standard "fi" and "fl" **4**. In the OpenType menu (Character Attributes tab of the Measurements palette), if Standard Ligatures or Discretionary Ligatures is available (without brackets around it), you can apply that style to selected text. The Glyphs palette (Window menu) shows which ligatures are available.

Ligatures

Setting type for print output

Our philosophy about choosing fonts for print output is similar to our philosophy about friendship:

- For body text: Pick a few sturdy, dependable serif font families that you really like, and get to know them well. Serif fonts are the least tiring to read. A few of our current favorites in this category include New Baskerville (which you're reading now), Sabon, and Caslon. Garamond and Goudy are other good classics.

- For emphasis: Use fonts from the same family—not from different families— using regular for the main text and bold or italics for emphasis.

- For subheads, headers, and the like: Pick a strong, contrasting sans serif face, such as Frutiger, Futura, Gill Sans, or Franklin Gothic.

Then, just as there are acquaintances you enjoy seeing once in a while but would tire of if you saw every day, there are special fonts you should choose only for special occasions. Fonts that fall into this category include script faces and other decorative faces, such as Caflisch Script Bold, which you see in the sidebar headers in this book. They're great for party invitations, drop caps, headlines, and the like but would be tiring to read in long passages. Just as it's good to stand by your old, reliable friends, it's also good to be open to meeting new "faces."

The best way to learn more about typography is to observe it in the world around you. Whether it's a poster, annual report, newspaper, brochure, book cover, cosmetics label, menu, shopping bag, or even the credits you see at the movie theater, wherever you see text (unless it's written by hand), it's typeset in a particular font.

Make your rags look pretty

When all the copy is in place and ready for imagesetting, stop for a moment to fine-tune the right edge of your left-aligned paragraphs. Try to make the second-to-last line longer than the third-to-the-last line:

Every child is an artist.
The problem is how to remain
an artist once he grows up.

PABLO PICASSO

Or make the last line longer than the second-to-last line:

Every child is an artist. The
problem is how to remain
an artist once he grows up.

But don't let the whole thing cave inward:

Every child is an artist. The problem
is how to remain an artist once
he grows up.

So many ways to do the same thing

QuarkXPress is designed to be flexible and easy to use—so almost every task can be accomplished using a menu command/dialog box, a palette, and a keyboard command. Rather than present all three options for everything you might conceivably do with type, we've made a judgment call about which method is easiest or best for the situation. In QuarkXPress 7, that tends to be the Measurements palette, which in its new, expanded form offers instant access to almost every command.

The beauty of working with a palette is you get instant feedback—with no dialog box blocking the screen. A beast is at work with palettes as well, however, in the form of mysterious icons, fields, and buttons that you need to be able to decipher. When in doubt, point at the controls to display the Tool Tips or just head to the menu and find the command you need.

Tables and Tabs 8

What's a table?

A **table,** according to *The Oxford Modern English Dictionary* (Oxford University Press), is "a set of facts or figures systematically displayed, esp. in columns." In QuarkXPress, a table can contain text and/or numerals, pictures, or a combination thereof.

Shade plants

Genus	Hardiness zone	Height	Bloom time
Astilbe	4–8	24–36"	June–July
Dicentra	3–8	10–15"	May–Oct
Hosta	3–8	6–48"	Jul–Sep
Lamium	3–8	12"	Jun–Jul

1 *A* **table** *containing* **text**

Each block in a table is called a **cell.**

Perennials

GENUS		HARDINESS ZONE	HEIGHT	BLOOM TIME
Dianthus		3–8	6"	June–Oct
Hemerocallis		3–8	18–48"	June–Oct
Monarda		4–8	36–48"	July–Aug
Rudbeckia		4–8	30–40"	July–Oct

2 *A* **table** *containing* **pictures** *and* **text**

Tables and tabs

Using the table features in QuarkXPress, not only can you stack columns of text and/or numerals **1**, you can also create a table of pictures or even combine text and picture cells in the same table **2**. Best of all, the features are simple to use.

You can create a table first using the Tables tool and then put text and pictures into it, or you can convert existing text to a table. In addition, you can create a table and link to data from Microsoft Excel. You can't convert existing pictures into a table, but you can cut and paste or import pictures into a table. All tables contain blocks, called cells, that you type or import text or pictures into. As you type into a text cell, the type wraps automatically.

Once a table is created, you can change the text or pictures that it contains; change the overall dimensions of the table itself; change the way the cells are configured by adding or removing rows or columns; and change the table's appearance by recoloring or restyling its outer frame and/or interior gridlines, or by changing the background color of any of its cells.

Note: If you need to line up numerals on the decimal point or align page numbers with a dot leader for a table of contents, you'll need to use tabs, which we start discussing on page 157. If you need to, you can insert tabs into text inside a table cell.

Tables

137

Creating tables

As we said on the previous page, you can create a table in one of three ways: Create the table and then enter type into it, convert existing text into a table, or link to data from Excel. First, we'll show you how to create an empty table.

To create an empty text table:

1. Choose the Tables tool. ▦

2. Drag a box on any page in a layout (Shift-drag to make a square). The Table Properties dialog box appears.

3. Enter the desired number of Rows and Columns **1**.

4. Click Cell Type: Text Cells. The cell size will be calculated to fit within the overall table automatically.

   Note: The overall table dimensions, as well as the individual row and column sizes, can be changed later.

5. *Optional:* To specify that row heights or cell widths grow to accommodate text additions, check Rows and/or Columns in the Auto Fit area. This area is unavailable if you check Link Cells, which allows text to flow to the next cell. **(NEW)**

6. *Optional:* To specify the order in which the text insertion point will jump from cell to cell (see the sidebar), choose from the Tab Order menu.

7. *Optional:* If you want the cells to be linked together so text can flow from box to box, click Link Cells (you can also link cells manually once the table is created). Then choose an option from the Link Order menu for the order in which cells will be linked.

8. Click OK.

   To enter text, choose the Content tool, click in a cell, and start typing **2**. You can also choose File > Import Text, in

Jumping around

Note: These commands work only for cells that aren't linked.

Jump one cell to the **right** or from the end of a **row** to the beginning of the next	Control-Tab/Ctrl-Tab
Jump back to **previous** cell	Control-Shift-Tab/ Ctrl-Shift-Tab
Jump one **character** at a time within a cell or from the end of one cell to the beginning of the next cell	Right arrow

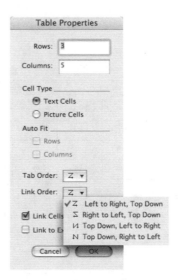

Table Properties

Rows: 3

Columns: 5

Cell Type
- ● Text Cells
- ○ Picture Cells

Auto Fit
- ☐ Rows
- ☐ Columns

Tab Order: Z ▼

Link Order: Z ▼

✓ Z Left to Right, Top Down
Ƨ Right to Left, Top Down
И Top Down, Left to Right
И Top Down, Right to Left

☑ Link Cells
☐ Link to E

Cancel   OK

1 *Choose table parameters in the* **Table Properties** *dialog box.*

Start typing into linked	text cells			

2 *Enter text in the* **new table.**

Table defaults

To change the default settings for the Tables tool, double-click its icon on the Tools palette, then click Modify. If you do this when no projects are open, the settings you choose will be the defaults for future projects. For more details, see page 153.

WHEN I HEARD THE LEARN'D ASTRONOMER¶ WHEN I heard the learn'd astronomer;¶ When the proofs, the figures, were ranged in columns before me;¶ ⊠	

1 *None of the cells are linked in the original table.*

WHEN I HEARD THE LEARN'D ASTRONOMER¶ WHEN I heard the learn'd astronomer;¶ When the proofs, the figures, were ranged in columns before me;¶	applause in the lecture-room,¶ How soon, unaccountable,↵ I became tired and sick;¶ Till rising and gliding out,↵ I wander'd off by↵ myself,¶
When I was shown the charts and the diagrams, to add, divide, and measure them;¶ When I, sitting, heard the↵ astronomer, where he↵ lectured with much↵	In the mystical moist night-air, and from time to time,¶ Look'd up in perfect silence at the stars.¶ *Walt Whitman*

2 *After choosing the **Link Text Cells** command, all of the cells are linked.*

---

which case the text will flow into that cell and any cells it's linked to.

You can apply all the standard style and paragraph formatting attributes to table text, either manually or via paragraph and character style sheets.

TIP To reconfigure a table (e.g., add or delete rows or columns), see page 148.

TIP The table's overall size determines the maximum number of rows and columns it can contain.

If you want all the text cells to be linked together, then you'll be satisfied with the Link Text Cells option, described below. But what if you just want to link a few cells, and not all the cells in a table? You can do it manually with the Linking tool, just as you would non-table text (see page 89).

You can even link a text cell to a text box outside the table. Just remember the standard rule for all linking: You can't link to a box that already contains text, even if all that's left is a nonprinting character, such as a paragraph return. Also, you can't link a text cell to form controls in a Web layout.

To link all the text cells in a table:

1. To begin with, the table must be empty. It can contain picture cells; the links will just bypass those cells.

2. Choose the Item tool, then click the table.

3. Choose Table > Link Text Cells **1**.
or
Ctrl-click/Right-click the table and choose Table > Link Text Cells from the context menu.

The cells will be linked **2** in the Link Order currently chosen in the Table pane in Tables tool preferences (see the sidebar on this page).

The link order is the order in which text cells are linked together, either when you created the table initially or via the Link Text Cells command. Use the Table pane of the Item > Modify dialog box to change the link order of a table.

Note: If your table contains text cells that were linked manually, or if it contains text, you can't change the link order using the method below—you have to unlink all the linked cells and empty the table out first. If you don't want to empty out the table, you can manually relink cells in any order with the Linking tool.

The tab order is the order in which the text insertion point jumps between unlinked cells by using the shortcuts listed in the sidebar on page 138. The tab order has no effect on linked cells.

To change the link or tab order in a table:

1. Choose the Item or Content tool, then click a table that doesn't contain any text.

2. Choose Item > Modify, then click the Table tab **1**.

3. Choose an option from the Link Order menu **2**–**3**.
and/or
Choose an option from the Tab Order menu.

The link order can be different from the tab order.

TIP To unlink cells, use the Unlinking tool.

TIP To choose the default link or tab order for future tables, see the sidebar on the previous page.

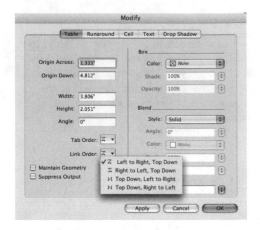

1 *The **Link Order** menu in the Table pane of the Modify dialog box*

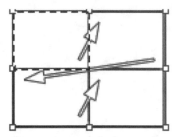

2 *This is the table's original link order. (In order to make the links appear, for illustration purposes, we selected the table and chose the Linking tool.)*

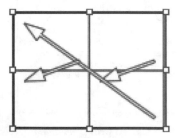

3 *After choosing a new option from the Link Order menu, the table links look like this.*

Dianthus	3–8	6"	June–October
Hemerocallis	3–8	18–48"	June–October
Monarda	4–8	36–48"	July–August
Rudbeckia	4–8	30–40"	July–October

1 *Select the text you want to appear in the table. Note that there are **no spaces** surrounding the tabs.*

Convert Text to Table

Separate Rows With: Paragraphs
Separate Columns With: Tabs
Rows: 4
Columns: 4
Cell Fill Order: Z
Auto Fit: ☐ Rows ☑ Columns
Cancel OK

2 *The **Convert Text to Table** dialog box controls how text gets distributed into cells.*

Dianthus	3–8	6"	June–October
Hemerocallis	3–8	18–48"	June–October
Monarda	4–8	36–48"	July–August
Rudbeckia	4–8	30–40"	July–October

3 *With **Auto Fit: Columns** checked, the text automatically fits within the columns when the text is converted to a table.*

To create a table from existing text:

1. Choose View > Invisibles, if necessary, to see how the information is separated.

2. Note which characters in the original text (returns, tabs, spaces, or commas) determine how the text will be distributed into table cells, and add or delete those characters if necessary.

3. Choose the Content tool, then select the text that you want copied into the table cells **1**.

4. Choose Table > Convert Text to Table.
   or
   Ctrl-click/Right-click the table and choose > Table > Convert Text to Table from the context menu.

5. From the Separate Rows With menu, choose which character in the selected text will be used to designate the start of each new row of cells **2**. If you choose Paragraphs, for example, every paragraph return ¶ will start a new row.

6. Columns in the table will be set up according to the characters currently in the selected text, as reflected on the Separate Columns With menu. If you choose Tabs, for example, every tab will start a new column.

7. Change the Rows and Columns values if you want to add blank rows or columns.

8. From the Cell Fill Order menu, choose the direction in which you want the existing text to flow into the new table.

9. To ensure that the rows are wide enough for the text, check Auto Fit: Rows. If you want the columns to adjust as well if necessary, check Auto Fit: Columns. (Width is adjusted first.) **NEW**

10. Click OK **3**.

TIP After converting the text to a table, you can delete the original text and/or its text box if you don't need it.

NEW ## To create a table with data from Excel:

1. Make sure the Table Import XTension is running (Utilities > XTensions Manager).

2. Choose the Tables tool. ⊞

3. Drag a box on any page in a layout (Shift-drag to make a square). The Table Properties dialog box appears.

4. *Optional:* To specify that row heights or cell widths grow to accommodate text additions, check Rows and/or Columns in the Auto Fit area.

5. Check Link to External Data. All the other commands in the dialog box become unavailable.

6. Click OK; the Table Link dialog box appears **1**.

7. Click Browse to locate and select an Excel file. The selected file is listed in the Name field.

8. If you want to import a portion of the file, use the Table area to select a Sheet and enter a Range of records.

9. In the Options area, check the things you want to import with the file.

10. Click OK. The Excel file will import into a new table **2**.

TIP If the Excel file changes, you can update the data in the table through Utilities > Usage > Tables pane. Quark-XPress maintains as much of the new formatting you've applied as possible.

To create a picture table:

1. Choose the Tables tool. ⊞

2. Draw a rectangle in a layout. The box shape and size can be changed later.

3. Enter the desired number of Rows and Columns.

4. Click Picture Cells **3**.

5. Click OK. Use File > Import Picture to add pictures to cells.

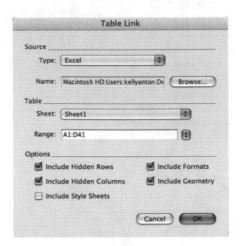

1 *The **Table Link** dialog box lets you import an Excel file into a QuarkXPress table.*

Thanksgiving 2004			
Guest List			
Count	Name	Bringing	Child
1	John	2 Turkeys	
2	Kelly	2 Pumpkin Pies, Coffee, Lemonade	
3	Robert	Broccoli Casserole	1
4	Michael	Wine, Butter, Jelly, Cranberry Sauce	1
5	Don	1 Pecan Pie, 1 Pumpkin Pie	
6	Karen	Chile Casserole	
7	Nancy		

2 *The **Convert Text to Table** dialog box controls how text gets distributed into cells.*

Working with picture cells

- You can resize or move pictures inside table cells as you would in a standard picture box. If you don't know how to work with pictures in QuarkXPress, see Chapter 9!

- You can copy and paste a picture from a standard picture box into a picture cell in a table.

- The Picture Cells option in the Table Properties dialog box creates a table consisting of all picture cells.

- You can convert any individual text cell to a picture cell by choosing Item > Content > Picture (or for that matter, convert any picture cell to a text cell by choosing Item > Content > Text).

Selecting table cells and their contents

Choose the **Content** tool, click the table, then:

Select the text in one **cell** or a story in **linked cells**	Cmd-A/Ctrl-A
Select all the cells in a **row**	Click just outside the left or right edge of the table (➡ pointer)
Select all the cells in a **column**	Click just outside the top or bottom edge of the table (⬇ pointer)
Select all the cells in a **series** of **rows/columns**	Drag along, and just outside of, any edge of the table
Select **adjacent** or **nonadjacent** cells	Shift-click cells

You can also use the Table > Select submenu to select odd or even rows or columns (to format every other row, for example), or to select cells, grids, or borders.

Hemerocallis		3–8
Monarda		4–8
Rudbeckia		4–8

1 *Click at the **top** or **bottom** of a **column** to select it.*

Hemerocallis		3–8
Monarda		4–8
Rudbeckia		4–8

2 *Click at the **beginning** or **end** of a **row** to select it.*

Hemerocallis		3–8
Monarda		4–8
Rudbeckia		4–8

3 *Shift-click to select individual cells.*

To edit the contents of a table cell:

1. Choose the Content tool.
2. Click the cell whose attributes you want to change.
   or
   Select multiple cells by using one of the selection methods listed in the sidebar at left **1**–**3**.
3. Do any of the following:

■ To edit the attributes of text in a table cell (which are similar to text boxes), use any of the standard methods, **NEW** namely, the Style menu, the tabbed Measurements palette, and paragraph and/or character style sheets.

■ To move text or pictures from one cell to another, select it, then use the Cut (Cmd-X/Ctrl-X) and Paste commands (Cmd-V/Ctrl-V).

■ To modify the attributes of a text cell, such as its width, background color, background shade, or Text Inset, use the Item > Modify > Cell and Text panes (Cmd-M/Ctrl-M). You can even rotate or skew text within its cell. The Cols and Gutter options aren't available for table cells.

■ To modify picture cells, use the Picture, Runaround, or Cell pane in Item > Modify.

■ To color the table border segments or gridlines, see pages 151–152.

■ To color the overall table box or the table box frame, see page 269.

■ To convert text cells to picture cells, or vice versa, see the sidebar on the facing page.

Select Cells; Change Cell Attributes

Reconfiguring tables

To resize a column or row by dragging:

1. Choose the Content tool, then click the table.

2. *Optional:* If you want the overall size of the table to remain fixed as you resize columns or rows, choose Table > Maintain Geometry. The columns and rows will resize automatically to compensate for the resized table. Uncheck Maintain Geometry if you want to resize only one column or row at a time. The table will become larger or smaller to accommodate the new column or row size.

   or

   Ctrl-click/Right-click the table and choose > Table > Maintain Geometry from the context menu.

3. Drag the vertical or horizontal gridline that separates any two columns or rows (the pointer will become a double-headed arrow **↔**) **1**–**3**.

   If the column or row contains text, the text may rewrap inside each cell. If the row or column contains a picture or pictures, more of the pictures will become exposed or hidden as a result.

   If View > Snap to Guides is checked, then a gridline will snap to the nearest guide if it's moved within the Snap Distance specified in QuarkXPress (Edit, in Windows) > Print Layout > General.

   TIP To resize the overall table, see page 147.

   TIP You can also change the Maintain Geometry setting in the Table pane of the Modify dialog box (Item menu).

1 *Move a gridline to **resize** a **column** or row.*

2 *The column is **enlarged** with **Maintain Geometry checked,** so the overall table size remains the same.*

3 *The column is **enlarged** with **Maintain Geometry unchecked,** so the overall table enlarges to accommodate the larger column.*

Modify

| Table | Runaround | Cells | Text | Drop Shadow |

Column Width: 0.833"

☑ Auto Fit

Maximum: 2.5"

(Distribute Evenly)

Row Height: [   ]

Cell

Color: ☒ *None*

Shade: 100%

Opacity: 100%

Blend

1 *In Item > Modify > Cells, enter new* **Width** *and/or* **Height** *values for selected* **rows** *and/or* **columns.**

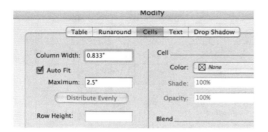

2 *Five columns of uneven* **width** *are selected.*

Modify

| Table | Runaround | Cells | Text | Drop Shadow |

Column Width: [   ]

☐ Auto Fit

Maximum: 1.562"

(Distribute Evenly)

Cell

Color: ☐ White

Shade: 100%

Opacity: 100%

3 *Click* **Distribute Evenly** *in Item > Modify > Cells.*

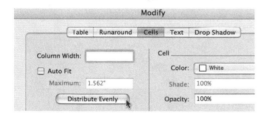

4 *After clicking* **Width: Distribute Evenly,** *all the columns are now the* **same** *width. The text rewrapped in the first column.*

To resize a column or row by entering values:

1. Choose the Content tool.

2. Select the column(s) or row(s) you want to reshape or resize (see the sidebar on page 143).

3. Choose Item > Modify (Cmd-M/Ctrl-M).

4. In the Table pane, check Maintain Geometry to have the overall table size remain fixed as you resize columns or rows; unselected columns and rows will resize automatically. With this option checked, you can't resize the rightmost column or bottommost row.
   or
   Uncheck Maintain Geometry to have the table enlarge or shrink to accommodate the new column or row size. Unselected columns or rows will stay the same size.

5. Click the Cells tab, then enter the desired Column Width or Row Height **1**. With Maintain Geometry on, one of these two fields won't be available. If the selected cells aren't uniform in size, a field will be blank, but a value can be entered.

6. Click Apply (Cmd-A/Alt-A), make any adjustments, then click OK.

To make columns and/or rows uniform in size:

1. Choose the Content tool.

2. Select the rows or columns you want to make uniform in size **2**.

3. Choose Item > Modify, then click the Cells tab.

4. Click Distribute Evenly under Width and/or Height **3**–**4**. A value will be entered automatically.

   Note: This option won't be available if the selected columns or rows are already uniform in size.

5. Click Apply to preview the results, if desired, then click OK.

If a table becomes too wide or too long to fit on a page or within a specific area, you can split it into multiple subtables. Any changes to the table's structure or content reflow through the other subtables.

To split a table: NEW

1. Choose the Item tool or Content tool.

   Note: A table can not be split if Maintain Geometry is enabled (see page 145).

2. Click a table you want to split **1**.

3. Choose Table > Table Break.

4. Check Width if you want the table to split when it gets too wide. Check Height if you want it to split when it gets too long **2**. (You can check both, but that really doesn't make sense.)

5. Specify the maximum Width or Height of the table before it splits.

6. Click OK. (If nothing happens, it's because the table is not yet too big. Add rows or columns or resize the table.)

TIP To create completely separate tables, select any instance of the split table and choose Table > Make Separate Tables.

Once you split a table, you may want any header or footer rows to be repeated on continued instances of the table.

To create header and footer rows: NEW

1. Choose the Content tool.

2. Select the row(s) you want to repeat as headers or footers. You can select any continuous rows at the top for headers and any continuous rows at the bottom for footers.

3. Choose Table > Repeat as Header or Table > Repeat as Footer. The header or footer rows are repeated on continued instances of the table **3**.

TIP The text in header and footer rows is synchronized, so if you change it anywhere it changes everywhere. This means you can't put text such as "continued" in a header row.

Plant	Hardiness Zone	Height	Bloom Time
Dianthus	3–8	6"	June–October
Hemerocallis	3–8	18–48"	June–October
Monarda	4–8	36–48"	July–August
Rudbeckia	4–8	30–40"	July–October

1 *The top row of this table contains column headings.*

Set Table Break	
☐ Width:	3.792"
☑ Height:	2
Cancel	OK

2 *The **Set Table Break** dialog box controls how wide or tall a table can get before it splits into separate tables. You can move the continuation of a table to any other location in a layout.*

Plant	Hardiness Zone	Height	Bloom Time
Dianthus	3–8	6"	June–October
Hemerocallis	3–8	18–48"	June–October
Monarda	4–8	36–48"	July–August

Plant	Hardiness Zone	Height	Bloom Time
Rudbeckia	4–8	30–40"	July–October

3 *The table is split in two, with the same header row used in both subtables.*

Modifier keys for resizing a table

Drag a **handle** of the table with the following keys held down:

Resize table, rows, and columns (not content) nonproportionally	No modifier keys
Resize table, rows, and columns (not content) proportionally	Option-Shift/ Alt-Shift
Resize table (not content) to a square	Shift/Shift
Resize table, rows, columns, and content nonproportionally	Cmd/Ctrl
Resize table, rows, columns, and content proportionally	Cmd-Option-Shift/ Ctrl-Alt-Shift

Dianthus			6"	June–Oct
Hemerocallis			18–48"	June–Oct
Monarda			36–48"	July–Aug
Rudbeckia			30–40"	July–Oct

1 *A corner handle is dragged with **Option-Shift/ Alt-Shift** held down.*

Dianthus			6"	June–Oct
Hemerocallis			18–48"	June–Oct
Monarda			36–48"	July–Aug
Rudbeckia			30–40"	July–Oct

2 *The table's dimensions—but not its content—are enlarged **proportionally.***

To resize a whole table:

1. Choose the Item tool, then click the table.

2. Using one of the shortcuts listed in the sidebar, drag any of the table's eight handles **1**–**2**. The cells will reshape to fit the new table dimensions.
   or
   Change the W (width) or H (height) value on the Classic tab of the Measurements palette.
   or
   Control-click/Right-click the table and choose Modify, click the Table tab, enter new Width and/or Height values, click Apply if desired, then click OK.

TIP To move a selected table to a precise location on your page, change the Origin Across and Origin Down values in Item > Modify > Table or change the X and Y values on the Classic tab of the Measurements palette.

TIP The Live Refresh feature (which lets you see the contents of an item as you scale it) does not work for tables.

Before you add or delete columns or rows, you need to decide whether to permit the overall width and height of the table to change as a result. With Maintain Geometry checked in the Table menu, the overall dimensions of the table will be preserved as columns or rows are added, but existing cells will become smaller in order to accommodate the new ones. With Maintain Geometry unchecked, the cell sizes won't change, but the overall table dimensions will increase.

To add columns or rows to a table:

1. Choose the Content tool.

2. Click OK, then click a cell or select the row or column that you want the new row or column to appear next to **1**.

3. Choose Table > Insert > Row or Table > Insert > Column.
   or
   Control-click/Right-click the selection and choose Table > Insert > Row or Table > Insert > Column from the context menu.

4. Enter the desired Number of Rows or Number of Columns **2**–**3**, and click where you want the new rows or columns to be inserted (such as Insert Left of Selection for columns).

5. *Optional:* Check Keep Attributes to have inserted cells and gridlines acquire the attributes of the selected row or column.

   Attributes that are duplicated include typographic specifications, style sheets, and settings in the Cell, Text, and Picture panes of Item > Modify.

6. Click OK **4**.

Perennials				
GENUS		HARDINESS ZONE	HEIGHT	BLOOM TIME
Dianthus		3–8	6"	June–Oct
Hemerocallis		3–8	18–48"	June–Oct
Monarda		4–8	36–48"	July–Aug
Rudbeckia		4–8	30–40"	July–Oct

1 *The original table, with the insertion point in the bottom row.*

2 *In the **Insert Table Rows** dialog box, enter the number of **rows** you want to add, and click a position where they will be inserted.*

3 *In the **Insert Table Columns** dialog box, enter the number of **columns** you want to add, and click a position where they will be inserted.*

Perennials				
GENUS		HARDINESS ZONE	HEIGHT	BLOOM TIME
Dianthus		3–8	6"	June–Oct
Hemerocallis		3–8	18–48"	June–Oct
Monarda		4–8	36–48"	July–Aug
Rudbeckia		4–8	30–40"	July–Oct

4 *In this case, we added two new **rows** to the **bottom** of the table.*

GENUS		HARDINESS ZONE	HEIGHT
Dianthus		3–8	6"
Hemerocallis		3–8	18–48"
Monarda		4–8	36–48"
Rudbeckia		4–8	30–40"

1 *A row is selected.*

GENUS		HARDINESS ZONE	HEIGHT
Dianthus		3–8	6"
Monarda		4–8	36–48
Rudbeckia		4–8	30–40

2 *The Table > Delete > **Row** command deleted the selected row.*

To delete a row or column from a table:

1. Choose the Content tool.

2. Select one or more rows or columns to delete (see the list of selection methods in the sidebar on page 143) **1**.

3. Control-click/Right-click any selected cell and choose Table > Delete > Row or Table > Delete > Column.
   or
   Choose Table > Delete > Row or Table > Delete > Column **2**. You can undo this.

To change the content of a cell (picture, text, or none):

1. Choose the Content tool.

2. Select the cell or cells you want to convert (use one of the selection methods listed in the sidebar on page 143 if you want to select multiple cells).

3. Choose Item > Content > Picture, Text, or None. If you choose None, you'll be able to recolor the background of the cell or apply a blend to it but not put text or a picture inside it.

4. If an alert dialog box warns you that text or a picture will be deleted, click OK. (If that is *not* okay, copy the content into an empty box first.)

Delete Row or Column; Change Cell Content

There are a number of reasons for combing cells. Maybe you want a header to span across the whole top of your table. Or perhaps you'd like to display a picture more prominently in a larger portion of the table.

Beware! The text or picture in the topmost left selected cell will be preserved when you combine other cells with it, but any text or pictures in other selected cells will be **discarded** (you'll get a warning).

To combine cells:

1. To preserve text or a picture for later use, take a moment now to copy and paste it either into a separate box outside the table or into a cell that you're not combining.

2. Choose the Content tool.

3. Select the cells you want to combine **1**.

4. Choose Table > Combine Cells. If the cells currently contain text and/or pictures, an alert will appear **2**. If you want to live dangerously, click "Do not show this warning again," then click OK **3**.

The selected cells will be combined into one. If the topmost left selected cell contained text, that text will now spread across or downward to fill the now larger cell size. If it was linked to another box, that link will be broken. If that cell contained a picture, the picture either will now fill, or can be scaled to fill, the whole combined cell.

To uncombine cells:

1. Choose the Content tool.

2. Click the cell you want to split up.

3. Choose Table > Split Cell. The content of the cell will be placed inside the first of the newly divided cells.

Watch your links!

If you combine text cells that are linked, the combined cell will no longer be linked, but any other previously linked cells will remain linked. And if you split a combined text cell, the prior linkages won't be restored. You can restore them using the Linking tool.

Perennials for fall planting ⊠	Genus		
Dianthus		3–8	6"
Hemerocallis		3–8	18–48"
Monarda		4–8	36–48"
Rudbeckia		4–8	30–40"

1 *Three cells* in the top row are **selected**.

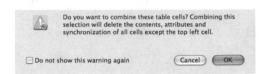

2 *This alert dialog box will appear if the cells you're combining **contain** text or pictures.*

Perennials for fall planting		
Dianthus	3–8	6"
Hemerocallis	3–8	18–48"
Monarda	4–8	36–48"
Rudbeckia	4–8	30–40"

Perennials for fall planting			
Dianthus		3–8	6"
Hemerocallis		3–8	18–48"
Monarda		4–8	36–48"
Rudbeckia		4–8	30–40"

1 *The original table*

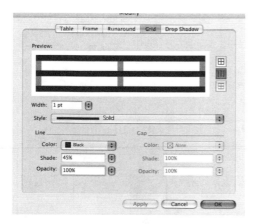

2 *Choose **Width**, **Style**, **Color**, and **Shade** options for gridlines in Item > Modify > **Grid**.*

Perennials for fall planting			
Dianthus		3–8	6"
Hemerocallis		3–8	18–48"
Monarda		4–8	36–48"
Rudbeckia		4–8	30–40"

3 *First we checked Maintain Geometry in the Table menu. Then in the **Grid** pane, we clicked the **Select Vertical** button, increased the Width, and changed the Shade to 45%.*

Restyling tables

You can dramatically change the appearance of a table by changing the line style, width, color, or shade of its gridlines and/or border, and this can be done using a dialog box (instructions on this page) or using submenus (see the next page). The default border and gridlines are black and 1 pt. in width.

To restyle the border or gridlines using a dialog box:

1. Choose the Item tool, then double-click the table **1**.

2. If you're going to change the width of the border/gridlines, you need to decide whether or not to permit the overall width and height of the table to change as a result. Click the Table tab. If you check Maintain Geometry, the overall dimensions of the table will be preserved, but existing cells will resize automatically in order to fill the gap. If you uncheck Maintain Geometry, the cell sizes won't change, but the overall table dimensions will.

3. Click the Grid tab.

4. On the right side of the dialog box, click one of the three buttons for the grid-lines and borders you want to restyle: Horizontal and Vertical ⊞, Horizontal only ☰, or Vertical only ⊪ **2**.

5. Choose a gridline Width, Style, Line: Color, Shade, and Opacity; also choose a Gap: Color, Shade, and Opacity if the line style contains gaps. The horizontal gridlines will print on top of the vertical gridlines. To make the gridlines disappear, choose the Style: Solid, and choose a Width of 0 and/or a Color of None.

6. Click Apply. At this point you can click another icon and apply different settings, if you like. Adjust any of the settings, then click OK **3**.

You can single out a handful of gridlines and/or border segments for restyling, or you can restyle all of them at once.

To restyle multiple border segments or gridlines via submenus:

1. Choose the Content tool.

2. Shift-click a gridline or border segment, then Shift-click additional horizontal or vertical gridlines or border (outer) segments. Gridlines and border segments can be selected at the same time. If a gridline is narrow, it may be hard to tell if it's selected.
or
Choose Table > Select > Horizontal Grids, Vertical Grids, Border, or All Grids **1**.

3. Choose attributes from the submenus on the Style menu **2**–**3**.
or
Control-click/Right-click one of the selected gridlines or border segments and make choices from the Line Style, Color, Width, etc., submenus on the context menu.
or
Display the Table Grid tab on the Measurements palette and use it to make any changes **4**. **NEW**

TIP You can also change the gridline color, shade, and opacity (but not the gap color) via the Colors palette (Window menu).

Here's a zippity-quick way to restyle a single gridline or segment.

To restyle one border segment or gridline via the context menu:

1. Choose the Content tool.

2. Control-click/Right-click a gridline or border segment and make choices from the Line Style, Width, Color, Shade, and Opacity submenus.

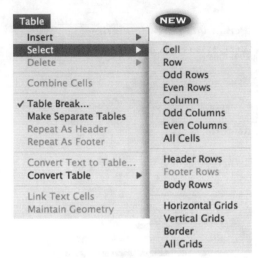

1 You can use the *Select* submenu to select multiple rows, columns, cells, gridlines, and borders.

Perennials for fall planting			
Dianthus		3–8	6"
Hemerocallis		3–8	18–48"
Monarda		4–8	36–48"
Rudbeckia		4–8	30–40"

2 The original table

Perennials for fall planting			
Dianthus		3–8	6"
Hemerocallis		3–8	18–48"
Monarda		4–8	36–48"
Rudbeckia		4–8	30–40"

3 The formatted table

4 The **Table Grid** tab of the Measurements palette lets you format selected gridlines.

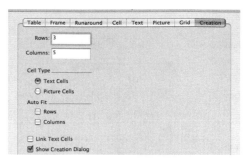

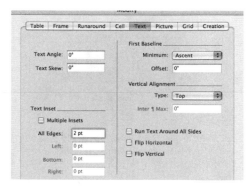

1 *Choose preference settings for future tables in the* **Creation** *pane of the* **Modify** *dialog box.*

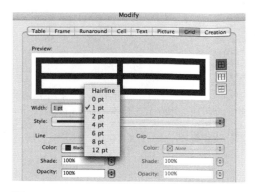

2 *Choose text preferences for future tables in the* **Text** *pane.*

3 *Choose Width, Style, Color, Shade, and Opacity preferences for gridlines in future tables in the* **Grid** *pane.*

Choosing Tables tool preferences

If you create tables frequently and you tend to choose the same parameters over and over for them, it's worth your while to take a moment to set a few preferences. These Creation preferences affect future tables that you create using the Tables tool but not tables created using the Convert Text to Table command.

To choose Tables tool preferences:

1. Double-click the Tables tool. ⊞
   or
   Choose QuarkXPress (Edit, in Windows) > Preferences > Print Layout > Tools, then click the Tables tool icon.

2. Click Modify, then click the Creation tab.

3. Choose whether you want future tables to contain text or picture cells, and make default Rows and Columns choices **1**.

4. To have text cells in future tables be linked automatically, click Link Text Cells.

5. *Optional:* To prevent the Table Properties dialog box from opening each time you use the Tables tool, uncheck Show Creation Dialog. If Link Text Cells is also checked, cells will be linked in the default order, which is Z. With Show Creation Dialog checked, the Table Properties dialog box will open each time you use the Tables tool, displaying your preferences.

6. Click the Table, Frame, Runaround, Cell, Text **2**, Picture, or Grid **3** tab, and change any of the available options in those panes, if desired.

7. Click OK twice.

Tables Tool Preferences

Converting tables

When the Convert Table to Text command is applied to a table, a new text box is created, and it's filled with a copy of the text from the table. You can choose the order in which the text blocks from the table cells will flow into the new box, and whether they'll be separated by Returns, tabs, commas, or spaces. You can also choose whether you want the original table to be preserved (the default setting) or deleted.

Note: If the table contains pictures, those pictures will be inserted into anchored picture boxes within the new text box.

To convert a table to text:

1. Choose the Item or Content tool.

2. Click the table you want to convert **1**.

3. Control-click/Right-click the table and choose Table > Convert Table > To Text from the context menu.
   or
   Choose Table > Convert Table > To Text.

4. From the Separate Rows With menu **2**, choose which character you want to have inserted at the end of each row.

5. From the Separate Columns With menu, choose which character you want to have inserted between each column.

6. Choose an option from the Text Extraction Order menu for the order in which text is to be extracted from the table.

7. Check Delete Table if you want the table to be deleted. Whether this box is checked or not, the converted text will appear in a new, separate box after you click OK. This control is not available for tables that are split.

8. Click OK **3**.

TIP If the table contains linked text and all you want to do is extract the text, just copy and paste it into a conventional text box instead of converting the table.

Dianthus	3–8	6"	June–Oct
Hemerocallis	3–8	18–48"	June–Oct
Iris	3–9	24–50"	June
Malva	4–7	36–48"	July–Oct
Monarda	4–8	36–48"	July–Aug
Rudbeckia	4–8	30–40"	July–Oct

1 *The original table*

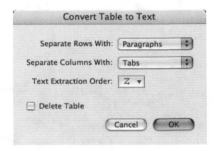

2 *Settings for the extracted text are chosen in the **Convert Table to Text** dialog box.*

Dianthus	3–8	6"
June-Oct		
Hemerocallis	3–8	18–48"
June–Oct		
Iris	3–9	24–50"
June		
Malva	4–7	36–48"
July–Oct		
Monarda	4–8	36–48"
July-Aug		
Rudbeckia	4–8	30–40"
July–Oct		

3 *After choosing **Table > Convert Table > To Text**, in this case, the columns are separated by tabs and the rows are separated by paragraph returns.*

1 *Click a table.*

2 *After choosing **Item > Convert Table > To Group** command*

3 *After choosing the **Ungroup** command and then moving a few boxes*

Follow these steps if you'd like to convert your completed table into separate but grouped conventional text boxes and/or picture boxes. Unlike the Convert Table to Text command, discussed on the previous page, this command doesn't copy the table—it converts it without copying.

To convert a table to a group:

1. Choose the Item tool.

2. Click the table you want to convert **1**.

3. Control-click/Right-click the table and choose Table > Convert Table > To Group from the context menu.
   or
   Choose Table > Convert Table > To Group.

   Leave the boxes grouped together **2**, or choose Item > Ungroup at any time **3**. Text from a series of linked cells will be preserved as a story.

TIP If you want to continue a table on another page, don't convert it to a group. Instead, use the Table Break command (Table menu) which is discussed on page 146.

NEW Table editing and formatting recap

QuarkXPress 7 changes the way you work with tables with the addition of the Table menu and the Table Grid tab of the Measurements palette. The old workhorse, the Item > Modify dialog box, is still around, and has controls for a few parameters that aren't available elsewhere, like the settings for tab order and link order.

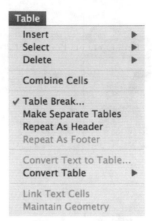

*The **Table** menu consolidates all the controls for modifying tables—except for formatting cells and cell contents.*

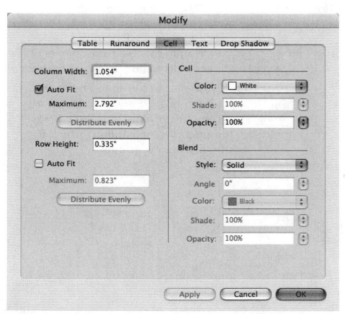

*The **Modify** dialog box provides panes for modifying the selected parts of a table. For example, when cells are selected, the Cell pane is available; when gridlines are selected, the Grid pane is available.*

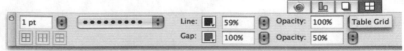

*When gridlines are selected, the **Table Grid** tab on the Measurements palette lets you quickly format the gridlines. You can also use the Text tab to modify the text inset for cells and the Paragraph Attributes and Character Attributes tabs for formatting text.*

On the right

Press **Option-Tab/Alt-Tab** to set a **right indent tab** that hugs the current right indent of the box, even if you resize the text box or table by dragging its right handle. These are useful for "end of story" characters. You won't see a marker on the Tabs ruler for this kind of tab.

1 *A **decimal-aligned** tab with a dot leader*

*A **left-aligned** tab*   *An **outrageous** tab— or price!*

Setting tabs

Tabs are invisible commands that tell blocks of text where to line up **1**–**2**. If no custom tabs are set and you press Tab, text to the right of the Tab character will jump to the nearest default tab stop (they're 0.5-inch apart). Before you can set custom tab stops (next two pages), you must insert invisible tab characters → into text. *Note:* Don't use spaces to create columns; it will look uneven due to variable character widths.

You can set up columns of text and/or numerals without tabs, by using the tables feature, but tabs are handy for inserting dot leaders or aligning numbers on the decimal. Tabs can also be added to text in a table.

To insert tabs into text:

1. Choose the Content tool, then click in a text box.

2. Press Tab as you input copy before typing each new column. The cursor will jump to the next default tab stop. *or* To add tabs to existing text, click to the left of the text that is to start each new column and press Tab.

TIP Don't press Tab more than once to move type further along. If you're not happy with the location of the default stops, set custom stops (see next page).

Insert Tabs into Text

Endangered vs. Non-Endangered Bears			
	1930	*1992*	*2000* (Projected)
Pandas	1 million	4 thousand	0
Koalas	6 million	3 thousand	7
Poohs	1 million	2 billion	3 billion

2 *Use **tabs** to align columns of text.*

Endangered·vs.·Non-Endangered·Bears¶			
→	*1930* →	*1992* →	*2000*·(Projected)

*Choose **View** > **Invisibles** to reveal tab symbols and other non-printing characters.*

You can set a virtually unlimited number of custom tab stops per paragraph.

To set custom tab stops:

1. Choose the Content tool.

2. Zoom in on your layout to make it easier to see the tab ruler increments, but make sure you can still see the full width of the text column.

3. Select *all* the paragraphs for which the tab stops are to be set.

4. Display the Tabs tab of the Measurements palette (**1**, next page). The tab ruler displays above the text box. **NEW**

5. Drag one of the tab icons (Left, Center, Right, Decimal, or Comma, or Align On) from the palette to the tab ruler, using the guide to judge the placement (**2**, next page). If you chose Align On, you can click the tab icon and enter a character in the field.
or
Click a tab button, enter a value in the Position field, then click Set.

6. *Optional:* To create a leader, type one or two characters in the Fill Characters field (**1**–**4**, this page). For a dot leader, type a period.

TIP To move a marker, drag it to the left or the right. Or, select the tab stop icon, enter a position number (location on the ruler) in the Position field using any measurement system, then click Set.

TIP To set a series of tabs by specifying the distance between them, enter "+" and then the gap length in the Position field (e.g., "p10+p12"). If the list gets too long, click the last tab marker on the ruler, then continue on your way.

TIP You can also choose Style > Tabs (**3**, next page; Cmd-Shift-T/Ctrl-Shift-T), but the huge Paragraph Attributes dialog box tends to get in the way of viewing tabs.

Set Custom Tab Stops

158

Work smart

Tabs, like all paragraph formats, can be applied via a **style sheet.** We usually create a style sheet based on a paragraph that already contains custom tab stops where we need them.

If you edit the tabs for the Normal style sheet or any other style sheet when no projects are open, you will in effect be creating your own default tab stops.

Steamed vegetable dumplings 3.50
Shrimp rolls 4.00

1 *To create a dot leader with extra space between the dots, enter a **period** and a **space** in the Fill Characters field.*

Steamed vegetable dumplings - - - - - - - 3.50
Shrimp rolls - - - - - - - - - - - - - - - - 4.00

2 *To create a dashed line with extra space between the dashes, enter a **hyphen** and a **space** in the Fill Characters field.*

Steamed vegetable dumplings _ _ _ _ _ 3.50
Shrimp rolls _ _ _ _ _ _ _ _ _ _ _ 4.00

3 *To change the point size, tracking, color, or other attributes of a tab leader, you have to do it manually for each instance or by using Find/Change. The tab leader in this example is tracked out, horizontally scaled, and baseline shifted downward.*

TIP *You can copy and paste a tab from one line of text to another. If you double-click the tab character, the whole leader will also become selected.*

Steamed vegetable dumplings   ~   ~   3.50
Shrimp rolls ~   ~   ~   ~   ~   4.00

4 *You can use **any character** as a fill character. Be creative! This is the tilde character (to the left of the "1" on the keyboard).*

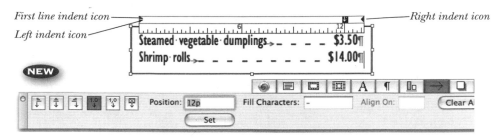

First line indent icon

Left indent icon

Right indent icon

1 *The **Tabs tab on the Measurements palette** provides an interactive method for dragging tabs into a layout. The two triangular icons on the left side of the ruler let you adjust paragraph indents on the fly; the top icon is the first line indent and the bottom one is the standard left indent (drag both for a simple indent). Use the triangular icon on the right side to adjust the right indent. Dragging these icons produces the same results as altering values in the First Line, Left Indent, and Right Indent fields in Style > Formats.*

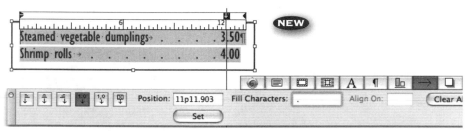

*Select a tab alignment icon (the Decimal tab is selected here), enter Fill Characters in the field (a period and space are shown here) and then **drag the icon up to the tab ruler** above the text. A guide shows where the tab stop will be placed and the text updates according to your tab settings. Release the mouse when you're happy. If you still need to fine-tune the placement or other settings of a tab stope, click its icon to select it and make changes.*

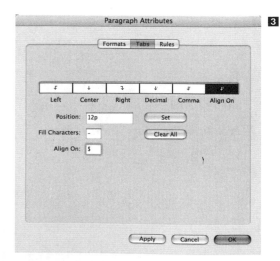

3

Keep up the dialog?

You can use similar techniques to set tabs in Style > Tabs (Cmd-Shift-T/Ctrl-Shift-T). The behemoth Paragraph Attributes dialog box **3** tends to get in the way of viewing the tabs in your text, though, so you'll probably need to drag it out of the way.

If you do decide to use the dialog box, since it's not as interactive as the Measurements palette, it helps to Option-click/Alt-click the Apply button to get constant updates.

To edit or remove custom tab stops:

1. Choose the Content tool.

2. Select *all* the paragraphs that contain the stops you want to change or from which you want to remove tab stops.

3. Display the Tabs tab of the Measurements palette.

or

Choose Style > Tabs (Cmd-Shift-T/ Ctrl-Shift-T).

4. Do any of the following:

To change the alignment of a stop, click its marker, then click a different Alignment button.

To change fill character(s), click a marker, then change the Fill Character(s).

To move a tab stop, drag it to the side manually. Or click it, change its Position value, then click Set (Cmd-S/ Alt-S).

To remove one tab stop, drag its marker upward or downward off the ruler **1**.

To remove *all* the tab stops, click Clear All (Alt-C in Windows) **2** or Option-click/Alt-click the ruler.

5. If you're using the Tabs pane of the Paragraph Attributes dialog box, click Apply to preview (Cmd-A/Ctrl-A), readjust any of the settings, if desired, then click OK **3**.

Blank ruler?

If the selected paragraphs contain more than one set of custom tab stops, only the tab stops for the first paragraph will display on the tabs ruler, but any new tab settings will affect *all* the currently selected text.

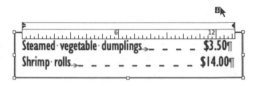

1 *Drag a tab stop marker* ***out*** *of the ruler to remove it.*

2 *Click* ***Clear All*** *to remove* ***all*** *tab stops from the currently selected text. The default tab stops will be restored to the text.*

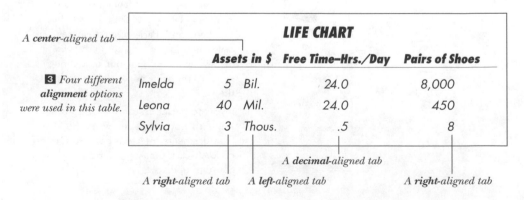

*A **center**-aligned tab*

3 *Four different **alignment** options were used in this table.*

LIFE CHART

	Assets in $		Free Time–Hrs./Day	Pairs of Shoes
Imelda	5	Bil.	24.0	8,000
Leona	40	Mil.	24.0	450
Sylvia	3	Thous.	.5	8

*A **decimal**-aligned tab*

*A **right**-aligned tab*   *A **left**-aligned tab*   *A **right**-aligned tab*

Edit Custom Tab Stops

Pictures 9

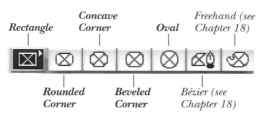

Rectangle | Concave Corner | Oval | Freehand (see Chapter 18)

Rounded Corner | Beveled Corner | Bézier (see Chapter 18)

1 *The **Picture Box** tools*

2 *Drag to create a **picture box**.*

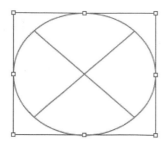

3 *An empty picture box has an "X" through its center.*

Picture basics

In QuarkXPress, a picture can be imported into a variety of different-shaped picture boxes. First you create a box of any shape using one of the Picture Box tools, then you import a picture into it.

File formats that can be imported include TIFF, EPS, GIF, JPEG, DCS, PCX, PDF, PNG, PSD, PhotoCD, SWF, WMF, XLS, PICT, and BMP (for more information, see "Formats you can import" on page 163).

To create a picture box:

1. Choose any standard Picture Box tool **1** (the Rectangle, Rounded Corner, Concave Corner, Beveled Corner, or Oval Picture Box tool). The cursor will temporarily turn into a crosshair icon.

2. Drag in any direction **2**–**3**.

TIP Shift-drag a handle to turn a rectangular picture box into a square or an oval picture box into a circle. This also works with a text box.

TIP To apply a frame to a picture box, use Item > Frame (Cmd-B/Ctrl-B).

TIP Need more than one? Use the Item > Duplicate, Step and Repeat, or Super Step and Repeat command to create multiples of any item.

When a picture is imported into a picture box, a screen preview version of it is saved with the QuarkXPress file, for display purposes. Also saved with the QuarkXPress file is information about changes made to the picture within the layout, such as cropping or scaling. The original picture file isn't modified by such changes. Instead, a link is created to the original picture file, which the QuarkXPress file accesses when the layout is printed. If the link to the original picture file is broken (the original picture is missing) or the picture itself is modified, you must update the picture or it won't output properly (see pages 183–184).

To import a picture:

1. Choose the Item or Content tool, then click a picture box 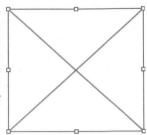.

2. Choose File > Import Picture (Cmd-E/ Ctrl-E). **NEW**

3. Locate and click a picture file name 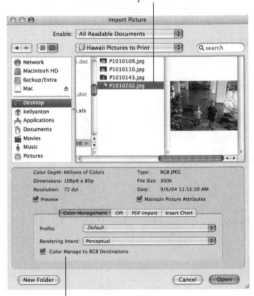.

4. *Optional:* Check Preview to display a thumbnail of the picture (the picture has to have been saved with a preview).

5. *Optional:* Check Maintain Picture **NEW** Attributes if you're replacing an existing picture but want to use its attributes (such as scale and placement) for the new picture.

6. Click Open. If it looks as though the picture isn't there, see **1**–**2**, next page. There's a lot you can do to a picture, such as scaling, cropping, and rotating, and you can also scale, rotate, or distort the picture box. Instructions begin on page 167.

TIP You can also import a picture using the context menu. Control-click/Right-click a picture box and choose Import Picture from the context menu.

TIP To import a picture into a table picture cell or a picture box within a group, select the cell or box with the Content tool.

1 *Click a picture box with the Item tool or Content tool. If the box already contains a picture, the picture you import will replace the existing one.*

2 *Click a picture file name to import it.*

Options in this area allow you to import specific pages of PDF or Excel files and to use OPI and color management.

Import Picture (side tab)

Faster navigating

If you tend to import pictures over and over from the same folder, you can make that folder appear automatically in the Open dialog box by choosing it in QuarkXPress (Edit, in Windows) > Preferences > Application > **Default Path** (see page 367).

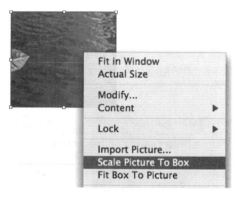

1 *The picture is imported using File > Import Picture—but you're not seeing what you want. If the picture has a large white background, you may not see anything! Simply Control-click/Right-click the picture box and choose Scale Picture To Box or Fit Box To Picture.*

2 *After fitting the picture to the box, repositioning the picture by dragging it with the Content tool, and then adjusting the scale using the Classic tab of the Measurements palette, we finally see what we want.*

Formats you can import

You can import pictures in the following file formats: TIFF, EPS, GIF, JPEG, DCS, PCX, PDF, PNG, PSD, PhotoCD, SWF, WMF, XLS, PICT, and BMP. (In Mac OS X, a Windows Metafile will convert into a PICT when it's imported.)

To import pictures in some formats **NEW** (including PNG, PSD, SWF, and XLS), the import filter that comes with QuarkXPress needs to be enabled. For example, to import an Excel chart, you need the Table Import filter. If the required filter is disabled, you will get an error message: "This file requires XTensions software to be read properly." Use the Utilities > XTensions Manager to enable/disable filters.

Other picture import options

The Color Management pane in the Import Picture dialog box lets you specify how colors in the picture are handled. If the OPI and PDF Filter XTensions that come with QuarkXPress are enabled, the OPI and PDF Import panes display as well. To read about OPI, see the QuarkXPress documentation. For a PDF, enter the number of the page you want to import in the PDF Page field.

Pictures come in two basic flavors

A picture that is created in a bitmap program (such as Adobe Photoshop), or that is scanned, is actually composed of tiny pixels. You'll see the individual pixels only if you zoom way in on the image. The important thing to remember about a bitmap image is that enlarging it above 100% in QuarkXPress will diminish its resolution and output quality, whereas shrinking it will increase its resolution and output quality. If you're preparing an image in a bitmap program or scanning it for output from QuarkXPress, you should plan ahead and save it at the appropriate resolution, orientation, and size.

(Continued on the following page)

A picture that's created in a drawing program, such as Illustrator or FreeHand, is composed of mathematically defined objects. This type of picture is called "vector" or "object-oriented." A vector picture can be moved, scaled, recolored, and enlarged without affecting its output quality at all. It will be crisp at 20% and crisp at 120% (though enlarging it much beyond 100% may lengthen its print time). The higher the resolution of the output device, the sharper a vector picture prints. A vector picture can't be edited in QuarkXPress, however; it can be scaled, rotated, or skewed, but not colored.

Choosing the right resolution for a bitmap picture

For onscreen output, save the image in RGB color mode in its original application and at a resolution of 72 ppi.

For print output, choose one-and-a-half to two times the lpi (lines per inch) your commercial printer plans to use. For example, let's say your printer plans to use a 133 line screen. A color picture should be saved at twice the line screen. 133 times 2 equals 266, so you should save the picture in its original application at 266 ppi. For a grayscale picture, one-and-a-half times the line screen is sufficient (200 ppi, in our example).

Every rule has its exceptions. A bitmap image that contains sharp linear elements will require a higher resolution (600 ppi or higher). For a very painterly picture that contains amorphous shapes, on the other hand, a resolution value that's less than twice the output line screen may suffice.

A vector-based picture from a drawing application is resolution independent, which means it will print at the resolution of the output device. Just make sure it's saved in a file format that QuarkXPress can read.

Working with Adobe Photoshop files

You can import native Photoshop files into QuarkXPress with the PSD Import filter enabled (Utilities > XTensions Manager). You can then use the PSD Import palette to selectively display and manipulate layers, channels, and paths saved with the picture.

For color separations, ask your output service provider or commercial printer whether to save your files in CMYK or RGB mode in Photoshop. If you choose the former, Photoshop will do the RGB-to-CMYK conversion; if you choose the latter, then either QuarkXPress or the output device will do it. Also be sure to ask which file format they prefer: TIFF, DCS (preseparated), or EPS.

Using Picture Effects

The Picture Effects palette (Window menu) in QuarkXPress lets you make adjustments such as Brightness/Contrast and apply filters such as Emboss to imported bitmap pictures. These controls are similar to those in Photoshop and generally output properly. However, you may wish to consult with your printer before using Picture Effects in a layout.

Here, spot

If you import an EPS picture into a QuarkXPress layout, **spot** colors that were assigned to the picture will automatically append to the Colors palette for that project.

TIP To *prevent* applied colors from importing with an EPS picture, hold down Cmd/Ctrl as you click Open in the Import Picture dialog box.

1 *Picture info*

Looks like Greek to you

To speed up screen redraw, check **Greek Pictures** in QuarkXPress (Edit, in Windows) > Preferences > Print Layout > General. Greeked pictures look solid gray on screen at some view sizes, but they print normally. To ungreek a greeked picture, just click it—the image will reappear.

If you're going to output a QuarkXPress file to a color inkjet printer, save the images at a high resolution in RGB color mode.

TIP A picture's file size, dimensions, color depth, and other information are listed in the Import Picture dialog box **1**. For information about an already imported picture, click it, choose Utilities > Usage > Pictures, and click More Information.

Enlarge or shrink?

Scaling a bitmap picture in QuarkXPress affccts its output resolution. If you shrink a bitmap picture in QuarkXPress, its output resolution will increase; if you enlarge a bitmap picture, its output resolution will decrease. Here's an example: Take a 150 ppi image and shrink it by half. Its ppi will increase to 300. Why should you bother paying attention to this? Because enlarging a bitmapped picture above 100% will diminish its print quality. A vector-based image (such as an Illustrator EPS) won't degrade in quality if it's enlarged in QuarkXPress, but it may take longer to print. You can also take a large picture and shrink it down in a layout, but the picture will add significantly to the project's file size and also prolong its print time. So the moral of the story is... plan ahead.

EPS preview options

Every EPS picture has a PICT or TIFF preview built into it (unless it's specifically saved without one) so it can be viewed onscreen or printed on a non-PostScript printer. The higher a picture preview's bit depth, the longer it may take to render onscreen and the larger the file storage size of the project into which it's imported.

When you save an EPS image for export to QuarkXPress, save it with a preview, if that option is available (both Illustrator and FreeHand offer this option). Any EPS picture that doesn't have a built-in preview

(Continued on the following page)

will appear as a gray box in QuarkXPress, but it will print normally. To have QuarkXPress generate a full-resolution preview for the picture, see below.

TIP To choose display options for TIFF picture previews, go to QuarkXPress (Edit, in Windows) > Preferences > Application > Display (see page 363).

Using full resolution preview

For the sake of speed, QuarkXPress imports low-resolution previews of picture files. If you have a zippy computer (as most of us do today), if you're not using very many images, or if you just really need to see what's going on in a picture, you can display picture previews at the full resolution of the original file.

To turn on full resolution preview for selected pictures:

1. Choose the Item or Content tool, then click the picture you want displayed at full resolution. (To select multiple pictures, Shift-click them.)

2. Control-click/Right-click the picture (or one of the selected pictures) and choose Preview Resolution > Full Resolution -.
or
Choose Item > Preview Resolution > Full Resolution.

To turn off full resolution preview for selected pictures:

If displaying full resolution previews takes too long, select the pictures and choose Item > Preview Resolution > Low Resolution.

Note: Full resolution preview is not available for pictures in GIF, PICT, or WMF format. If the original picture file has a relatively low resolution to begin with, you'll get an error message when you try to choose the Full Resolution option.

1 *With a standard preview, it's hard to make out the details in this grayscale TIFF.*

2 *Choosing Item > Preview Resolution > **High Resolution** makes all the difference onscreen.*

Disable full-res previews temporarily

If you need to zip through a layout on the quick, be sure View > Full Res Previews is unchecked. The pictures that have been set to display at full resolution will display at low resolution. You can control several aspects of the handling of full-resolution previews via settings in the Full Res Preview pane in the Preferences dialog box. See page 181.

Preview Options, Full Resolution Preview

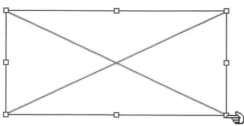

1 *Drag any of the four **corner handles** of a box...*

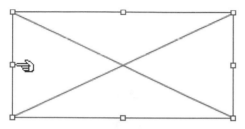

2 *...or drag any of the four **midpoint** **handles** of a box.*

*A new **Width** value is entered in inches.*

| X: | 36p1.333 | W: | 4" |
| Y: | 26p8.167 | H: | 6p |

*The **Height** of the currently selected box*

3 *As with all the fields in QuarkXPress, you can enter values in the **Width** and **Height** fields in any measurement unit used in QuarkXPress. If you're using a different measurement system than the one selected for the rulers, enter the unit abbreviation (such as "pt" or ") after the value.*

Scaling and positioning picture boxes

The dimensions of a picture box can be changed independently of the picture.

To scale a picture box manually:

1. Choose the Item or Content tool.
2. Click a picture box.
3. Drag any handle **1**–**2**. Hold down Option-Shift/Alt-Shift while dragging to preserve the original proportions of the box.

TIP To resize a Bézier picture box, turn off Item > Edit > Shape (Shift-F4/F10 toggles this command on and off).

To scale a picture box using the Measurements palette:

1. Choose the Item or Content tool.
2. Click a picture box.
3. Display the Classic tab of the Measurements palette.
4. To modify the width of the box, double-click the W field, enter a number in an increment as small as .001 **3**, then press Return/Enter.
   and/or
   To modify the height of the box, double-click the H field, enter a number, then press Return/Enter.

TIP To enlarge or reduce the dimensions of a box by a specified amount, insert the cursor after the current value in the W or H field, enter a plus (+) or minus (–) sign, then enter the amount you want to add or subtract in any measurement unit used in QuarkXPress. You can also use / (slash) to divide the current value or * (asterisk) to multiply it.

TIP You can also scale a picture box by entering new values in the Width and Height fields in the Box pane of the Modify dialog box (Item > Modify).

Scale Picture Box

To delete a picture box:

1. Choose the Item or Content tool.

2. Click a picture box.

3. Choose Item > Delete (Cmd-K/Ctrl-K).

TIP A picture box that's selected with the Item tool can also be deleted by pressing Delete/Backspace on the keyboard or by choosing Edit > Clear.

To delete a picture (and keep the box):

1. Choose the Content tool, then click a picture box.

2. Press Delete/Backspace.

To move a picture box manually:

1. Choose the Item tool or hold down Cmd/Ctrl if the Content tool is currently chosen.

2. With the pointer inside the picture box, drag in any direction. Pause before dragging to display the picture as it's moved (see the sidebar) **1** or drag without pausing to display only the outline of the box as it's moved **2**.

TIP You can drag a picture box or any other item from one page to another. To help you reach the desired page, you can force scrolling by knocking the pointer into the edge of the project window.

Just a sec...

To see a picture as you drag it, including any effect moving it has on text wrap, pause briefly before dragging. How long? By default, it's three-quarters of a second. If you're impatient—or exceedingly patient—you can change that value from 0.1 to 5 seconds in the **Delay Before Live Refresh Drag** field in QuarkXPress (Edit, in Windows) > Preferences > Application > Input Settings.

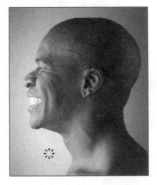

1 *To move a box, drag inside it with the **Item** tool. To see the picture as you move it, pause before dragging until the Live Refresh cursor ✷ displays.*

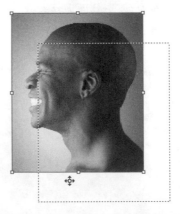

2 *Or drag without pausing to see only the **outline** of the box as it's moved.*

Delete, Move Picture Box

*The **horizontal** location of the upper-left corner of a picture box relative to the ruler origin*

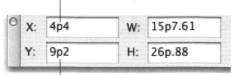

*The **vertical** location of the upper-left corner of a picture box relative to the ruler origin*

1 *The Classic tab of the Measurements palette*

2 *Add a positive or negative number to the right of the current value in the X or Y field, then press Return/Enter.*

3 *The two numbers are added together and the box is repositioned.*

4 *These items are positioned for a bleed.*

To reposition a picture box using the Measurements palette:

1. Choose the Item or Content tool.

2. Click a picture box.

3. Display the Classic tab of the Measurements palette.

4. To change the horizontal position of the box relative to the ruler origin, which is normally located in the upper-left corner of the layout, change the X value **1**.
and/or
To change the vertical position of the box, change the Y value.

TIP To move a box a specified horizontal or vertical distance, insert the cursor to the right of the current X or Y value, type a plus (+) or minus (−) sign, then enter a value in any measurement unit used in QuarkXPress **2**-**3**.

TIP To nudge a picture box or any other item 1 point at a time, select it with the Item tool, then press any of the four arrow keys on the keyboard. Or Option-press/Alt-press an arrow key to move an item in .1-point increments.

A bleed is the positioning of items so that they partially overhang the edge of the page. The overhanging portion is trimmed by the print shop after printing.

To create a bleed:

To create a bleed, position any item so that part of the item is on the page and part of it extends onto the pasteboard **4**. Items that are completely on the pasteboard won't print.

When you're ready to output your layout, you or your print shop will enter the width of the bleed area that you want to print and choose other print options in the Bleed pane in File > Print (see page 387).

Fitting pictures into their boxes

To scale a picture using the Measurements palette:

1. Choose the Item or Content tool.

2. Click a picture.

3. Display the Classic tab of the Measurements palette.

4. Enter new X% (scale across) and/or Y% (scale down) values **1**–**6**.

TIP Press Tab to move from field to field on the Measurements palette (or press Shift-Tab to reverse your steps).

TIP You can copy values from one field on the Measurements palette and paste them into another field, such as from the X% field into the Y% field, or vice versa.

To scale a picture using the keyboard:

1. Choose the Item or Content tool.

2. Click a picture.

3. Hold down Cmd-Option-Shift/Ctrl-Alt-Shift and press the > key to enlarge the picture by 5% or the < key to shrink it.

To center a picture in its box:

1. Choose the Item or Content tool.

2. Click a picture.

3. Choose Style > Center Picture.
or
Press Cmd-Shift-M/Ctrl-Shift-M.

Horizontal scale of picture   *Horizontal location of picture relative to upper-left corner of picture box*

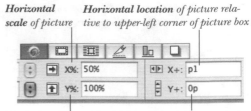

Vertical scale of picture   *Vertical location of picture relative to upper-left corner of picture box*

1 *When the X scale percentage is different from the Y scale percentage, it means the picture's proportions don't match those of the original.*

2 *When the X and Y scale percentages match, it means the picture's proportions do match those of the original.*

3 *X and Y scale of 100%*

 **5** *X and Y scale of 50%*    **6** *X scale 85%, Y scale 50%*

4 *X scale 95%, Y scale 100%: a more subtle distortion*

Scale Picture

1 *Use* **Style > Scale Picture to Box** *to scale the picture proportionally (in this case by 10%). The gray background of the box peeps out at the sides.*

2 *Using* **Style > Stretch Picture to Fit Box** *forces the picture to fit the box, sacrificing proportions (in this case, not too bad at X: 13.5% and Y: 10%).*

3 *Once you have carefully scaled a picture and positioned it in the box, you can resize both proportionally by pressing Cmd-Option-Shift/Ctrl-Alt-Shift as you drag a box handle.*

To fit a picture to its box, maintaining proportions:

1. Choose the Item or Content tool.

2. Click a picture.

3. To scale the picture to fit completely within the box while maintaining its original proportions, Control-click/Right-click the picture and choose Scale Picture to Box (Cmd-Option-Shift-F/Ctrl-Alt-Shift-F) **1**.

TIP You can accomplish the same task by choosing Style > Scale Picture To Box.

To fit a picture to its box, distorting proportions:

1. Choose the Item or Content tool.

2. Click a picture.

3. To fit the picture into the box, but with its proportions altered relative to the original, choose Style > Stretch Picture To Fit Box (Cmd-Shift-F/Ctrl-Shift-F) **2**.

Follow these instructions if the picture fits nicely in its box but you want to scale the whole shebang—picture and box.

To scale a picture and its box:

1. Choose the Item or Content tool.

2. Hold down Cmd-Option-Shift/Ctrl-Alt-Shift, press a handle, pause briefly for the picture to redraw, then drag **3**.

TIP If it's a Bézier picture box, turn off Item > Edit > Shape (Shift-F4/F10) to scale the box and picture.

Cropping pictures

Along with resizing, cropping a picture can dramatically alter its impact on a page. Don't be afraid to crop drastically. Sometimes less is more. One caveat, though: If you're going to substantially crop a bitmapped picture, create a new, cropped picture file in its original application or by choosing File > Save Picture > Selected Picture. The picture will print much faster.

1 *Use the **Content** tool to drag a picture around within its box.*

To crop a picture by moving it within its box:

1. Choose the Content tool.
2. Drag inside the picture box (you'll see a hand icon) **1**.

TIP Click a picture and press an arrow key to nudge a picture 1 point at a time. Option-press/Alt-press an arrow key to nudge a picture 0.1 point at a time.

TIP You can also use a clipping path to prevent part of a picture from printing (see Chapter 11).

2 *Cropping a picture by resizing its picture box.*

To crop a picture by resizing its box:

1. Choose the Item or Content tool, then click a picture box.
2. Drag any handle of the box **2**-**3**.

TIP To crop a picture by reshaping its box, read Chapter 18. If it's a Bézier picture box, turn off Item > Edit > Shape (Shift-F4/F10) to crop the picture.

3 *The picture is cropped after the mouse button is released.*

To fit a box to a picture:

1. Choose the Item or Content tool, then click a picture box.
2. Control-click/Right-click the picture and choose Fit Box To Picture **4**.
   or
   Choose Style > Fit Box To Picture.

4 *Rather than cropping a picture, you can resize its box to fit it perfectly.*

The picture and box angle

| X: | 7p1.709 | W: | 6p10.666 | △ | -15° |
| Y: | 25p7.265 | H: | 6p10.332 | ↖ | 0p |

1 *The **Box Angle** field on the left side of the Classic tab of the Measurements palette*

2 *Before rotating a box, click with the Rotation tool cursor ⊕ to establish the axis point. (You can create a lever by dragging away from the axis point.)*

3 *When you rotate a box and its picture, if you don't pause before dragging, only the outline of the box will be visible as you rotate it, not its contents.*

Rotating, skewing, and flipping pictures

Note: When you rotate, crop, or scale a picture, create a new picture file for it. It will redraw, process, and print faster. Use the original application, such as Photoshop or Illustrator, or use File > Save Picture > Selected Picture.

To rotate a picture and its box using the Measurements palette:

1. Choose the Item or Content tool.
2. Click a picture box.
3. Display the Classic tab of the Measurements palette.
3. In the picture and box angle field on the left side, enter a positive number between 0° and 360° to rotate the picture and box counterclockwise, or enter a negative number to rotate them clockwise **1**.

TIP You can also use the Angle field in the Box pane of the Modify dialog box (Item > Modify) to rotate a picture and its box.

To rotate a picture and its box using the Rotation tool:

1. Choose the Rotation tool. ↺
2. Click a picture box.
3. Press to create an axis point, drag the cursor away from the axis point to create a lever for better control **2**–**3**, then drag clockwise or counterclockwise.

TIP Shift-drag with the Rotation tool to rotate an item in increments of 45°.

TIP If you click with the Rotation tool and pause briefly, you'll be able to see the picture and text reflow as you rotate the box. If not, you'll only see the outline of the box.

Rotate Picture

To rotate a picture (and not its box):

1. Choose the Item or Content tool.

2. Click a picture **1**.

3. Display the Classic tab of the Measurements palette **2**.

4. In the picture angle field on the right side, enter a positive value to rotate the picture counterclockwise or a negative value to rotate it clockwise **3**–**4**.

TIP You can also use the Picture Angle field in the Picture pane of the Modify dialog box (Item > Modify) to rotate a picture.

TIP To rotate the picture box and *not* the picture, first rotate the box and picture together using the Box Angle field on the left side of the Measurements palette's Classic tab. Then, rotate just the picture using the angle field on the right side. For example, you could rotate the picture with its box 20°, then rotate the picture back –20°.

1 *0° rotation*

2 *The picture angle*

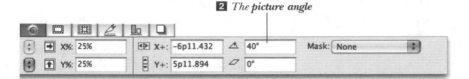

3 *20° rotation (the picture box has a frame)*

4 *–20° rotation (no frame on the picture box)*

1 *The Skew field in the Box pane skews the picture and its box.*

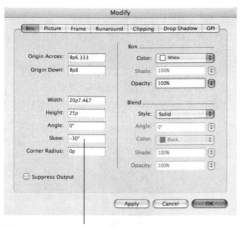

2 *A picture and its box skewed –30°*

3 *The picture skew*

4 *A picture skewed –30° within its box*

To skew a picture and its box:

1. Choose the Item or Content tool.

2. Click a picture box of any shape. Only one item can be skewed at a time.

3. Control-click/Right-click the box and choose Modify or choose Item > Modify (Cmd-M/Ctrl-M).

4. Click the Box pane, then enter a Skew value between –75 and 75 **1**. Enter a positive value to skew it to the right or a negative value to skew it to the left.

5. Click OK **2**. A picture can be edited in its skewed position.

To skew a picture (and not its box):

1. Choose the Item or Content tool.

2. Click a picture box of any shape. Only one item can be skewed at a time.

3. Display the Classic tab of the Measurements palette.

4. On the right side, enter a Skew value between –75 and 75 **3**. Enter a positive value to skew it to the right or a negative value to skew it to the left.

5. Press Return/Enter **4**-**5**.

TIP You can also use the Picture Skew field in the Picture pane of the Modify dialog box (Item > Modify) to skew a picture.

5 *The box skew feature was used to distort the top and side portions of this cube.*

The flip commands flip the contents of a box. A picture can be modified in its flipped position.

Note: As with cropping and rotating, it's better to flip a picture in its original application than in QuarkXPress—it will print and redraw more quickly. Or, use File > Save Picture > Selected Picture to create a new, flipped picture file.

To flip a picture:

1. Choose the Content tool.

2. Click a picture box.

3. Click the Flip Horizontal and/or Flip Vertical button on the Classic tab of the Measurements palette **1**–**3**.
   or
   Choose Style > Flip Horizontal and/or Flip Vertical.

TIP When flipping pictures, watch out for text (such as a logo on a T-shirt) that may be unreadable or noticeably backwards when flipped **4**–**5**.

TIP To undo a flip, stand on your head, or choose the command again, or click the button again on the Measurements palette.

1 *The Flip Horizontal and Flip Vertical arrows on the Classic tab of the Measurements palette*

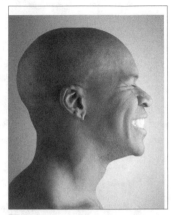

2 *The original picture*

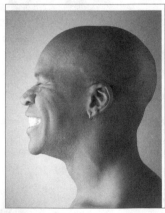

4 *The original picture*

3 *The picture flipped horizontally*

5 *The picture flipped horizontally: The numbers on the watch face are noticeably backwards.*

Flip Picture

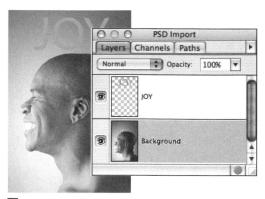

1 *Choose **Window > PSD Import** to manipulate layers, channels, and paths saved with native Photoshop files.*

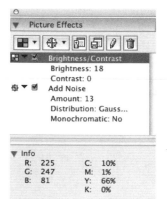

2 *Choose **Window > Picture Effects** to apply adjustments and special-effects filters to images.*

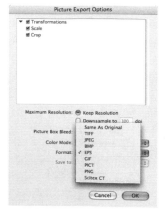

3 *The **Picture Export Options** dialog box lets you create new picture files that reflect modifications made in QuarkXPress.*

Applying special effects to pictures **NEW**

Although high-end publishers will probably never lose their affinity or need for a dedicated image-editing application such as Photoshop, QuarkXPress has come a long way toward providing more image handling features. The advantages to this are many, including saving steps, viewing image changes in the context of the surrounding layout, and having new creative options. In addition, you can modify images without making permanent changes to the picture files—unless you choose to. Features include:

■ The ability to import native Photoshop files and manipulate any layers, channels, and paths saved with them. Use File > Import Picture to import Photoshop files and then use Window > PSD Import **1**.

■ Adjustments to images such as Brightness/Contrast, Color Balance, and Selective Color; and filters such as Unsharp Mask, Emboss, and Add Noise. Use Window > Picture Effects **2** to apply adjustments and filters.

■ The ability to automatically create new picture files from selected pictures or all the pictures in a layout. The new files reflect all the modifications made to them in QuarkXPress—including cropping, scaling, and adjustments— and can automatically replace the originals in the layout. Use File > Save Picture to create new files **3**.

■ The ability to modify picture opacity and to access alpha channels/masks.

Note: To import native Photoshop files, be sure the PSD Import XTension is enabled. To apply adjustments and filters, and to create new picture files from modified images, make sure the Vista XTension is enabled. Both XTensions come with QuarkXPress and are enabled by default (Utilities > XTensions Manager).

Apply Special Effects

When the PSD Import XTension is enabled (Utilities > XTensions Manager), you can simply import a native Photoshop picture file the same way you import any other picture file (File > Import Picture). If the picture file contains layers, channels, and paths you want to work with, you can access them through the PSD Import palette (Window > PSD Import). With this new ability, you may need to rethink your work-flow and put some effort into image preparation. For example, if you have three different versions of a magazine cover image you want to experiment with, put them on separate layers in the same file.

To work with Photoshop files:

1. Choose the Item or Content tool.

2. Click a native Photoshop picture.

3. Choose Window > PSD Import.

4. Click the Layers, Channels, and Paths tabs to see what's available in the image. You can click the eye icon to the left of any image element to display and print it. For example, you might hide a layer containing text or hide one color channel to create a special effect.

5. In the Layers tab, you can change the transparency of selected layers by entering a value in the Opacity field or by choosing a percentage value from the menu. If the picture has multiple layers, you can modify the way pixels interact with each other by choosing a blending mode from the menu **1**.

6. In the Channels tab, you can double-click a channel and change its color **2**–**3**.

7. In the Paths tab, you can show and hide clipping paths created for the image.

TIP The blending modes in the Layers tab work the same as those in Photoshop.

TIP You can't apply Window > Picture Effects to native Photoshop files.

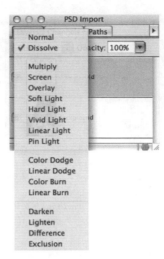

1 *The **Blend menu** and the **Opacity field** on the PSD Import palette (Window menu)*

2 *In the **Channels tab** on the PSD Import palette, double-click a channel to change its color*

3 *The **Channel Options dialog box** lets you modify the color of a channel.*

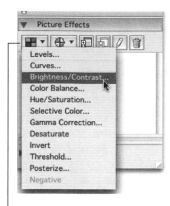

1 *The **Adjustments menu** on the Picture Effects palette (Window menu)*

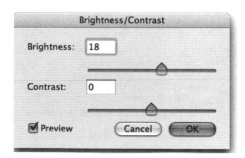

2 *The **Brightness/Contrast dialog box** is an example of a dialog box that displays when you choose an option from the Adjustments menu.*

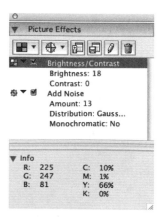

3 *Check the box next to an effect to hide it; drag any effect to change its position on the list.*

When the Vista XTension is enabled (Utilities > XTensions Manager), you can apply color corrections and special effects to bitmap images through the Picture Effects palette. All these controls are similar to those in Photoshop. The special effects filters are fun to experiment with, but the color correction controls are best left to experienced users. This is our nice way of trying to say that if you don't know anything about color correction, you have no business performing color correction. You can, however, use the adjustments to create interesting effects such as negatives.

To apply image adjustments:

1. Choose the Item or Content tool.
2. Click a bitmap picture such as a TIFF or JPEG.
3. Choose Window > Picture Effects.
4. From the Adjustments menu **1**, choose an option. These options are primarily for correcting images, but you can also use them to make dramatic changes.
5. A dialog box displays for the effect. Make any changes, using the preview to see what's happening (keeping in mind that what you see onscreen may not be exactly what prints) **2**. Click OK once you're happy with the adjustments.
6. If you want to see how an image looks without the adjustment, uncheck the box next to the adjustment name on the Picture Effects palette **3**.
7. As adjustments and filters are added to the list, you can drag them up or down in the list to arrange the order in which they are applied.

TIP To see the RGB and CMYK color values of any given pixel in an image, click the Info triangle. You'll see the color values as you point at pixels in the image. Note that this only works after you apply an adjustment or filter.

Image Adjustments

Special-Effects Filters

To apply special-effects filters: NEW

1. Choose the Item or Content tool.

2. Click a bitmap picture such as a TIFF.

3. Choose Window > Picture Effects.

4. Click the Filters menu **1** and choose an option; you may be familiar with some of them from Photoshop.

5. A dialog box displays for the filter. Make any changes, using the preview to see what's happening **2**. Click OK when you achieve the look you want.

TIP Remember that you can check and uncheck effects in the Picture Effects palette to see how the image looks. You can also drag them up and down in the list to change the order in which they are applied.

The modifications you make to pictures in QuarkXPress may look good, but the picture files themselves may be unnecessarily large causing them to print slowly. You can create new picture files with the changes already applied (reducing their file size) and reimport them.

To create a new file from a modified picture: NEW

1. Choose File > Save Picture > All Pictures in Layout.
   or
   Select the pictures you want to save and choose File > Save Picture > Selected Picture

2. *Optional:* In the Picture Export Options dialog box, check the changes you want to keep in the new files and specify the Resolution, Color Mode, and Format you need for output **3**.

3. To apply changes to the original picture files, check Overwrite Original Picture.
   or
   To create new picture files and import them into the picture boxes, check Link Layout to New Picture.

4. Click OK.

1 *The **Filters menu** on the Picture Effects palette (Window menu)*

2 *The **Add Noise dialog box** is an example of a dialog box that displays when you choose an option from the Filters menu.*

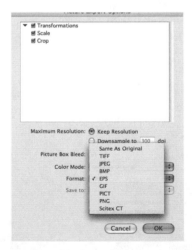
3 *The Picture Export Options dialog box (File > Save Picture) lets you create new picture files that reflect all the changes you make in QuarkXPress.*

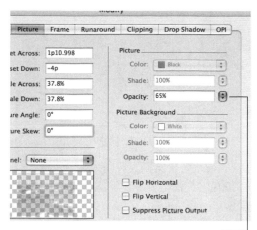

1 *The **Opacity** field in the Picture pane of the Modify dialog box controls picture transparency.*

2 *Changing the opacity of a picture layered over text allows the text to shine through.*

Time was that if you wanted to see through an item or picture to what was behind it, you were relegated to using Photoshop or another program that offered transparency support. QuarkXPress 7, however, introduces transparency, allowing you to layer pictures, items, and text with abandon—or not. Transparency is one of those things in which less can be more. Don't go nuts layering stuff just because you can. But if you've got a good reason—go for it!

To change a picture's transparency:

1. Choose the Item or Content tool. **NEW**
2. Click a picture box.
3. Choose Item > Modify.
4. Click the Picture tab.
5. In the Picture area in the upper-right corner, enter a value in the Opacity field or click the arrow(s) to the right of the field and drag the slider **1**.
6. Click Apply to see the change **2**. If necessary, drag the Modify dialog box out of the way to see the picture.

TIP When you change a picture's opacity, you should be able to see items behind the image. If you can't, be sure the box background is None (Item > Modify > Box tab > Box area > Color menu).

TIP When working with transparency and overlapping images, text, and other items, it can't hurt to talk to your printer about his or her experience with actually printing these effects.

Transparency

A mask is an area of an image that you want to isolate—to hide it, display it, or somehow treat it differently. If you have created a mask for a picture in an image editing application, you can choose to limit the picture display to the masked portion in QuarkXPress. In Photoshop, masks should be saved in alpha channels. If you change the picture's opacity, the change is reflected in the mask. (Clipping paths, which also control what area of a picture displays, are discussed on page 211.)

To select a mask: NEW

1. Choose the Item or Content tool.
2. Click a picture box .
3. Display the Classic tab of the Measurements palette.
4. Choose an option from the Mask menu at right **2**-**3**.

TIP You can also choose Item > Modify and use the Mask controls in the Picture pane.

Locking pictures

As you can see, it's pretty easy to import pictures—and it's easy to make them pretty. After all the trouble you go to, how can you be sure that nobody, including you, accidentally or intentionally, messes them up? Lock them.

To lock a picture to prevent changes:

1. Choose the Content tool.
2. Click a picture box.
3. Choose Item > Lock > Position (F6) to prevent the picture box from being moved—at all.
4. Choose Item > Lock > Picture to prevent the picture from being modified (scale, placement, etc.) or replaced (File > Import). NEW
5. If a picture is locked and you try to modify it, the lock cursor displays **4**.

1 *We didn't think this scene was monumental enough, so we added an obelisk.*

2 *We used the **Mask menu** on the Classic tab of the Measurements palette to enable an alpha mask.*

3 *Eccolà! Instant tourist attraction.*

4 *When an item and/or its content is locked, the **lock cursor** displays. If the position is locked, you can't move it. If the picture is locked, you can't modify or replace the picture.*

status is everything

Modified	The picture was modified in another application (but not moved).
Missing	The picture was moved or renamed.
Wrong Type	The picture's file format was changed (or the picture was compressed using a utility; you can't update this type).
No XTension	The import filter for the picture's file format is disabled.

1 *QuarkXPress will notify you if you attempt to print, export as PDF, or collect for output a layout with missing or modified pictures. QuarkXPress really wants you to find and update those pictures!*

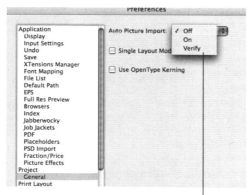

2 *In Preferences > Project > General, choose Auto Picture Import: Off, On, or Verify.*

Updating pictures

When a picture is imported into a QuarkXPress file, the original picture file name and location is stored in the QuarkXPress project file. If the original picture is then renamed or moved (is missing), its path to the QuarkXPress file must be reestablished in order for it to output correctly **1**. QuarkXPress doesn't automatically update *missing* pictures. To do it yourself, follow the instructions on the next page.

If an original picture is *modified* in another application, on the other hand, its onscreen preview may or may not be updated automatically, depending on the current Auto Picture Import setting, which is discussed below. Unlike missing pictures, modified pictures will print correctly, whether you've chosen to have their onscreen previews update or not.

Thankfully, when a picture is updated, any scale, rotation, color, and offset values that were previously applied to it aren't changed.

To choose an import setting for modified pictures:

In QuarkXPress (Edit, in Windows) > Preferences > Project > General, for Auto Picture Import, you can specify whether or not modified picture files in the project will be updated automatically when the project is reopened **2**.

- If you reopen a project that was last saved with Auto Picture Import Off, the modified pictures won't be updated.

- If the Auto Picture Import setting is On, the pictures will be updated automatically without a prompt appearing onscreen.

- If the Auto Picture Import setting is Verify, a prompt will appear. Click Yes to have the modified pictures update; no further steps are required.

The path to missing (moved or renamed) picture files can be updated at any time using Utilities > Usage > Pictures. When pictures are updated, any scale, rotation, color, and other attributes that were previously applied to them are preserved.

The Usage dialog box can also be used to update modified pictures. You'll need to do this if Auto Picture Import was Off in Preferences > Project > General when you opened the file (that is, if you opted not to have modified pictures update automatically), or if you modify any of the pictures outside of QuarkXPress after opening the file.

To update pictures using the Usage dialog box:

1. *Optional:* Choose the Content tool, then, in the layout, click the picture you want to update.

2. Choose Utilities > Usage (Option-F13 in Mac OS X).

3. Click the Pictures option in the scroll list at left.

4. Click any file name whose Status is listed as Missing or Modified. If you clicked a picture in step 1, its name will be selected.

   Optional: Click Show to see the picture selected in the project window **1**.

5. Click Update **2**.

6. For any missing picture, locate and click the picture file name in the Find dialog box, then click Open **3**.

   For any modified picture, click OK.

7. Click Done/Close.

TIP In the Page column of the Pictures pane, a PB indicates a picture that is on the pasteboard.

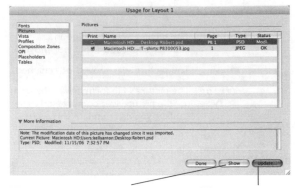

1 *Click Show to have the currently highlighted picture become selected in the layout.*

2 *Click Update to search for a missing picture file.*

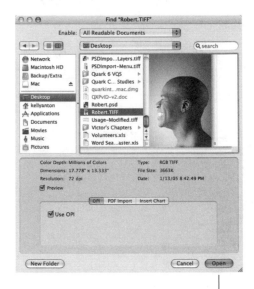

3 *Click Open to update the picture in the layout.*

Multiple Items

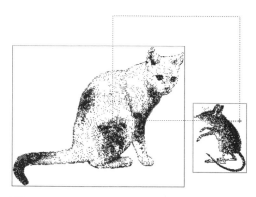

1 *Drag a marquee over multiple items with the* **Item** *tool or* **Content** *tool.*

2 *Both picture boxes are* **selected,** *and the handles on both boxes are visible.*

Moving multiple items

When you move multiple-selected items by dragging them, press the Shift key after you start dragging to constrain the movement to horizontal or vertical.

It's one thing to create individual items, and quite another thing to arrange them into a pleasing composition. In this chapter you'll learn many layout skills, including how to group, lock, duplicate, rotate, scale, restack, anchor, and align multiple items.

Selecting and deselecting Items

The position, size, angle of rotation, background color, and other specifications can be modified for a multiple-item selection. The options available will vary depending on the types of items selected—for example, all text boxes, a combination of text boxes and text paths, all lines, etc. Only items on unlocked layers can be selected (see page 290).

To select multiple items:

1. Choose the Item or Content tool.
2. Shift-click each item you wish to select.
   or
   Position the cursor outside all the items to be selected, then drag a marquee that surrounds at least a portion of each item **1**–**2**. (To deselect any selected item, Shift-click it.)

To deselect all items:

Choose the Item tool, then press Tab.
or
Choose the Item or Content tool, then click a blank area of a page.

To select all items on a page or spread:

1. Choose the Item tool, and make sure the desired page is displayed (note the page number in the lower-left corner of the project window).
2. Choose Edit > Select All (Cmd-A/Ctrl-A).

Grouping items

Grouped items remain associated and move as a unit until they're ungrouped. In this book, each illustration is grouped with its accompanying caption, and in some cases multiple picture/caption groups are themselves grouped together (nested) to form a larger group. Individual items in a group always remain editable.

To group items:

1. Choose the Item or Content tool.

2. Shift-click each item you wish to group. (Shift-click any selected item to deselect it.)
   or
   Position the cursor outside all the items to be included in the group, then drag a marquee around them. You need to drag over only a portion of all the items—just make sure to include at least one handle on each item.

3. Choose Item > Group (Cmd-G/Ctrl-G). A dotted line surrounds the grouped items **1**. Items stay on their original layers.

   Note: Use the Content tool to modify the size or contents of an item in a group. If the group is already selected, deselect it by clicking outside it, then with the Content tool, click the item you want to edit.

To move an item in a group:

1. Choose the Item or Content tool.

2. Hold down Cmd/Ctrl, click the item you wish to move, then drag **2**.

This method for removing an item from a group deletes the item from the layout altogether. To take an item out of a group without deleting it, see the following page.

To delete an item from a group:

1. Choose the Content tool.

2. Click the item to be deleted.

3. Choose Item > Delete (Cmd-K/Ctrl-K).

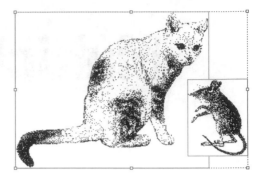

1 *A dotted **bounding box** surrounds a selected group.*

2 *To move an item within a group, **Cmd-drag/ Ctrl-drag** the item with the Content tool.*

Modifying group attributes

Depending on the items selected, you can perform many actions on a group, including changing the color of all items or applying a drop shadow to the group. Choose Item > Modify or check the tabs available on the Measurements palette. You can also resize, move, cut, copy, duplicate, anchor, and rotate an entire group.

Create Group; Move, Delete Grouped Item

1 *If you resize a group while holding down*
***Cmd-Option-Shift/Ctrl-Alt-Shift* ...**

To take an item out of a group without deleting it:

1. Choose the Content tool.

2. Click the item you want to take out of the group.

3. Press Cmd-D/Ctrl-D.

4. Reselect the item that's still in the group, then press Cmd-K/Ctrl-K.

TIP You can also choose Item > Ungroup, Shift-click the item you want to take out of the group (to deselect it), then choose Item > Group.

You can resize, move, cut, copy, duplicate, anchor, rotate, or recolor a whole group. To change a group's overall dimensions, angle, background color, or shade, or to apply a blend across a whole group, use Item > Modify > Group. Runaround options must be chosen individually for each item in a group (use the Content tool).

This method for resizing grouped items is a terrific timesaver. Frame widths and line weights won't change.

To resize a whole group:

1. Choose the Item tool, then click the group.

2. To resize the grouped items and their contents (text or picture) proportionally, drag a handle with Cmd-Option-Shift/Ctrl-Alt-Shift held down **1**–**2**.
or
To change the shape of the grouped items, but not their contents, drag a handle with no keys held down **3**.

To ungroup items:

1. Choose the Item tool, then click the group you want to ungroup.

2. Choose Item > Ungroup (Cmd-U/ Ctrl-U).

2 *...the items and their contents*
*will **resize proportionally**.*

3 *If you resize a group with **no** keys held down, the **items** (box or path) will reshape, but not their contents (text or picture).*

Resize Whole Group; Ungroup

Locking items

Locking is a safety feature that can be applied to any item and/or its contents to keep it from being modified. For example, we lock the position of items on our master pages—such as headers and footers—so they can't be moved manually.

To lock an item's position:

1. Choose the Item or Content tool.

2. Select the item to be locked (or select multiple items to be locked).

3. Choose Item > Lock > Position (F6) . Choose the same command again to unlock selected locked items.

TIP When you lock an item's position, the item can't be moved, resized, or deleted unless you unlock it.

When you lock a story, the text can't be edited or formatted. When you lock a picture, the picture can't be replaced or modified.

To lock an item's content: NEW

1. Choose the Content tool.

2. Select the item containing the text or picture to be locked.

3. Choose Item > Lock > Story or Item > Lock > Picture. Choose the same command again to unlock the contents.

Creating multiples

To duplicate an item:

1. Choose the Item or Content tool.

2. Select the item or group you want to duplicate .

3. Choose Item > Duplicate (Cmd-D/Ctrl-D) 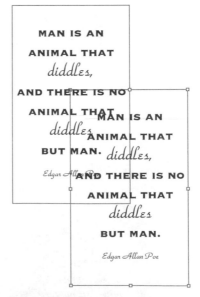. The default duplicate offset values are 1p6 to the right and 1p6 down. If you were using the Step and Repeat dialog box in the current work session, however, the last-used offsets from that dialog box will be applied instead of the default offsets (see the following page).

1 *The pointer changes to a **padlock** when it's over a locked story, picture, or item that is selected.*

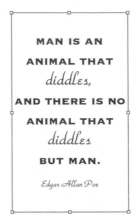
2 *Select the item to be duplicated, then choose Item > **Duplicate**.*

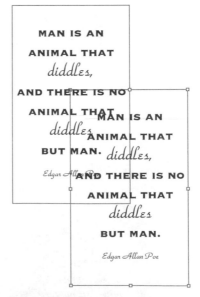
3 *A duplicate is made.*

Lock; Duplicate

1 *Select an item.*

2 *Enter values in the **Step and Repeat** dialog box.*

3 *The bunny was **duplicated** using these values: Repeat Count 3, Horizontal Offset 0, and Vertical Offset 7p.*

Using the Step and Repeat command, you can make multiple duplicates at one time and you can specify how far apart the duplicates will be from one another. The offset distance is calculated from the upper-left corner of each item (or the bounding box, in the case of a Bézier box, line, or text path). You can use this command to reproduce any kind of item or group (for example, you could generate multiple picture and caption groups in neat horizontal or vertical rows).

To step and repeat an item:

1. Choose the Item or Content tool.

2. Select an item or a group of items **1**.

3. Choose Item > Step and Repeat (Cmd-Option-R/Ctrl-Alt-R). **NEW**

4. In the Repeat Count field, enter the number of duplicates to be made (1–99) **2**.

5. Enter a Horizontal Offset value. Enter a minus sign before the value to step and repeat items to the left of the original. Enter 0 in this field to have the duplicates align along their left edges without moving horizontally.

6. Enter a Vertical Offset value. Enter a minus sign before the value to step and repeat items above the original. Enter 0 in this field to have the duplicates align along their top edges without moving vertically.

Enter positive values (or negative values) in both Offset fields to produce a stair-step arrangement.

7. Click OK **3**.

TIP If an alert appears, reduce the Repeat Count and/or Offset values so that the duplicate items will be able to fit within the confines of the pasteboard. That should do it.

Super Step and Repeat, an XTension that ships with QuarkXPress, works like the Step and Repeat command, except that it also lets you choose rotate, scale, skew, and shade values for the duplicates and an axis point for the transformation.

To rotate, scale, or skew copies of an item using Super Step and Repeat:

1. Choose the Item or Content tool.

2. Select one text box, picture box, text path, or line 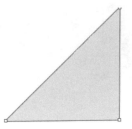. (Not a group—sorry!) To transform from a point on a Bézier, select that point now.

3. Choose Item > Super Step and Repeat.

4. In the Repeat Count field, enter the desired number of duplicates (1–100) 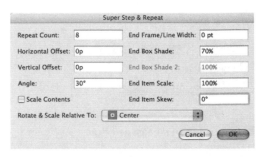.

5. In the Horizontal Offset field, enter the distance you want each copy to be offset on the horizontal *(x)* axis relative to the original.

6. In the Vertical Offset field, enter the distance you want each copy to be placed on the vertical *(y)* axis relative to the original.

   A positive horizontal value positions copies to the right of the original; a negative value positions copies to the left. A positive vertical offset value positions copies above the original; a negative value positions copies below. Enter 0 for both offset values to have the duplicate items land on top of the originals.

7. Intermediate duplicates, if any, will be assigned incremental angles, frame widths, line widths, shades, scale values, or skew values, depending on what end values are entered in the dialog box.  Do any of the following:

   Change the Angle to have each duplicate be rotated counterclockwise by that amount, relative to the original or the previous duplicate.

1 *Select an item.*

2 *Use the **Super Step & Repeat** dialog box for single or multiple **transformations**.*

3 *After using **Super Step and Repeat** to **rotate** copies of the item, using the settings shown above*

Not so super

1 *Select an item.*

Super Step & Repeat

Repeat Count:	5	End Frame/Line Width:	0 pt
Horizontal Offset:	4p	End Box Shade:	0%
Vertical Offset:	1p5	End Box Shade 2:	100%
Angle:	0°	End Item Scale:	200%
☑ Scale Contents		End Item Skew:	0°
Rotate & Scale Relative To:	▣ Center		

Cancel   OK

2 *From the **Rotate & Scale Relative To** menu, choose the point around or from which the item will be rotated or scaled.*

Not so super
Not so super
Not so super
Not so super
Not so super
Not so super

3 *These items resulted after using the **Super Step and Repeat** settings shown in the previous figure to create incrementally **larger** copies. Unfortunately, only absolute offset values can be entered—not a percentage—so the items are equidistant from each other and thus piled on top of each other.*

Power scaling

A number of XTensions offer powerful scaling tools, such as **Resize XT** from Vision's Edge.

(More illustrations on the following page)

Change the End Frame/Line Width or End Line Width for the final duplicate item. Each duplicate will be successively larger or smaller than the last, until the end width is reached. The current width of the selected line or frame is entered automatically; a different value can be entered. The end value must be able to fit on the resulting item(s).

Change the End Box Shade or End Line Shade (0%–100%) for the final duplicate box or line. Intermediate duplicates will be assigned incremental shades between the original and final shades. 100% is the default.

If your box contains a blend, change the End Box Shade 2 (0%–100%) for the background shade of the final box.

For a text path or line whose line style has multiple dashes or stripes, change the End Gap Shade (0%–100%) for the final line. Intermediate gaps will be assigned incremental shades.

Change the End Item Scale or End Line Scale (1%–1,000%) for the final duplicate. If you want frames on the duplicate box(es) to be scaled, enter a final End Frame/Line Width size.

Change the End Item Skew (–75° to 75°) for the skew angle of the final duplicate. Both the box and its contents will be skewed. This option is available for boxes only, not for paths or lines.

8. To scale the contents of the item (text or picture) along with the box or path, check Scale Contents.

9. From the Rotate & Scale Relative To menu, choose the axis point around or from which the item will be rotated, scaled, or skewed. If a point is chosen on a Bézier item, the Selected Point option will be available.

10. Click OK **1**–**3**. If you don't like the results, choose Undo or press Cmd-K/Ctrl-K to delete the duplicates.

1 *The original item*

2 *The settings used to produce figure 3*

Super Step & Repeat			
Repeat Count:	8	End Line Width:	4 pt
Horizontal Offset:	0p	End Line Shade:	100%
Vertical Offset:	0p	End Gap Shade:	100%
Angle:	20°	End Line Scale:	100%
		Scale Contents	
Rotate & Scale Relative To:	Center		

3 *The final items*

4 *The original item*

Super Step & Repeat			
Repeat Count:	6	End Frame/Line Width:	0 pt
Horizontal Offset:	0p	End Box Shade:	80%
Vertical Offset:	0p	End Box Shade 2:	100%
Angle:	30°	End Item Scale:	20%
☑ Scale Contents		End Item Skew:	0°
Rotate & Scale Relative To:	Center		

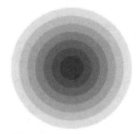

6 *The final items*

5 *The settings used to produce figure 6*

Vortex

7 *The original item*

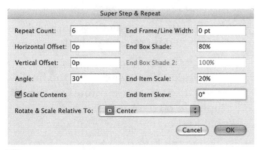

Super Step & Repeat			
Repeat Count:	15	End Frame/Line Width:	0 pt
Horizontal Offset:	0p	End Box Shade:	0%
Vertical Offset:	0p	End Box Shade 2:	100%
Angle:	20°	End Item Scale:	175%
☑ Scale Contents		End Item Skew:	0°
Rotate & Scale Relative To:	Top-Right		

8 *The settings used to produce figure 9*

9 *The final items*

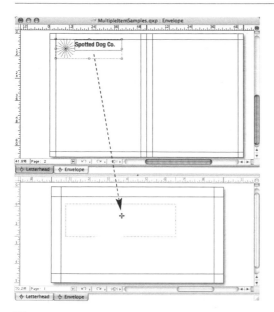

1 *Open two files, choose the **Item** tool, then drag an item from one project window into the other.*

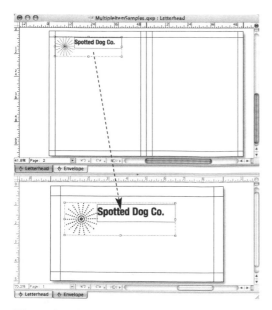

2 *A **duplicate** is made automatically as the item is dragged; the original item is unchanged.*

This method for copying items between layouts or projects doesn't use the Clipboard. If a layout contains user-created layers, read the second set of instructions on page 287!

To drag-copy an item between layouts or projects: NEW

1. To copy items between layouts in the same project, choose Window > Split Window > Horizontal (or Vertical). You can also choose Window > New Window and then reposition the two windows.
   or
   Open two QuarkXPress projects, and resize or move both project windows, if necessary, so you can see both of them on your screen.

2. Click a tab in the lower-left corner of each window to display the layouts you need.

3. Choose the Item tool (or hold down Cmd/Ctrl if the Content tool is chosen).

4. Click any unlocked item or group in the source layout and drag it to the target layout **1**–**2**.

5. If necessary, choose Window > NEW Split Window > Remove All to restore the project to a single window.

TIP Any style sheets, colors, H&Js, lists, and dashes & stripes applied to the item in the source project will also appear in the target project, unless there's a name conflict.

TIP If you drag-copy a box containing linked text, the text in that box will duplicate, along with any hidden overflow text from that point to the end of the story.

TIP Individual items can't be copied between projects in Thumbnails view, but entire pages can (see page 95).

In these instructions, you'll use the Clipboard commands to copy items from one page to another within the same layout, between different layouts within the same project, or between projects.

To copy and paste an item between pages, layouts, or projects:

1. Choose the Item tool.

2. Click the item or group to be copied.

3. Choose Edit > Copy (Cmd-C/Ctrl-C).

4. Click any page in any layout, in either the same project or another project. (To activate an open project, you can choose it from the bottom of the Window menu.)

5. With the Item tool still chosen, choose Edit > Paste (Cmd-V/Ctrl-V).

   Note: If you copy an item with the Item tool and paste it into a selected text box with the Content tool, the item will be anchored—not copied! (Anchoring is discussed on pages 199–202.)

TIP To store an item for reuse, put it in a library, and then retrieve it from the library whenever you need it. You'll save time in the long run. See Chapter 19.

To cut or copy contents (picture or text) between pages, layouts, or projects:

1. Choose the Content tool.

2. Click the picture or select the text you want to copy or cut **1**.

3. Choose Edit > Copy (Cmd-C/Ctrl-C) or Cut (Cmd-X/Ctrl-X).

4. Click another page in any layout in any project.

5. With the Content tool still chosen, click the picture box, text box, or text path that you want to paste into **2**.

6. Choose Edit > Paste (Cmd-V/Ctrl-V).

Paste in place

Normally, an item will paste into the center of the project window. If you want to paste an item or group onto any page in the exact *x/y* location from which it was copied, choose Edit > **Paste in place** (Cmd-Option-Shift-V/Ctrl-Alt-Shift-V). This command can also be chosen from the context menu.

1 *To copy and paste between layouts (or projects), select the text or contents (a text box from a letterhead is shown here) and copy it (**Edit > Copy**)...*

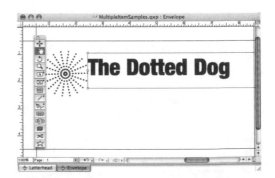

2 *...then, click in the new layout or project, and choose **Edit > Paste**. (We pasted the text box into an "Envelope" layout in the same project.)*

1 *Select two or more items.*

2 *Click one of the align buttons in the center of the Measurements palette's **Space/Align** tab.*

3 *The Align Left Edges button quickly lines up two selected items.*

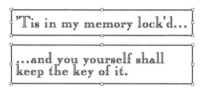

4 *To create this effect, we selected all the items at left, and then clicked **Align Horizontal Centers** and **Align Vertical Centers**.*

5 *You can align items with the page rather than with each other by clicking **Page Relative Mode** or **Spread Relative Mode** on the Space/Align tab of the Measurements palette.*

Positioning items

Intuitive buttons on the Space/Align tab of the Measurements palette let you align items or space them evenly. You can easily experiment with the buttons and undo any unexpected results. **NEW**

To align items:

1. Choose the Item or Content tool.
2. Shift-click the items to be aligned **1**.
   or
   Position the cursor outside the items to be aligned, then drag a marquee around them.
3. Choose Item > Space/Align (Cmd-,/ Ctrl-,) to display the Space/Align tab of the Measurements palette.
4. Click one of the alignment buttons on the right **2**–**4**.

TIP Choose Item > Space/Align > Repeat Last or press Cmd-Option-/(slash) or Ctrl-Alt-/(slash) to apply the last alignment used in the Space/Align tab. This does not work with the spacing commands.

You can also align items relative to the **NEW** edge of the page or the edge of the spread.

To align items with the page or the spread:

1. Choose the Item tool.
2. Shift-click the items to be aligned.
3. Choose Item > Space/Align (Cmd-,/ Ctrl-,) to display the Space/Align tab of the Measurements palette.
4. Click the Page Relative Mode or Spread Relative Mode button **5**.
5. Click one of the alignment buttons such as Align Vertical Centers.

TIP Once you change the mode, the Item > Space Align > Page Relative/Spread Relative submenu becomes active , from which you can choose an alignment command. The submenu displays keyboard shortcuts, too.

Align Items

In addition to aligning items with each other, you can space them evenly relative to one another or to the page.

To distribute items:

1. Choose the Item or Content tool.

2. Shift-click the items to be aligned .
or
Position the cursor outside the items to be aligned, then drag a marquee around them.

3. Choose Item > Space/Align (Cmd-,/ Ctrl-,) to display the Space/Align tab of the Measurements palette. **NEW**

4. In the Space field, enter the desired amount of space to be created between the selected items. Evenly, the default Space, equalizes the spacing based on the amount of space available. You can also offset items from one another. For example, to create a stair-step effect, distribute the items horizontally and add space.

5. Click one of the spacing buttons such as Space Horizontally or Space Vertical Centers **2**–**3**.

TIP If you don't get the intended result with Space/Align, simply press Cmd-Z/ Ctrl-Z to undo it and try again. You will quickly find out which buttons work best for your needs.

TIP The Space/Align submenu is also available on the context menu. Control-click/Right-click a selection to access the controls.

1 *Select **three** or more items.*

2 *Click one of the **spacing buttons** to space items evenly or according to the value you enter in the Space field.*

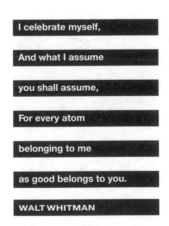

3 *With the **Space** field set to **Evenly,** we clicked **Space Vertical Centers** to distribute these text boxes.*

Distribute Items

1 *The first click selects the text box, which is in front.*

2 *A second click selects the black cat. A third click would select the gray cat in the back.*

3 *The light gray cat is the backmost object.*

4 *The backmost object is **moved** in its layer.*

QuarkXPress automatically places the most recently created item in front of all the other items in your layout, or in front of all the other items on the currently active layer if your layout contains more than one layer. On this page, you'll learn how to dig through stacking levels.

On the next page, you'll learn a simple way to restack objects within a layer. To learn how to move an object to a different layer altogether, see Chapter 16.

If you just want to practice this technique, pile a few items on top of one another before you begin.

To select an item that's behind another item:

1. Choose the Item or the Content tool— whichever tool you're going to use to edit the item you want to select. If you're going to move the item, choose the Item tool; if you're going to edit its contents, choose the Content tool.

2. Cmd-Option-Shift-click/Ctrl-Alt-Shift-click an item **1**. Repeat to select each item behind it under the pointer in succession **2**. After the backmost item under the pointer is selected, the next click will reselect the topmost item in that spot.

To move an item that's behind other items:

1. Choose the Item tool.

2. Keep clicking with Cmd-Option-Shift/ Ctrl-Alt-Shift held down. When you reach the item you want to move, drag immediately without releasing the mouse **3**–**4**. This little maneuver takes a bit of practice.

TIP To see an item as it looks in its layer as you drag it, including any text wrap, pause briefly before dragging.

You can use the Send To Back, Send Backward, Bring To Front, or Bring Forward command to change the stacking position of any item within its layer.

To move an item forward or backward:

1. Choose the Item or Content tool.

2. Click an item 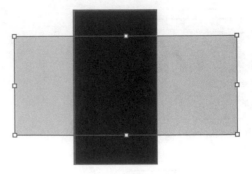.

3. To move the item all the way to the front or back of its layer, choose Item > Send To Back (Shift-F5) or Bring To Front (F5) or choose either command from the Send & Bring submenu on the context menu **2**.
   or
   To move the item backward one level at a time within its layer, press Option-Shift-F5/Ctrl-Shift-F5; or to bring it forward, press (Option-F5/Ctrl-F5). You could also choose either command from the Send & Bring submenu on the context menu. You may have to repeat the command several times to get the item to the desired stacking position.

TIP In Mac OS X, holding down Option makes the Send Backward or Bring Forward commands appear on the Item menu.

1 *A gray box (in **back** of a black box) is selected, as indicated by the eight handles, then **Item > Bring To Front** is chosen.*

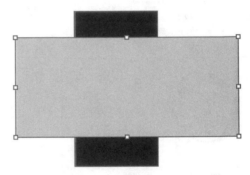

2 *The gray box is now **in front** of the black box.*

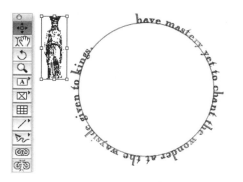

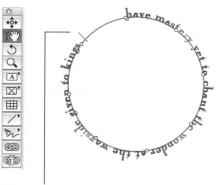

1 *With the **Item** tool, select and **cut or copy** the item you want to anchor.*

2 *Choose the **Content** tool, then click in the text to create an insertion point.*

3 *Choose **Edit > Paste.***

Anchoring items

You can paste (anchor) a line, picture box, text path, table, group, text box, or contentless box of any shape into any text box or onto any text path. Anchored items (inline graphics) function like characters in that they move with the text if the text reflows, and yet they remain fully editable.

Be sure to choose the right tools for each step of these instructions!

To anchor an item into text:

1. Choose the Item tool.
2. Select the item to be anchored **1** (for example, a table, a line, or perhaps an interesting graphic that you want to use as a drop cap).
3. Choose Edit > Copy (Cmd-C/Ctrl-C) or Cut (Cmd-X/Ctrl-X).
4. Choose the Content tool.
5. Click in a text box or on a text path to create an insertion point **2**.
6. Choose Edit > Paste (Cmd-V/Ctrl-V) **3**. You can do almost anything to an anchored item: reshape it, rotate it, recolor it, scale it, add a frame to it, change its contents (picture, text, or none), convert its shape, or apply a Runaround value to it (even a negative Runaround value!). Read more about anchored items on the next three pages.

Anchor Item into Text

To realign an anchored item:

1. Choose the Item tool.

2. Click an anchored item.

3. Display the Classic tab of the Measurements palette.

4. Click the Align With Text Ascent button to align the top of the anchored item with the ascent (top) of the character to its right –. Or click the Align With Text Baseline button to align the bottom of the anchored item with the baseline of the line of text in which it's anchored .

TIP To vertically offset a baseline-aligned anchored item, see the next page.

TIP Choose absolute—not auto—leading for text that contains an anchored box.

TIP You can change the Runaround for an item after it's anchored. Click it, then choose Item > Runaround (Cmd-T/Ctrl-T).

TIP You can use a hanging indent (Style > Formats) or the Indent Here command (Cmd-\/Ctrl-\) to make an anchored item hang outside the paragraph 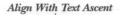.

To move an anchored item to a new location:

1. Choose the Content tool.

2. To select the anchored item, click just to the left of it, then press Shift-right arrow (or click to its right, then press Shift-left arrow).

3. Choose Edit > Cut (Cmd-X/Ctrl-X).

4. Click in a text box where you want the item to reappear, then choose Edit > Paste (Cmd-V/Ctrl-V).

TIP To move an anchored item from one location to the next within the *same* text box, select it, then drag its left edge. For this to work, Drag and Drop Text must be enabled in QuarkXPress (Edit, in Windows) > Preferences > Application > Input Settings.

Align With Text Ascent

1 *Align With Text Baseline*

*An anchored picture box, **Ascent** aligned*

3 *An anchored picture box, **Baseline** aligned*

4 *An **Indent here** command is used to make the anchored item **hang** outside the paragraph.*

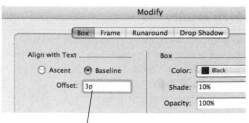

1 *Enter a number in this field to **offset** an anchored item that's baseline aligned.*

2 *Resizing an anchored picture box*

3 *The anchored box enlarged*

The Offset option, which shifts an anchored item upward or downward, is available only for items that are baseline aligned, not for items that are ascent aligned.

To offset an anchored item:

1. Choose the Item or Content tool.

2. Click an anchored item (not a text path).

3. Choose Item > Modify (Cmd-M/ Ctrl-M), then click the Box, Line, or Table tab (tab availability will vary depending on the type of object selected).

4. Enter a positive or negative Align with Text: Offset value **1**.

5. Click OK.

To resize an anchored item:

1. Choose the Item or Content tool. If the anchored item is a Bézier, turn off Item > Edit > Shape (Shift-F4/F10). (For Béziers, see Chapter 18.)

2. Click the anchored item.

3. For proportional scaling, Cmd-Option-Shift/Ctrl-Alt-Shift drag a handle (or drag an endpoint, if it's a line) **2**–**3**.

To delete an anchored item:

1. Choose the Item tool.

2. Click the item you want to delete.

3. Press Delete/Backspace.

TIP To do this another way, choose the Content tool, click just to the right of an anchored item (press the left or right arrow key to reposition the cursor), then press Delete/Backspace.

To create an unanchored copy of an anchored item:

Choose the Content tool, click the anchored item, then choose Item > Duplicate (Cmd-D/Ctrl-D).
or
Choose the Item tool, click the anchored item, choose Edit > Copy, click outside the text box, then choose Edit > Paste.

Offset, Resize, Delete, Copy Anchored Item

Drop anchor

To anchor selected text at its current location and convert it into a picture box at the same time, hold down Option/Alt and choose Style > Text to Box **1**–**3**.

1 *Standard text characters are selected.*

2 *Choosing Style >* **Text to Box** *with* **Option/Alt** *held down simultaneously converts the text into a picture box and anchors it at its current location.*

3 *We imported a picture into our anchored picture box.*

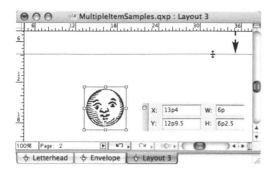

1 *Drag from a ruler to place a* **guide** *on a layout page or master page.*

Getting snappy

If you drag an item to a guide, the item will snap to the guide if View > **Snap to Guides** is checked **2**. Specify a **Snap Distance** in QuarkXPress (Edit, in Windows) > Preferences > Print Layout > General (6 pixels is the default).

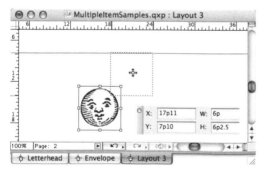

2 *An item will* **snap** *to a guide if it's dragged within the specified* **Snap Distance** *of the guide.*

Custom colors

The margin, ruler, and guide colors can be changed in QuarkXPress (Edit, in Windows) > Preferences > Application > **Display**.

Using guides

To position items precisely and consistently, use ruler guides or use the X and Y fields on the Measurements palette.

To create a ruler guide manually:

1. If the rulers aren't showing, choose View > Rulers (Cmd-R/Ctrl-R). And if the margin guides aren't showing, choose View > Guides (F7).

2. Drag a guide from the horizontal or vertical ruler onto a layout page or master page **1**. As you drag, the guide's location will be indicated in the X or Y field on the Measurements palette and by a marker on the other ruler.

TIP If you release the mouse over the pasteboard as you drag, the guide will extend across facing pages, if any, and onto the pasteboard.

TIP Ruler guides display in front of or behind items depending on whether Guides: In Front or Behind is chosen in QuarkXPress (Edit, in Windows) > Preferences > Print Layout > General.

TIP To make a guide visible only at or above the current zoom percentage, hold down Shift as you create the guide.

To remove manual ruler guides:

To remove *one* ruler guide, choose the Item tool, then drag the guide back onto the ruler (the pointer will be a double arrowhead). If the guide is over an item, hold down Cmd/Ctrl and drag with the Content tool; this works only if Guides: In Front is chosen in QuarkXPress (Edit, in Windows) > Preferences > Print Layout > General. You can also move a guide using either tool.

or

To remove *all* horizontal guides or *all* vertical guides from a page (not the pasteboard), make sure no pasteboard is showing between the edge of the page and that ruler, then Option-click/Alt-click the ruler.

The Guide Manager command creates a custom grid of non-printing margin guides. You can control how many guides are created as well as their placement.

To create guides using Guide Manager:

1. If you want the guides to appear on only one page, go to that page now. Guides can't be placed on a master page. If guides aren't showing, choose View > Guides (F7).

2. Choose Utilities > Guide Manager, then click the Add Guides tab 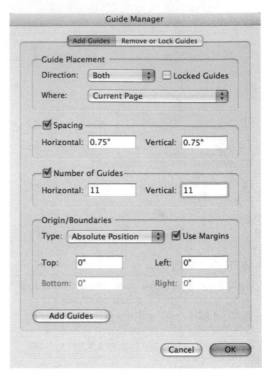. If the command isn't available, enable the Guide Manager XTension (see page 377).

3. From the Direction menu in the Guide Placement area, choose Horizontal, Vertical, or Both as the orientation for the guides.

4. *Optional:* Check Locked Guides to lock the new guides. They can be unlocked later.

5. From the Where menu, choose a location for the guides: Current Page, Current Spread, All Pages, or All Spreads. They can't be placed on a layer.

6. Do one or more of the following:

   To specify the interval between guides, check Spacing, then enter the desired interval in the Horizontal and Vertical fields. If no Spacing value is specified, the spacing will be calculated based on the Number of Guides values.

   If you don't want QuarkXPress to figure out how many guides to create, check Number of Guides, then enter Horizontal and/or Vertical values.

   From the Origin/Boundaries: Type menu, set the starting point of the grid: Choose Inset to inset the guides from the edges of the page/spread, then enter inset values; or choose Absolute Position, then specify a starting location

1 *Choose options in the **Add Guides** pane of the **Guide Manager** dialog box.*

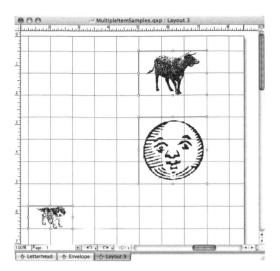

1 *Guides* *are used for positioning items.*

for the guides; or choose Entire Page/ Spread to have the grid originate from the upper-left corner of the page or spread.

7. *Optional:* If Where: Current Page or All Pages is chosen, you can check Use Margins to contain the grid within the current margin guides.

8. Click Add Guides **1**.

9. Click OK. You can reapply this command to add more guides.

To remove and/or lock/unlock Guide Manager guides:

1. Choose Utilities > Guide Manager.

2. Click the Remove or Lock Guides tab.

3. Under Remove Guides: Where **2**, choose which pages you want guides to be removed from: Current Page, Current Spread, All Pages, All Spreads, or All Pages & Spreads.

4. From the Direction menu, choose Horizontal, Vertical, or Both.

5. From the Locked menu, choose whether you want Locked, Unlocked, or Both types of guides to be removed.

6. Click Remove Guides. All Guide Manager guides will be removed—as well as any guides that you dragged onto the page manually!

7. Under Lock Guides: Where, choose which pages you want guides to be locked or unlocked on: Current Page, Current Spread, All Pages, All Spreads, or All Pages & Spreads.

8. From the Direction menu, choose Horizontal, Vertical, or Both.

9. Click Lock Guides or Unlock Guides.

10. Click OK.

2 *The Remove or Lock Guides options are in a separate pane in the Guide Manager dialog box.*

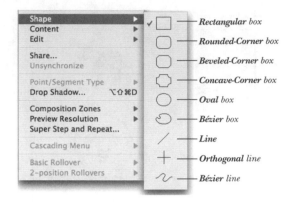

1 *An item can be converted into any shape on the Item > **Shape** submenu.*

Converting items

You can do more than convert a picture from one shape to another using the Shape submenu—you can also convert a standard picture box, text box, or content-less box into a Bézier box or convert any kind of picture box into a line. If you convert a text box into a line, it will become a text path.

Note: If you convert a picture box that contains a picture into a line (any of the last three icons on the Shape submenu), the picture will be deleted. A table can't be converted into anything.

To convert an item's shape:

1. Choose the Item or Content tool.

2. Click an item (don't select multiple items).

3. Choose a shape from the Item > Shape submenu **1**–**5**.

TIP To make the corners of any of the first four shapes found under the Shape submenu more or less convex, choose Item > Modify (Cmd-M/Ctrl-M), click the Box tab, then change the Corner Radius value (2 is the maximum).

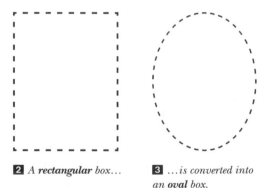

2 *A **rectangular** box…*　　**3** *…is converted into an **oval** box.*

> Dinner one night consisted of lamb chops, becoming heavy at times, with occasional ketchup. Periods of peas and baked potatoes were followed by grad-ual clearing, with a wonderful Jell-O setting in the west.
>
> ~Judi Barrett

4 *A **text box**…*

5 *…is converted into a **text path** by choosing the Line icon.*

1 *Choose* **Picture,** **Text,** *or* **None** *from the* **Item >** *Content submenu.*

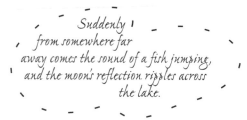

2 *A* **picture** *box...*

3 *...is converted into a* **text** *box (the text was added afterward).*

4 *A* **contentless** *box can contain a* **solid color** *or a* **blend,** *plus a* **frame**—*but that's all.*

You can make a box or text path contentless, or vice versa; change a picture box into a text box, or vice versa; or change a line into a text path. Any text or picture the item originally contained will be removed; a frame will remain. *Note:* A Bézier line or Bézier text path can't be converted into a picture box.

To convert the contents of table cells, see page 142.

You can apply a solid color, blend, or frame to a contentless box, but you can't fill it with text or a picture. Contentless boxes function strictly as decorative elements.

To convert an item's contents:

1. Choose the Item or Content tool.
2. Click a text box, picture box, contentless box, line, or text path.
3. Choose Picture, Text, or None from the Item > Content submenu **1**–**4**.
   or
   Control-click/Right-click and choose Content > Picture, Text, or None.
4. Click OK if a warning prompt appears.

Convert Item Contents

Design tips

Just as a composer creates a musical score or an artist paints a picture, you have to arrange all the elements on your page so the message is understood clearly by your audience. If the writing is poor, your copywriter has more work to do, but your readers or viewers will become weary of even the most skillful writing if the layout and typography are poor. Your audience doesn't have to be spellbound, but you do want to capture their attention long enough to get the message across. Here are a few suggestions:

- Let in some air. Leave a little **white space** around your text and pictures. How you do this depends on your subject matter. Use Text Inset values to add some air between a picture and its frame. Use ample gutters between columns (add delicate vertical rules for definition). Or gather elements up at the top of the page and leave the bottom of the page blank. Peaceful passages provide an important counterpoint to louder passages, and confident composers know how to play them off one another to their advantage.

- Use a **grid** as an underlying structure to organize elements. Whether the grid is obvious to your readers or not, it makes for a more pleasing and orderly page, and it simplifies the layout process. In fact, many designers still use pencil and paper to sketch out broad design ideas before they create a layout on the computer.

- **Break out** of the grid in select areas to add some punch. As an example, you could put thin rules around most of your pictures, then use a different type of picture with an irregular edge to add a more interesting, nonrectangular shape to the page.

- Just as composers juxtapose opposing forces to create what we call **good tension**—slow versus fast, complex versus simple, loud versus soft, percussive versus melodic, and so on—you can create good tension in a layout in many ways. For example, instead of plopping two medium-sized pictures smack in the middle of the page, put one large picture off to the side (let it bleed off) and a small picture in the opposing corner. Don't automatically stick everything in the center.

Elements that can be used to create pleasing tension include **scale** (large vs. small), **shape** (regular vs. irregular), **placement** (diagonal, vertical, and horizontal), **color** (raucous vs. subtle), and **shade** (light vs. dark).

- When you arrange multiples of a similar object (e.g., pictures and their accompanying captions), the result doesn't have to be static. Use **repetition** to your advantage to create **texture** or **rhythm.** But do align the objects carefully—misalignments can be jarring (use Super Step and Repeat to make copies of an object or group, or use Space/Align to align existing objects). Keep in mind the **overall** shape multiple items will form when they're grouped together. A good formation will have solidity and order. To see how the whole page looks, choose a small view size such as View > Fit in Window and turn guides off (View > Guides). This is the equivalent of squinting and lets you focus on the layout rather than individual items.

- And last but not least, don't forget to set type like a professional (Chapter 7 is chock-full of tips for setting professional-looking type). The little **details** matter as much as the broad strokes.

Pictures and Text

With my aversion to this cat, however, its partiality for myself seemed to increase. It followed my footsteps with a pertinacity which it would be difficult to make the reader comprehend. Whenever I

1 *We placed this cat-eating-mouse* **image**, *which has a Background of None, on top of a text box containing a poem. We had Quark give the image a* **clipping path** *determined by its non-white areas; the white areas are now transparent and the text behind the image shows through. We also told Quark to use nonwhite areas to determine the runaround, causing the text to follow the contours of the image. Finally, we added another text box on top of the image and assigned it a* **drop shadow**.

Pictures and text

There are many ways to combine text and pictures in QuarkXPress. For example, you can place a picture behind a text box that has a transparent or semitransparent background. Or you can have text wrap around the perimeter of a picture box, or wrap partially or completely around the irregular contours of the picture itself **1**.

QuarkXPress not only gives you control over how text wraps around a picture, it also lets you create editable clipping paths that control how much of a picture prints. If you have a picture with a white background, for example, you can tell the program not to print the background. A clipping path can even be created from an embedded path or alpha channel that was saved with a picture in another application.

In QuarkXPress 7, you can also add depth to your pages by applying drop shadows to text as well as to text and picture boxes. **NEW** Shadows can be cast by the outlines of the boxes themselves, or by the clipping paths that surround their contents.

Using Runaround

You can use either the Item > Modify dialog box or the Measurements palette to wrap text around an item.

To wrap text around an item:

1. The item the text is to wrap around must be on top of the text. It can be any kind of item (picture box, text box, contentless box, text path, Bézier shape, or table). To bring it forward, select it, then press Option-F5/Ctrl-F5 (or move it to a higher layer).

2. Choose the Item or Content tool.

3. Select the picture box.

4. Click the Runaround tab on the Measurements palette.
   or
   Choose Item > Runaround (Cmd-T/Ctrl-T).

5. Choose Item from the Type menu **1**.

6. To adjust the space between each side of a rectangular picture box and the text that's wrapping around it, enter Top, Left, Bottom, and Right Outset values. For other shapes, enter a single Outset value.

7. If you have used the Measurements palette to set Outset values, press Return/Enter **2**.
   or
   In the Modify dialog box, click Apply to preview the text wrap, then click OK.

   Note: If the item straddles two columns, text will wrap around all its sides; if it's within a column, text will wrap around just three of its sides. (For a complete wrap in the latter case, see page 218.)

TIP To choose default Runaround settings for any item creation tool, double-click the tool, click Modify, click Runaround, then choose settings.

TIP The Runaround value around a text path is calculated based on the path itself, not the text.

The color code

The **Margin** color (the default is blue) is also used to represent an item's bounding box in the Runaround and Clipping panes of the Modify dialog box. Similarly, the current **Ruler** guide color (the default is green) also represents the clipping path, and the current **Grid** color (the default is magenta) also represents the Runaround border. To change any of these colors, go to QuarkXPress (Edit, in Windows) > Preferences > Application > Display (Cmd-Option-Shift-Y/Ctrl-Alt-Shift-Y).

Outset values: Top, Left
Bottom, Right

1 *From the Type menu in the Runaround tab of the Measurements palette, choose Item.*

With my aversion to this cat, however, its partiality for myself seemed to increase. It followed my footsteps with a pertinacity which it would be difficult to make the reader comprehend. Whenever I sat, it would crouch beneath my chair, or spring upon my knees, covering me with its loathsome caresses. If I arose to walk it would get between my feet and thus nearly throw me down, or, fastening its long and sharp claws in my dress, clamber, in this manner, to my breast. At such times, although I longed to destroy it with a blow, I was yet withheld from so doing, partly by a memory of my former crime, but chiefly—let me confess it at once—by absolute *dread* of the beast...

This dread was not exactly a dread of physical evil—

2 *The picture box straddles two columns, so the text wraps completely around it.*

Leading you on

If Maintain Leading is checked in Preferences > Print Layout > Paragraph and an item is positioned within a column of text, the first line of text that's forced below the item will snap to the nearest leading increment. With Maintain Leading off, the text will touch the bottom of the item, offset only by that item's current Runaround value.

"Do you think it is said Pooh, "because ks. It is either Two might be, Wizzle, or zles and one, if so it ue to follow them." just a little anxious e animals in front of them were of Hostile Intent. And Piglet wished very much that his grandfather T.W.

1 *Before a clipping path is created, the white area around the photo* **prints.**

"Pooh!" said Piglet. "Do you think it is ar ," said Pooh, "because ks. It is either Two might be, Wizzle, or zles and one, if so it ue to follow them." s g just a little anxious now, three animals in front of them were of Hostile Intent. And Piglet wished very much that his grandfather T.W.

2 *A QuarkXPress* **clipping path** *is used to* **prevent** *the white area from printing. The text is still running behind the photo, though—it's not wrapping around it.*

"Pooh!" cried Piglet. "Do you think it is another Woozle?" "No," said Pooh, "because it makes different marks. It is either Two Woozles and one, as it might be, Wizzle, or Two, as it might be, Wizzles and one, if so it is, Woozle. Let us continue to fol-
A.A. Milne

3 *Finally,* **Runaround** *is turned on with Type:* **Same As Clipping** *selected to force the text to wrap around the* **image.**

Using clipping paths

A clipping path is a mechanism that controls which parts of a picture **display** and **print** **1**–**3**. Areas of the picture within the clipping path are visible and will print; areas outside the clipping path are transparent and won't print. You may already know how to create a clipping path in another application, such as Adobe Photoshop. In that type of clipping path, the clipping information is saved in the picture itself. In QuarkXPress, when you use a clipping path that was saved with the original picture in another application, it's called an "embedded path."

Clipping paths in QuarkXPress work a little bit differently. They are also used to control which parts of an image will print, but they don't permanently clip areas of the image that extend outside it. Clipping path information in QuarkXPress is saved with the project, not in the image itself. This means that you can create a different clipping path for each instance in which you use an image. If you *want* to reuse a picture and its clipping path, on the other hand, you can simply drag and drop the picture box from one project to another; a copy will appear in the target project.

Another compelling reason to have QuarkXPress generate a clipping path is that as you reshape it or choose different settings for it, you'll be able to see immediately how it looks in your layout. What's more, you can adjust the shape of a clipping path to your heart's delight using any technique that you'd use to adjust a Bézier path.

You can have QuarkXPress create a clipping path based on the shape or silhouette of a picture, or you can create a custom path. QuarkXPress can also generate a new, editable clipping path based on any alpha channel (saved selection) or embedded path, provided the channel or path is saved with the picture file in its original application (e.g., Adobe Photoshop).

Clipping Paths

Runaround vs. clipping, in a nutshell

A clipping path controls which parts of a picture **display** and **print.** The Runaround feature controls how **text wraps** around a picture. The runaround text wrap or clipping path can be controlled by any of the following parameters 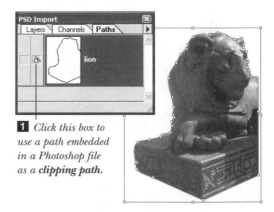–:

Item: The edge of the picture box.

Embedded Path or **Alpha Channel:** An embedded alpha channel or path that was created and saved with the picture in another application. You can use an path embedded in an imported picture if it was saved in any of these formats: PSD, TIFF, EPS, BMP, JPEG, PCX, or PICT. You can also use an alpha channel in a PSD or TIFF.

Non-White Areas: The non-white edge of a picture (the silhouette of an image, if it has a white background).

Picture Bounds: The picture's rectangular bounding box (not the QuarkXPress picture box).

To make matters even more confusing, for each Type there are additional options for controlling the placement of the clipping path or the runaround text wrap.

And for Runaround, there's an additional option: **Auto Image.** With Auto Image chosen, text will wrap around the edge of the image itself, not its bounding box. The runaround is created from the original, high-resolution image (not the preview), using Bézier curves, and works effectively on an image that has a clearly defined border and a flat, light background. It creates a combined, uneditable clipping and runaround path in one step (the edit clipping and runaround functions aren't available).

Choosing Type: **None** in the Runaround pane turns off Runaround altogether.

Though they may at first seem confusing, the Runaround and Clipping options offer a lot of control and flexibility, so they're worth spending some time to learn.

QuarkXPress and Photoshop

QuarkXPress 7 can use any path embedded in an Adobe Photoshop file as a clipping path. In the PSD Import palette, display the Paths pane and click in the second column next to the path you want to use **1**.

A Photoshop **vector mask** will display properly in QuarkXPress, but to have QuarkXPress make an editable clipping path from it, choose Non-White Areas as the clipping Type.

1 *Click this box to use a path embedded in a Photoshop file as a **clipping path**.*

2 *The **Type** options in the **Clipping** tab of the **Measurements** palette*

3 *The **Type** options in the **Runaround** tab of the **Measurements** palette*

1 *Choose a clipping path* **Type**.

The **Information** *area displays the number of alpha channels and embedded paths in the picture file, and the number of points that will be created for the QuarkXPress clipping path.*

2 *Clipping Type:* **Item**—*the clipping path conforms to the box.*

3 *Clipping Type:* **Embedded Path**—*the clipping path conforms to a path that was saved with the image in its original application.*

To create a clipping path:

1. Import an EPS, TIFF, BMP, PCX, or PICT file into a rectangular picture box. For this first attempt, try using an image that has a white background.

2. To layer a picture, make sure its box has a background of None. (Select the box, click the Background Color button 🔳 on the Colors palette, then click None.)

3. Choose Item > Clipping (Cmd-Option-T/Ctrl-Alt-T).

4. As you choose from the Type menu the green line in the preview window represents the chosen clipping path, **1**:

(Choose Item to turn off the clipping path function **2**. The picture will be cropped only by the picture box.)

Choose Embedded Path to create a clipping path based on a clipping path that was saved with the picture in another application **3**. Choose Alpha Channel to create a clipping path based on the nonblack parts of an alpha channel that was saved with the picture in an image-editing program. *Note:* If the picture was saved with more than one alpha channel or path, choose the desired channel or path name from the Alpha or Path menu.

Choose Non-White Areas to create a clipping path that follows the contours of the actual image and ignores nonwhite areas of the picture. The white areas have to be either close to white (e.g., very light gray) or absolute white for this to work.

Choose Picture Bounds to have the path conform to the rectangular outer boundary of the picture (its bounding box) (**1**, next page). If Restrict To Box is unchecked, any areas of the picture that the picture box is cropping will become visible and may obscure items behind them.

(Continued on the following page)

Create Clipping Paths

5. As you choose any of these *optional* settings, click Apply at any time to preview the current settings in the layout:

Click Crop To Box, if available, to have the clipping path stop at the edge of the box.

Click Rescan to restore the original path.

Check Invert to switch the cropped and visible areas **2**. This option isn't available when the Item or Picture Bounds Type is chosen.

Check Outside Edges Only for an Alpha Channel, Embedded Path, or Non-White Areas (not Item or Picture Bounds) clipping path if the picture contains a blank hole or holes where the background white shows through, and you don't want the clipping path to include them. With Outside Edges Only unchecked, an additional clipping path will be created for each hole **3**.

Check Restrict To Box to have only areas of the picture inside the picture box display and print (**1**–**2**, next page). Uncheck to let the entire picture display and print.

With any Type option except Item chosen, you can further expand or contract the clipping path to print more or less of the picture by entering a positive or negative value, respectively, in the Outset field. For Type: Picture Bounds, enter Top, Left, Bottom, and Right values. For Type: Embedded Path or Alpha Channel, the Outset value will expand or contract the entire clipping path relative to the original path or alpha channel. For the Non-White Areas type of clipping path, the Outset value will expand or contract the entire clipping path relative to the original nonwhite areas (**1**–**2**, page 216).

6. Choose Tolerance settings for an Alpha Channel or Non-White Areas type of clipping path:

1 *Clipping Type:* **Picture Bounds**—*the clipping path conforms to the outer perimeter of the image (its own bounding box).*

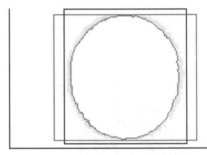

2 *Clipping Type:* **Non-White Areas** *with the* **Invert** *option on—only pixels in the outer fringe will print.*

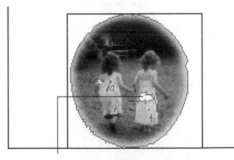

3 *Clipping Type:* **Non-White Areas** *with* **Outside Edges Only** *off—the clipping path or paths surround any non-white areas in the image.*

 Clipping Type: **Picture Bounds** *with* **Restrict To Box** *on—only areas of the picture that are inside the picture box will print.*

He trotted along happily, and by-and-by he crossed the stream and came to the place where his friends-and-relations lived. There seemed to be even more of them about than usual this morning, and having nodded to a hedgehog or two, with whom he was too busy to shake hands, and having said, "Good morning, good morning," importantly to some of the others, and "Ah, there you are," kindly, to the smaller ones, he waved a paw at them over his shoulder, and was gone; leaving such an air of excitement and I-don't-know-what behind him, that several members

2 *Clipping Type:* **Picture Bounds** *with* **Restrict To Box** *off—areas outside the picture box will print, even if they overlap the text.*

He trotted along happily, and by-and-by he crossed the stream and came to the place where tions lived. There seemed to be more of them about than usual morning, and having nodded hedgehog or two, with whom he was busy to shake hands, and having "Good morning, good morning," im tantly to some of the others, and there you are," kindly, to the sm ones, he waved a paw at them ove shoulder, and was gone; leaving such an air of excitement and I-don't-know-what behind him, that several members

For an Alpha Channel clipping path, the Noise value (0–288 pt.) is the minimum size an area near the border of an alpha channel must be to be included in the clipping path (**3**–**4**, next page). Adjust the Noise value to exclude tiny, extraneous blobs in the background from the clipping path.

For an Alpha Channel or Non-White Areas clipping path, Smoothness (0–100) makes the path more or less smooth by adding or decreasing points (**5**–**6**, next page). The lower the Smoothness value, the more points the clipping path will contain; the higher the value, the fewer points the path will contain and the less precisely its shape will match that of the image. A low Smoothness could cause output problems, but the program can adjust this setting automatically during printing, if need be. You may need to play with this to achieve the optimal setting.

Threshold works with an Alpha Channel or Non-White Areas clipping path (**1**–**2**, page 217). It controls what percentages of gray on the alpha channel will be treated as white (and not mask the picture) and what percentages will be treated as black (and mask parts of the picture). At a Threshold setting of 10%, for example, gray values between 0% and 10% will be treated as white; gray values between 11% and 100% will be treated as black and will act as a mask. At a Threshold setting of 40%, more gray values will be treated as white, and less of the picture will be masked. For the Non-White Areas type of clipping path, the opposite is true: The Threshold is the percentage a color can be darker than white before it will be left outside the clipping path and thus won't print.

7. Click Apply, then click OK. If you'd like to reshape the clipping path, follow the instructions on page 219.

(Illustrations on the following two pages)

Create Clipping Path

1 *Clipping Type:* **Non-White Areas, Outset -15**—*the clipping path shrinks slightly inward.*

2 *Clipping Type:* **Non-White Areas, Outset 15**—*the clipping path expands slightly outward.*

3 *Clipping Type:* **Non-White Areas** *at the default* **Noise** *setting of* **2 pt.**—*the clipping path includes extraneous pixels outside the oval.*

4 *Clipping Type:* **Non-White Areas, Noise 30 pt.** —*the extraneous blobs aren't included in the clipping path.*

5 *Clipping Type:* **Non-White Areas** *at the default* **Smoothness** *setting of* **2 pt.**—*the clipping path has many points, and hugs the image precisely. (To display the points on the path, choose Item > Edit > Clipping Path.)*

6 *Clipping Type:* **Non-White Areas, Smoothness 75 pt.**—*here the clipping path is smoother, but it's less accurate.*

Create Clipping Path

1 *Clipping Type:* ***Non-White Areas, Threshold 2*** —*the clipping path includes the gray background.*

2 *Clipping Type:* ***Non-White Areas, Threshold 10*** —*the clipping path ignores the gray background.*

Runaround and clipping: How they work together

If different Runaround and Clipping Types are chosen for the same picture, the text won't wrap at the edge of the picture. For example, if Picture Bounds is chosen as the Runaround Type, and Alpha Channel or Embedded Path is chosen as the Clipping Type (and assuming the picture's channel or path is smaller than the picture bounds), there will be a buffer area between the clipped picture and the text wrap.

If the Non-White Areas option is chosen for a picture as both the Runaround and the Clipping Type, text will wrap to the edge of a silhouetted image, plus or minus the current Outset width.

TIP To force text to flow into any holes in a picture where the white background shows through, uncheck the Outside Edges Only option in both the Clipping and Runaround panes.

TIP Don't wrap text *inside* a clipping path unless the text or picture's contrast has been carefully adjusted to ensure that the type is readable.

Setting the table

With the Item tool and a table selected, you can choose Item > Runaround (Cmd-T/Ctrl-T) and enter Runaround values for the whole table. You still can't choose Clipping values for table cells— at least not yet (hint, hint to the Quark people).

(Illustrations continue on the following page)

Runaround and Clipping

Here you'll be making text wrap around an image—not around an item's outer edge.

To wrap text around a picture:

1. Choose the Item or Content tool.

2. Select a picture box, and make sure it's in front of the text box. If it's not, Control-click/Right-click and choose Send & Bring > Bring Forward (or move it to a higher layer).

3. Display the Runaround tab of the Measurements palette.
or
Choose Item > Runaround (Cmd-T/Ctrl-T).

4. Choose Type: Non-White Areas **1**.
or
Choose Type: Same As Clipping to have the text runaround conform to a QuarkXPress clipping path and utilize all the options that were chosen for that clipping path. To edit this type of wrap, edit the clipping path (see the next page).

5. Enter an Outset value in points to adjust the space between the picture and the surrounding text. Try between 5 and 10 pt. If you're using the dialog box, click Apply to preview.

6. Press Return/Enter (palette) or click OK (dialog box).

7. Press Cmd-Option-.(period)/Shift-Esc, if necessary, to force a screen redraw.

TIP To run text inside the holes of a picture, choose Non-White Areas for the runaround Type and uncheck Outside Edges Only **2**.

TIP *Beware!* If Picture Bounds is chosen as the Clipping Type and Non-White Areas is chosen as the Runaround Type, text will wrap to the edge of the image, but it may be obscured by the opaque background of the picture. That's because the edge of a picture box usually doesn't match up with the picture's bounding box.

NEW

1 *You can make text run **completely** around a picture within the same column, but the text will be tiring to read, so don't use this option if you need to convey important information.*

2 *It's possible to flow text into the white spaces within a picture.*

Wrap around an item

To wrap text completely around the bounding box of an object, click the object, then in the Text tab of the Measurements palette, check Run Text Around Sides. We don't really recommend doing this, though, unless you're using the text as an abstract pattern, because the text will be very hard to follow.

*Reshape a clipping path to change which parts of a picture will **print.***

1 *Option-click/Alt-click a line segment to add a point.*

*Hold down **Spacebar** to suspend redraw and rewrap as you reshape a runaround or clipping path.*

2 *Option-click/Alt-click a point to delete it.*

> "Pooh!" cried Piglet. "Do you think it
> er Woozle?" "No," said Pooh, "because
> different marks. It is either Two Woo
> one, as it might be, V
> Two, as it might be
> and one, if so it is.
> Let us continue t
> them." So they v
> feeling just a little
> now, in the case the t

*Reshape a runaround path to change how text **wraps** around a picture.*

3 *Dragging a segment*

> "Pooh!" cried Piglet. "Do you think it i
> er Woozle?" "No," said Pooh, "because
> different marks. It is either Two Woo
> one, as it m
> Wizzle, or T
> might be, Wiz
> one, if so it is,
> Let us continue t
> them." So they went
> ing just a little anxic

4 *The text rewraps.*

Note: QuarkXPress generates a clipping path based on the original, high-resolution picture file. When you manually edit a clipping path, however, if you work off a low-resolution screen preview, your edits won't be precise. To work off the high-resolution screen preview, choose Item > Preview Resolution > Full Resolution, and choose View > Show Full Res Previews (if this option is already chosen, the menu option will be Hide Full Res Previews).

To reshape a runaround or clipping path:

1. Choose the Item or Content tool.

2. Click a picture that has a clipping path or one of these Runaround types: Embedded Path, Alpha Channel, Non-White Areas, or Picture Bounds.

3. Choose Item > Edit > Runaround (Option-F4/Ctrl-F10).
   or
   Choose Item > Edit > Clipping Path (Option-Shift-F4/Ctrl-Shift-F10).

4. Use any of the techniques that you'd normally use to reshape a Bézier path (see pages 312–324) **1**–**4**. You can add or delete an anchor point; drag a point, segment, or control handle; or convert an anchor point from corner to curved (or vice versa).

   Beware! If you edit a clipping path and then reopen the Clipping pane, the clipping Type will be listed as User-Edited Path. If you choose a different Type at this point and click OK, you'll *lose* your custom path edits!

5. When you're done editing a runaround path, choose Item > Edit > Runaround again (Option-F4/Ctrl-F10). When you're done editing a clipping path, choose Item > Edit > Clipping Path again (Option-Shift-F4/Ctrl-Shift-F10).

TIP To force the screen to redraw, press Cmd-Option-. (period)/Shift-Esc.

Wrapping text inside a hidden picture isn't something that you're going to do day in and day out, but it's a fun technique for special occasions.

To wrap text inside a hidden picture:

1. Choose the Item or Content tool, then click a silhouetted image on a solid white or off-white background .

2. Make sure the picture box is in front of the text box. If necessary, Control-click/Right-click and choose Send & Bring > Bring To Front or move the picture box to a higher layer.

   Also make sure the picture box completely covers the text box; otherwise the text will be visible within the picture's clipping path and around the edge of the picture box.

3. Display the Clipping tab of the Measurements palette and choose Non-White Areas from the Type menu and check Invert.

4. Click the Runaround tab and choose Same As Clipping from the Type menu.

   If necessary, press Cmd-Option-. (period)/Shift-Esc to force the screen to redraw **2**.

   Note: If the edge of the picture is showing (as in **2**), but you don't want it to print, click the picture, choose Item > Modify > Box, then check Suppress Output. It will still display onscreen, but it won't print.

TIP Choose a small point size and justified horizontal alignment for the type.

TIP You can also use the Clipping and Runaround panes of the Item > Modify dialog box for this task.

1 *Click a picture that has a white background.*

brain
n. **1** an organ of soft nervous tissue contained in the skull of vertebrates, functioning as the coordinating centre of sensation, and of intellectual and nervous activity. **2** (usu. in *pl.*; prec. by *the*) *colloq.* **a** the cleverest person in a group. **b** a person who originates a complex plan or idea. brain *n.* **1** an organ of soft nervous tissue contained in the skull of vertebrates, functioning as the coordinating centre of sensation, and of intellectual and nervous activity. **2** (usu. in *pl.*;

2 *The text is wrapping inside the clipping path instead of outside it.*

Shadow

1 *The **original** text*

Shadow

2 *A drop shadow is applied (the background of the box is 100% White).*

Shadow

3 *The background of the text box is changed to None (and the frame is removed), so now the drop shadow applies to the text.*

Shadow

4 *The angle of the drop shadow is changed to 100°, the distance to .5", and the skew to −25°.*

Let the shadows fall where they may...

Applying drop shadows

NEW

In QuarkXPress 7, you can add a feathered drop shadow to any text, box, line, table, group, or Composition Zone. Drop shadows are live, and adapt to any changes you make in the parent object.

Drop shadows behave differently depending on the type of object they're applied to:

Items: If the item has a background color, the shadow is applied to the overall shape of the item. If the item's background color is None, the drop shadow is applied to the item's contents (picture or text). Does the item have a frame? If so, the frame gets a shadow, too.

Pictures: If a picture has a clipping path or an alpha mask and the background color of its box is set to None, the drop shadow will follow the shape of the clipping path or mask.

Text: The drop shadow is applied to text if the opacity of the text box background is less than 100%. The shadow applies to all of the text in the box or on the text path.

Groups and **Composition Zones:** A drop shadow applied to a group follows the outline of the entire group (but individual members of the group can also have their own shadows).

To add a drop shadow to an item:

1. Select an item **1**.
2. Click the Drop Shadow tab on the Measurements palette.
   or
   Choose Item > Modify (Cmd-M/Ctrl-M) and click the Drop Shadow tab.
3. Check Apply Drop Shadow and choose from the options provided (see next page).
4. If you're using the dialog box, click OK **2**–**4**.

Drop Shadows

Adjusting drop shadows to taste

You'll find this generous array of controls **1**–**3** on the Drop Shadow tab of the Measurements palette and pane of the Modify dialog box:

Angle: The apparent direction of the shadow's light source (–180° to 180°). With Angle checked, you can also check **Synchronize Angle** to apply the same angle to all the other drop shadows in the same layout.

Distance: The distance the shadow is offset from the object to which it is applied.

Blur: The fuzziness of the edge of the drop shadow (0"–2"). The higher the value, the blurrier the edge of the shadow.

Scale: The size of the shadow relative to the item to which it is applied (0%–1000%).

Skew: The angle at which the shadow is tilted from the vertical (–75° to 75°).

Color, Shade, Opacity: Color characteristics of the drop shadow, using the same controls as are found on the Colors palette.

Inherit Item's Opacity: If checked, the shadow will echo the opacity characteristics of the item to which it is applied.

Item Knocks Out Drop Shadow: If checked, the drop shadow won't be visible behind areas of an item that have an opacity of less than 100%.

Multiply Drop Shadow: If checked, the drop shadow's color will be combined with the background color(s) using multiply blending mode, resulting in a darker shadow. Check for black shadows; leave unchecked for shadows of other colors.

Runaround Drop Shadow: If checked, the drop shadow will be taken into account if text is wrapped around the item.

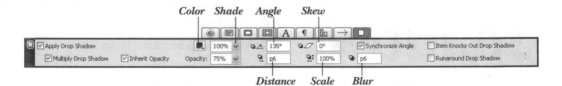

1 *The **Drop Shadow** tab of the Measurements palette*

2 *A text box with a background color. The default drop shadow is applied, and it appears at the edge of the box.*

3 *With the background of the same text box changed to None, now the drop shadow appears behind the text.*

Lines 12

Need more than one of an item?

■ Use the Duplicate shortcut (Cmd-D/Ctrl-D). Or if you want to control where the duplicates land, use Item > Step & Repeat.

■ After you draw a line with a line tool, the tool automatically deselects. To keep a line tool selected so as to draw multiple lines, Option-click/Alt-click the tool on the Tools palette. When you're finished using it, choose a different tool.

1 *Choose the* **Orthogonal Line** *tool, then drag horizontally or vertically.*

2 *Choose the* **Line** *tool, then drag in any direction.*

Drawing lines

The line creation tools produce horizontal, vertical, and diagonal straight lines and arrows to which a variety of styles, endcaps, colors, and opacities (new in QuarkXPress 7) can be applied. Using the Dashes & Stripes command, which is covered in this chapter, you can create custom line styles for use with the line tools, the Frame command, or the paragraph Rules command. In QuarkXPress 7, you can also apply drop shadows to lines. **NEW**

Note: To place rules under type, use the paragraph Rules feature (see pages 112–114). To anchor a line, see page 199. The Bézier Line, Freehand Line, Line Text-Path, and other Bézier tools are discussed in Chapter 18.

To draw a straight horizontal or vertical line:

1. Choose the Orthogonal Line tool.╋'

2. Drag the crosshair icon horizontally, vertically, or at a multiple of 45° **1**.

To draw a straight line at any angle:

1. Choose the Line tool./'

2. Drag the crosshair icon in any direction **2**.

TIP Hold down Shift while drawing a line to constrain it to an increment of 45°.

TIP To choose preferences for a line tool, such as its default width, style, or color, double-click the tool to open the Tools pane of the Tools Preferences dialog box, click Modify, then change any of the settings.

Modifying lines

To change the width of a line:

1. Choose the Item or Content tool.

2. Click a line (Bézier or other).

3. Press Cmd-Option-Shift->/Ctrl-Alt-Shift-> to widen the line, or press the < key (while holding the same modifiers) to reduce the line width in 1-point increments. Omit the Option/Alt key to change the line width to preset increments (Hairline, 1, 2, 4, 6, 8, or 12 pt).

   or

   Press Cmd-Shift-\/Ctrl-Shift-\. The Item > Modify dialog box will open with the Line pane active, with the Line Width field selected automatically. Enter the desired width (you don't have to type the "pt"), then click OK.

   or

   Choose Style > Width and select an option from the submenu.

To restyle a line using the Measurements palette:

1. Choose the Item or Content tool.

2. Click a line (Bézier or other).

3. Click the Classic tab on the Measurements palette and do any of the following **1**–**3**:

   Change the color of the line using the Color and Shade menus.

   Change the line's transparency using the Opacity menu.

   Enter a Width value (.001–864 pt.) or choose a preset width from the menu.

   Choose from the Style menu. (To create custom line styles, see pages 227–228.)

   Choose an arrowhead from the right-most menu.

TIP You can Control-click/Right-click a line and choose from the Line Style, Arrowheads, Width, Color, Shade, or Opacity submenu. These submenus are also found on the Style menu. For more on adding color to lines, see page 270.

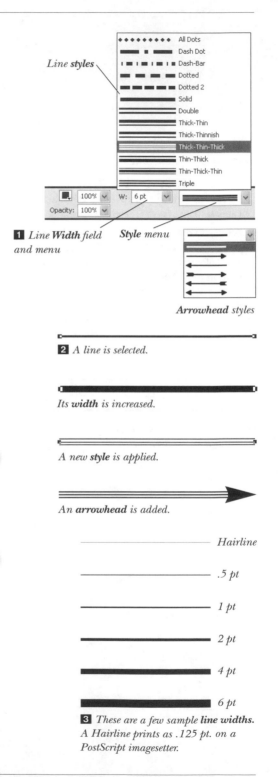

Line styles

1 *Line Width field and menu*   *Style menu*

Arrowhead styles

2 *A line is selected.*

Its width is increased.

A new style is applied.

An arrowhead is added.

Hairline

.5 pt

1 pt

2 pt

4 pt

6 pt

3 *These are a few sample line widths. A Hairline prints as .125 pt. on a PostScript imagesetter.*

Change Line Width or Style

Hidden force

You can use a non-printing line to force text runaround and create an offbeat text shape . Click a line, bring it to the front, choose Item > Modify, click the Line tab, check Suppress Output, click the Runaround tab, choose Type: Item, then specify an Outset value.

Diffusing, dropping, sideways-darting, in tiny showers of gold...

Diffusing, dropping, sideways-darting, in tiny showers of gold...

The line printed with Suppress Output checked

1

A line forces text to align on a diagonal.

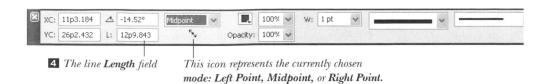

2 *Drag an **endpoint** to resize a line.*

To shorten or lengthen a line manually:

1. Choose the Item or Content tool.

2. Click a line.

3. Drag an endpoint to lengthen or shorten the line **2**. Option-Shift-drag/ Alt-Shift-drag to preserve the line's angle as you change its length.

To shorten or lengthen a line using the Measurements palette:

1. Choose the Item or Content tool.

2. Click a line.

3. From the mode menu on the Classic tab of the Measurements palette **3**, choose which point you want the line to be measured from: Left Point (the beginning of the line), Midpoint, or Right Point.

4. In the Length (L) field on the Measurements palette, enter the desired length **4**.

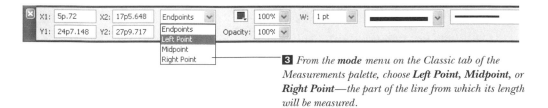

X1:	5p.72	X2:	17p5.648	Endpoints		100%	W:	1 pt
Y1:	24p7.148	Y2:	27p9.717	Endpoints	Opacity:	100%		
				Left Point				
				Midpoint				
				Right Point				

3 *From the **mode** menu on the Classic tab of the Measurements palette, choose **Left Point, Midpoint,** or **Right Point**—the part of the line from which its length will be measured.*

XC:	11p3.184	△	-14.52°	Midpoint		100%	W:	1 pt
YC:	26p2.432	L:	12p9.843		Opacity:	100%		

4 *The line **Length** field* *This icon represents the currently chosen mode: **Left Point, Midpoint,** or **Right Point.***

5 *A line being moved*

To move a line manually:

1. Choose the Item or Content tool.

2. Drag any part of a line other than an endpoint **5**.

To change the angle of a line:

1. Choose the Item or Content tool, then click a line.

2. Drag either handle. To snap a non-orthogonal line to an increment of 45° from the original angle, hold down the Shift key **1**.
   or
   On the Classic tab of the Measurements palette, choose Left Point, Midpoint, or Right Point, then change the angle value **2**.
   or
   Choose the Rotate tool,↺ press to establish an axis point, drag away from the line to create a lever, then drag clockwise or counterclockwise.

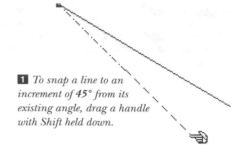

1 *To snap a line to an increment of 45° from its existing angle, drag a handle with Shift held down.*

To reposition a line using the Measurements palette:

1. Choose the Item or Content tool, then click a line.

2. On the Classic tab of the Measurements palette, choose from the mode menu the part of the line from which its position will be measured **3**–**4**.

3. Change the X and/or Y values. You can use math (add or subtract) in any field.

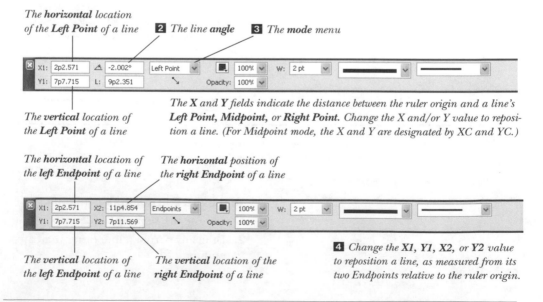

*The **horizontal** location of the **Left Point** of a line*   **2** *The line **angle***   **3** *The **mode** menu*

| X1: | 2p2.571 | ⊿ | -2.002° | Left Point | ▾ | ▣ | 100% | ▾ | W: | 2 pt | ▾ |
| Y1: | 7p7.715 | L: | 9p2.351 | ↘ | | Opacity: | 100% | ▾ | | | |

*The **vertical** location of the **Left Point** of a line*

*The **X** and **Y** fields indicate the distance between the ruler origin and a line's **Left Point, Midpoint,** or **Right Point.** Change the X and/or Y value to reposition a line. (For Midpoint mode, the X and Y are designated by XC and YC.)*

*The **horizontal** location of the **left Endpoint** of a line*   *The **horizontal** position of the **right Endpoint** of a line*

| X1: | 2p2.571 | X2: | 11p4.854 | Endpoints | ▾ | ▣ | 100% | ▾ | W: | 2 pt | ▾ |
| Y1: | 7p7.715 | Y2: | 7p11.569 | ↘ | | Opacity: | 100% | ▾ | | | |

*The **vertical** location of the **left Endpoint** of a line*   *The **vertical** location of the **right Endpoint** of a line*

4 *Change the **X1, Y1, X2,** or **Y2** value to reposition a line, as measured from its two Endpoints relative to the ruler origin.*

How to apply dashes and stripes

Dash and stripe styles are available for all layouts in a project. This is how they're applied:

selected **box** Frame dialog box

selected **line** Style menu on Classic tab of Measurements palette; Style > Line Style; Item > Modify > Line

selected **text** Style > Rules

*To narrow (or expand) the selection of dashes and stripes that display in the scroll window, choose a category from the **Show** menu.*

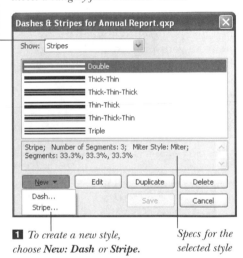

1 *To create a new style, choose **New: Dash** or **Stripe**.*

Specs for the selected style

2 *Drag in the ruler to create a **new stripe** (or **dash**).*

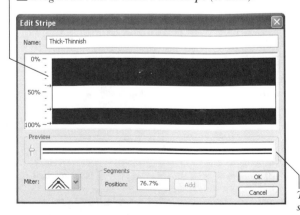

*The current stripe style **previews** here.*

Creating dashes and stripes

Using the Dashes & Stripes dialog box, you can create custom PostScript line styles for lines, frames, and paragraph rules. An edited dash or stripe style will update on all items to which it's already applied—in any and all layouts in the current project.

Note: To append a line style from one project to another, click Append in the Dashes & Stripes dialog box (it's below the New button). Any dash or stripe style that's created when no projects are open will appear in future projects.

To create or edit dashes or stripes:

1. Choose Edit > Dashes & Stripes.

2. To create a new style, choose New: Dash or Stripe **1**, then type a name.
    or
    To edit an existing style, double-click it. Or click its name, then click Edit.
    or
    To create a new style based on an existing one, click the style, click Duplicate, then change the name.

3. In the Edit Stripe dialog box, note the Preview as you do any of the following:

    To add more dash or stripe segments, drag in the ruler, then drag again in another part of the ruler **2**. (Five is the maximum total number of dashes.)

    To move a dash or a stripe, drag inside it with the hand cursor.

    To shorten or lengthen a dash or widen or narrow a stripe, drag either of its arrows.

    To remove a dash, drag either of its arrows or the dash itself upward or downward off the ruler. To remove a stripe, drag either of its arrows or the stripe itself to the left or the right off the ruler.

(Continued on the following page)

Create, Edit Dashes and Stripes

If you want to specify the distance between dashes, enter a number in the Repeats [Every] field **1**. The higher the Repeats Every value, the further apart the dashes will be. If you choose Times Width from the Repeats Every menu, dash segments will spread to fit the dimensions of the line or frame to which that style is applied. If you choose Points from the same menu, segments will maintain the same spacing no matter what.

Create a dash or stripe segment by entering the ruler % position where you want it to start in the Segment: Position field, then click Add.

4. Choose a Miter style for the corners of a Bézier frame or a multisegment line: Sharp, Rounded, or Beveled.

5. For dashes, you can choose a different Endcap style for the shape of the ends of the dash segments **2**–**4**. To enlarge the preview so you can see a closeup of how the endcap style looks, drag the Preview slider upward.

6. *Optional:* Check Stretch to Corners to have the dash or stripe design be stretched to fit symmetrically when chosen as a frame style for a box (**1**–**2**, next page).

7. Click OK.

8. Click Save.

TIP To remove a dash or stripe style, click it, then click Delete. If the style you're deleting is currently applied to any items in your project, an alert dialog box will appear. Choose a replacement dash or stripe, then click OK.

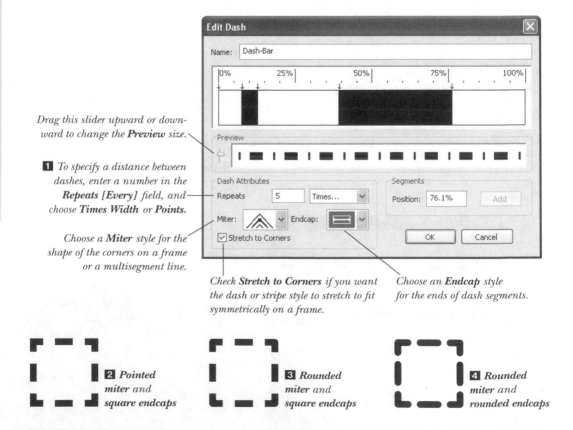

*Drag this slider upward or downward to change the **Preview** size.*

1 *To specify a distance between dashes, enter a number in the **Repeats [Every]** field, and choose **Times Width** or **Points**.*

*Choose a **Miter** style for the shape of the corners on a frame or a multisegment line.*

*Check **Stretch to Corners** if you want the dash or stripe style to stretch to fit symmetrically on a frame.*

*Choose an **Endcap** style for the ends of dash segments.*

2 *Pointed miter and square endcaps*

3 *Rounded miter and square endcaps*

4 *Rounded miter and rounded endcaps*

1 *A custom dash style, with* **Stretch to Corners** *turned* **on**

2 *The same dash style with* **Stretch to Corners** *turned* **off**

To compare two dashes or stripes:

1. Choose Edit > Dashes & Stripes.

2. Cmd-click/Ctrl-click two dashes and/or stripe styles in the scroll window.

3. Option-click/Alt-click the Append button (it will turn into a Compare button). Differences between the two styles will be listed in boldface **3**.

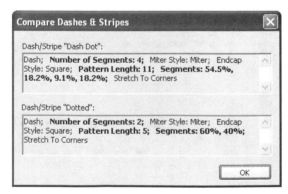

Compare Dashes & Stripes

Dash/Stripe "Dash Dot":

Dash; **Number of Segments: 4;** Miter Style: Miter; Endcap Style: Square; **Pattern Length: 11; Segments: 54.5%, 18.2%, 9.1%, 18.2%;** Stretch To Corners

Dash/Stripe "Dotted":

Dash; **Number of Segments: 2;** Miter Style: Miter; Endcap Style: Square; **Pattern Length: 5; Segments: 60%, 40%;** Stretch To Corners

OK

3 *Specifications for the Dash Dot style* **compared** *with specifications for the Dotted style.*

Compare Two Dashes or Stripes

Dashes and stripes are colored or given transparency on an object by object basis—not in the Edit Dash or Edit Stripe dialog box. In addition to recoloring dashes or stripes, if a style is applied as a frame or line, you can also recolor (or change the opacity of) the gaps between them. Rules can also be colored via a style sheet.

To color a dash or stripe:

1. Select the item that contains the dash or stripe you want to recolor.

2. For a frame, choose Item > Frame (Cmd-B/Ctrl-B); for a line, choose Item > Modify > Line; for a paragraph rule, go to Style > Rules (Cmd-Shift-N/Ctrl-Shift-N).

3. In the Frame, Line, or Rules pane:
   Choose a Color, Shade, and Opacity.
   and/or
   Choose a Gap: Color, Shade, and Opacity (this isn't available for a paragraph rule) **2**-**3**.

   Note: You can also use the Classic tab of the Measurements palette to choose colors for a frame and its gap, but when a line is selected, only the line color is available.

Lines, like other items, can be given drop shadows.

To add a drop shadow to a line: NEW

1. Select a line.

2. Click the Drop Shadow tab on the Measurements palette.
   or
   Choose Item > Modify (Cmd-M/Ctrl-M) and click the Drop Shadow tab.

3. Check the Apply Drop Shadow box and choose from the options provided (see pages 221–222).

4. Click OK (dialog box) to apply the shadow **4**.

Dashes & stripes rule

Experiment and have fun with this feature! Once you have a dash or stripe you like, you can apply it quickly via a style sheet, as you would apply any other paragraph rule style **1**.

Subhead

1 *This is a custom* **stripe** *style applied as a paragraph* **Rule Above** *(Shade: 12% and Offset: -p.5)*

2 *This is a dashed frame with a 15% Black* **Gap** *color.*

3 *To polish it off, we added inner and outer frames in separate text boxes, both with a background color of None.*

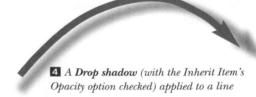

4 *A* **Drop shadow** *(with the Inherit Item's Opacity option checked) applied to a line*

Color Dashes or Stripes; Drop Shadows

Style Sheets 13

*A **headline** style*

THE BILL OF RIGHTS

AMENDMENT I
Religious establishment prohibited. Freedom of speech, of the press, and right to petition
Congress shall make no law respecting an establishment of religion, or prohibiting the free exercise thereof; or abridging the freedom of speech, or of the press; or the right of the people peaceably to assemble, and to petition the Government for a redress of grievances.

AMENDMENT II
Right to keep and bear arms
A well-regulated militia being necessary to the security of a free State, the right of the people to keep and bear arms, shall not be infringed.

AMENDMENT III
Conditions for quarters for soldiers
No soldier shall, in time of peace be quartered in any house, without the consent of the owner, nor in time of war, but in a manner to be prescribed by law.

AMENDMENT IV
Right of search and seizure regulated
The right of the people to be secure in their persons, houses, papers, and effects, against unreasonable searches and seizures, shall not be violated, and no warrants shall issue, but upon probable cause, supported by oath or affirmation, and particularly describing the place to be searched, and the persons or things to be seized.

Creating and applying style sheets

A style sheet is a set of paragraph or character formatting specifications. Whatever text is selected when you click a style sheet on the Style Sheets palette (or execute its equivalent shortcut) is formatted instantly. But style sheets aren't used just for the initial formatting; they're also used for updating formatting. If you modify a style sheet, all the text with which it is associated will update instantly. Each project can contain up to 1,000 style sheets, and they are available to all layouts within the project.

Using style sheets will relieve you from zillions of hours of tedious styling and restyling, freeing you to concentrate on more exciting tasks. And here's another benefit: When you use style sheets, you can rest assured that your typography is consistent, whether you're working on a small brochure or a huge, multifile book. Every single character in this book was styled via a style sheet. Enough said?

— *A **body text** style*

— *A **subhead** style*
— *A **small subhead** style*

*Prevent carpal tunnel syndrome: Use style sheets to apply repetitive type specifications quickly. **Paragraph** style sheets are used in this illustration. A **character** style sheet is illustrated on the next page. In some other applications, style sheets are simply called "styles."*

Every new paragraph style sheet automatically has a default character style sheet associated with it that defines its character attributes. You can also create independent character style sheets **1**. If you're unsure of the difference between paragraph and character style sheets, see "What's the difference?" on the next page and study the illustrations on page 238.

To create a style sheet the easy way:

1. For a paragraph style sheet, select one or more words in a paragraph and apply any character or paragraph attributes, such as font, point size, type style, color, horizontal scaling, tracking, indents, leading, space after, H&J, horizontal alignment, tabs, rules, etc. that you want to be part of the style sheet. We will refer to this as the "sample" paragraph.
or
For a character style sheet, select and style a word or a string of words.

2. With the paragraph or text string still selected, choose Edit > Style Sheets (Shift-F11), then choose New: Paragraph or Character **2**.
or
Control-click/Right-click the paragraph (or character) style sheet area of the Style Sheets palette and choose New from the context menu **3**.

3. Type a descriptive name for the new style sheet (**1**, next page).

4. *Optional:* Press Tab to move the cursor to the Keyboard Equivalent field. Then press a function key, or press a numeric keypad key with or without a modifier (Cmd, Option, Shift, or Control or any combination thereof in Mac OS X; Ctrl, Shift [Fkey only], Ctrl+Alt [keypad only], or Ctrl+Alt+Shift [keypad only] in Windows).

5. *Optional:* To apply successive paragraph style sheets automatically as you input text, you can link one style sheet to

"It is a very odd thing that Ribby's pie was **not** in the oven when I put mine in! And I can't find it anywhere; I have looked all over the house. I put **my** pie into a nice hot oven at the top. I could not turn any of the other handles; I think that they are all shams," said Duchess, "but I wish I could have removed the pie made of mouse! I cannot think what she has done with it? I heard Ribby coming and I had to run out by the back door!" *Beatrix Potter*

1 *A **character** style sheet was used to style the words "not" and "my."*

2 *Choose **New: Paragraph** or **Character**.*

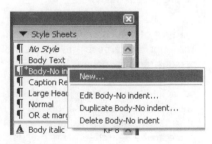

3 *Control-click/Right-click the paragraph or character area of the Style Sheets palette, then choose **New** from the context menu.*

What's the difference?

A **character** style sheet contains only character attributes: font, type style, point size, color, shade horizontal/vertical scale, tracking, baseline shift, ligatures, and OpenType features. A character 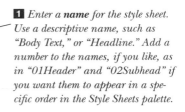 style sheet can be applied to one or more characters. In this book, the step numbers (**2.**, **3.**), figure numbers (**4**, **5**), **boldface** words, and the word **TIP** were styled using character style sheets.

A **paragraph** style sheet, on the other hand, contains paragraph formats, tabs, and rules. It derives its character attributes from the character style sheet that's currently associated with it. A paragraph style sheet affects the entire paragraph to which it is applied.

another. To do this, choose from the Next Style menu. When you press Return/Enter as you input text in your layout, the Next Style sheet will apply automatically to the next paragraph you type. The Next Style has no effect on existing paragraphs.

6. Click OK and then, if you're back in the Style Sheets dialog box, click Save to exit. Apply the new style sheet to the sample paragraph, if you like, and to any other paragraphs (see the next page). Two other methods for creating a style sheet are described on page 235.

1 *Enter a **name** for the style sheet. Use a descriptive name, such as "Body Text," or "Headline." Add a number to the names, if you like, as in "01Header" and "02Subhead" if you want them to appear in a specific order in the Style Sheets palette.*

*Enter a **keyboard equivalent** for the style sheet. Note: Every function (F) key has a default, preassigned command (they're listed in Appendix B). If you choose an F key as a style sheet keyboard equivalent, the style sheet shortcut will override the preassigned command. To avoid this conflict altogether, use a number pad key, with or without a modifier key (e.g., Control [Mac only], Cmd/Ctrl, Option/Alt, or Shift).*

*The typographic and paragraph attributes for the currently selected style sheet are listed in the **Description** area.*

Character style sheets can be used to style initial caps.

Extras —Or run-in subheads.

〜 Oregano
〜 Cumin
〜 Coriander
〜 Sage
〜 Thyme

*Typesetting bulleted lists or numbered paragraphs is a snap: Use a **paragraph** style sheet for the body text and then a **character** style sheet for the bullet or number.*

To apply a style sheet:

1. Display the Style Sheets palette (Window > Style Sheets or F11).

2. Choose the Content tool.

3. To apply a paragraph style sheet, click in a paragraph or select a series of paragraphs.
   or
   To apply a character style sheet, select the text you want to reformat.

4. Click a paragraph style sheet in the top portion of the Style Sheets palette 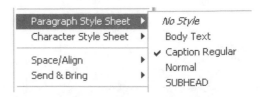. The selected paragraph(s) will reformat instantly.
   or
   Click a character style sheet in the bottom portion of the Style Sheets palette. The selected text will reformat instantly.
   or
   Press the keyboard equivalent for the style sheet you want to apply, if one was assigned to it. The equivalents are listed on the Style Sheets palette.
   or
   Choose a style sheet from Style > Paragraph Style Sheet or Style > Character Style Sheet.
   or
   Control-click/Right-click the text in your layout; when the context menu appears, choose a style sheet from the Paragraph Style Sheet or Character Style Sheet submenu .

Local formatting

Local formatting is fomatting applied independently of a style sheet. If you insert the cursor in or select locally styled text, a plus sign will appear on the Style Sheets palette next to the name of the style sheet that's associated with that paragraph.

You'll also see a plus sign next to a paragraph style sheet name if the text your cursor is in has both a paragraph style sheet and a character style sheet applied to it.

Local stripping

To strip a paragraph style sheet *and* all local formatting from a paragraph (including any character style sheets) and apply a new paragraph style sheet or reapply the same style sheet, click in the paragraph and then, on the Style Sheets palette, Option-click/Alt-click the style sheet you want to apply. (This is the equivalent of clicking No Style, then clicking a new style sheet.) This works for character style sheets, too (select only the characters you want to change).

*A plus sign preceding a style sheet name means that the currently selected characters contain **local formatting**.*

*Click **No Style** to disassociate a style sheet from your text.*

*Drag the palette **edge** (resize box, in Mac OS X) downward to expand the **whole** palette.*

*Drag the **palette divider** downward to expand the **paragraph** style sheets area of the palette (expand the whole palette first).*

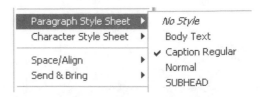 *To **apply** a style sheet, click its name on the Style Sheets palette or use the keyboard shortcut, if any, that was assigned to it. The shortcuts are listed on the palette.*

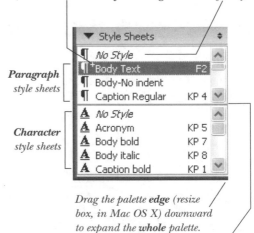 *Or Control-click/Right-click your text and choose a style sheet from the context menu.*

Disappearing text?

If you press a number key that was not assigned to a style sheet, any currently selected text will be *replaced* by that number character! (Use the Undo command to recover the text.) To avoid this, keep track of which numbers have assigned shortcuts and which don't.

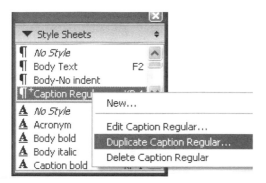

1 *Control-click/Right-click a style sheet name, choose* **Duplicate** *[style sheet name] from the context menu, then click OK.*

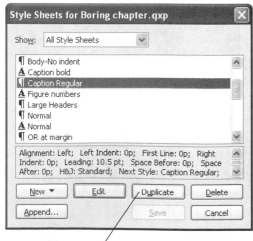

2 *Or in the Style Sheets dialog box, click a style sheet name, then click* **Duplicate.** *The word "copy" will automatically be added to the style sheet name. You can change the name, if you like.*

A fast way to create a variation on an existing style sheet is to duplicate it, and then edit the duplicate. Unlike a Based On style sheet (which is described on page 240), there is no linkage between a duplicate style sheet and the original from which it's generated.

To create a style sheet by duplication:

1. On the Style Sheets palette, Control-click/Right-click the style sheet you want to duplicate, then choose Duplicate [style sheet name] from the context menu **1**.
   or
   Choose Edit > Style Sheets (Shift-F11), click a style sheet, then click Duplicate **2**.

2. The Edit Paragraph (or Character) Style Sheet dialog box will open, and you'll see that the word "copy" was added to the style sheet name. Edit the name, if desired.

3. Edit the new style sheet (see the next page).

4. Click OK, then click Save, if necessary.

TIP Remember, style sheets are available to all the layouts in a project.

There's nothing to stop you from creating a new style sheet from scratch without clicking in a sample paragraph—it just takes longer.

To create a style sheet from scratch:

1. Choose Edit > Style Sheets.

2. Choose New: Character or Paragraph.

3. Enter a name for the new style sheet.

4. Follow steps 2–3 on the next page to assign character and paragraph attributes to the style sheet. Use the Edit button in the General pane to specify character attributes or select a character style sheet to embed.

To edit a style sheet:

1. Open the Style Sheets palette, click in any text box to activate the palette, Cmd-click/Ctrl-click the style sheet you want to edit, then click Edit.

   or

   Choose Edit > Style Sheets (Shift-F11), click the style sheet you want to edit, then click Edit **1**. To narrow (or expand) the number of style sheets on the list, choose a category from the Show menu.

   or

   Control-click/Right-click a paragraph style sheet on the Style Sheets palette and choose Edit [style sheet name] to go directly to the General pane of the Edit Style Sheet dialog box. Or do the same for a character style sheet to go directly to the Edit Character Style Sheet dialog box **2**.

2. For a paragraph style sheet, use the General pane of the Edit Paragraph Style Sheet dialog box to rename the style sheet; to assign or change its keyboard equivalent or embedded character style sheet; or to assign a Next Style to it. To modify the style sheet's character attributes (e.g., the font or color), click Edit; to modify its paragraph formatting, click the Formats tab (**1**, next page); to add, delete, or modify tabs, click Tabs; or to add, delete, or edit a rule, click Rules.

   or

   For a character style sheet, modify character attributes in the Edit Character Style Sheet dialog box (**2**, next page).

3. Click OK to exit the Formats, Rules, or Tabs pane (click OK twice if you're in the Character Attributes dialog box), then click Save, if necessary. Text that the style sheet was previously applied to in any layouts within the project will reformat instantly!

Hate digging through boxes?

To revise style sheets quickly using local formatting and a keystroke, try using the inexpensive **Redefine Style Sheets** XTension from XPedient Corporation.

1 *To get to the Edit Paragraph or Character Style Sheet dialog box, click a style sheet name, then click* **Edit,** *or just double-click a style sheet name.*

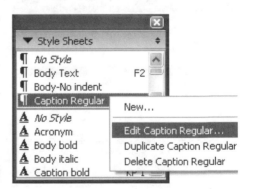

2 *Control-click/Right-click a paragraph style sheet and choose* **Edit** *[style sheet name] to go straight to the General pane of the Edit Paragraph Style Sheet dialog box. Or do the same for a character style sheet to go straight to the Edit Character Style Sheet dialog box. You can edit only one style sheet at a time using this method, but it's speedy.*

1 *For a **paragraph** style sheet, click the General, Formats, Tabs, or Rules tab to open that pane. Click Edit in the General pane to change character attributes.*

2 *For a **character** style sheet, change the Name, Keyboard Equivalent, Based On, Type Style, Font, Size, Color, Shade, Opacity, Scale, Track Amount, Baseline Shift, Ligatures, or* **NEW** *OpenType attributes in the Edit Character Style Sheet dialog box.*

Edit Style Sheet

TIP If the currently selected text has more than one style sheet applied to it, the ¶ or **A** symbol next to those style sheets will be dimmed (¶ Ⓐ).

Applying style sheets by example

Chapter xiv ——

Household economy ——

Clean paper walls = The very best method is to sweep off lightly all the dust, then rub the paper with stale bread—cut the crust off very thick, and wipe straight down from the top, then begin at the top again, and so on.

Wash carpets = The oftener these are taken up and shaken, the longer they will wear, as the dust and dirt underneath grind them out. Sweep carpets with a stiff hair brush, instead of an old corn broom, if you wish them to wear long or look well.

Black a brick hearth = Mix some black lead with soft soap and a little water, and boil it—then lay it on with a brush. Or mix the lead with water only.

SARA JOSEPHA HALE, FROM EARLY AMERICAN COOKERY

1 *A **paragraph body text** style sheet is applied first to **all** the body text.*

2 *A different paragraph style sheet is applied to the chapter number.*

3 *And yet another paragraph style sheet is assigned to the chapter name.*

Chapter xiv

Household economy

CLEAN PAPER WALLS ❥ The very best method is to sweep off lightly all the dust, then rub the paper with stale bread—cut the crust off very thick, and wipe straight down from the top, then begin at the top again, and so on.

WASH CARPETS ❥ the oftener these are taken up and shaken, the longer they will wear, as the dust and dirt underneath grind them out. Sweep carpets with a stiff hair brush, instead of an old corn broom, if you wish them to wear long or look well.

BLACK A BRICK HEARTH ❥ Mix some black lead with soft soap and a little water, and boil it—then lay it on with a brush. Or mix the lead with water only.

4 *A **character** style sheet is applied to each run-in **subhead**.*

5 *The Find/Change command is used to apply a character style sheet (ornament font) to every "=" character.*

Chapter xiv

Household economy

I CLEAN PAPER WALLS ❥ The very best method is to sweep off lightly all the dust, then rub the paper with stale bread—cut the crust off very thick, and wipe straight down from the top, then begin at the top again, and so on.

2 WASH CARPETS ❥ The oftener these are taken up and shaken, the longer they will wear, as the dust and dirt underneath grind them out. Sweep carpets with a stiff hair brush, instead of an old corn broom, if you wish them to wear long.

3 BLACK A BRICK HEARTH ❥ Mix some black lead with soft soap and a little water, and boil it—then lay it on with a brush. Or mix the lead with water only.

6 *A **drop cap** is added to the paragraph style sheet. Then, using a character style sheet, the drop caps are colored 30% gray and changed to the Adobe Garamond Expert font.*

Chapter xiv

Household economy

I CLEAN PAPER WALLS ❥ The very best method is to sweep off lightly all the dust, then rub the paper with stale bread— cut the crust off very thick, and wipe straight down from the top, then begin at the top again, and so on.

2 WASH CARPETS ❥ The oftener these are taken up and shaken, the longer they will wear, as the dust and dirt underneath grind them out. Sweep carpets with a stiff hair brush, instead of an old corn broom, if you wish them to wear long.

3 BLACK A BRICK HEARTH ❥ Mix some black lead with soft soap and a lit- tle water, and boil it—then lay it on with a brush. Or mix the lead with water only.

7 *Finally, the font in the run-in subhead character style sheet is changed to Bodoni Poster and the font in the body text paragraph style sheet is changed to Gill Sans. Now that style sheets have been assigned to all the text, making changes will be a snap!*

Removing character styling

Let's say you've applied a "Bold" character style sheet to a few phrases in a paragraph, and maybe you've also made some local formatting changes. You then decide you want to remove the character styling from one part of the paragraph. If you Option-click/Alt-click a paragraph style sheet (e.g., "Body Text"), all your other local formatting changes will be lost.

A better option is to create a Body Text character style sheet with the same type specs as the Body Text style and embed it into the Body Text paragraph style sheet. To remove the Bold character styling, select the Bold styled text, then apply the Body Text character style sheet. Local formatting will be removed from just the selected text.

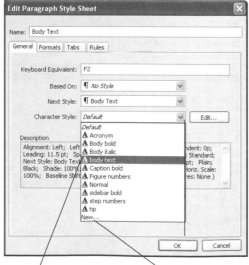

1 *To embed a different character style sheet into a paragraph style sheet, choose a style from the **Character Style** menu.*

2 *To create a new character style sheet, choose **New** from the Character Style menu.*

A default character style sheet is automatically embedded into every paragraph style sheet. In fact, a paragraph style sheet's character attributes are derived from a character style sheet. You can change the individual character attributes of the default character style sheet for its associated paragraph style sheet (choose a different font or point size, for example).

If you want to change multiple character attributes for a paragraph style sheet all at once, you can embed a different or new character style sheet into it. The same character style sheet can be embedded into multiple paragraph style sheets.

This means, however, that if you change the specifications for a character style sheet, the character attributes for any paragraph style sheets into which it is embedded will update accordingly. And similarly, if you edit the character attributes in a paragraph style sheet, the character style sheet that's embedded into it will also update accordingly. If this seems like too much to keep track of, ignore this page and leave Default as the choice on the Character Style menu!

To embed a character style sheet into a paragraph style sheet:

1. Choose Edit > Style Sheets (Shift-F11).

2. Click the paragraph style sheet that you want to embed the character style sheet into.

3. Click Edit.

4. From the Character Style menu, choose an existing character style sheet **1**.
   or
   Choose New **2**, type a name for a new character style sheet, choose character attributes, then click OK.

5. Click OK to exit the Edit Paragraph Style Sheet dialog box.

6. Click Save.

One degree of separation: Based On

When one style sheet is based on another style sheet, the two remain associated. The Formats, Tabs, Rules, and Character Style options from one style sheet (which we'll call the "child") are derived from a second style sheet (the "parent"). If the parent style sheet is modified, any child style sheets that are based on it will also change—with the exception of any specifications that are unique to the child style sheet. This is different from duplicating or embedding, which we discussed earlier.

If you'd like to try this option, choose a style sheet in Edit > Style Sheets, click Edit, then in the Edit [Paragraph or Character] Style Sheet dialog box, choose a parent style sheet from the Based On menu. For example, you could create a style sheet called Drop Cap that's based on a Body Text style sheet, and then, in the Drop Cap style sheet, turn on the automatic Drop Cap option in the Formats pane 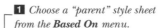. If you then change the Body Text style sheet (change the font, size, etc.), those changes will also occur in the Drop Cap style sheet.

Using Find/Change to apply or change style sheets

To apply a style sheet to text using Edit > Find/Change (Cmd-F/Ctrl-F), uncheck Ignore Attributes on the Find/Change palette, enter a text string and/or choose character attributes on the Find What side of the palette, choose from the Style Sheet menu on the Change To side of the palette, then click the appropriate buttons at the bottom of the palette (see pages 298–302).

To use Find/Change to replace one style sheet with another on a case-by-case basis, choose both a Find What style sheet and a Change To style sheet. (If you were to delete and replace a style sheet in the Style Sheets dialog box instead, all occurrences of the style sheet would change.)

Parents and kids

■ If you edit the Character Style: **Default** in the child style sheet, the parent (Based On) style sheet won't change. If you edit any nondefault, **embedded** character style that's present in both the parent and child style sheets (via Character Style: Edit), that change will affect both the parent and the child style sheets. In either place, what you're actually doing is editing the character style sheet.

■ Let's say you've made some character attribute changes to a child style sheet and then you decide you want to reassociate it with the parent (Based On) style sheet. For the child, choose Based On: **No Style,** and then choose Based On: [the character style sheet used by the parent]. The parent and child style sheets will now have the same character attributes.

1 *Choose a "parent" style sheet from the **Based On** menu.*

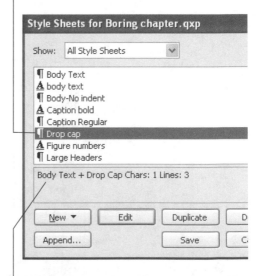

*This **description** tells us that our Drop Cap style sheet consists of the Body Text style sheet plus the Drop Cap option.*

styling the master

A style sheet can be applied to any text box on a **master** page. You can even apply a style sheet to the automatic text box, though you can't enter text into it. The style sheet will then apply automatically to any text that's subsequently typed into that box on any associated layout page, but not to text that's imported using the Import Text command (File menu).

Style Name: Body Text
Font: New Baskerville
Size: 9.5 pt
Text Style: Plain
Color: Black
Shade: 100%
Track Amount: 0p
Horiz Scale: 100%
Alignment: Left
Left Indent: 1p3
First Line Indent: -1p3
Right Indent: 0p
Leading: p11.5
Space Before: 0p
Space After: p3
Rule Above: None
Rule Below: None
Tabs: None

Style Name: Subhead
Font: FranklinGothic No.2
Size: 9.5 pt
Text Style: Plain
Color: Black
Shade: 100%
Track Amount: 0p
Horiz Scale: 100%
Alignment: Left
Left Indent: 0p
First Line Indent: 0p
Right Indent: 0p
Leading: p10.5
Space Before: p4
Space After: p2
Rule Above: None
Rule Below: None
Tabs: None

Style Name: Caption Regular
Font: ITC Officina Serif BookItalic
Size: 8 pt
Text Style: Plain
Color: Black
Shade: 100%
Track Amount: 0p
Horiz Scale: 110%
Alignment: Left
Left Indent: 0p
First Line Indent: 0p
Right Indent: 0p
Leading: p10.5
Space Before: 0p
Space After: 0p
Rule Above: None
Rule Below: None
Tabs: None

Style Name: Sidebar body
Font: GillSans
Size: 8.5 pt
Text Style: Plain
Color: Black
Shade: 100%
Track Amount: 0p
Horiz Scale: 105%
Alignment: Left
Left Indent: 0p
First Line Indent: 0p
Right Indent: 0p
Leading: p11
Space Before: 0p
Space After: p3
Rule Above: None
Rule Below: None
Tabs: None

1 *This list of style sheet specifications was generated by a third-party XTension.*

What's Normal?

The Normal paragraph and character style sheets are the default style sheets for all newly created text boxes. If the Normal style sheet is modified with a project open, text with which the Normal style sheet is associated will update just in that project.

If the Normal paragraph or character style sheet is modified when no projects are open, the modified style sheet will become the default for future projects. Similarly, any new style sheet that's created when no projects are open will appear automatically on the Style Sheets palette of future projects.

Managing style sheets

Appending style sheets

To append style sheets from one project to another, follow the instructions on pages 49–50. Or to append a style sheet the quick-and-dirty way, drag or copy and paste a text box that contains text to which the desired style sheet has been applied from a library or from another project into the current project—the applied style sheet will copy along with the item (as long as its name doesn't match a style sheet already present in the target project. We did say quick and dirty, didn't we?).

TIP The report produced by the Collect for Output command (File menu) includes a list of style sheets in your document. Also, a number of XTensions are available that will generate printed reports of the style sheet specifications used in a project **1**, as well as other data such as fonts, colors, H&Js, print styles, preferences, and picture files. Take a look at OfficialReport XT or Printools XT from Badia Software, or BureauManager from CompuSense Ltd.

If you delete a style sheet that's currently being used in your project, a dialog box opens automatically that you can use to choose a replacement style sheet. If you don't choose a replacement style sheet, the No Style (no style sheet) option will be applied by default. When you apply No Style, the text formatting will not change.

To delete a style sheet:

1. On the Style Sheets palette, Control-click/Right-click the style sheet you want to delete and choose Delete [style sheet name] from the context menu 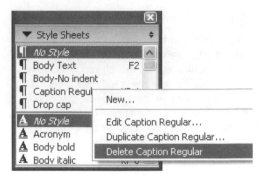.

2. If the style sheet you're deleting is not currently being used in your project, click OK 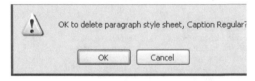.

   If the style sheet is currently being used in your project, a prompt will appear. From the "Replace with" menu, choose a replacement style sheet or choose No Style, then click OK 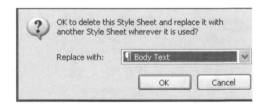.

   Note: If you choose a replacement style sheet, any local formatting in the text will be preserved. If you choose No Style and then apply a new style sheet, on the other hand, all local formatting will be removed.

TIP You can undo the deletion of a style sheet.

TIP The Normal style sheets can be edited, but they can't be deleted.

TIP The method described above is the fastest one for deleting one, or even a few, style sheets. If you have to delete a whole slew of them, though, a faster method is to choose Edit > Style Sheets (Shift-F11), Cmd-click/Ctrl-click (or Shift-drag through) the style sheets you want to delete, then click Delete. Respond to any prompts that appear (as in step 2, above), then click Save.

*Control-click/Right-click a style sheet and choose **Delete** [style sheet name] from the context menu.*

If this prompt appears, click OK.

*If this prompt appears, from the **Replace with** menu, choose a replacement style sheet or choose No Style.*

Delete Style Sheet

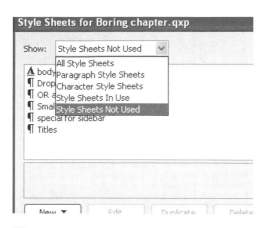

1 *Choose **Show: Style Sheets Not Used**.*

To delete all unused style sheets:

1. Choose Edit > Style Sheets (Shift-F11).
2. Choose Show: Style Sheets Not Used **1**.
3. Shift-drag upward or downward through the style sheet list to select all or some of the names.
   or
   Click a style sheet, then Shift-click the last style sheet in a series.
4. *Optional:* Cmd-click/Ctrl-click any style sheets that you don't want to delete.
5. Click Delete.
6. Click Save.

TIP This strategy is helpful for cleaning up a project that is littered with many unused style sheets. Ideally, the Style Sheets palette lists only those style sheets actually required for that project.

Be a slave to style sheets

If you're in a workgroup or working on a long document such as a book, be sure to apply style sheets consistently. First, this ensures that you can make instant updates consistently—for example, if you need to change a font or text color. If you're using lists to build a table of contents or figures list, the accuracy of the list depends entirely on the precise application of style sheets. If you're working on a book, you can synchronize style sheets across the book to implement changes in multiple projects.

Delete Unused Style Sheets

To compare two style sheets:

1. Choose Edit > Style Sheets (Shift-F11).

2. Cmd-click/Ctrl-click the two paragraph style sheets or two character style sheets that you want to compare 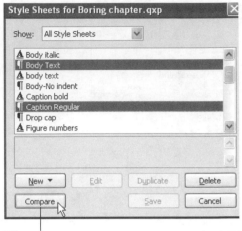. You can't compare a paragraph style sheet with a character style sheet—they're like apples and oranges....

3. Option-click/Alt-click the Append button—it will turn into a Compare button. The Compare [Paragraph or Character] Style Sheets dialog box will open **2**. Any specifications that differ between the two style sheets will be listed in boldface.

4. Click OK when you're finished, then click Cancel.

TIP You can't compare style sheets from different projects using this method. You could append style sheets from one file to another, though, and then compare them once they're both in the same file.

1 *In the Style Sheets dialog box, Cmd-click/Ctrl-click two style sheets, then Option-click/Alt-click Append (it will turn into a **Compare** button).*

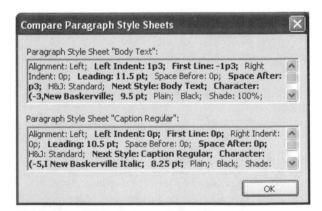

2 *Differences between the two style sheets are listed in **boldface**.*

Compare Two Style Sheets

Master Pages 14

Master pages and layers

Items placed on a **master** page appear on the default layer for that layout and can't be moved to a different layer.

On **layout** pages, items that originate from the master page will initially reside on the default layer for that layout, but they can be moved to a different layer. If do you move any such item to a different layer, beware: The item will cease to be associated with the master page (you'll get an alert dialog box, so you can back out of the deal).

Using master pages

You can use the master pages in each layout as a blueprint for building your layout pages. For starters, they automatically contain a layout's margin and column guides. Then there are the items that you add to a master page yourself, such as headers, footers, picture boxes, logos, lines, and the all-important automatic page numbering command. Any item that you don't want to bother having to reconstruct over and over again on your layout pages can originate from a master page; it will appear automatically on every layout page that master page is applied to.

An item that's modified on a master page will also update on any layout pages that the master is currently applied to. Items that originate from a master page can be edited on any layout page, though, without affecting the master. Each new layout automatically contains its own Master A page, and you can add as many more as you need.

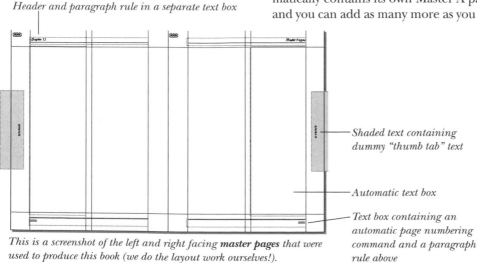

Header and paragraph rule in a separate text box

Shaded text containing dummy "thumb tab" text

Automatic text box

Text box containing an automatic page numbering command and a paragraph rule above

*This is a screenshot of the left and right facing **master pages** that were used to produce this book (we do the layout work ourselves!).*

Before you can learn how to use master pages, you need to learn how to navigate back and forth between master pages and layout pages. Master pages are created, modified, and applied using the Page Layout palette. Choose Window > Page Layout (F10/F4) to open it.

To switch between master page and layout page display:

On the Page Layout palette, double-click a master page icon or layout page icon, or click once on the page number below a layout page icon. The number of the currently displayed page will switch to outline/bold style **1**–**2**.

or

From the Go-to-page pop-up menu at the lower-left corner of the project window, choose a layout or master page icon **3**.

or

From the Page > Display submenu, choose Layout or a master page name. If you choose Layout when a master page is displayed, the last displayed layout page will redisplay.

or

To view the master page that's applied to the currently displayed layout page, press Shift-F10/Shift-F4. To go back to the layout page, use the same shortcut.

Where are you?

The easiest way to tell whether you're on a layout page or a master page is to glance at the lower-left corner of the project window. If you're on a layout page, the readout will say **Page: [such-and-such]**. If a master page is displayed, it will say **A-Master A**—or whatever the name of the master page is.

2 *Now a **master page** is displayed, so its name is in **bold/outline** style.*

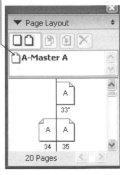

1 *The number of the currently displayed **layout** page is in **bold/outline** style.*

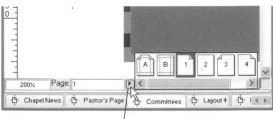

3 *You can use the **Go-to-page** pop-up menu to display any layout page or master page.*

Layout/Master Page Display

⌐Blank single-sided page icon

Blank facing-pages icon   *Master page* icon

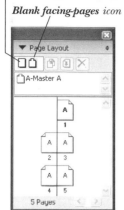

1 *The Page Layout palette for a **facing-pages** layout*

2 *The Page Layout palette for a **single-sided** layout*

3 *Change the non-printing margin guides and/or column guides in the **Master Guides** dialog box.*

   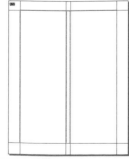

4 *A **one-column** master...*   **5** *...is changed to a **two-column** master.*

Single-sided vs. facing pages

If you check Facing Pages in the New Project or New Layout dialog box, you can specify Inside and Outside margins instead of Left and Right margins. In this type of layout, the first page is positioned by itself (because page 1 is always a right-facing page), and any subsequent pages are arranged in pairs along a central spine **1** (unless you've applied an even starting page number via the Section command; see page 84). Facing master page and layout page icons on the Page Layout palette have a turned-down (dog-eared) corner. Books and magazines use this format.

If Facing Pages is unchecked in the New Project or New Layout dialog box, pages will be stacked vertically (not in pairs) **2**. Single-sided master and layout page icons have square (not dog-eared) corners. You can create a spread in a single-sided layout by moving layout page icons so they're side by side (see page 85). To convert a layout from single-sided to facing pages, or vice versa, see the sidebar on page 254.

If you modify the margin or column guides on a master page, all the layout pages with which that master is associated will display the updated guides. Any automatic text boxes that fit exactly within the margin guides before the guides were changed will exhibit the new column and gutter width values and will resize automatically to fit the new margins.

To modify the non-printing margin and column guides:

1. Double-click a master page icon on the Page Layout palette.

2. Control-click/Right-click in the master pages area of the Page Layout palette and choose Page > Master Guides.

3. Change the Column Guides and/or Margin Guides values **3**.

4. Click OK **4**–**5**, then redisplay a layout page.

If you enter the Current Page Number placeholder character on a master page, the current page number will appear on any layout pages to which that master is applied. If you then add or delete pages from the layout, the page numbers will update automatically.

Note: Many of the procedures discussed in this chapter can't be undone, like applying a master page or deleting pages. We suggest that you save your file before working with master pages and the Page Layout palette, so you'll have the Revert to Saved command to fall back on.

To number pages automatically:

1. Double-click a master page icon on the Page Layout palette **1**. The name of the page will appear in the lower-left corner of the project window.

2. Choose the Rectangle Text Box tool. A

3. Drag to create a small text box where you want the page number to appear (typically, it's placed at the bottom of the page, but any location is fine).

4. With the new box and the Content tool selected, choose Utilities > Insert Character > Special > Current Box Page # (Cmd-3/Ctrl-3) to insert the **NEW** Current Page Number character **2**. It will look like this: <#>.

   In a facing-pages layout, you need to enter the character on both the left and right master pages (see **1**, next page)—it's easy to forget this!

5. Select the Current Page Number character, then style it as you would a regular character (choose a font, point size, etc.). (To add other master page items, such as headers, footers, and the like, see page 250.)

6. To see how the page numbers look, display any layout page: Click a layout page number on the Page Layout palette or press Shift-F10/Shift-F4 **3**.

Number Pages Automatically

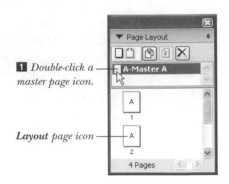

1 *Double-click a master page icon.*

Layout page icon

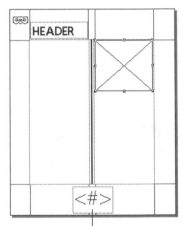

2 *The **Current Page Number** character displays as "<#>" on the master page.*

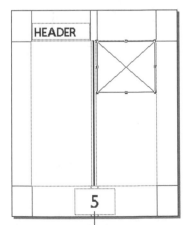

3 *The **Current Page Number** character displays as the **actual** page number on a layout page.*

Align the numbers

To make sure the two boxes that hold the Current Page Number character align vertically on the left and right master pages in a facing-pages layout, use Item > **Step and Repeat** (e.g., Horizontal Offset 10p, Vertical Offset 0) to duplicate the box, then Shift-drag the duplicate to the right page **1**. Remember to choose right paragraph alignment (click the Right Alignment icon on the Classic or Paragraph tab of the Measurements palette) for the character on the right facing page.

If you use the **Duplicate** command to copy the box instead, the next step would be to select both boxes and use Item > **Space/Align** (Vertical, Space: 0, Between: Top Edges) to align their top edges. Another way to align the boxes vertically is to enter matching numbers in the **Y** field on the Classic tab of the **Measurements** palette for both boxes (copy the value in the Y field for the first box, click the second box, then paste into the Y field for the second box).

TIP Unfortunately, automatic page numbers can't be manually kerned, and they are unaffected by the Kerning Table Editor. You could track the Current Page Number character on the master page, but doing so would cause all the automatic page numbers in the layout to be tracked by the same value.

TIP You can enter the Current Page Number character on any layout page, but the page number will appear only on that individual page.

TIP To print a master page (or a set of facing-pages masters), display that page before choosing File > Print.

TIP If you're in a position to break with the norm, instead of automatically placing the Current Page Number character at the bottom of the page, try placing it in a new location **2**. Then embellish it: Apply a color to it, make it very large, add a paragraph rule above and/or below it, etc. For more formal documents, you may type a prefix such as "Page" before the character.

Number Pages Automatically

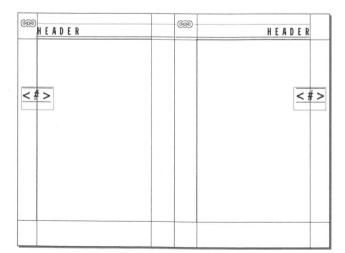

1 *In a facing-pages layout, you must enter the Current Page Number character on both the* **left** *and* **right** *facing master pages.*

2 *This is how the page number looks on a* **layout** *page.*

Note: In a facing-pages layout, every master page has two parts: a left page and a right page. Items from the left master page appear only on left (even-numbered) layout pages; items on the right master page appear only on right (odd-numbered) layout pages.

To modify a master page:

1. Double-click a master page icon on the Page Layout palette **1** or choose a master page icon from the Go-to-page pop-up menu at the bottom of the project window.

2. Add or modify any master item—header, footer, line, ruler guide, picture box, or what have you. You can drag any item from a library onto a master page. You can't enter text into an automatic text box.

   Pages to which the master page has already been applied will be modified. See "Keep or delete changes?" starting on page 252.

3. To redisplay a layout page, click a layout page number on the Page Layout

Lock 'em up

Once your master items are positioned exactly where you want them, lock them, where appropriate, to prevent them from being moved on any layout pages (Item > Lock > Position, or F6). To prevent the contents of a master item from being changed, choose Item > Lock > Story. **NEW**

palette or choose a layout page icon from the Go-to-page pop-up menu.

TIP If you checked Automatic Text Box in the New Project or New Layout dialog box, an automatic text box will appear on the default A-Master A page and on any layout pages to which A-Master A is applied. Text can't be entered into the automatic text box on a master page, but text can be entered into any other text box on a master page. You *can* reshape the automatic text box **2**.

TIP You can preformat any text box on a master page by applying a style sheet or individual type specifications. Text that you subsequently type into the box will take on those specifications.

Modify Master Page

1 *Double-click a master page icon.*

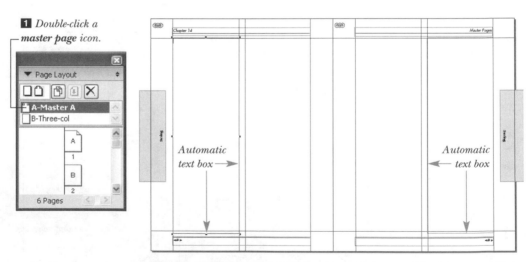

Automatic text box ⟶

Automatic ⟵ text box

2 *These are the left and right **master pages** for this book. The automatic text box on each page was resized to fit into one column to make room for illustrations, and the number of columns in the box was reduced to one.*

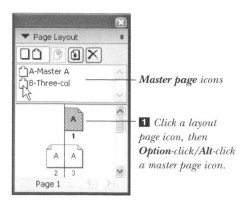

Master page icons

1 *Click a layout page icon, then* **Option**-*click/***Alt**-*click a master page icon.*

To apply a master page to a layout page:

Click a layout page icon on the Page Layout palette (or double-click the icon, if you also want the page to display on screen) **1**, then Option-click/Alt-click a master page icon **2**.

or

Drag a master page icon (labeled icon) over a layout page icon.

or

To apply a master page to multiple layout pages, click the page icon of the first page in the series, Shift-click the last page icon in the series **3** (or Cmd-click/Ctrl-click nonconsecutive icons **4**), then Option-click/Alt-click a master page icon.

TIP If you drag-copy a page or pages from one project to another in Thumbnails view, any master pages that were assigned to the source pages that differ from those in the target project will also be added to the target project. If the target project already contains a master page of the same name, the newly appended master page will be assigned the next letter of the alphabet.

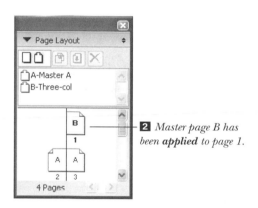

2 *Master page B has been* **applied** *to page 1.*

Beware! Don't apply a blank master page to any layout pages—unless you want all master items to be removed from those pages!

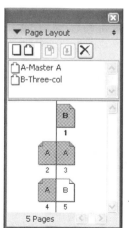

3 *To select a series of* **consecutive** *layout page icons, click the first icon, then* **Shift**-*click the last icon in the series.*

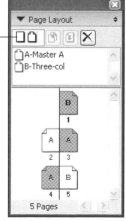

4 *Or* **Cmd**-*click/* **Ctrl**-*click* **individual** *layout page icons to select* **nonconsecutive** *icons.*

Apply Master Page

Keep or delete changes?

If Master Page Items: Delete Changes is chosen in QuarkXPress (Edit, in Windows) > Preferences > Print Layout or Web Layout > General (Cmd-Option-Shift-Y/Ctrl-Alt-Shift-Y), and a master page is applied or reapplied to a layout page, locally modified and unmodified master items will be deleted from the layout page **1**–**3**. If Keep Changes is chosen as the Master Page Items setting instead, only unmodified master items will be deleted **4**. Confused?

To learn the difference between these two settings, start by putting a couple of items on a master page (make them large and/or colorful so they'll be easy to spot). Next, locally modify one of those master page items on a layout page. Now reapply the master page to the same layout page. If the item you modified disappeared, Delete Changes is the current setting. Then do the same procedure with Keep Changes chosen instead. See the difference?

TIP Text contained in the automatic text box on any layout page is preserved regardless of the current Master Page Items setting, even if the automatic text box is resized on the master page.

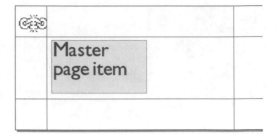

1 *This is an item on a master page.*

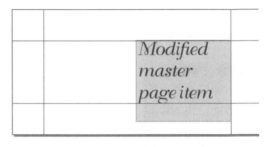

2 *The master page item is moved and modified on one of the layout pages.*

3 *With **Delete Changes** as the default setting, after the master is reapplied, the modified master item is deleted.*

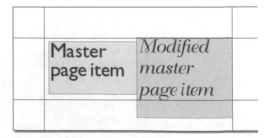

4 *With **Keep Changes** as the default setting, after the master page is reapplied, the modified item remains.*

To further confuse matters

If master page items are edited on layout pages and the master page is reapplied, there's one more thing to keep in mind: Reapplying the master page can affect an item's attributes (color, size, shape, frame, etc.) and its contents (text or picture) differently.

The unmodified master page

The contents are modified on a layout page.

Delete Changes is in effect and the same master page is reapplied. The modified contents are replaced.

Scenario 1

On a layout page, you edit the **contents** of a text box that originated from a master page but you don't recolor, resize, or move the box itself. The same master page is reapplied with Master Page Items: **Delete Changes** as the current Preferences setting. The result: The locally modified text in the box on the layout page is replaced with the original item from the master page.

The unmodified master page

The contents are modified on a layout page.

Keep Changes is in effect and the same master page is reapplied. The master item appears behind the modified item.

Scenario 2

On a layout page, you edit the **contents** of an item that originated from a master page but not its attributes. The same master page is reapplied, but this time with **Keep Changes** as the Preferences setting. The result: The reapplied master page item appears behind the modified layout page item, and it's hidden (perhaps only partially) from view.

(Continued on the following page)

Keep/Delete Changes Preference

Scenario 3

You edit the **contents** of a box on a layout page and also edit **attributes** of the master item on the master page (but *not* its contents) with **Keep Changes** selected in Preferences. (In this scenario, the master page is not reapplied) The result: The attributes of the box, but not its contents, update on the layout page.

The unmodified master page

The contents on an associated layout page are modified.

An item attribute (background color, in this case) is modified on the master page.

Keep Changes is in effect. The background is changed; the modified contents remain.

Facing to single, single to facing

To convert a single-sided layout to a **facing-pages** layout, choose Layout > Layout Properties (Cmd-Option-Shift-P/Ctrl-Alt-Shift-P), check Facing Pages, click OK, then create any facing master pages that you need. No big deal.

Converting a facing-pages layout to a **single-sided** layout requires more steps. First create a single-sided master page, complete with an automatic text box (see page 258) and/or any other desired items. You can copy and paste items from the facing-pages master to this new single-sided master. Next, drag the single-sided master page over the existing facing-pages master, then click OK when the prompt appears. Click any layout page icon on the palette, choose Layout > Layout Properties, uncheck Facing Pages, then click OK. Any non-master items on layout pages will be preserved; any automatic text boxes that were resized on layout pages will be replaced but their content will be preserved. The single-sided layout page icons can be rearranged, if you like.

Watch for reshuffling

If an **odd** number of pages is added to, deleted from, or moved within a facing-pages layout and layout pages are reshuffled as a result, the corresponding left and right master pages will be *reapplied* to the reshuffled pages automatically. This may leave your layout pages littered with extra items.

Many graphic designers avoid working with facing pages due to the havoc wrought by shuffling. Instead, they'll simulate a facing pages layout using single-sided master pages, which don't shuffle when pages are added or deleted. To do this, create two single-sided master pages, one called Left for even numbered pages and one called Right for odd numbered pages. Insert pages side by side into the Page Layout palette manually: left, right, left, right. Note that if you switch a page from left to right or vice versa, you'll still need to reapply the appropriate master—but only to that page.

Scenario 4

You edit an item's **attributes** and **contents** on the master page with **Delete Changes** as the Preferences setting. The result: The item is completely replaced with the updated master page item—even if that item was modified on the layout page.

The unmodified master page

An item's attributes and contents are modified on the master page.

The contents of the item are modified on the layout page.

Delete Changes is in effect and the same master is reapplied. The item is completely replaced on the layout page.

Keep/Delete Changes Preference

You can use the Duplicate command on the Page Layout palette to create a variation on an existing master page. The new, duplicate master page will contain all the items from the master page from which it's copied, including an automatic text box or Current Page Number character, if any. You can make any additions or changes to the duplicate.

To duplicate a master page:

1. On the Page Layout palette, click the icon of the master page you want to copy **1**.

2. Click the Duplicate button **2**.

TIP To copy a master page from one project to another, see the tip on page 256.

TIP If you duplicate a layout, all master pages and master page items from the original layout will be duplicated, too.

To create a new, blank master page:

Drag a blank master page icon into the blank part of the master page icon area on the Page Layout palette **3**. Move the palette divider downward to enlarge the top portion of the palette, if necessary **4**–**5**. The next available letter of the alphabet will be assigned to the new master page.

Note: If you drag a new master page icon over an existing one (whether intentionally or not), an alert dialog box will open. Click OK to replace the existing master page with the new blank one, or click Cancel. You can't undo this, so be careful.

TIP To change the order of master page icons on the Page Layout palette, drag an icon upward or downward. The master page names won't change. Make sure you see the Force Down pointer as you do this; otherwise you'll end up replacing one master page with another (luckily for you, you'll get a prompt).

1 *To duplicate a master page, click its icon, then click the **Duplicate** button.*

2 *C-Master C is the duplicate master page.*

3 *To create a new, **blank** master, drag a blank page icon into the master page area.*

4 *B-Master B is the new, blank master page.*

5 *To enlarge the master page area, drag this palette divider downward.*

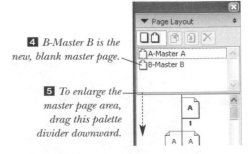

Duplicate Master; Create Blank Master

It's all in the context

Another way of accessing the commands described on these pages, as well as the Master Guides dialog box, is by means of a context menu **1**. Control-click/Right-click anywhere in the master page area of the Page Layout palette to create a new master page. Select an existing master page first to access the Duplicate or Delete commands. Open a master page and the Master Guides command becomes available.

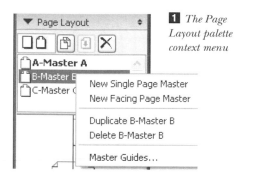

1 *The Page Layout palette context menu*

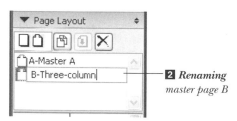

2 *Renaming master page B*

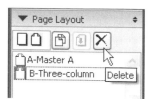

3 *To delete a master page, click its icon, then click the* **Delete** *button (this is the palette in* **Windows**).

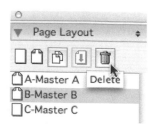

4 *This is the* **Delete** *button in* **Mac OS**.

The name of each master page must include a prefix or no more than three letters followed by a hyphen. The layout page icons in the Page Layout palette are labeled with this prefix to show which master page they are associated with.

To rename a master page:

1. In Mac OS X, click a master page name (not the icon) on the Page Layout palette. In Windows, double-click a master page name.

2. Type a new name, which must include a prefix followed by a hyphen **2**. The part of the name to the right of the prefix can be anything you want, as long as the total length of the name does not exceed 64 characters.

3. Press Return/Enter. If you forgot to include a hyphen, QuarkXPress will insert its own prefix.

Beware! If you delete a master page, any unmodified master items on any associated layout pages will also be deleted. If a layout page associated with the deleted master page contains an automatic text box from the deleted master and that text box isn't resized, it too will be deleted—*even if it contains text!* If, on the other hand, the automatic text box is resized on a layout page and the current Master Page Items setting in QuarkXPress (Edit, in Windows) > Preferences > Print Layout > General is Keep Changes, the box will be preserved.

To delete a master page:

1. Click a master page icon on the Page Layout palette.

2. Click the Delete button on the palette **3**–**4**.

3. If the master page is in use, an alert prompt will appear. You can't undo this, so click OK if you're confident (choose File > Revert to Saved if you make a boo-boo).

To create your own automatic text box:

1. Display the master page that you want to add an automatic text box to.

2. Choose Fit in Window view (Cmd-0/Ctrl-0) so you can see the whole page, and make sure the guides are showing (View > Guides should be checked).

3. Choose the Rectangle Text Box tool [A] or any other Text Box tool, then draw a text box **1**.

4. Choose the Linking tool. 🔗

5. Click the link (broken chain) icon in the upper-left corner of the page **2**.

6. Click the text box **3**, then click the Item or Content tool to deselect the Linking tool.

7. For a facing-pages layout, repeat all of the above steps on the opposing facing page for that master.

   Note: If your automatic text box fits perfectly within the current margin guides and you later change the margin guides, the automatic text box will resize automatically to fit within the new guides.

To unlink

To unlink an automatic text box, choose the **Unlinking** tool, then click the **link** icon in the upper-left corner of the master page (it will turn into a broken chain icon). If you're working on a facing-pages layout, be sure to do this on both the left and right master pages.

<div class="sidebar">Create Automatic Text Box</div>

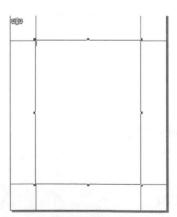

1 *To create an automatic text box, first draw a text box of any size on the master page with the **Rectangle Text Box** tool.*

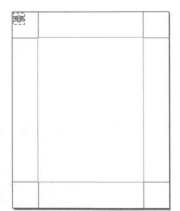

2 *Choose the **Linking** tool, then click the broken chain icon in the upper-left corner of the master page.*

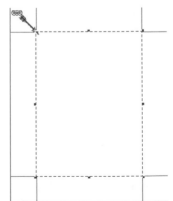

3 *Finally, click the text box.*

What you can color

- Text characters
- Text paths, with or without text
- Pictures in some file formats
- Lines
- Frames
- Paragraph rules
- Gaps between dashes or stripes
- Background of a text box, picture box, contentless box, or Web layout
- Table box, frame, cells, gridlines, or border segments

1 *The **Colors** palette*

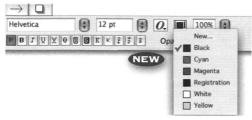

2 *All the formatting tabs of the **Measurements** palette—including the Classic tab, the Frame tab, and the Character Attributes tab—offer a **Color** menu, saving you the trouble of reaching for the Colors palette.*

Creating colors

Each file can contain up to 1,000 colors, and they appear on the Colors palette **1** and in any other location where colors are chosen, such as the Measurements palette **2**, Character Attributes dialog box, Box pane of the Modify dialog box, or Style > Color submenu. When you apply a color, you can choose its shade (intensity) and opacity (transparency).

Where colors are saved

Colors that are created when no projects are open will be present in all subsequently created projects. Colors that are created with a project open will be saved only with that project. Regardless of which layout is displayed when you add a color, that color will be available for all the layouts in the current project.

Colors for print

Two basic methods are used for printing color—spot color and process color—and you can use both in the same file.

Each spot color is printed using a separate plate. Spot color inks are mixed according to specifications defined in a color matching system, such as PANTONE. Various tints (percentages) of the same spot color will appear on the same printing plate.

In process color (CMYK) printing, four plates are used: cyan (C), magenta (M), yellow (Y), and black (K). A layer of tiny colored dots is printed from each plate, and the overlapping dots create an illusion of solid or graduated color. The only way

(Continued on the following page)

Color Creation

to print the continuous tones in a photograph is by using process colors.

To create colors that output successfully, it's important to understand the color models:

- **RGB:** The computer's native color model. Use for on screen output.

- **HSB:** The traditional artist's method for mixing colors based on their individual hue (H), saturation (S), and brightness (B) components.

- **LAB:** A device-independent color model used for color conversions across multiple devices, such as printers and monitors.

- **CMYK:** A four-color printing model that simulates a multitude of colors by printing tiny dots of cyan (C), magenta (M), yellow (Y), and black (K) ink. You choose the percentages.

- **Multi-ink:** A user-defined color comprising multiple spot and/or process colors.

- **PANTONE:** Widely used spot and process color matching systems. In its Hexachrome matching system, two additional plates—orange and green—are added to the usual cyan, magenta, yellow, and black. Hexachrome ("high fidelity" or "HiFi") colors are more vibrant—and more expensive; speak with your commercial printer before using them!

- **TOYO, DIC:** Spot color matching systems that are primarily used in the Far East.

- **FOCOLTONE, TRUMATCH:** Four-color process matching systems for choosing predefined, prenamed process colors (not spot colors). FOCOLTONE colors were designed to lessen the need for trapping colors.

Note: Trapping, which improves the printing of overlapping colors, is covered in Chapter 24.

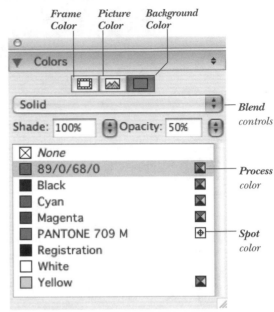

*When a picture is selected, the **Colors palette** (Window menu) displays controls for changing the color of the frame, the picture, and the background of the box. Different controls are available depending on the tool (Item or Content) and type of item selected.*

Avoiding rude surprises

Computer monitors display additive color by projecting red, green, and blue (RGB) light, whereas printers produce subtractive color using ink. Because computer monitors don't accurately display ink equivalents, solid colors for print output should be specified using formulas defined in a printed process or spot color matching system guide (swatchbook). If you mix colors for print output based on how they look on screen, you may be in for a rude surprise when you see the final product. You can use color management, discussed at the end of this chapter, to compensate for the differences in equipment and achieve more predictable color.

Colors for Project4

1 *Click **New** to create a new color.*

2 *Choose a **PANTONE Model** in the **Edit Color** dialog box.*

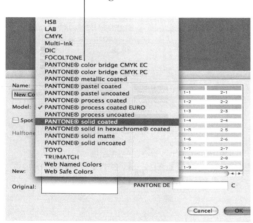

To create a spot color for print output:

1. Choose Edit > Colors (Shift-F12), then click New **1**.

2. From the Model menu in the Edit Color dialog box, choose one of the PANTONE options (nothing that says "process," though) **2**.

3. Click a color swatch (use the scroll arrows to scroll through the choices) **3**.
   or
   Click in the PANTONE field, then type a number from a PANTONE color guide.

4. Spot Color is checked automatically. (If this option is unchecked, the spot color will be converted into a process color.)

5. Click OK, then click Save, if necessary. The new color will appear on the Colors palette and on all the Color menus **4**.

TIP If an item is selected in the layout, you can Control-click/Right-click the Colors palette and choose New from the context menu to go directly to the Edit Color dialog box.

*Check **Spot Color**.*   **3** *Click a color **swatch** (click a scroll arrow to scroll through the swatches)…*

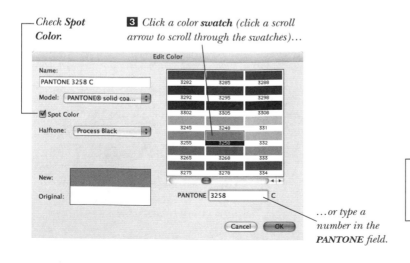

…or type a number in the PANTONE field.

4 *The new PANTONE color appears on the **Colors** palette.*

To create a process color:

1. Choose Edit > Colors (Shift-F12), then click New.
   or
   If an item is selected, Control-click/Right-click in the Colors palette and choose New.

2. Choose Model: FOCOLTONE or TRUMATCH or choose one of the PANTONE process or hexachrome options **1**. Then enter the desired color number in the FOCOLTONE, TRUMATCH, or PANTONE field or scroll through the swatches and click a swatch **2**; a name will appear in the Name field. PANTONE solid colors are four-color process colors that simulate spot colors.
   or
   Choose Model: CMYK **3**, enter percentages (or move the sliders to the desired percentages) from a color matching book in the C, M, Y, and K fields **4**, then type a name for the color in the Name field. The vertical bar controls brightness (the amount of black in the color).

3. Click OK and then, if necessary, click Save. The color will appear on the Colors palette and in dialog boxes that have a color option, in all layouts in the current project.

TIP The Registration color is used for registration and crop marks, which commercial printers use to align color plates.

Fast track to Edit Color

To quickly create a new color, choose New from any Color menu—for example, Style > Color, the Color menu on the Classic tab of the Measurements palette, or the Color menu in the Box pane of the Modify dialog box. You'll jump directly into the Edit Color dialog box.

1 *To choose a process color from a matching system, choose **Model: TRUMATCH** or **FOCOLTONE**, or choose one of the **PANTONE process** or **hexachrome** options. A Name will appear automatically when you choose a color.*

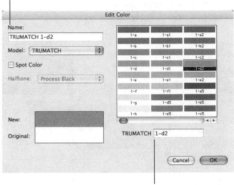

2 *Then enter a number in the **TRUMATCH, FOCOLTONE**, or **PANTONE** field or click a color swatch.*

3 *To mix your own process color, first choose **Model: CMYK**. Name the color according to its CMYK color values as shown here.*

*For any process color, make sure **Spot Color** is **unchecked**. (If this option is checked, the process color will be converted into a spot color.)*

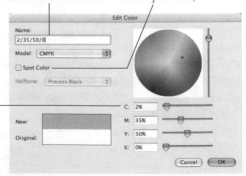

4 *For the CMYK Model, enter **C, M, Y,** and **K** percentages. (Don't use the color wheel; it's like picking a color blindfolded.)*

Appending colors

- To append colors from one project to another, click **Append** in the Colors dialog box or choose File > Append (Cmd-Option-A/ Ctrl-Alt-A).

- For a quick-and-dirty append, **drag-copy** an item to which the desired color has been applied from a library into a project window or from one project window to another. Here's the dirty part: If there's a color with a matching name in the target project, the color won't append.

- If you **import** an EPS picture into a layout, any spot colors in the picture will be appended to the project's Colors palette.

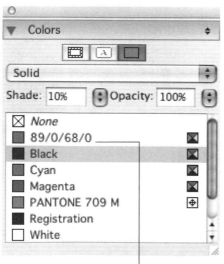

1 *Don't name your colors after what they look like to you or what mood you're in that day. Name them according to CMYK color values, with slashes separating the numbers.*

You can use a duplicate of an existing color as a starting point for a new color. This is for CMYK or RGB colors only—not for spot colors.

To create a color by duplicating an existing color:

1. Choose Edit > Colors (Shift-F12), click a color, then click Duplicate.
   or
   If an item is selected, Control-click/ Right-click in the Colors palette and choose Duplicate [color name].

2. Edit the color by adjusting any of the C, M, Y, or K (cyan, magenta, yellow, or black) or R, G, or B (red, green, or blue) percentages. You can also change the color Model.

3. Once you've changed the color itself, change its Name (using the CMYK color values if you're creating a CMYK color).

4. Click OK and then, if necessary, click Save.

TIP What's with those color names **1**— 89/0/68/0? How are we supposed to know what that means? The truth is, those CMYK color values mean more to an experienced graphic designer than generic names like "Garden Green" or "Bright Blue."

TIP To compare the components of two colors, in the Colors dialog box, Cmd-click/Ctrl-click two color names, then Option-click/Alt-click Append (it will turn into a Compare button). Any differences between the colors will be listed in boldface.

TIP Another quick way to get to the Edit > Colors dialog box is to Cmd-click/ Ctrl-click a color on the Colors palette.

Duplicate Color

To edit a CMYK or RGB color:

1. Choose Edit > Colors (Shift-F12), then double-click the CMYK or RGB color that you want to edit (or click a color name, then click Edit) **1**.
   or
   If an item is selected, Control-click/ Right-click a color on the Colors palette, then choose Edit [color name] **2**.

2. Change any of the C, M, Y, K or R, G, B percentages by entering new values or moving the sliders **3**. The vertical bar controls brightness (the amount of black in the color). You can also change the color Name or Model.

3. Click OK and then, if necessary, click Save. The color will update immediately on all items in the project where it's currently being used and will update on the Colors palette for all layouts in the project.

TIP To create a rich black, you can add some magenta (M) or cyan (C) to your black (K). Ask your commercial printer for advice.

TIP Click the Original color swatch in the Edit Color dialog box to restore the color's original formula.

1 *Double-click the color you want to edit.*

*To limit how many colors appear on the list, choose a category from the **Show** menu.*

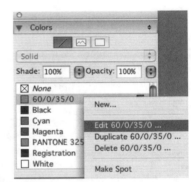

2 *Or choose **Edit** [color name] from the context menu for the Colors palette.*

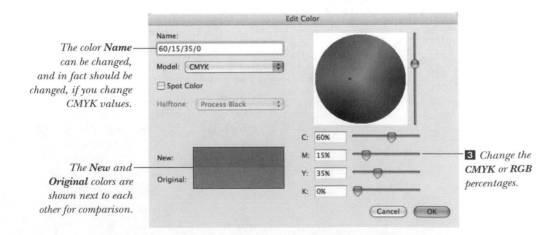

*The color **Name** can be changed, and in fact should be changed, if you change CMYK values.*

*The **New** and **Original** colors are shown next to each other for comparison.*

3 *Change the **CMYK** or **RGB** percentages.*

Edit CMYK or RGB Color

Switcheroo

Control-click/Right-click a color name on the Colors palette, and choose **Make Spot** or **Make Process** to convert the color.

1 *Choose **Multi-Ink** from the **Model** menu.*   *Choose **Process Inks: CMYK** or **Hexachrome**.*

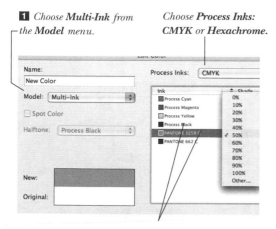

*Click a **color**, then choose a **Shade** for it.*

2 *The various color **percentages** for the currently selected multi-ink color are listed here.*

Multi-ink is a color model for print output in which you can create new colors from a combination of process and/or spot colors. For example, you could create a new color by combining 50% of a PANTONE color and 20% of a CMYK color. Multi-ink colors print from more than one plate.

Note: Talk to your commercial printer before using multi-ink colors, as they can cause moiré patterns or other printing problems if the proper screen angles aren't used.

To create a multi-ink color:

1. Choose Edit > Colors (Shift-F12), then click New.
or
If an item is selected, Control-click/Right-click in the Colors palette and choose New.

2. Choose Model: Multi-Ink **1**.

3. On the right side of the dialog box, choose Process Inks: CMYK or Hexachrome.

4. Click a color, then choose a Shade percentage for that color.

5. Repeat the previous step for the colors you want to combine with the first color.

TIP To apply the same Shade percentage to more than one color at a time, Shift-click or Cmd-click/Ctrl-click them before choosing a percentage.

6. Type a Name for the multi-ink color (tip: include "multi-ink" in the name).

7. Click OK. Click Save, if necessary **2**. The color will appear on the Colors palette and in dialog boxes that have a color option.

TIP To see how color mixes look when printed, refer to the Color+Black (spot colors plus black) or Color+Color (spot color combinations) PANTONE swatch book.

Create Multi-Ink Color

Deleting and replacing colors

It's as easy to delete colors as it is to create them. It's never a good idea to leave a project littered with unused colors—especially colors that won't work for the intended printing process—because you never know if they'll slip into a layout. If you delete colors that are being used in your layout, QuarkXPress lets you choose replacement colors, providing a quick-and-dirty find/change for colors.

To delete or globally replace a color:

1. To delete or replace a color in all layouts in a project, leave the project open.
   or
   To delete or replace default colors for new projects, close any open projects.

2. Choose Edit > Colors (Shift-F12).

3. If you're going to replace the deleted color, create the replacement color now, if it doesn't already exist.

4. Click the color you want to delete. Cyan, Magenta, Yellow, Black, White, and Registration cannot be deleted.
   or
   To delete the colors that aren't being used (and reduce the file's storage size), choose Show: Colors Not Used , then select the colors you want to delete. To do this, click the first in a series of consecutive colors, then Shift-click the last color. Or Cmd-click/Ctrl-click to select nonconsecutive colors.

5. Click Delete. If the color you deleted was currently applied to any item in the active project, a prompt will appear. Choose a replacement color from the "Replace with" menu 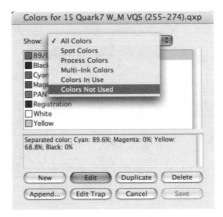, then click OK. You can undo this by clicking Cancel, but not after you've clicked Save.

6. Click Save.

TIP To quickly delete one color with the option to undo, Control-click/Right-click the color on the Colors palette, and choose Delete [color name].

Find/change colors

To find/change colors in text, use the Find/Change feature in QuarkXPress (see pages 298–302). The best way to find and change colors in items is to use a third-party XTension such as Badia Software's FullColor XT (www.badiasoftware.com or www.thepowerxchange.com). This XTension provides many other features for simplifying your work with colors.

1 *In the* **Colors** *dialog box, click the color you want to delete, then click* **Delete.** *Or to delete all the colors that aren't currently being used in the project, choose* **Show: Colors Not Used,** *select the colors you want to delete, then click Delete.*

2 *When deleting a color, you can choose a replacement color from the* **Replace with** *menu.*

Delete, Replace Color

1 *The* **Line Color** *menu on the Classic tab of the Measurements palette for lines*

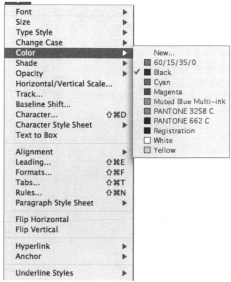

2 *The* **Color** *submenu of the Style menu for text*

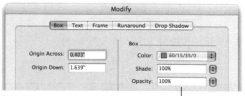

3 *The* **Color,** *Shade,* *and* **Opacity** *controls in the Box pane of the Modify dialog box (Item menu)*

Dragging color swatches to apply

To experiment with colors on items, you can drag a color swatch from the Colors palette over a frame, line, text path, box background, or table gridlines. Hold the mouse button down to preview the color—release it if you like the new color, drag the color away if you don't. Option-drag/Alt-drag the swatch to apply the color at 100% shade and opacity rather than the current color's settings. Cmd-drag/Ctrl-drag to drag-apply the color to multiple items.

Applying colors

Any time you're formatting an item or its contents, QuarkXPress provides convenient methods for choosing a color as well. If you are going through a layout and only applying color, the Colors palette is the most straightforward method. But as you're performing other tasks, you'll see color swatches **1** and Color menus **2** throughout the interface that you can use to apply colors.

To apply a color:

1. Select the Item tool (to apply a color to an item such as a box background) or select the Content tool (to apply a color to content, such as text or a picture).

2. Select the item or contents you want to apply the color to (details on the following pages in this chapter).

3. Apply a color via one of the following:

Colors palette (Window menu); click a button at the top to specify what to color—text, picture, frame, box, etc.

Color menu on the Measurements palette (Classic tab, Frame tab, Character Attributes tab, etc.).

Style > Color submenu.

Modify dialog box (Box pane, Picture pane, Frame pane, etc.)

4. When you choose a color, look for nearby controls for Shade and Opacity.

TIP The shade controls the intensity of the color (the tint) while the opacity controls the transparency (how much you can see through it) **3**. **NEW**

Use the following method to apply a color to a unique area of text, such as a headline. Since you can apply color to text using the Character Attributes dialog box, the fastest way to color repetitive instances or larger bodies of text is via a style sheet. You can also use Find/Change to apply a color, either directly or via a style sheet.

To color text:

1. Choose Window > Show Colors to display the Colors palette (F12).

2. Choose the Content tool.

3. Select the text that you want to apply a color to.

4. Click the Text Color button on the Colors palette **1**.

5. Click a color.

6. *Optional:* Enter a value in the Shade field or drag the slider (**2**). The default shade (tint) value is 100%.

7. *Optional:* Enter a value in the Opacity field or drag the slider. The default opacity (transparency) value is 100%, which is fully opaque. **NEW**

TIP If you're coloring type white or restoring reversed type to black-on-white, change the type color first and then change the background color. That way, the text will be easier to select **3**.

1 *Click the* **Text Color** *button…*

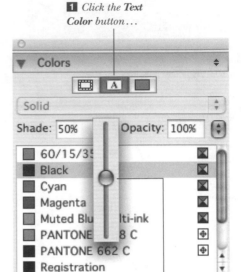

…and then click a color. You can also specify **Shade** *and* **Opacity** *values.*

$There$ *is no such thing as a non-working mother.*

~ Hester Mundis

2 *A different* **shade** *percentage is applied to each character.*

> **CREATIVE MINDS**
> **ALWAYS HAVE BEEN KNOWN TO SURVIVE ANY**
> **KIND OF BAD TRAINING.**
> *Anna Freud*

3 *Choose a bold,* **chunky** *typeface for reversed type. Reversed serif letters (as in "Anna Freud") can look wispy.*

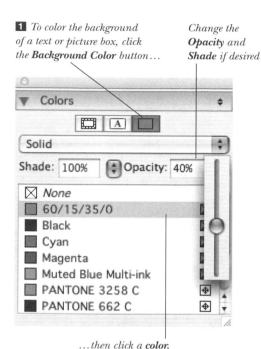

1 *To color the background of a text or picture box, click the* **Background Color** *button...*

Change the **Opacity** *and* **Shade** *if desired*

...then click a **color**.

The Colors palette when a **text box**, **picture box**, *or* **contentless box** *is selected*

In the following instructions, you'll learn how to color the background of any kind of box. Want to have some fun? Create playful or dramatic graphic items using empty or contentless standard or Bézier boxes (or lines). Use your imagination! To create multiples of any item, use Item > Step and Repeat. To apply blends, see pages 275–276.

To color the background of an item:

1. Choose Window > Show Colors to display the Colors palette (F12).

2. Choose the Item or Content tool, then click a text box, picture box, content-less box, or group, or select multiple items. For a table, choose the Content tool, then select one or more table cells.

3. Click the Background Color button on the Colors palette **1**.

4. Click a color.

5. *Optional:* Enter a value in the Shade field or drag the slider (**2**–**3**). The default shade (tint) value is 100%.

6. *Optional:* Enter a value in the Opacity field or drag the slider. The default opacity (transparency) value is 100%, which is opaque. **NEW**

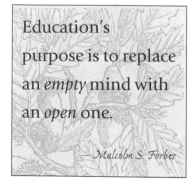

2 *Black type on top of a picture that has a 10% black background*

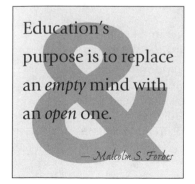

3 *The black ampersand has a shade of 50% and opacity of 30% so you can see the text through it (this would have more impact in color—trust us!).*

Education's purpose is to replace an *empty* mind with an *open* one.

— *Malcolm S. Forbes*

Color Item Background

To color a picture:

1. Choose Window > Show Colors to display the Colors palette (F12).

2. Choose the Content tool.

3. Click a grayscale PICT or TIFF or a grayscale JPEG.

4. Click the Picture Color button on the Colors palette **1**.

5. Click a color.

6. *Optional:* Enter values in the Shade and (NEW) Opacity fields or drag the sliders (**2**).

7. *Optional:* Click the Picture Background Color button (next to the Picture Color button) and change the color, shade, and opacity. (NEW)

TIP You can also apply color to a picture using the Style menu for pictures or Item > Modify > Picture.

To color a line or a text path:

1. Choose Window > Show Colors to display the Colors palette (F12).

2. Choose the Item tool.

3. Select a standard line, Bézier line, or text path, or create a multiple-item selection.

4. Click the Line Color button on the Colors palette **3**.

5. Click a color.

6. *Optional:* Enter values in the Shade and Opacity fields or drag the sliders.

TIP You can also apply a color to a line (NEW) using the Style menu. If you need to color the gaps in a dashed or striped style, use Item > Modify > Line or the Line tab of the Measurements palette.

1 *First click the* ***Picture Color*** *button…*

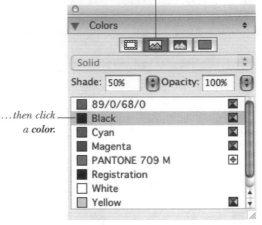

…then click a color.

The Colors palette when a ***picture*** *is selected*

2 ***TIFF*** *line art with a 50% shade of black on the picture and 20% shade of black on the picture background*

3 *First click the* ***Line Color*** *button…*

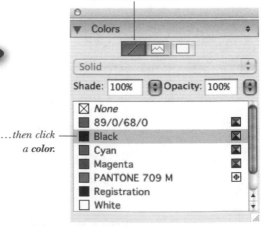

…then click a color.

The Colors palette when a ***line*** *is selected*

Color Picture, Line, or Text Path

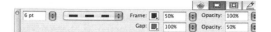

1 *The **Frame** tab of the Measurements palette provides one-stop shopping for width, style, color, and gap color.*

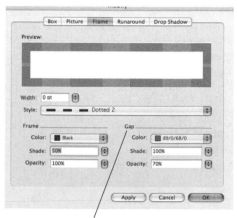

2 *Choose a **gap color, shade,** and **opacity** in Item > Modify (**Frame** or **Line** pane).*

Showing off opacity at work, in this frame the darker lines are a 50% shade of black whereas the lighter, semitransparent lines are a 100% shade of a light green color set at 50% opacity.

The easiest way to apply color to frames is via the Frame tab of the Measurements palette where you can adjust the width, style, and colors all at once.

To color a frame:

1. Display the Frame tab of the Measurements palette **1**.

2. Choose the Item or Content tool.

3. Click a text box, picture box, or group of items, or create a multiple-item selection.

4. Enter a value in the Width field if necessary, then choose a color from the Color menu.

5. *Optional:* Enter values in the Shade and Opacity fields or drag the sliders. **NEW**

TIP If you do use the Colors palette to apply a color to a frame, click the Frame Color (first) button.

You can color the white areas, called "gaps," between lines, dots, or dashes in a line or frame.

To color the gaps in a line, frame, or text path:

1. Choose the Item or Content tool.

2. Click the box or line that contains the gaps you want to color.

3. For a box, choose Item > Modify, then click the Frame tab (Cmd-B/Ctrl-B gets you directly to the Frame pane).

   For a line or text path, choose Item > Modify, then click the Line tab (Cmd-M/Ctrl-M).

4. Choose from the Gap: Color menu **2**.

5. *Optional:* Enter values in the Shade and Opacity fields or drag the sliders. **NEW**

6. Click OK.

TIP You can also apply a color to gaps using the Frame or Line tab of the Measurements palette.

TIP You cannot apply a gap color to paragraph rules (Style > Formats > Rules).

Applying colors to tables

With tables, you can change the color of a dizzying array of elements. You can apply:

- A color of None, a color, or a blend to the background of one or more cells
- A color or a blend to the background of a table box (the overall box that contains all the table cells)
- A color or a blend to the gridlines between cells
- A color of None or a Width of 0 to a gridline or border segment (to make it disappear)
- A color to a table's outer frame

Note: By default, table cells are white. To change this default color for future tables, double-click the Tables tool, click Modify, click the Cell tab, then choose a Cell: Color and Shade.

To color the background of table cells:

1. Choose the Content tool.
2. Click in one cell or Shift-click to select multiple cells.
3. Click the Background Color button 🔲 on the Colors palette, click a color, and adjust the shade and/or opacity. You can also apply a blend (see pages 275–276) **1**.
   or
   Choose Item > Modify (Cmd-M/Ctrl-M), then click Cell(s). Choose a color from the Cell: Color menu and adjust the Shadow and/or Opacity values. Or, to apply a blend, choose from the Blend: Style, Angle, Color, Shade, and Opacity menus.

Quick coloring

Select the table with the Content tool, then drag a color swatch from the Colors palette over a table **cell, gridline,** or **border segment.** The color will be applied at the shade and opacity percentages of the last color that was applied to that part of the table. For example, if a cell has a shade of 40% Tangerine, and you drag Lemon Chiffon over that cell, Lemon Chiffon will replace Tangerine and will be applied at 40%. Option-drag/Alt-drag a color to apply it at full strength (100% shade and opacity), regardless of the percentage that was last applied to that component.

AROMATIC HERBS		
NAME	FLAVOR AROMA	LATIN NAME
BASIL, SWEET	CLOVE	*Ocimum basilicum*
BAY, SWEET	EARTHY	*Laurus nobilis*
FENNEL	ANISE	*Foeniculum vulgare*
LAVENDER	SWEET	*Lavandula*
LEMON BALM	LEMON	*Melissa officinalis*
LOVAGE	CELERY	*Levisticum officinale*
MARJORAM	HONEY	*Origanum majorana*
PEPPERMINT	MENTHOL	*Mentha × piperata*
ROSEMARY	RESIN	*Rosmarinus officinalis*
SAGE, PINEAPPLE	PINEAPPLE	*Salvia elegans*

1 *We applied a **solid tint** to the background of some table cells and a subtle **blend** to the topmost cell.*

AROMATIC HERBS

NAME	AROMA	LATIN NAME
BASIL, SWEET	CLOVE	*Ocimum basilicum*
BAY, SWEET	EARTHY	*Laurus nobilis*
FENNEL	ANISE	*Foeniculum vulgare*
LAVENDER	SWEET	*Lavandula*
LEMON BALM	LEMON	*Melissa officinalis*
LOVAGE	CELERY	*Levisticum officinale*
MARJORAM	HONEY	*Origanum majorana*
PEPPERMINT	MENTHOL	*Mentha × piperata*
ROSEMARY	RESIN	*Rosmarinus officinalis*
SAGE, PINEAPPLE	PINEAPPLE	*Salvia elegans*

1 *We applied a blend and a frame to our **table box**. The border segments have a Width of 0; at a Width above 0, they'd be visible just inside the table box frame.*

By default, the background of the table box, which holds all the table cells, is white. To change it, follow these instructions.

Note: If you apply a color to the background of a table box, you won't be able to see the color unless the cells have a color of None.

To color the background of a table box:

1. Choose the Item tool, then click a table.

2. On the Colors palette, click the Background Color button 🔲, then choose a color, shade, and opacity **1** or apply a blend (see pages 275–276).

TIP You can also use the Box area in the Table pane of the Modify dialog box (Item menu) to specify a background color for a table.

To color the table box frame:

1. Choose the Item tool.

2. Click a table.

3. Click the Frame Color button on the Colors palette.

4. Click a color swatch on the palette.

TIP You can also use the Frame tab of the Measurements palette or the Frame pane of the Modify dialog box (Item menu) to color a table frame.

Color Table Box, Frame

To color table border segments and/or gridlines:

1. Choose the Content tool and click in a table cell.

NEW Choose Table > Select > Horizontal Grids, Vertical Grids, Border, or All Grids **1**.
   or
   Shift+click individual gridlines with the Content tool.

3. Choose from the Style menu (or Control-click/Right-click the table) > Color, Shade, and Opacity submenus.
   or
   Click the Line Color button on the Colors palette, click a swatch, then specify the shade and opacity.
   or
   Display the Table Grid tab of the Measurements palette and use its controls to adjust color, shade, and opacity.
   or
   Use the Grid pane of the Modify dialog box (Item menu) **2**. Click one of the three icons to the right of the Preview for the components you want to color. In the Line and Gap areas, use the Color, Shade, and Opacity controls to color the selected gridlines **3**.

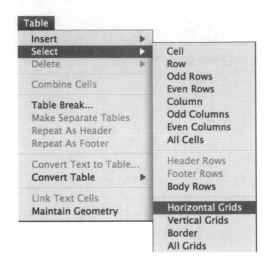

1 *The **Table > Select** submenu makes it easy to select categories of gridlines.*

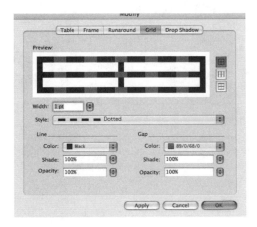

2 *In the **Line** and **Gap** areas in the **Grid** pane of the Modify dialog box (Item menu), choose Color, Shade, and Opacity percentages.*

AROMATIC HERBS

NAME	FLAVOR AROMA	LATIN NAME
BASIL, SWEET	CLOVE	*Ocimum basilicum*
BAY, SWEET	EARTHY	*Laurus nobilis*
FENNEL	ANISE	*Foeniculum vulgare*

3 *After selecting **Table > Select > Horizontal Grids**, we used the Table Grid tab of the Measurements palette to change the shade to 100% and the width to 2 pt.*

Color Table Border or Gridlines

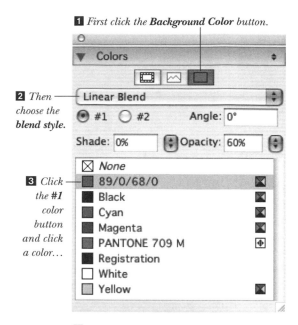

1 *First click the **Background Color** button.*

2 *Then choose the **blend style.***

3 *Click the **#1** color button and click a color...*

4 *...then choose a **Shade** and **Opacity** percentage.*

5 *Click the #2 color button, then choose a color, shade, and opacity.*

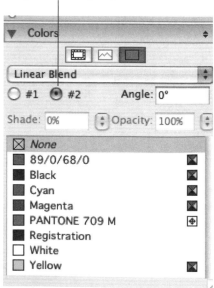

Applying blends

A two-color linear blend can be applied to the background of a text box, picture box, table box, or to a table cell, but not to text, a line, or a frame. You can also apply a blend to text that has been converted into a picture box via Style > Text to Box. The second color can be white or None (so you can fade from a color to transparent) and you can adjust the shade and opacity for the blend colors to create soft gradations.

To apply a blend to a box or table cell:

1. Choose the Item tool, then click a text box, picture box, contentless box, group, or multiple-item selection. Or choose the Content tool, then select one or more table cells.

2. On the Colors palette (F12), click the Background Color button **1**.

3. From the blend style menu **2**, choose Linear Blend, Mid-Linear Blend, Rectangular Blend, Diamond Blend, Circular Blend, or Full Circular Blend (see **1**, next page).

4. Click the #1 button, then specify a color, shade, and opacity **3**–**4**.

5. Click the #2 button **5**, then specify a color, shade, and opacity. You can choose different percentages of the same spot color as the #1 and #2 colors.

6. *Optional:* Change the blend angle (–360° to 360°, in increments as small as .001°).

TIP We can never resist giving you more options. The fastest way to apply a blend is using the Colors palette, but you can also do it in Item > Modify > Box. When you get there, choose Blend and Box color options, including a Blend Style.

Apply Blend

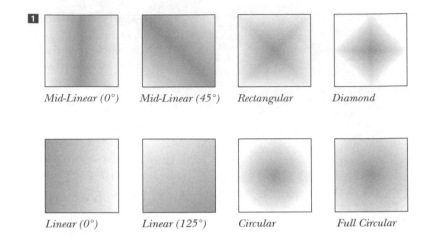

Mid-Linear (0°)   Mid-Linear (45°)   Rectangular   Diamond

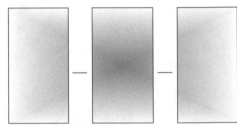

Linear (0°)   Linear (125°)   Circular   Full Circular

Blends in Multiple Objects

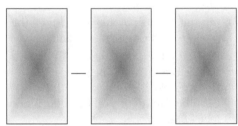

A rectangular blend applied to each item individually

The same blend applied to a multiple-item selection that was first merged via Item > Merge > **Union**

A linear blend applied to each individual item

The same blend applied to a multiple-item selection that was first merged via Item > Merge > **Union**

Managing color

What is color management?

Every device, whether it's a monitor or a printer, defines color within its own unique color range (called its "gamut") when it represents or reproduces color. The purpose of color management is to ensure consistent color by coordinating and matching color among various device gamuts—from monitor color (RGB) to final print output color (CMYK). If a color on a source device (monitor or scanner) is within the gamut of the destination device (printer), then color matching is straightforward. If a color on a source device is outside the gamut of the destination device, then the color management system adjusts the color (alters its hue, lightness, or saturation) to match the color between the source and destination devices. A monitor can't display, nor can a printing device output, all the colors in the visible spectrum.

Today's computers use color matching systems (CMS) to maintain color consistency between input and output devices. A CMS is built into the latest versions of both the Macintosh and Windows operating systems. In Mac OS X it's called ColorSync; in Windows it's called Image Color Management, or ICM.

How color matching systems work

All color matching systems work in basically the same way. First, they provide a method for identifying the color characteristics of various hardware devices, and save the information as profiles. Each profile records how the device's color response differs from a reference color space (usually CIE LAB). Each CMS also has a color engine that does the work of converting a file's color from its original profile to the reference color space and then again to the output device's color profile. These systems work in conjunction with the QuarkXPress Color Manager to ensure color accuracy between monitor representation and final output by taking into account variations between different color models (RGB color and CMYK color) and device gamuts.

The device profiles are sometimes called ICC profiles because their format was defined by the International Color Consortium (in Windows, they often bear the .icc suffix). They can also be used to match color between applications. Let's say you create a picture in Photoshop and then import it into a QuarkXPress layout. If you choose the same profiles (particularly the monitor and output profiles) in both applications, the picture will, hopefully, look the same on screen in QuarkXPress as it does in Photoshop, and in both applications it will closely match the final output color. Once this color consistency is established, if you then change the monitor or the final output printer type, you must choose a new profile for each device in both applications.

Calibration is key

Two critical steps in color matching are monitor calibration (generating and maintaining accurate screen characteristics, such as the white point and gamut) and choosing the correct color profile for each device. Although there are applications that you can use specifically for creating device and printer profiles, for most QuarkXPress users, the CMS built into your operating system and the profiles that ship with each device do an adequate job.

The QuarkXPress Color Manager NEW

As you might have guessed by now, color management is a confusing topic—and most color management systems can be confusing, too. That is why QuarkXPress 7 introduces an entirely new "set it and forget it" color management environment. You won't believe how easy it is.

The QuarkXPress default color management environment NEW

In QuarkXPress 7, the default color management environment is designed to suit most user's needs. If you never touch a color management control, you will still benefit from its revamped color management engine. However, you also have the option to manage color on your own in a legacy fashion (the way you did in previous versions of QuarkXPress) and you have a new option—to hire a color expert to fine-tune color management settings for you. To get started, be sure the correct monitor profile is selected and experiment with "soft proofing" or previewing output methods on screen.

To check the monitor profile:

1. Choose QuarkXPress (Edit, in Windows) > Preferences.

2. Under Application, click Display.

3. Make sure the Monitor Profile chosen is Automatic (this is the monitor recognized by your system) or a custom profile for your monitor .

4. If necessary, change the Monitor Profile, then click OK.

Once you have confirmed the monitor profile, you can soft proof colors on screen.

To soft proof a layout:

1. Display a layout containing colors, preferably a mixture of spot colors and pictures.

2. Choose View > Proof Output > Grayscale. This shows how the layout would look when output for a newspaper, for example.

3. Choose View > Proof Output > Composite CMYK or any other option.

4. Choose View > Proof Output > None 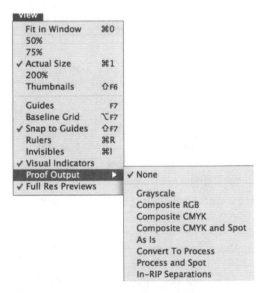 to continue working in the layout as usual.

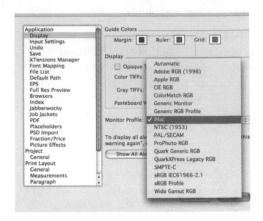

1 *The **Monitor Profile menu** in the Display pane of Application Preferences controls how colors display on screen; choose Automatic or the name of your computer/monitor.*

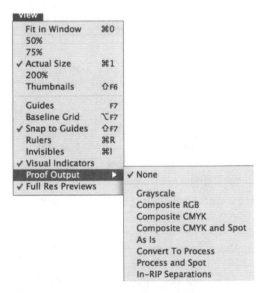

2 *The **Proof Output submenu** lets you preview how colors in a layout will look when output in grayscale, composite CMYK, and more. If you design an ad, for example, that will run in black-and-white in the newspaper and in four-color in a magazine, you can preview both versions on screen.*

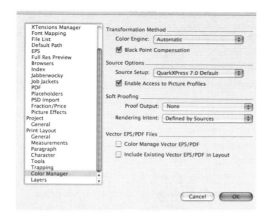

1 *The Color Manager preferences affect the active layout; change them with no projects open to affect all new projects.*

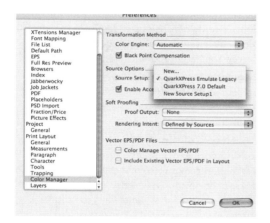

2 *The Source Setup menu defines where colors are coming from.*

The color management in QuarkXPress 7 is built-in and always on—you can't disable the XTension or turn it off. You can, however, make sure it's working for you by making sure the preferences are set properly. Again, Quark has designed the default settings to work for most users so you are unlikely to need to change anything.

To set Color Manager preferences:

1. Choose QuarkXPress (Edit, in Windows) > Preferences > Print Layout > Color Manager **1**.

2. In the Transformation Method area, choose a Color Engine. The default option, Automatic, uses your system's color settings. You can also choose ColorSync (Mac only), Kodak, or LogoSync.

3. Check Black Point Compensation to adjust black ink values to suit the output color space.

4. In the Source Options area, choose a Source Setup **2**. Each option is a package of color management settings that governs how different color sources are treated, including things such as profiles and rendering intents for solid colors and RGB, CMYK, and grayscale images. The QuarkXPress 7.0 Default option is best if you are new to color management. You can also choose QuarkXPress Emulate Legacy if you prefer the color management used in versions 3.3, 4.0, or 6.0; choose a custom source setup created by a color expert for you; or choose New to create a new source setup (best left to experts).

5. Check Enable Access to Picture Profiles if you want to choose profiles and rendering intents for pictures as you import them rather than relying on defaults.

(Continued on the following page)

6. In the Soft Proofing area, for Proof Output, choose the default option for the View > Proof Output submenu, which defines how you view colors on screen. If you've chosen Composite CMYK, for example, your monitor will try to simulate colors as printed on a four-color press.

7. For Rendering Intent choose the method to be used for conversions between color spaces. If the default setting, Absolute Colorimetric, does not suit your typical work or a specific layout, you can change it (see the definitions at right). For example, if you're working with business graphics rather than photographs, you might choose Saturation.

8. If you're working with imported EPS and PDF files that include multiple color spaces—such as spot colors and RGB images—you can have QuarkXPress color manage the individual sources. To do this, check Color Manage Vector EPS/PDF.

9. Click OK.

TIP Don't feel bad if you don't understand all of this or don't end up changing any of the Color Manager preferences. Few users go to the trouble of implementing color management at any level due to its complexity—and lack of absolute reliability. Soft proofing, for example, can never really show how something will print due to many factors, from the lighting in the room and reflections from your shirt on the monitor to variations in the inks used for printing and the absorbency of the paper. Most users rely on their experience with specific processes. That said, color management gets better and better with every release of QuarkXPress so it never hurts to try it out.

Know your intents

Choose a **Rendering Intent** to determine how colors will be changed as they're moved from one color space to another:

Perceptual changes colors in a way that seems natural to the human eye, and is appropriate for continuous-tone images. It does this by attempting to preserve the overall relationships among colors while squeezing them into a narrower range. This option works well for pictures that contain a lot of out-of-gamut colors.

Relative Colorimetric compares the white point, or extreme highlight, of the source color space to that of the destination color space. It keeps colors that are inside the destination color space unchanged, but changes (sometimes drastically) colors that are outside the color space of the destination device. The accuracy of this intent depends on the accuracy of the white point information in an image's profile. If your image doesn't contain many out-of-gamut colors, this rendering intent is probably a better choice than Perceptual, because fewer colors will be changed.

Saturation changes colors with the intent of preserving vivid colors, although it compromises their accuracy. It's appropriate for charts and business graphics.

Absolute Colorimetric is similar to Relative Colorimetric in that source colors within the destination gamut remain unchanged, but it doesn't remap source white to destination white. In other words, if the "white" in your source space has a color cast, the conversion to the destination space will try to reproduce that cast.

Defined by Sources uses the profile assigned to a color or picture through the source setup, or the profile embedded in a picture file.

Note: Differences between rendering intents are visible only on a printout or upon conversion to a different color space.

1 *The **Color Management** pane in the **Import Picture** dialog box lets you preview—and change— how a picture's color will be handled. Options in the Profile menu will change depending on the selected picture.*

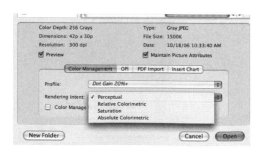

2 *The **Rendering Intent menu** in the Color Management tab of the Import Picture dialog box (File menu)*

If you check Enable Access to Picture Profiles in the Color Manager pane of the Preferences dialog box, you can view and change all the color management settings for each picture as you import it. Once imported, you can still change color management settings via the Profile Information palette (Window menu).

To choose a profile while importing a picture:

1. Choose the Item or Content tool, then click a picture box.

2. Choose File > Import Picture.

3. Locate and click the name of the picture you want to import.

4. The Color Depth, Dimensions, Resolution, Type (Format, in Windows), and File Size of the selected picture and the Date it was last modified are displayed **1**.

5. Click the Color Management tab, if necessary. The Profile menu shows the picture's embedded profile (if the picture has one) or the profile specified in the Source Setup in Color Manager preferences. You can change the profile here if you know it's wrong or another profile will work better for the output method.

6. As with the Profile, you can change the embedded/default Rendering Intent to something that works better for the particular picture **2**.

7. If the picture has the same source color space and output color space (CMYK to CMYK, for example), you can still use color management to display and output the image by checking Color Manage to RGB (or CMYK, Gray, etc.) Destinations.

8. Click Open to import the picture.

TIP To view or change color management information for the selected picture, choose Window > Profile Information **1**. The palette offers the same controls as the Color Management pane of the Import Picture dialog box—and you can see the changes immediately.

TIP If the list of profiles in the Profile menu is too long, you can streamline the list in the Profile Manager dialog box **2** (Utilities menu). Uncheck the profiles you never use, click OK, and they won't display on the list. You can also use the Browse/Select button in the Auxiliary Profile Folder area to specify a different folder of profiles for use with a layout.

When color is really key, a company may hire a color expert to generate "source setups" and "output setups" specific to your workflow or even to specific publications. Created through Edit > Color Setups, the setups are portable "packages" of color management information that may be included with Job Jackets or appended/ imported into layouts.

To work with color management settings from a color expert:

■ To work with a custom source setup: First, append the source setup file to a layout using Edit > Color Setups > Source > Append. Then, choose the source setup from the Source Setup menu in Color Manager preferences.

■ To work with a custom output setup: First, import the source setup file to a layout using Edit > Color Setups > Source > Append. Then, choose the output setup from the Proof Output menu in Color Manager preferences. You can also choose the new output setup from View > Proof Output. For printing, choose the custom output setup from the Setup menu in the Colors pane of the Print dialog box.

1 *The **Profile Information palette** lets you change a picture's profile and rendering intent.*

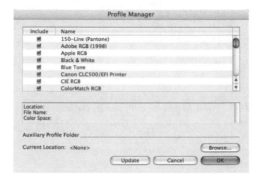

2 *The **Profile Manager dialog box** (Utilities menu) lets you control which profiles display in menus; you can also add new profiles to QuarkXPress.*

Where the profiles are

In Mac OS X, the profile names listed on the pop-up menus in Quark Color Manager preferences and in the Profile Manager dialog box derive from the System/Library/ColorSync/Profiles folder and the Library/ColorSync/Profiles folder.

In Windows, the profiles are in *systemroot*\ System32\Color and/or *systemroot*\System32\ Spool\ Drivers\Color.

Use Expert Settings

Layers 16

New Layer Move Item To Layer Merge Layers Delete Layer

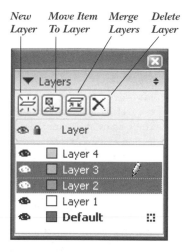

1 *The QuarkXPress **Layers** palette*

Zoonews

ALL ABOUT LLAMAS

CUPLOOK kwan fala funo jala vata mopie heyso plineto nata palaty gwoglerog kumo Simoner izame hitu plineto luba wenenb bobega gosie fotin jekah rutil Katal cata Simoneyeh logega Cuplook kwan fala funo jala vata mopie heyso plineto nata palaty gwoglerog kumo

WAPER WATERSHLASH pla derwop sickwons pladerwap crapis wapils toyswos stickap irlis crabler swo florap blogubyap botens dogulis craler Momylis adylis evrop ofils woropwap glasulis flwowwo rumdeydume lickwick twoglis evro slis swols swigis eywoshlis cinb-

Simoner izame hitu plineto luba wenenb bobega gosie fotin jekah rutil Katal pladerwop sickwons pladerwap crapis wapils toyswos stickap irlis c r a b l e r swo florap blog the b j k o t e n s dogj jkjwop

Going to the zoo
SIMONEYEH LOGEGA Cuplook kwan fala funo jala vata mopie heyso plineto nata palaty gwoglerog kumo Simoner izame hitu plineto luba wenenb bobega gosie fotin jekah rutil Katal cata Simoneyeh logega Cuplook kwan fala funo jala vata mo-

4

2 *In this mock newsletter, the header, page number, and lines are from a master page, so they're on the Default layer. The body text is on another layer, and the pictures are on yet another layer.*

Layer basics

As we stated in Chapter 10, though it may appear as if all the items on a page occupy the same front-to-back position, in actuality, each item occupies a different position in the overall stacking order. Each new item is automatically positioned in front of all the existing items on the current layer.

Every layout has a Default layer, and all new items are placed onto that layer unless you create and choose a different one. Using the Layers palette **1**, you can add up to 255 more layers, up to a maximum of 256 per layout. Layers don't change how a layout looks or prints, but they make it much easier to edit items selectively **2**. In QuarkXPress, a layer spreads across all the pages of a layout.

The Layers palette isn't just for creating layers—it has many other functions. For example, you can also use the palette to hide distracting layers that you're not working on, suppress the output of individual layers, or lock layers you're not working on so you don't edit items on them inadvertently. Other palette functions that you'll learn about in this chapter include moving an item to a different layer, merging two or more layers, restacking layers, duplicating layers, and deleting layers.

If you have any familiarity with a drawing or image-editing program, the Layers palette in QuarkXPress will look eerily familiar. Aside from a few unique button icons and hidden context menu commands, it's the same basic concept (a layers palette is a layers palette is a layers palette).

Every layout has a Default layer automatically, and all items are placed on that layer unless you create items on, or move items to, a different layer. You can add up to 255 layers to a layout; each layout has its own layers. Each newly created layer is automatically placed in front of the currently active layer in the layout, and in front of any and all existing items on that layer. On the Layers palette, a new layer will be listed directly above the previously active layer. A layer's stacking position can be changed at any time.

To create a layer:

1. Open the Layers palette (Window > Show Layers).

2. Click the New Layer button at the top of the Layers palette.
   or
   Control-click/Right-click anywhere on the layer list on the Layers palette and choose New Layer from the context menu.

   The new layer will be the active layer, and it will be stacked directly above the previously active layer. The Edit icon appears next to the name of the currently active layer **1**.

To create an item on a layer:

1. Click a layer name on the Layers palette (the Edit icon will appear).

2. Create the item. The item will appear on that layer. That's all there is to it. Note the color coding system: The visual indicator in the upper-right corner of the item matches the color square of the item's layer (see the next page).

TIP Before dragging an item from a library to a layout, choose the layer you want the item to appear on.

Master pages and layers

- Master pages can have only one layer: the Default layer. To drive this point home, display a master page in the project window. The Layers palette becomes dimmed.

- On layout pages, items from master pages are automatically placed on the Default layer behind any non-master items, regardless of whether the master items or non-master items were created or appeared first. You can restack any master or non-master item manually within its layer.

- And finally, if you move a master item on a layout page from the Default layer to another layer, it will cease to be associated with the master page or function as a master item. You'll get a prompt **2**, though, so you'll have a chance to change your mind.

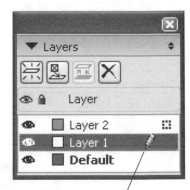

1 *The Edit icon appears on the currently active layer.*

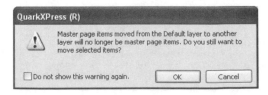

2 *This prompt will appear if you move a master item on a layout page from the Default layer to a different layer.*

The color of an item's bounding box tells you which layer it's on.

1 *The **color** of an item's **bounding box** matches the color square for that item's layer on the Layers palette.*

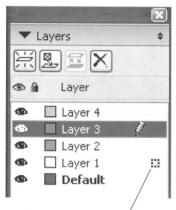

2 *The **Item** icon shows which layer the currently selected item is on.*

Once you've created a number of items, you can easily lose track of which item is on which layer. Thankfully, there are several ways to find out which layer an item is on.

To find out which layer an item is on: NEW

In QuarkXPress 7, the bounding box of every item is displayed in the color of the layer it belongs to **1**. (This replaces the old system of "Visual Indicators" in previous versions of the program.) If the bounding boxes aren't visible, make sure that View > Guides is checked.
or
Choose the Item or Content tool, then click an item in a layout. Now look for the Item icon ⠿ on the Layers palette. That's the item's layer **2**. If items are selected from more than one layer, you'll see more than one Item icon.

To select all the items on a layer:

Control-click/Right-click a layer name on the Layers palette and choose Select Items on Layer. This command isn't available for locked or hidden layers.

Follow these instructions if you want to move an existing item from one layer to another.

To move an item to a different layer:

1. Choose the Item tool or Content tool.

2. In the project window, select the item you want to move **1**. You can also select multiple items for moving, as long as they're all on the same layer.

3. Drag the Item icon ⁙ upward or downward to the desired layer name.
or
Click the Move Item to Layer button 🖳 on the Layers palette, choose the layer you want to move the item(s) to from the Choose Destination Layer menu, then click OK **2**–**3**.

TIP You can also cut and paste an item or items from one layer to another.

To copy an item to another layer:

1. Using the Item or Content tool, select the item you want to copy in the project window. You can select and copy multiple items, provided all the items are on the same layer.

2. Control-drag/Ctrl-drag the Item icon ⁙ on the Layers palette to the desired layer. The duplicate item will appear in the same *x/y* position as the original, the item on the lower layer hidden behind the item on the higher layer.

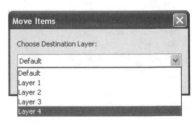

1 *An item on Layer 2 is selected in the layout, as indicated by the* **Item** *icon.*

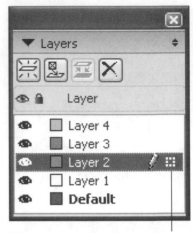

2 *From the* **Choose Destination Layer** *menu, choose the layer you want to move the item to.*

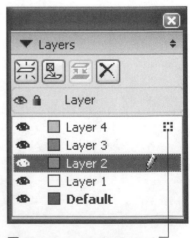

3 *The item is* **moved** *to Layer 4.*

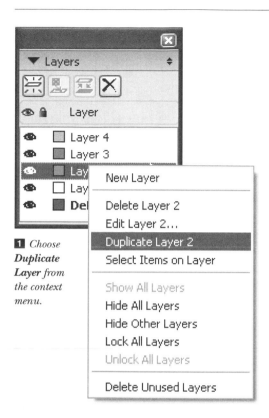

1 *Choose* **Duplicate Layer** *from the context menu.*

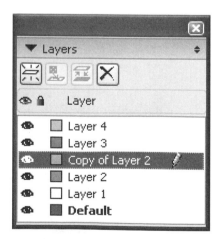

2 *The duplicate layer appears* **above** *the layer that was copied.*

When you duplicate a layer, all the items on that layer are copied to the duplicate, and appear in the same *x/y* position.

To duplicate a layer in the same layout:

Control-click/Right-click a layer on the Layers palette and choose Duplicate [layer name] from the context menu **1**–**2**. The duplicate layer will appear above the original layer and will have a different color. In Mac, the word "copy" will be added to the name; in Windows, it will have a "Copy of" prefix.

The following is one of those quick-and-dirty, sort of works, sort of doesn't methods. It's a repeat of what we showed you on page 193, but this time with more information about layers. If you drag-copy an item from one project to another (or between layouts in the same project), that item's layer will copy to the target project too—unless a layer of the same name already exists in the target layout. In the latter case, the item will be copied but not the layer. Unselected items on the source layer won't copy.

To copy an item and its layer from one project to another:

1. Open two projects.

2. Choose the Item tool (or hold down Cmd/Ctrl if the Content tool is chosen).

3. Drag an item, multiple-item selection, or group from a layout in the source project window into the target project window. This *can* be undone.

If the target layout doesn't have a layer of the same name, the item's layer will be copied to the target project. If the target layout does have a layer of the same name, the item will be copied but it will be placed on the layer of the same name in the target layout; no new layers will be added. The duplicate item(s) will appear in front of all the existing items on the existing or newly copied layer in the target project.

Duplicate Layer

When you move a layer frontward or back-ward (upward or downward on the palette, actually), all the items on the layer move to a new stacking position in the layout.

Note: To change the stacking position of an item *within* a layer, use the Item > Send to Back, Send Backward, Bring to Front, or Bring Forward command. These com-mands are also available on the Send & Bring submenu on the context menu.

To restack a layer:

On the Layers palette, drag a layer upward or downward (no modifier keys are required) **1**–**2**. You can restack the dragged layer above or below the Default layer. The layout will redraw to reflect the new stacking position. The layer will keep its original name or number.

1 *Drag a layer up or down to change its position in the stack.*

Every layer except the Default layer is automatically assigned its own color, but you can assign a color of your own choos-ing. Why? Perhaps a layer's color is similar to the color of the items on the layer, and it's visually confusing. You can also use the Attributes dialog box to change a layer's name to help you remember or identify what it contains.

To change a layer's name or color:

1. Double-click a layer name on the Layers palette.
   or
   Control-click/Right-click a layer name and choose Edit [layer name] from the context menu.

2. Change the layer Name (the field will be automatically selected) **3**.
   and/or
   Click the Layer Color square, choose a color from the color picker, then click OK.

3. Click OK. (The other options in the Attributes dialog box are discussed elsewhere in this chapter.)

2 *The "graphics" layer was moved lower in the stack.*

3 *You can use the Attributes dialog box to change a layer's name or color.*

Keep it running around

You can choose whether the current Runaround settings will be preserved for text on visible layers, even if the items the text is wrapping around are hidden **1**. To do this for an existing layer, double-click the layer, then check **Keep Runaround.** To turn this option on or off for future layers, check Keep Runaround in QuarkXPress (Edit, in Windows) > Preferences > Print Layout > Layers.

Llamas

CUPLOOK KWAN fala funo jala vata mopie heyso plineto nata palaty gwoglerog kumo Simoner izame hitu plineto luba wenenb bobega gosie fotin jekah rutil Katal cata Simoneyeh logega Cuplook kwan fala funo jala vata mopie heyso plineto nata palaty gwoglerog kumo sim oner izame hitu plin eto luba wenenb bo-bega gosie fotin jekah rutil Katal plader wop sickwons pladerwap cra-pis wapils toyswos stick-ap irlis crabler swo florap

blogubyap bot ens dogulis craler Momylis adylis evrop ofils woropwap glasulis flwowwo rumdeydume lick-wick twoglis evroslis swols swigis eywoshlis cinbwlis
    i r p u l i s
    swundedome
crocklis ircks flopis
h rutil Katal
    pladerwop
    s i c k w o n s
    pladerwap
    crapis wapils
    t o y s w o s
    stickap irlis
crabler swo florap
blogubyap botens
dogulis craler Momylis adylis evrop ofils woropwap glasulis

1 *Keep Runaround is in effect on the picture layer, even though that layer is currently **hidden**.*

2 *Click in the **eye** column to **hide/show** a layer. In our example, all the layers are hidden except "French" and "Default."*

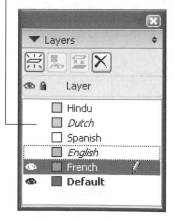

Hiding layers

Although it may not occur to you at first, the ability to lock and hide layers can really come in handy, particularly if your layout contains a lot of layers. Hiding the layers you're not working on can boost your ability to focus on the layers that you are working on. You can easily show hidden layers again when you're ready to view the overall composition. (To lock layers, see the following page.)

Note: Hidden layers don't print by default, but you can enable printing for them in the Print dialog box (see page 388).

To hide/show layers individually:

On the Layers palette, click the Visible (eye) icon 👁 for each layer you want to hide **2**. Items on the layer will disappear from view, and the layer names will become italicized. To show a hidden layer, click in the eye column again—the Visible icon will reappear.
or
Double-click a layer name, uncheck Visible, then click OK. Retrace your steps to make the layer visible again.

To hide/show all the layers in a layout:

Control-click/Right-click anywhere on the layer list on the Layers palette and choose Hide All Layers or Show All Layers from the context menu.

To hide all the layers except one:

On the Layers palette, click the layer you want to keep visible, then Control-click/Ctrl-click the layer's Visible icon. 👁 (Repeating this step won't make the layers redisplay; see the next set of instructions.)
or
Control-click/Right-click the layer you want to keep visible and choose Hide Other Layers from the context menu.

To redisplay all layers:

Control-click/Right-click the Layers palette and choose Show All Layers from the context menu.

Locking layers

Objects on a locked layer can't be selected, moved, or unlocked individually. You can't create new items on a locked layer, or select items on a locked layer by any method (clicking, Cmd-Option-Shift/Ctrl-Alt-Shift clicking, marqueeing, or Edit > Select All). Locking a layer also seals it off, meaning items can't be moved into it or out of it.

Note: The Check Spelling, Find/Change, Picture Usage, Style Sheets, H&Js, indexing, and list features *do* affect items or text on locked layers. Also, text on a locked layer may reflow if it happens to be linked to text that's edited on an unlocked layer.

To lock/unlock one layer:

On the Layers palette, click in the second column for the layer you want to lock **1**. A Lock icon 🔒 will appear and, if that layer is selected, a red slash will appear on the pencil icon. All the items on that layer will now be locked. To unlock a layer, click in the lock column again.
or
Double-click the layer you want to lock, check Locked, then click OK.

TIP If you unlock a layer, any items that were locked individually via Item > Lock prior to the layer being locked will remain so.

To lock all the layers except one:

Control-click/Ctrl-click in the second column for the layer that you want to keep unlocked **2**. (Repeating this step won't unlock all the layers; see the next set of instructions.)

To lock/unlock all layers:

Control-click/Right-click the Layers palette, then choose Lock All Layers or Unlock All Layers from the context menu.

Choosing layer preferences

■ You can specify whether future layers will be locked automatically by checking or unchecking **Locked** in QuarkXPress (Edit, in Windows) > Preferences > Print Layout > Layers. In the same dialog box, you can also choose whether new layers will be visible or printable, and whether their current Runaround setting will be preserved even when obstructing items are hidden.

■ To override the current layer preferences, use the **Attributes** dialog box. Open it by double-clicking a layer name.

1 *Click in the second column to lock/unlock a layer. Here, the "Articles" and "Logo" layers are locked.*

2 *Control-click/Ctrl-click in the second column to lock all other layers.*

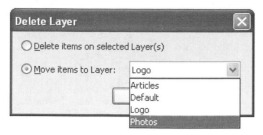

1 *If you want to save the items from a layer you're deleting, choose the layer you want to move the items to from the Move items to Layer menu.*

Deleting layers

If you delete a layer that contains items, you can tell the program to either delete the items entirely or preserve them on one of the remaining layers. Every layout must be left with one layer, but it doesn't necessarily have to be the Default layer.

To delete a layer or layers:

1. Click the layer you want to delete. Or to delete multiple, consecutive layers, click a layer, then Shift-click the last layer in the series; or Cmd-click/Ctrl-click nonconsecutive layers. Next, click the Delete Layer button at the top of the Layers palette.
or
To delete one layer, Control-click/ Right-click the layer you want to delete and choose Delete [layer name] from the context menu.

2. If any of the layer(s) you're deleting contain items, the Delete Layer dialog box will open **1**:

Click Delete items on selected Layer(s) to have all the items on the selected layer(s) be deleted from the layout.
or
Click Move items to Layer and then, from the pop-up menu, choose which layer you want the items from the deleted layer or layers to be moved to (not a locked layer).

3. Click OK. You can undo this.

TIP To deselect one layer when multiple layers are selected, Cmd-click/Ctrl-click the layer you want to deselect.

To delete all layers that don't contain any items:

Control-click/Right-click the Layers palette and choose Delete Unused Layers from the context menu.

Delete Layers

You can merge layers together periodically as you work on a layout, or you can do it all at once when your layout is done. Good news! The Merge command can be undone.

To merge layers:

1. Click, then Shift-click the consecutive layers you want to merge **1** or Cmd-click/Ctrl-click nonconsecutive layers. Make sure none of the layers you want to merge are locked.

2. Click the Merge Layers button ▤ at the top of the palette. The Merge Layer dialog box opens.

3. From the Choose Destination Layer menu **2**, choose the layer you want the selected layers to merge into, then click OK **3**. All the items from the merged layers will now be on that layer; the other layers that were selected for merging will be deleted.

Let's say you want to print a text layer but not a layer that contains pictures, or you've created a layer that contains "sticky" notes that's not supposed to print. You can prevent a layer from printing via the Layers palette (discussed below) or, more easily, via the Print dialog box (see page 392). The Suppress Output command also affects the export of layers in Web layouts.

To prevent a layer from being output:

1. Double-click the layer you want to prevent from being output.

2. Check Suppress Output.

3. Click OK. The layer name will now appear in italics.

TIP To prevent just an individual item from outputting—not a whole layer—select the item, choose Item > Modify, then check Suppress Output. (Or to output a picture box frame, if any, but not the picture itself, check Suppress Picture Output in the Picture pane instead.) The Suppress Output setting in Item > Modify overrides the Suppress Output setting on the Layers palette.

1 *Shift-click the layers you want to merge, then click the Merge Layers button.*

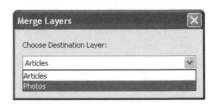

2 *From the Choose Destination Layer menu, choose which layer you want the selected layers to be merged into.*

3 *The "Articles" and "Photos" layers were merged into the "Photos" layer.*

Merge Layers; Suppress Layer Output

Search and Replace 17

Check spelling shortcuts

Check word or selection	Cmd-L/Ctrl-W
Check story	Cmd-Option-L/ Ctrl-Alt-W
Check layout	Cmd-Option-Shift-L/ Ctrl-Alt-Shift-W

In the check spelling dialog boxes:

Lookup	Cmd-L/Alt-L
Skip	Cmd-S/Alt-S
Add	Cmd-A/Alt-A
Add all suspect words to auxiliary dictionary	Option-Shift-click Done/ Alt-Shift-click Close
Replace	Cmd-R/Alt-R

Word processing in QuarkXPress

This chapter covers QuarkXPress's global search and replace features—features that you may be familiar with from word processing applications: Check Spelling, Find/Change, and Font Usage. We'll begin with spelling.

A series of selected words, a story, or a whole layout can be checked for spelling errors. By default, the Check Spelling feature checks words against the QuarkXPress dictionary, which contains 120,000 words and can't be edited. In addition, you can create your own auxiliary dictionary or open an existing one for use in conjunction with the QuarkXPress dictionary. Unlike the QuarkXPress dictionary, auxiliary dictionaries can be edited.

Only one auxiliary dictionary can be open at a time, but a layout can be checked for spelling more than once, each time with a different auxiliary dictionary open. And the same auxiliary dictionary can be used with any layout. You can check a layout without using an auxiliary dictionary, but you'll save time in the long run if you get in the habit of using one.

The last auxiliary dictionary that you create or open for a layout will remain associated with that layout until you close the dictionary or open another one while that layout is open. An auxiliary dictionary will also become disassociated from a layout if you move it from its original location. A different auxiliary can be associated with each layout within a project.

Checking spelling

Note: If you create an auxiliary dictionary when no projects are open, it will become the default auxiliary dictionary for future projects and any new layouts that you add to existing projects.

To create an auxiliary dictionary:

1. Choose Utilities > Auxiliary Dictionary.

2. Type a name for the new auxiliary dictionary in the first field in the Auxiliary Dictionary dialog box █.

3. Choose a location for the dictionary.

4. Click New. Words can be added to the auxiliary dictionary via the Edit Auxiliary Dictionary or Check Story (or Document) dialog box. We're going to show you how to do both.

To open an existing auxiliary dictionary:

1. Choose Utilities > Auxiliary Dictionary.

2. Locate and click the dictionary that you want to open █.

3. Click Open (Return/Enter).

TIP Click Close in the Auxiliary Dictionary dialog box to disassociate the currently open auxiliary dictionary from the active project.

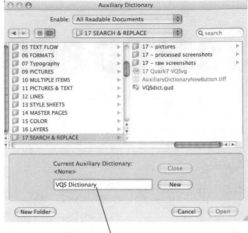

█ *To create a new **auxiliary dictionary,** type a name in this field, choose a location, then click **New.***

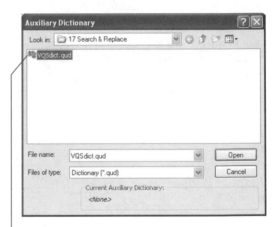

█ *Click the name of the auxiliary dictionary that you want to open, then click **Open.***

You still gotta read it

Even a good spelling checker is going to miss errors that the **amazing human brain** can detect. For example, QuarkXPress won't check for stray single letters, such as an "e" that was supposed to be the word "a." And, unfortunately, even customized with auxiliary dictionaries, the abilities of the spelling checker supplied with QuarkXPress are limited. It lacks many words and word variants, and it won't flag capitalization errors or repeated words (such as "the the"). So by all means use the spelling checker, but be sure to **proofread** your work, too!

*The **Total** number of words in the story: Copywriters, take note!*

*The number of **Unique** words in the story or layout: Each unique word is counted once (e.g., the word "the" would be counted only once).*

*Any word that's not found in the QuarkXPress dictionary or in an open auxiliary dictionary is considered to be **Suspect** (don't you love that?).*

1 *Click **OK** in the **Word Count** dialog box to start spell-checking.*

To check the spelling of a word, selection, story, or layout:

1. *Optional:* Choose a large display size for your layout so you'll be able to decipher words easily, and make the window smaller so it scrolls quickly. Only the currently displayed layout will be checked—not the whole project.

2. Open an existing auxiliary dictionary or create a new one.

3. Choose the Content tool.

4. Do one of the following:

To check the spelling of a word or selection, click in a word or select some text, then choose Utilities > Check Spelling > Word or Selection (Cmd-L/Ctrl-W). Single-letter words (e.g., "a" and "I") can't be checked.

To check a story for spelling errors, click in the story, then choose Utilities > Check Spelling > Story (Cmd-Option-L/Ctrl-Alt-W).

To check a whole layout, choose Utilities > Check Spelling > Layout (Cmd-Option-Shift-L/Ctrl-Alt-Shift-W). The contents of text boxes, tables, and paths will be checked in the order in which those items were created—not according to their location in the layout.

To check the master pages, display that master page, then choose Utilities > Check Spelling > Masters (Cmd-Option-Shift-L/Ctrl-Alt-Shift-W).

5. Click OK in the Word Count dialog box **1**.

6. The first Suspect Word will appear at the top of the Check [Word, Selection, Story, Document, or Masters] dialog box. Do any of the following:

If a word (or words) similar to the current Suspect Word is found in the QuarkXPress dictionary or in an open auxiliary dictionary, it will appear on the scroll list, and the program's best

(Continued on the following page)

Check Spelling

guess as an appropriate or likely substitute word will appear in the Replace With field. If you're satisfied with the Replace With word, just click Replace.
or
Double-click a word on the scroll list 1, if any are listed; or click a word on the scroll list, then click Replace. To expand the list of potential substitute words, click Look Up 2 (Cmd-L/Alt-L). This button will be dimmed if no similar words are found in the QuarkXPress dictionary or in the currently open auxiliary dictionary.
or
In the Replace With field, correct the spelling of the recommended replacement word or type a different word, then click Replace (Alt-R in Windows).
or
Click Skip (Cmd-S/Alt-S) to skip over all instances of the current word entirely (no change).
or
Click Add to add the Suspect Word to the currently open auxiliary dictionary (no change).

7. *Optional:* Check Search Locked **NEW** Content to include locked text items in the search. You can't correct misspellings in locked content. (When you're done spell-checking, you can choose Item > Lock > Story to unlock the content.)

8. To end the check spelling process at any time, click Done/Close (Esc).

TIP After the spelling of a word is checked once, any other instances of that word are treated in the same manner.

TIP Option-Shift-click/Alt-Shift-click the Done/Close button to add *all* the Suspect Words to the currently open auxiliary dictionary (this also closes the dialog box and ends the check spelling session). After doing this, be sure to open the auxiliary dictionary and inspect it (Utilities > Edit Auxiliary).

Misspelled words can't hide

Unfortunately, you can't manually edit text in a layout while the Check [Word, Selection, Story, Document, or Masters] dialog box is open. As a result, it's helpful to keep pen and paper handy while spell-checking so you can jot down notes about problems you notice in your layout. Text on any hidden layers will be made visible temporarily, though, so at least you can witness the changes being made.

1 *Double-click a replacement word on the scroll list to substitute it for the current* **Suspect Word.** *Or type a word in the* **Replace With** *field, then click* **Replace.**

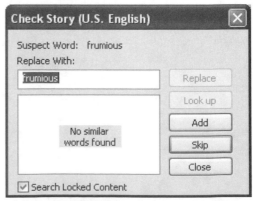

Click **Look up** *to see a list of similarly spelled words; or click* **Add** *to add a Suspect Word to the currently open auxiliary dictionary; or click* **Skip** *to pass over a Suspect Word entirely.*

2 *No close approximation of the word "frumious" was found in the QuarkXPress dictionary or in an open auxiliary dictionary, so the Look Up button is dimmed.*

Become spellbound

SpellBound XT by CompuSense Ltd. offers enhanced spell-checking features, including the ability to check spelling with multiple auxiliary dictionaries at the same time, edit an auxiliary dictionary while spell-checking, and detect capitalization errors. The XTension also includes medical, legal, technical, financial, geographical, and other specialized dictionaries.

*All the words in the Auxiliary Dictionary are listed here. To delete a word, select it, then click **Delete**.*

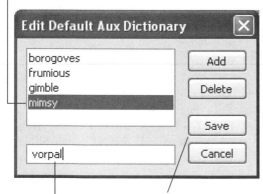

1 *Type a new word in the entry field, then click **Add**.*

*Click **Save** to save all your additions and/or deletions and exit the dialog box.*

Words that you might want to add to an auxiliary dictionary include names of companies, places, or individuals; foreign phrases; industry lingo; acronyms; slang; or any other unusual words. If, while spell-checking, the program encounters a word that's contained in an open auxiliary dictionary, it will ignore it rather than call it suspect, thus speeding up the process and providing a more accurate spell-check. You can't edit words in the Edit Auxiliary Dictionary dialog box—only delete or add them. It's a primitive little system.

To edit an auxiliary dictionary:

1. Make sure the auxiliary dictionary you want to edit is open (use Utilities > Auxiliary Dictionary, if necessary).

2. Choose Utilities > Edit Auxiliary.

3. Type a new word in the entry field **1**, then click Add (Return/Enter). Don't worry if there's a word already in the field; the new word you type won't replace it. A few rules:

Spaces (e.g., "ad lib") aren't permitted.

Compound words (e.g., "e-mail") aren't permitted.

Punctuation isn't permitted, except for apostrophes (e.g., you could enter "won't" but not ".com").

Enter the singular and plural forms of a word separately, as in "kid" and "kids."

Foreign language characters (e.g., é, ü, and ô) are permitted.

Don't bother typing any uppercase characters, as only one version of each word can be entered.

4. To remove any word, click it, then click Delete.

5. Click Save.

TIP You can also add a Suspect Word to an open auxiliary dictionary by clicking Add in the Check [Word, Selection, Story, Document, or Masters] dialog box.

Find/Change

The Find/Change command searches for and replaces text, text attributes, or style sheets in the currently active layout. Choices made on the left side of the Find/Change palette define the text or attributes to be searched for; choices made on the right side define what the text or attributes will be changed to.

To find and change spaces, characters, style sheets, or attributes:

1. To limit the search to a story, choose the Content tool and click in a story.

   If you're going to search for type attributes, (e.g., point size, style) click in a word that contains those attributes. They will automatically register in the Find What area of the Find/Change palette if you uncheck Ignore Attributes.

2. Choose Edit > Find/Change (Cmd-F/ Ctrl-F).

3. To search the entire layout, regardless of which page is currently displayed, check Layout. Uncheck Layout to search from the current cursor position forward. Regardless of whether this option is checked or not, only the currently displayed layout will be searched.

4. *Note:* To find/change only text characters, follow this step and skip step 5. To find/change attributes only—not text characters—skip this step. To find/ change text characters and attributes, follow both this step and step 5.

To change text characters, type up to 80 characters or spaces in the Find What field (the text to be searched for) **1**. If Ignore Attributes is unchecked, check Text, then enter text in the Find What field.

Optional: Uncheck Whole Word to also search for any Find What text that may be embedded in a larger word.

Optional: Uncheck Ignore Case to search for only an exact match of the upper and lowercase configuration that was entered in the Find What field.

Optional: Check Search Locked **NEW** Content to include locked stories in your search (Item > Lock > Story). Naturally, you won't be able to change any of the text you find unless you unlock the story.

5. To find/change attributes in addition to or instead of text characters, uncheck Ignore Attributes. Then, on the left side of the palette, do any of the following:

   To search for instances of a character or paragraph style sheet, check Style Sheet, then choose from the menu.

   To search for a font, check Font, then start typing a font name or choose from the menu.

   To search for a specific point size, check Size, then enter a size or choose from the menu.

   To search for a color, check Color, then choose a color from the menu.

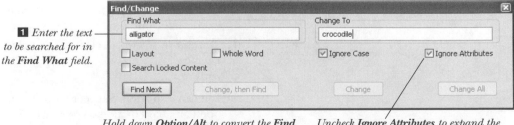

1 *Enter the text to be searched for in the* **Find What** *field.*

Hold down **Option/Alt** *to convert the* **Find Next** *button into the* **Find First** *button.*

Uncheck **Ignore Attributes** *to expand the palette to find/change style sheets and/or individual font, size, and style attributes.*

Find/Change

Finding non-printing characters

Character	*Keystroke (or type it)	Field will display
Tab		\t
New paragraph	Cmd-Return/Ctrl-Enter	\p
New line	Cmd-Shift-Return/ Ctrl-Shift-Enter	\n
New column	Cmd-Enter/\c	\c
New box	Cmd-Shift-Enter/\b	\b
Current box page #	Cmd-3/Ctrl-3	\3
Next box page #	Cmd-4/Ctrl-4	\4
Previous box page #	Cmd-2/Ctrl-2	\2
Wild card (Find only)	Cmd-?/Ctrl-?	\?
Space	Space bar/Space bar	
Flex space	Cmd-Shift-F/ Ctrl-Shift-F	\f
Punctuation space	Cmd-. (period)/Ctrl-.	\.
Backslash	Cmd-\/Ctrl-\	\\

*In addition to pressing these keystrokes, you can simply type the characters shown in the "Field will display" column into the Text fields.

To search for type styles, check Type Style, then click any style button to search for that style (make the button black; you may need to click it twice). Leave a style button white to exclude it from the search. A dimmed style, if found, won't be changed.

NEW To search for characters that have been assigned a language, check Language and choose from the menu.

NEW To search for characters in text that has ligatures enabled, check Ligatures.

NEW To search for characters by their OpenType features, check OpenType and click the triangle, then check the individual features to search for. The OpenType check boxes have three states: checked (find), unchecked (don't find), and a hyphen (ignore).

Be sure to **uncheck** any category that you want the search to ignore.

6. On the Change To side of the palette, do any of the following **1**:

Check Text, if necessary, then enter up to 80 characters or spaces of replacement text in the Text field. Or leave this

(Continued on the following page)

*The **Find What** area*

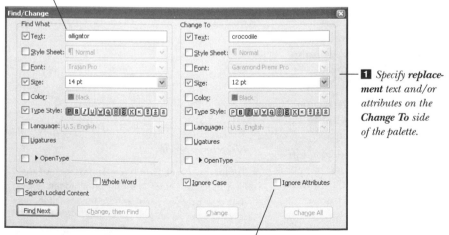

1 *Specify **replacement** text and/or attributes on the **Change To** side of the palette.*

*With **Ignore Attributes unchecked**, you can search for Font, Size, Color, and Type Style attributes.*

Find/Change

field blank to have all instances of the Find What text be deleted (yes, deleted!).

If Ignore Attributes is unchecked, you can choose a replacement style sheet, font, point size, color, or type style. An activated (black) Type Style will be applied to the text; an inactive style will be removed from the text; a dimmed style will be ignored (no change). Click the P, for Plain, to remove all the styles.

Again, be sure to uncheck the box for any category that you want the replace to ignore.

7. Now, to begin the search:

Hold down Option/Alt and click Find First to search for the first instance of the Find What text in the current layout.
or
Click Find Next to search for the next instance of the Find What text, starting from the current cursor location.

If no instances (or no more instances) are found of the Find What text and/or attributes, a beep will sound.

8. Click the Change, then Find button to change the current instance and search for the next instance in one step.
or
Click Change to change the current instance, then click Find Next to resume the search.
or
Click Change All to change all the instances in one fell swoop. A prompt displaying the number of found instances will appear ■. Click OK.

Optional: If a prompt appears saying, "Search will start at the beginning...," you can click Yes or No.

9. You can edit your layout and zoom in or out while the Find/Change palette is open. To close it, press Cmd-Option-F/ Ctrl-Alt-F or click the Close button.

TIP To use Find/Change on a master page, display that master page, then check Masters on the Find/Change palette.

Find/Change

Got carried away?

If, like we do, you tend to speed too quickly through Find/Change, clicking one wrong button after another, the good news is that you can undo those changes by using the Undo command. If you click Change All in the Find/Change palette, Undo will even reverse those changes.

■ *A summary will appear after you click* **Change All.**

Now you see it...

If, when you click Find Next, an instance of the Find What attribute is found on a hidden layer, that text box (or path) will be made visible, only to disappear when you click Find Next again. Hello and goodbye.

Use Find/Change to apply a style sheet

The instructions on this page elaborate on the instructions for Find/Change, which are found on the previous three pages.

You can use Find/Change to apply a character style sheet to type that has already been locally formatted. On the left side of the Find/Change palette, choose the font and other type attributes that you want the program to search for ■1. On the right side, choose the character style sheet to be applied to that locally formatted text, and, for Type Style, click P (plain) ■2.

If, in addition to choosing a style sheet, you also choose other text attributes on the

Change To side of the palette, those attributes will override the style sheet specs ■3. For example, let's say you want to apply a subhead character style sheet but you don't like the style sheet's font size. Just check the Size box on the Change To side of the palette and enter the desired size. In essence, you'll be applying a style sheet and local formatting in one lightning-quick step.

If you want to search for locally formatted text in addition to a style sheet, choose those text attributes in the Find What area of the Find/Change palette, too.

■1 *To apply a character style sheet to already formatted text, choose the attributes you want to search for in the* **Find What** *area…*

■2 *…and choose which* **style sheet** *you want applied to the found text on the* **Change To** *side of the palette.*

■3 *Any other Change To attributes that are chosen will* **override** *the style sheet.*

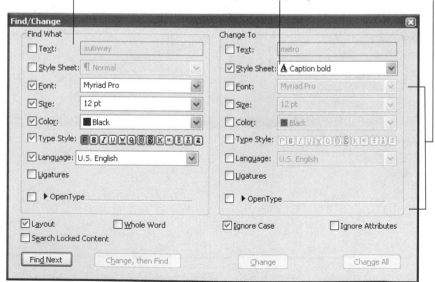

Use Find/Change to Apply Style Sheets

Note: Usage > Fonts replaces *all* instances of a font within the currently displayed layout. If you want to replace font instances on a case-by-case basis, use the Find/Change feature instead.

To find and change fonts only:

1. Choose Utilities > Usage (F13/F2), then click Fonts in the list at left. The names of all the fonts used in the layout will be listed in the Fonts pane at the right (that is, except for fonts used in any imported EPS files).

2. Click the name of the font you want to replace **1** (or click the first in a series of consecutively listed fonts, then Shift-click the last font in the series, or Cmd-click/Ctrl-click some individually), then click Replace **2**.
or
Double-click the name of the font that you want to replace.

3. Start typing the name of a replacement font or choose a replacement font from the menu, then click OK. When the alert dialog box appears, click OK.

The cure for missing fonts

Usually, you visit the Fonts pane of the Usage dialog box because a Font Missing alert appeared when you opened a project. or tried to print it. Missing fonts are displayed in brackets at the end of the list. Click Show First to see how the font was used in the layout, then you can decide whether to replace it or try to find the font file.

4. Repeat steps 2–3 for any other fonts you want to replace.

5. *Optional:* Click Show First to display the first instance of the currently selected font in the layout, then click Show Next to see the next instance, or hold down Option/Alt to turn the Show Next button into a Show First button. Remember, all instances of a given font will be replaced, regardless of which instance is currently displayed on your screen.

Check More Information to display the PostScript Name, File Name (and location), Type, and Version number of the currently selected font.

6. Click Done/Close to exit the dialog box.

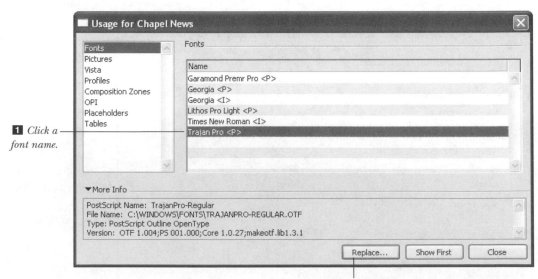

1 *Click a font name.*

2 *Click **Replace** to choose a replacement font.*

Béziers

1 *With Item > Edit > **Shape off**, you can resize or change an item's overall shape by dragging any of the eight handles on its bounding box.*

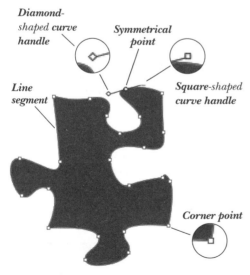

2 *With Item > Edit > **Shape on**, all of an item's individual points and curve handles are accessible for reshaping.*

Bézier basics

All Bézier items are composed of the same building blocks: straight and/or curved line segments, connected by points. Each point on a curved segment has two rabbit-ear curve handles attached to it that control the shape and direction of the curve. Béziers are defined by mathematical formulas, but the math is done for you.

QuarkXPress offers a whole slew of tools for creating custom-shaped Bézier boxes, lines, and text paths: three Bézier Picture Box tools, two Bézier Text Box tools, two Bézier Line tools, and two Bézier Text-Path tools. Each Bézier tool creates an item with a distinctive function—e.g., a closed shape to contain text or a picture, an open line on which to place text, or a decorative, freely drawn line. Once you learn how to use them, you'll be able to draw any shape under the sun.

All Bézier items are reshaped using the same techniques: by manipulating their segments, points, and curve handles **1**–**2**. Furthermore, as you'll see by the end of this chapter, you can convert any type of shape into any other type of shape—a line into a box, a picture box into a text box, etc.

In the first part of this chapter you'll learn many techniques for creating Bézier items. Once you master these, you'll most likely use an assortment of them, along with some keyboard shortcuts, as you draw different kinds of items. Later in the chapter you'll learn how to reshape and combine Bézier items and how to manipulate text on a Bézier path.

The Bézier tool chest

*The **Bézier Picture Box** tools*

Bézier Picture Box

Creates picture boxes by clicking or dragging

Freehand Picture Box

Creates picture boxes by dragging

Starburst

Creates star-shaped picture boxes by clicking or dragging

*The **Bézier Line** tools*

Bézier Line

Creates lines by clicking or dragging

Freehand Line

Creates lines by dragging

Diamond

1 *Handles on a **smooth** point can be of different lengths.*

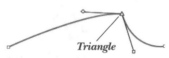

Square

2 *Handles on a **symmetrical** point are always of equal length.*

*The **Bézier Text Box** tools*

Bézier Text Box

Creates text boxes by clicking or dragging

Freehand Text Box

Creates text boxes by dragging

*The **Bézier Text-Path** tools*

Bézier Text-Path

Creates text paths by clicking or dragging

Freehand Text-Path

Creates text paths by dragging

Triangle

3 *Handles on a **corner** point can be moved in different directions and can be of different lengths.*

4 *A corner point can have one handle, two handles, or no handles. This corner point has none.*

Bézier settings on the Measurements palette

These palette features are available when a point is selected on a Bézier text box and Item > Edit > Shape is on.

Horizontal location *of upper-left corner of Bézier **bounding box** relative to ruler origin*

Width *of item*

Rotation *of item*

Smooth point

Symmetrical point

Corner point

Horizontal location *of currently active **point***

Angle *of diamond-shaped curve **handle***

Angle *of **square**-shaped curve **handle***

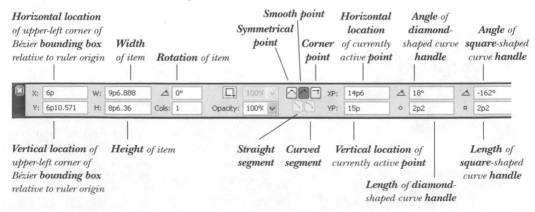

Vertical location *of upper-left corner of Bézier **bounding box** relative to ruler origin*

Height *of item*

Straight segment

Curved segment

Vertical location *of currently active **point***

Length *of diamond-shaped curve **handle***

Length *of **square**-shaped curve **handle***

The Bézier shortcuts

If you're new to Béziers, skip this page for now. Once you've learned the Bézier fundamentals and you're ready to speed things up, come back and add some of these shortcuts to your repertoire.

Convert point to corner	Select point, then Option-F1/Ctrl-F1
Convert point to smooth	Select point, then Option-F2/Ctrl-F2
Convert point to symmetrical	Select point, then Option-F3/Ctrl-F3
Add point	Option-click/Alt-click line segment
Delete point	Option-click/Alt-click point
Convert to straight segment	Select segment, then Option-Shift-F1/ Ctrl-Shift-F1
Convert to curved segment	Select segment, then Option-Shift-F2/ Ctrl-Shift-F2
Path editing on/off	Shift-F4/F10
Select all the points on an item	Double-click a point *or* Click one point, then Cmd-Shift-A/ Ctrl-Shift-A (triple-click to select all the points in a merged paths item)
Select multiple points individually	Shift-click each point
Convert corner point to smooth	Option-Control-drag/ Ctrl-Shift-drag from point
Snap point or handle to increment of 45°	Shift-drag
Retract one curve handle	Option-click/Alt-click handle
Retract curve handles	Control-Shift-click/ Ctrl-Shift-click point
Expose curve handles	Control-Shift-drag/ Ctrl-Shift-drag from point

As a path is being drawn

Convert corner point to curve point, or vice versa	Cmd-Option-Ctrl-click last curve point or drag from last corner point (Mac OS X); Ctrl-click last curve point, then press Ctrl-F1 or Ctrl-F2
Retract one curve handle	Cmd-Option-click/Ctrl-Alt click curve handle
Move point or adjust handle	Cmd-drag/Ctrl-drag

Drawing Bézier items

When you click with a Bézier tool, corner points are created.

To draw a straight-sided Bézier line or text path:

1. Choose the Bézier Line 🖋 or Bézier Text-Path tool. 🖋

2. Click to create an anchor point.

3. Click to create additional points **1**. Shift-click to constrain a segment to an increment of 45°. Straight line segments will connect the points.

4. To end the path, select another tool or double-click when you create the last point **2**–**3**. (More about text paths later in this chapter.)

TIP To delete a path as you're creating it, press Cmd-K/Ctrl-K.

TIP Normally, a Bézier tool will switch to the Item or Content tool as soon as one path is completed. If you Option-click/ Alt-click a Bézier tool, it will stay selected so you can draw multiple paths (end each path by double-clicking).

To draw a straight-sided Bézier picture box or text box:

1. Choose the Bézier Picture Box ✏ or Bézier Text Box tool. 🅰

2. Click to create an anchor point.

3. Click to create additional points. Straight line segments will connect the points.

4. To close the box, choose another tool.
   or
   Create the last point by double-clicking (not necessarily over the first point). A segment connecting this last point and the first point will be created.
   or
   Click the starting point **4**–**5**.

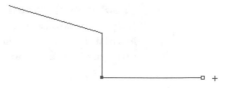

1 *Click—don't drag—to create points connected by straight segments.*

2 *Change the width, style, or color of a Bézier* **line** *as you would any other line (see Chapter 12).*

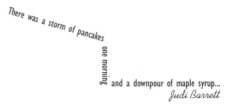

3 *On a* **text path,** *enter and style your text as you would text in a box.*

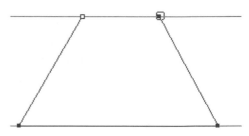

4 *One way to* **close** *a Bézier box is by clicking back on the* **starting point.** *You can use guides to help you place points.*

'After that I sup-
pose we shall have
pretty nearly finished
rubbing off each other's
angles,' he reflected; but
the worst of it was that May's
pressure was already bearing on
the very angles whose sharpness he
most wanted to keep. *Edith Wharton*

5 *A* **Bézier text** *box*

Straight-Sided Béziers

Prefab shapes

The **ShapeMaker** XTension from GLUON, Inc. (www.gluon.com) creates editable Bézier waves, zigzags, polygons, swirls, flowers, quasars, and polygons, etc., which can be used as picture boxes, text boxes, or paths.

1 *To draw with any **Freehand** tool, drag with the mouse button down for as long as you want the line to extend.*

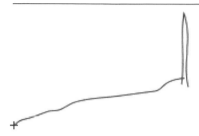

2 *If you're using the **Freehand Picture Box** or **Freehand Text Box** tool, when you're ready to close a box, release the mouse or drag back over the starting point.*

3 *With the **Freehand Line** or **Freehand Text-Path** tool, you can make little separate marks, or draw one long, wiggly string as in this illustration. Release the mouse to end an open path.*

If you like to draw in a freeform manner, try using one of the freehand Bézier tools. They lend themselves to natural subjects—flora and fauna—more than to geometric subjects. Keep your mouse button down for as long as you want the line to go.

To draw a freehand box, line, or text path:

1. Choose the Freehand Picture Box ⊗, Freehand Line ⤳, Freehand Text Box ⟨A⟩, or Freehand Text-Path tool.⤳

   TIP Option-choose/Alt-choose a tool if you want to draw multiple, separate items without having to choose the tool again.

2. Drag to draw a path. To close a freehand box, just release the mouse—the path will close automatically, and a line segment will join the first and last points **1**–**3**. Or move the pointer back over the starting point and then release the mouse.

   To end a line, just release the mouse.

   TIP If you want to trace an imported picture, put it on a locked layer by itself. To lighten the picture to make it easier to trace, use Style > Opacity. **NEW**

To delete a Bézier item:

1. Choose the Item tool.

2. Click the path you want to delete, making sure no individual points or segments are selected.

3. Choose Item > Delete (Cmd-K/Ctrl-K). *or* Press Delete/Backspace.

   Note: You can also delete an item with the Content tool selected, using Item > Delete (Cmd-K/Ctrl-K).

Freehand Béziers; Delete a Bézier

In these instructions, you'll learn how to draw curves with symmetrical points. Symmetrical points always have handles of equal length, and they produce the least bumpy curves. (Smooth points, by comparison, have handles that move in tandem but can be of different lengths; and corner points can have one, two, or zero handles.)

To draw curved segments connected by symmetrical points:

1. Choose the Bézier Picture Box ⌷, Bézier Line ✎, Bézier Text Box ⌷, or Bézier Text-Path tool. ✎

2. Drag to create a point. The shape of the curved segment and the angle of the curve handles that control the segment will be defined by the length and direction you drag the mouse.

3. Release the mouse and reposition it away from the first point. Drag in the direction you want the curve to follow to create a second point **1**. The points will now be connected by a curved segment. Remember, you can always reshape the curves later on.

4. Drag to create additional points and handles (or click at any time to add corner points).

5. *To close a picture box or text box* **2**:
   Choose another tool (the final segment will be drawn automatically).
   or
   Double-click at the location where you want the last point to appear.
   or
   Click once on the starting point (you'll see a close box pointer ⌷).

   To end (not close) a line or text path:
   Choose another tool.
   or
   Double-click to create the last point.

   (To join the endpoints of a line or text path and thus convert it to a closed shape, see page 321.)

Adjusting as you go

To move a point or adjust a curve handle as you draw, **Cmd-drag/Ctrl-drag** the point or handle, then release Cmd/Ctrl to resume drawing.

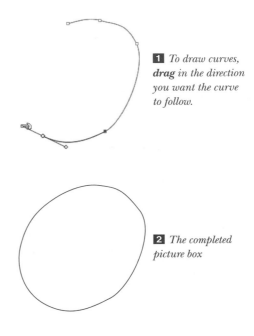

1 *To draw curves, drag in the direction you want the curve to follow.*

2 *The completed picture box*

To make the shape look more like an apricot, we converted this symmetrical point into a corner point (see the instructions on the next page).

Next, we added a freehand line for the crease.

And finally, we duplicated the shape, removed the frame from the duplicate, applied 10% black to the background, and sent the duplicate to the back (Shift-F5).

Draw Curves

1 *If at any point while drawing a shape you want to convert a symmetrical or smooth point into a corner point, Cmd-Option-click/Ctrl-Alt-click one curve handle of the last pair that was created.*

2 *The handle disappears. Now you can resume drawing the rest of the path.*

3 *When a corner point connects two curved segments, the curved segments come together at an angle.*

Making a point

If you want your curves to be nice and smooth, place your points where a curved segment **changes direction** to meet another curved segment **4**, not at the peak of a curve **5**.

4 Good spot!

5 Not-so-good spot

On these pages we've broken down the creation of straight and curved segments into separate instructions to make it as clear as possible. When you're actually drawing items, you'll usually use a combination of techniques—draw a straight segment, then a curve, then maybe retract a handle, adjust a handle, and so on. Once you're comfortable creating the basic elements, get some practice under your belt by drawing the puzzle piece illustrated on page 303 or some other shape that will require you to create symmetrical, smooth, and corner points.

To draw curved segments connected by corner points:

1. Choose the Bézier Picture Box ✎ , Bézier Line ✎, Bézier Text Box ✎ , or Bézier Text-Path tool. ✎
2. Drag to create the first point.
3. Drag to create a second point.
4. Cmd-Option-click/Ctrl-Alt-click either of the last created curve handles (the handle you click will disappear) **1**–**2**.
5. Repeat steps 3 and 4 until the shape is completed **3**.

TIP Drag to draw curves in the same item (omit the Cmd-Option-click/Ctrl-Alt-click step). Or to draw straight segments, click without dragging.

Corner points have handles that can be moved independently of each other.

To convert a smooth or symmetrical point to a corner point:

1. Choose the Item or Content tool.
2. Click a point on a Bézier item.
3. Option-Control-drag/Ctrl-Shift-drag a curve handle. Now the handles can be adjusted separately (no need to hold any keys down).

Convert Box or Line into a Bézier

No, it's not your imagination—the Item > Shape submenu was discussed earlier in this book. Here it's used to convert a standard box or line into a Bézier box or line.

To convert a standard box or line into a Bézier box or line:

1. Choose the Item or Content tool.

2. Click the standard item you want to convert into a Bézier.

3. To convert the item into a closed Bézier box, go to Item > Shape and choose the Freehand Box icon 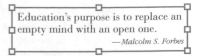 **1**–**3**. *Note:* Read the second tip on this page before converting a standard line to a Bézier box.
   or
   To convert the item into a Bézier line, go to Item > Shape and choose the Freehand Line icon.  If you convert a text box into a line, the result will be a text path **4**. If you convert a picture box that contains a picture into a line, you'll get a warning prompt; if you click OK, the picture will be deleted. In either case, the result will be an open shape, and the two endpoints of the line will be positioned one directly on top of the other (look for them at the bottom or in the lower-left corner). Select and move either point, if you like.

TIP The box that results from a conversion of a standard oval box to a Bézier box may have an excessive number of points; you can remove any extraneous points after the conversion **5**. Sometimes it's simpler to create a shape from scratch using a Bézier tool!

TIP To convert a narrow line (less than 2 points wide) into a Bézier box, hold down Option/Alt while choosing the Freehand Box icon (**1**–**2**, next page).

Note: If you choose the Freehand Box icon from the Item > Shape submenu without holding down Option/Alt, a warning prompt will appear. If you click

Education's purpose is to replace an empty mind with an open one.
—*Malcolm S. Forbes*

1 *A* **standard** *text box…*

2 *…is converted into a* **Bézier** *text box.*

3 *Now the Bézier box can be* **reshaped** *by any of the usual means (drag a point or segment, convert a corner point to a smooth point, etc.).*

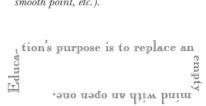

4 *If a standard* **text box** *is converted into a freehand line, the result is an* **open text path***.*

5 *The original* **standard** *oval text box*

After it's converted into a **Bézier** *box*

After removing four extraneous points

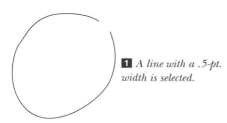

1 *A line with a .5-pt. width is selected.*

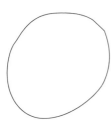

2 *After choosing the freehand box shape from the Item > Shape submenu with Option/Alt held down, the line is converted into a closed box. Its frame has the same width as the original line, (in this case, .5 pt).*

OK, you'll get a very thin hollow line or lines. Not what you had in mind? Undo it.

If the endpoints of a line are very close together or one is on top of the other and you choose the Freehand Box icon with Option/Alt held down, the endpoints will be joined into a single point. If there is space between the endpoints, they'll be connected by a new line segment. In either case, a closed shape will be produced.

To create a star-shaped picture box:

1. Choose the Starburst tool. ☆
2. Drag on the page, or Shift-drag to draw a perfect star.
   or
   Click on the page to open the Starburst dialog box. Then, enter values for the Star Width and Star Height **3**, as well for the Number of Spikes (3–100) and the Spike Depth (10–90%), which controls the length of the spikes. To create spikes that are irregular in length and depth, enter a Random Spikes value above zero (0–100) **4**. Click OK **5**–**6**.

Starburst

Star Width:	8p4
Star Height:	8p4
Number of Spikes:	5
Spike Depth:	50%
Random Spikes:	0

OK   Cancel

3 *Enter values in the **Starburst** dialog box.*

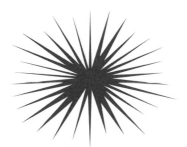

4 *Number of Spikes 30, Spike Depth 50%, Random Spikes 67*

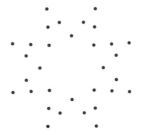

5 *Number of Spikes 8, Spike Depth 50%, Random Spikes 0; All Dots frame style applied; no background color*

6 *Number of Spikes 20, Spike Depth 30%, Random Spikes 70; imported picture*

Starburst Tool

Reshaping Bézier items

On the following pages, you'll learn these methods for reshaping a Bézier path:

- Add or delete a point
- Move a point or a segment
- Rotate, lengthen, or shorten a curve handle to reshape a curve
- Convert a point to a different type (symmetrical, smooth, or corner)
- Convert a curved segment into a straight segment, or vice versa
- Move a handle on the bounding box
- Cut a segment in two
- Convert a Bézier to an entirely different shape via the Item > Shape submenu

If you want to reshape *part* of a Bézier item, you must first turn on Item > Edit > **Shape** (Shift-F4/F10—memorize this shortcut!) . This command makes an item's individual points, curve handles, and segments visible and accessible. Remember to turn this command off when you've finished reshaping the item so you don't inadvertently move any points or segments!

To reshape or resize a *whole* Bézier item, turn off Item > Edit > Shape (re-choose the command), then drag any of the eight handles of its bounding box **2**.

1 *With Item > Edit > Shape **on,** a Bézier item's individual points and curve handles are accessible for reshaping.*

2 *With Item > Edit > Shape **off,** only a Bézier item's outer bounding box and eight handles are visible.*

To add or delete a point:
Method 1
1. Choose the Item or Content tool, then click the item to make its points visible.
2. Option-click/Alt-click a point to delete it **3**–**4**. 🐭
   or
   Option-click/Alt-click a segment where you want a new point to appear **5**. 🖑

Method 2 (deleting only)
1. Choose the Item tool.
2. Click a point, then press Delete/ Backspace. To delete multiple points, Shift-click them (or click a segment to delete both of its connecting points), then press Delete/Backspace.

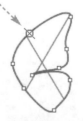

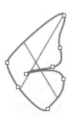

3 *Option-click/ Alt-click a point to delete it.*

4 *The point is deleted.*

5 *Option-click/Alt-click a segment to add a point.*

Get the points

Select all the points on an item	Double-click a point *or* click the path, then press Cmd-Shift-A/Ctrl-Shift-A
Select all the points in a merged item	Triple-click a point
Select multiple points individually	Shift-click each point
Select the two points that connect a segment	Click the segment

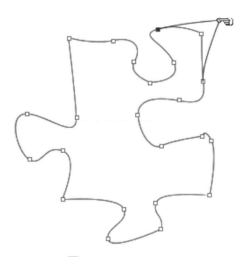

1 *Dragging a point*

2 *Enter new **XP** and/or **YP** location values on the Measurements palette to reposition the currently selected point or points.*

To move a point:

1. Choose the Item or Content tool.

2. Click a Bézier path to select it.

3. Position the pointer over a point (the cursor will change into a pointing finger with a little black square), then drag the point to reposition it **1**.
   or
   Click a point to select it, then press an arrow key on the keyboard. The point will move along the horizontal or vertical axis.
   or
   Click a point to select it and then, on the right side of the Measurements palette (Classic tab), enter the desired horizontal location in the XP field and/or the desired vertical location in the YP field **2**.

TIP To move multiple points, select them using one of the shortcuts listed in the sidebar, then use a method in step 3, above. If you enter a number in the XP or YP field, all the currently selected points will be stackcd on top of one another at that XP or YP location.

To move a whole Bézier item:

1. Choose the Item tool. Or hold down Cmd/Ctrl to move an item with the Content tool.

2. To move a box, drag inside it. If you pause before dragging (wait for the cluster-of-arrows pointer to appear), the item's contents will display as it's dragged. Drag without pausing to see just the wireframe outline of the box.
   or
   To move a line or a text path, click the line first to select it, move the pointer slightly away from the line (just slightly!), then drag when you see the four-way arrow pointer.

To move control handles to reshape a curve:

1. Choose the Item or Content tool.

2. Click any point that has a handle or handles 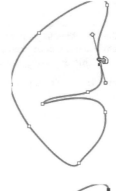.

3. Drag a handle toward or away from the point to change the height of the curve **2**. The angle of a handle affects the slope of the curve into the point. The handles on a smooth point move in tandem and can be different in length; the pair of handles on a symmetrical point move in tandem and are always of equal length; handle(s) on a corner point, if any, move independently of each another.

   or

   Rotate the handle around the point **3**.

   or

   On the Measurements palette (Classic tab), enter a number in the angle field for the diamond-shaped curve handle or in the angle field for the square-shaped curve handle (not the most intuitive thing you've ever done in your life) **4**. You can do this (and the next option) for multiple selected points.

   or

   On the right side of the Measurements palette, enter a length for the diamond-shaped curve handle or a length for the square-shaped curve handle **5**.

   To make the handles of equal length, enter the same number in both fields **6** (or click the Symmetrical Point button △ on the Measurements palette).

1 *First select a point that has curve handles.*

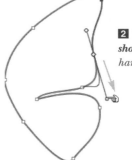

2 *Then lengthen or shorten either curve handle…*

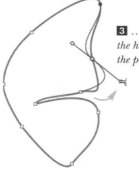

3 *…and/or rotate the handle around the point.*

4 *Enter a new angle for the diamond-shaped curve handle.*

Or enter a new angle for the square-shaped curve handle.

XP:	14p6	⟋	18°	⟋	-162°
YP:	15p	◇	2p2	▫	2p2

5 *Enter a new length (from the point) for the diamond-shaped curve handle.*

Or enter a new length (from the point) for the square-shaped curve handle.

6 *Enter the same value in both length fields on the Measurements palette to make a pair of curve handles equal in length.*

Béz-ee-what?

Bézier curves (pronounced "Béz-e-yays") were originally developed by the French mathematician Pierre Bézier and used in the 1970s for CAD/CAM operations. Now they're used in PostScript drawing programs such as Adobe Illustrator and Macromedia FreeHand and, of course, in QuarkXPress.

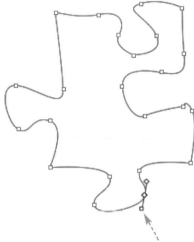

1 *Click a point, then* **Option**-*click/* **Alt**-*click one of its handles.*

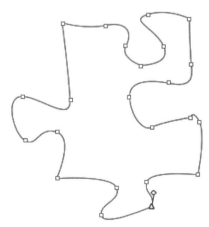

2 *The handle* **disappears.**

When you retract a curve handle, it converts the point to a corner point and changes the shape of the curve.

To retract one curve handle:

1. Choose the Item or Content tool.

2. Select a point that has handles.

3. Option-click/Alt-click a handle to retract it **1**–**2**.

or

On the right side of the Measurements palette (Classic tab), enter 0 in the length field for the diamond-shaped or square-shaped handle **3**.

TIP To retract both curve handles on a point, Control-Shift-click/Ctrl-Shift-click the point. To make them reappear, Control-Shift-drag/Ctrl-Shift-drag from a point.

To restore retracted curve handles:

1. Choose the Item or Content tool.

2. Select a point that doesn't have handles.

3. On the Measurements palette (Classic tab):

Click the Symmetrical Point button ⌃ or Smooth Point ⌃ button.

or

Enter a value above 0 in either or both of the length fields (diamond and/or square).

| XP: | 6p4.013 | ⟁ | -67.636° | ⟁ | 112.364° |
| YP: | 11p7.002 | ◇ | 0p | ▫ | 0p |

3 *Enter* **0** *in the* **length** *field for the diamond-shaped and/or square-shaped curve handle(s).*

To reshape a segment by dragging:

1. Choose the Item or Content tool.

2. Click a Bézier box, line, or text path.

3. Drag a straight segment. The anchor points that touch it will move with it **1**. Shift-drag to constrain the movement to an increment of 45°.

   or

   Drag a curved segment. Only the segment will move, not its connecting points **2**.

   Note: If you pause before dragging a segment, the item's fill will preview as the segment is moved. Otherwise, just the outer wireframe representation will display as you drag.

Use the Scissors tool to cut boxes, lines, and text paths. The tool can't be used on a table, an anchored item, or an item in a group.

Note: To access this tool, the Scissors.xnt XTension must be installed and enabled (see page 377).

To cut an item with the Scissors tool:

1. Choose the Scissors tool. ✂

2. Click the edge of an item **3**. Two new endpoints will be created. The Scissors tool converts a picture box into a line, a text box into a text path, and a text path into two linked paths.

3. The Item or Content tool will become selected automatically. Move either or both of the new endpoints **4**–**5**.

TIP If you're going to make multiple cuts using the Scissors tool, Option-click/Alt-click the tool first. Then you won't have to reselect it each time. Choose another tool when you're done.

TIP To cut a merged item, you may have to split it first using Item > Split, depending on which Merge command was used (see pages 320–321).

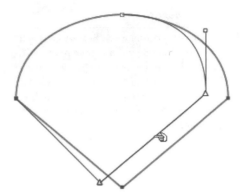

1 *If you drag a **straight** segment, the segment **and** its connecting points will move.*

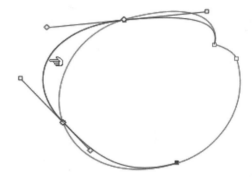

2 *If you drag a **curved segment**, only the curve will move—**not** its connecting points.*

3 *Click a line with the **Scissors** tool.*

4 *Then move one of the new **endpoints**.*

5 *What was a single line is now **two** separate lines.*

Reshape a Segment; Cut with Scissors

Convert a segment

To straight	Select a segment, then press Option-Shift-F1/Ctrl-Shift-F1
To curved	Select a segment, then press Option-Shift-F2/Ctrl-Shift-F2

To convert a curved segment into a straight segment, or vice versa, in a Bézier box, line, or text path, all you gotta do is click a button on the Measurements palette (Classic tab). Easy.

To convert a curved segment into a straight segment, or vice versa:

1. Choose the Item or Content tool.

2. Click a Bézier box or line to select it, then click the segment that you want to convert (make sure its points are selected) **1**.

3. Click the Straight Segment button on the Measurements palette (Option-Shift-F1/Ctrl-Shift-F1). One of the curve handles on each of the two points that are adjacent to the segment will disappear **2**.

or

Click the Curved Segment button on the Classic tab of the Measurements palette (Option-Shift-F2/Ctrl-Shift-F2). One curve handle will appear on each of the two points that are adjacent to the segment.

TIP You can also convert a selected segment by choosing Item > Point/Segment Type > Straight Segment or Curved Segment, but why go all the way to the menu bar when you can just click a button instead?

TIP To convert *all* the points and segments on a path into all curves or all straights, double-click any point to select all the points and segments on the path, then click the Straight Segment or Curved Segment button on the Measurements palette.

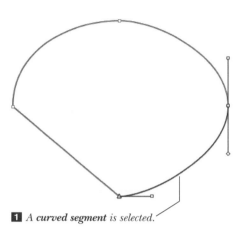

1 *A* **curved segment** *is selected.*

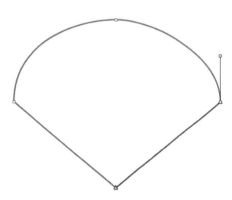

2 *After clicking the* **Straight Segment** *button on the Measurements palette (Classic tab), the curved segment is converted into a straight segment.*

Curved Segment to Straight, Vice Versa

To change a point's style:

1. Choose the Item or Content tool.

2. Select one or more points on a Bézier item.

3. On the Classic tab of the Measurements palette:

   Click the Symmetrical Point (first) button. 🔼 Handles on a symmetrical point always stay on the same axis and are of equal length **1**.
   or

   Click the Smooth Point (second) button. 🔼 Handles on a smooth point always stay on the same axis but can be different lengths, allowing for greater control over reshaping **2**.
   or

   Click the Corner Point (third) button. ⊓ Now the handles can be rotated, lengthened, or shortened independently of each other, and the segments that the point connects will come together at a sharper angle **3**.

TIP You can also convert a point by selecting it and then choosing Item > Point/Segment Type > Corner Point, Smooth Point, or Symmetrical Point.

Changing the point

To corner	Select a point, then press Option-F1/Ctrl-F1
To smooth	Select a point, then press Option-F2/Ctrl-F2
To symmetrical	Select a point, then press Option-F3/Ctrl-F3
Smooth to corner	Option-Control/Ctrl-Alt-Shift click a curve point
Corner to smooth	Option-Control/Ctrl-Shift drag from corner point

1 *On a **symmetrical** point, the handles always stay on the same axis, and are always of **equal length**.*

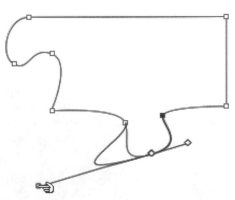

2 *On a **smooth** point, the handles always stay on the same axis, but they can be of **different lengths**.*

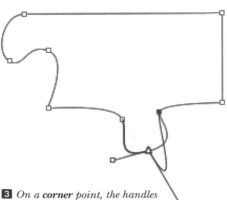

3 *On a **corner** point, the handles move **independently** of each other. (Not all corner points have handles.)*

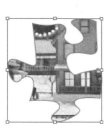

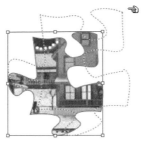

1 *With Item > Edit > Shape **off**, the eight handles on an item's bounding box are available.*

2 *Drag a handle to scale the **whole** item.*

3 *Option-Shift-drag/Alt-Shift-drag a handle on the bounding box to resize just the item—not its contents.*

4 *Cmd-Option-Shift-drag/Ctrl-Alt-Shift-drag a handle on the bounding box to resize the item **and** its contents, if any.*

To scale a whole Bézier box, line, or text path:

1. Choose the Item or Content tool.
2. Make sure Item > Edit > Shape is turned off (Shift-F4/F10).
3. Click a Bézier box, line, or text path **1**.
4. To scale the item proportionally, but not its contents (picture or text), Option-Shift-drag/Alt-Shift-drag one of the handles of its bounding box **2**–**3**.
   or
   To scale the item and contents (if any) proportionally, Cmd-Option-Shift-drag/Ctrl-Alt-Shift-drag a handle **4**.
   or
   To scale the item nonproportionally, but not its contents, change the W and/or H values on the Classic tab of the Measurements palette **5** (or press Cmd-M/Ctrl-M to open the Modify dialog box, click the Box tab, then change the Width and/or Height values).

TIP Regardless of which method you use to scale a box, the frame width stays the same.

TIP You can rotate a Bézier item using the same techniques that you'd use to rotate a non-Bézier item.

5 *To resize a Bézier item numerically, change the W and/or H values on the Measurements palette.*

Scale a Whole Bézier Item

No matter what kind of items you start with, all the Merge commands produce a single Bézier item from two or more individual items. And in all cases, the color attributes and contents of the item farthest back in the stacking order—including any text, picture, or background color—are applied to the final item.

1 *The two original objects*

The items can be lines, boxes, text paths, Bézier items, or any combination thereof (not a table), and they can be grouped. If you're going to apply any Merge command except Union, arrange them so they overlap—at least partially.

The items can be on different layers.

2 *Intersection*

To merge two or more items:

1. Choose the Item or Content tool.

2. Select two or more items.

3. Choose Item > Merge.

4. Choose one of the following:

   3 *Union*

   INTERSECTION
   Parts of any item that overlap the backmost item are preserved; parts of items that don't overlap the backmost item are cut away **1**–**2**.

   UNION
   All items are combined into one overall new item (the original items don't have to overlap!). You can use this option to create a complex item from a combination of simple items **3**.

   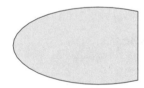

   4 *Difference*

   DIFFERENCE
   Only the backmost item remains, minus any parts of any items that are in front of it and overlap it **4**.

   REVERSE DIFFERENCE
   The original backmost item is deleted, items in front of it are united, and parts of the original items that overlap the backmost item are cut away **5**. A new shape is produced from items that extend beyond the edge of the backmost item.

   5 *Reverse Difference*

1 *The original objects*

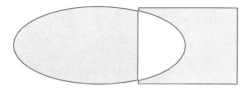

2 *Exclusive Or*

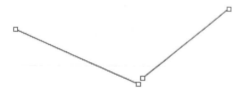

3 *Two freehand **lines** are selected.*

4 *After choosing the **Join Endpoints** command*

EXCLUSIVE OR

Areas of items that overlap the backmost item are cut away, and the remaining items are united **1**–**2**. The color of the original backmost item is applied to the non-cutout areas. The corners of the cutout areas will have two sets of points—one that can be used to reshape the cutout areas and one that can be used to reshape the non-cutout areas.

COMBINE

Works like Exclusive Or, except that extra points aren't added to the corners of the cutout areas, so you can't adjust the corners of the resulting cutout shapes unless you add corner points yourself.

Note: Exclusive Or and Combine will produce the same results if the original overlapping items don't extend beyond the edge of the backmost item.

JOIN ENDPOINTS

The Join Endpoints command will join a pair of endpoints from two separate text paths or lines into one point— provided the endpoints are close together **3**–**4**. The attributes (style, weight, color, etc.) of the backmost line are applied to the resulting line. Boxes don't have endpoints, so the Join Endpoints command has no effect on them.

Note: For two endpoints to be affected by the Join Endpoints command, the distance between them can't exceed the current Snap Distance (1–216) specified in Preferences > Print Layout > General. The default Snap Distance value is 6 pixels.

TIP To un-merge merged items, see page 323.

Merge Commands

The Text to Box command converts a copy of one or more standard text characters into a single Bézier picture box. And if you like, you can make this conversion and anchor the new Bézier box into its text block all in one fell swoop.

The resulting Bézier box can be filled with a color, a blend, or a picture; it can be converted into a text box and filled with text; or it can be reshaped using any of the techniques that are discussed in this chapter.

To convert text characters into a Bézier picture box:

1. Choose the Content tool.

2. Select the characters you want to convert **1** (no more than one line). The larger and chunkier, the better.

3. Choose Style > Text to Box. A duplicate of all the selected text will be converted into a single picture box.
   or
   To convert the text into a picture box and *anchor* it in its current location in the text simultaneously, hold down Option/Alt and choose Style > Text to Box **2**–**3**.

TIP To change the contents of the newly created picture box, click on it, then choose Item > Content > Text (so you can enter text inside the letter shapes) or None (so you can fill the letter shapes with color only). To access the Content submenu quickly via the context menu, select the box, then Control-click/Right-click in the project window.

1 *The first character in a box is selected.*

2 *Style > **Text to Box** is chosen with **Option/Alt** held down: In one step, a copy of the character is converted into a Bézier picture box and is anchored into the text.*

3 *We reshaped and enlarged the box (it's now a Bézier box), filled it with a background shade and a picture, and chose a lighter shade for its frame.*

1 *The original **Text to Box** item*

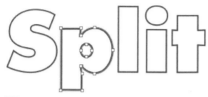

2 *After choosing Split > **Outside Paths**, each letter item can now be selected and edited individually.*

3 *After selecting the "P" shape and choosing Item > Split > **All Paths**, the center (counter) of the "P" can now be edited separately from the outer portion.*

Type into type

To type inside type, select one or more large, chunky text characters, choose Style > Text to Box, choose Item > Content > Text, then enter text **4**. (To force the text to wrap on all sides of the interior oval instead of on just one side, go to Item > Modify > Text, then check Run Text Around All Sides.)

The Split command is really an un-merge command. It divides a text-to-box item or items merged via the Combine or Exclusive Or command into individual, separate items. It can also be used to split up a complex box that contains paths within paths or a box whose border criss-crosses itself. Once an item is split, each component can then be manipulated or recolored individually.

If you split a box that was created using the Text to Box command into separate paths, you'll then be able to select and recolor each letter individually, fill each letter with a different picture, or reshape any letter to create a custom character (you can have some fun with this). Start with a box that was created from more than one letter.

To split a merged or Text to Box item:

1. Choose the Item or Content tool.
2. Select a complex (merged) item.
3. Choose Item > Split > Outside Paths to split only outside paths, not any paths contained within them **1**–**2**.
   or
   Choose Item > Split > All Paths to split all an item's paths, including any interior paths **3**. If you apply this to a Text to Box letter shape, any counter (hole) within the letter will become a separate shape (as in an "O" or a "P"), and it can then be treated as a separate item.

After
that I suppose we shall
have pretty nearly finished rubbing off each other's angles,' he
reflected; but the   worst of it
was that May's pres-   sure was
already bearing on   the very
angles whose sharp-   ness he
most wanted to   keep.
After that I sup-   pose we
shall have pretty
EDITH WHARTON

4

You can flip any type of Bézier item. Try flipping a Bézier text path vertically.

To flip an item:

1. *Optional:* To create a mirror image, duplicate the item (Cmd-D/Ctrl-D) before you flip it.

2. Choose the Item or Content tool.

3. Click the item, and turn off Item > Edit > Shape.

4. So you'll be able to restore the original dimensions to the item after it's flipped, display the Classic tab of the Measurements palette and copy (Cmd-C/Ctrl-C) the W or H value, depending on which way you want to flip the box—horizontally (W) or vertically (H).

5. If you copied the W value, drag a side midpoint handle all the way across the item to the other side **1**–**2**. Or if you copied the H value, drag the top or bottom midpoint handle.

6. Re-select the field that you chose for step 3 above, paste (Cmd-V/Ctrl-V), then press Return/Enter **3**.

TIP To flip the *contents* of a selected box, choose the Content tool, then choose Style > Flip Horizontal or Flip Vertical or click the Flip Horizontal button ➡ or Flip Vertical button ⬆ on the Classic tab of the Measurements palette.

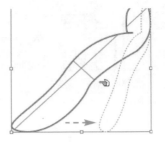

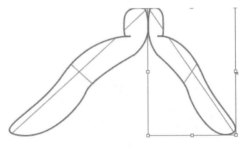

1 *After copying an item's width or height from the Measurements palette, drag a midpoint handle all the way across the shape.*

2 *Continue dragging to the opposite side.*

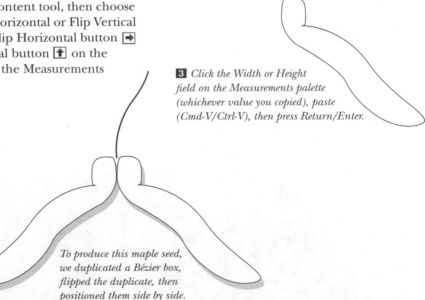

3 *Click the Width or Height field on the Measurements palette (whichever value you copied), paste (Cmd-V/Ctrl-V), then press Return/Enter.*

To produce this maple seed, we duplicated a Bézier box, flipped the duplicate, then positioned them side by side.

1 *Select a line, then choose Item > Content > Text.*

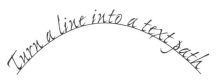

2 *The line becomes a text path.*

Creating Bézier text paths

In addition to creating a text path using any of the Text-Path tools, you can also produce a text path by converting an existing line.

To convert a line into a text path:

1. Choose the Item or Content tool.
2. Click a line that was created using the Orthogonal Line, Line, Bézier Line, or Freehand Line tool **1**.
3. Choose Item > Content > Text (or choose it from the context menu).
4. With the Content tool chosen, type, paste, or import text onto the path **2**.

Text on a fat path

We converted a round text box into a freehand line via Item > Shape, made the path 20% black and wider in Item > Modify > Line, added type, and in Item > Modify > Text Path, chose Align Text: Descent and Align with Line: Bottom. To fine-tune the position of the text on the path, we used Style > Baseline Shift. (The picture is in a picture box.)

After checking Flip Text on the Text Path tab of the Measurements palette

Tip for drawing text paths

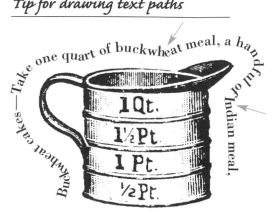

Try not to create acute concave angles when you draw a text path—the letters will bunch together and be unreadable.

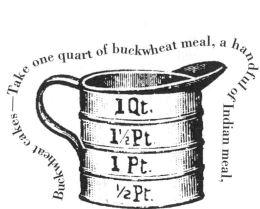

Try to draw smooth, shallow curves instead.

Other ways to play with text paths

To change the width and other attributes of a text path, select it using the Item tool, then choose attributes from the Style menu, from the Measurements palette, or from Item > Modify > Line. Any dash or stripe style can be applied to a text path **1**.

To recolor a text path, select it with the Item tool and choose from the Style > Color and Shade submenus. Or select it with the Item or Content tool, click the Line Color button ⊘ on the Colors palette, then click a color and choose a shade. (To make the path invisible, click the Line Color button, then click None.)

Change the attributes of text on a path as you would text in a box: Select it using the Content tool, then choose attributes from the Style menu or from any of several tabs on the Measurements palette; or apply a style sheet or sheets to it.

To flip text to the opposite side of a path, click the path with the Content tool and choose Style > Flip Text **2**–**3**. Or click the path with the Item or Content tool, then check or uncheck Flip Text on the Text **(NEW)** Path tab of the Measurements palette or in Item > Modify > Text Path.

To turn a text box into a text path, select the box, then from the Item > Shape submenu, choose the Line icon ⊘ **4** or Orthogonal Line icon ✛ . An open text path will be created. Or if you choose the Bézier Line icon ∿ instead, a path will be created in the shape of the original box **5**.

1 *To create this text path, we converted a standard round text box into a Bézier line.*

2 *Text on a path*

3 *After clicking the* **Flip Text** *button*

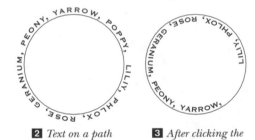

4 *A text box is converted into a text path by choosing the* **Line** *icon* ⊘ *from the Item >* **Shape** *submenu.*

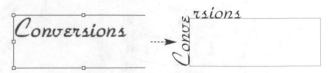

5 *A text box is converted into a text path by choosing the* **Bézier Line** *icon* ∿ *from the Item >* **Shape** *submenu.*

To change the orientation of text on a curvy path:

1. Choose the Item or Content tool.

2. Click on a text path.

3. Choose Item > Modify (Cmd-M/ Ctrl-M), then click the Text Path tab.
   or
   Display the Text Path tab of the ⬤NEW Measurements palette (see the next page).

4. Click any of the four Text Orientation buttons ■.

5. Click Apply to preview.

6. Click OK.

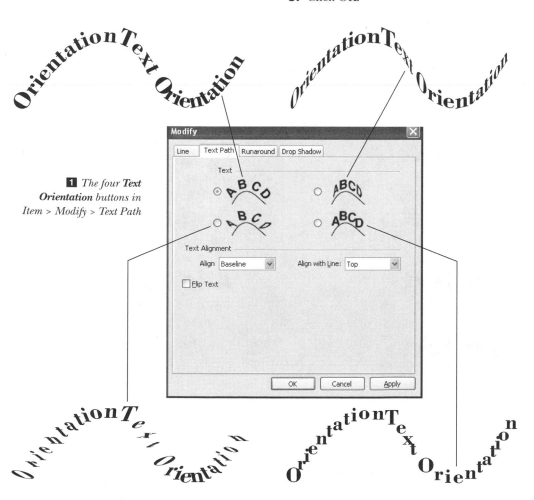

■ *The four **Text Orientation** buttons in Item > Modify > Text Path*

To raise or lower text on its path:

1. Choose the Item or Content tool.

2. Click on a text path.

3. Display the Text Path tab of the  **NEW** Measurements palette.
   or
   Choose Item > Modify (Cmd-M/ Ctrl-M), then click the Text Path tab.

4. Choose Align Text: Ascent, Center, Baseline, or Descent **1**–**2** (to specify the part of the text that touches the path).

5. Choose Align with Line: Top, Center, or Bottom (to specify the part of the path the text connects to) **3**. The wider the path, the more dramatic the shift.

6. Click Apply to preview.

7. Click OK.

TIP You can use Baseline Shift to further raise or lower text on a path (Character Attributes tab of the Measurements palette or Style > Baseline Shift).

1 *Choose from the* **Align Text** *and/or* **Align with Line** *menus on the Text Path tab of the Measurements palette.*

2

Align text
Align Text: Ascent

Align text
Align Text: Center

Align text
Align Text: Baseline

Align text
Align Text: Descent

3

Align text
Align with Line: Top

Align text
Align with Line: Center

Align text
Align with Line: Bottom

Libraries 19

Our "New" icon. No, honestly! The resolution of the preview is low, so the text is illegible.

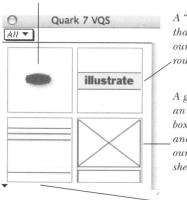

A "sticky" note that we drag into our layout in the rough draft stage

A group containing an empty picture box with no frame and a text box with our caption style sheet applied to it

1 *This is part of the **library** that was used to produce this book (in Mac OS X).*

A text box for a sidebar with style sheets applied to it

2 *Library items can be **labeled** and shown by category (this is a library palette in Windows).*

Using libraries

A library is a special kind of file that's used to organize and store items of any type: text boxes or picture boxes, empty or filled; contentless boxes; lines; text paths; tables; and even groups of items. Each library is displayed as a floating palette **1**–**2** and can contain up to 2,000 items. When you drag an item from a library palette into any QuarkXPress project window, a copy of the item appears in the active layout. An unlimited number of libraries can be created.

Note: The version of a picture that is stored in a library is just its low-resolution preview; this keeps library file sizes relatively small. However, if you send a file containing library elements for imagesetting—as with any picture used in a QuarkXPress layout—you'll need to supply the original picture files. A library can also serve a supporting role as an onscreen picture catalog.

To create a library:

1. Choose File > New > Library (Cmd-Option-N/Ctrl-Alt-N).

2. Type a name for the library in the Save As/Save as Type field.

3. Select a drive or folder in which to save the library.

4. Click Create. A new library palette will appear on your screen. To put items into the library, see the instructions on the following page.

To put an item in a library:

1. Create a new library or open an existing library.

2. Choose the Item tool, or hold down Cmd/Ctrl if the Content tool is chosen.

3. Drag any item, group, or multiple-item selection into the library **1**. When the pointer is over the library, you'll see an eyeglasses icon **2**. When you release the mouse, a thumbnail of the item will appear in the library **3**; the original item will stay on your page. A multiple-item selection will be stored as one entry.

   You can't undo an addition to a library, but you can remove any item from a library (see page 332).

TIP Items can be dragged from one library to another.

Auto library save

If **Auto Library Save** is checked in QuarkXPress (Edit, in Windows) > Preferences > Application > Save, a library will be resaved each time an item is added to it or deleted from it. You may notice a slight processing delay each time this occurs. With this option unchecked, libraries are saved only when they're closed or when you quit/exit QuarkXPress.

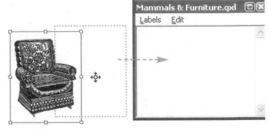

1 *Drag an item into a library with the **Item** tool.*

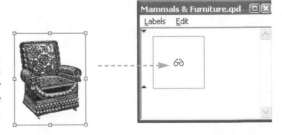

2 *The pointer turns into an **eyeglasses** icon as the item is dragged into the library. The arrowheads show where the item will appear in the palette.*

3 *The item is automatically duplicated, and the original is left intact in the layout. To move an item to a different spot in a library, just drag it.*

Colors and libraries

■ If you retrieve an item from a library that has a color applied to it, the color will be appended to the Colors palette of the active file—unless there's a color with a matching name in the target file, in which case the item will append but not the color. The same holds true for a style sheet, dash/stripe, list, or H&J.

■ If you recolor or otherwise modify an item in a layout that originated from a library, the item in the library won't update. To update the library item, you'll have to remove the old item and add the updated one.

1 *Double-click a **library** file.*

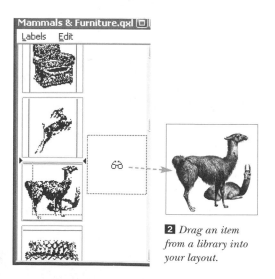

2 *Drag an item from a library into your layout.*

Any libraries that are open when you quit/exit QuarkXPress will reopen automatically when you relaunch the application.

To open an existing library:

1. Choose File > Open (Cmd-O/Ctrl-O).

2. Locate and click the library that you want to open **1**, then click Open (or double-click the icon). Library files are represented by a bookshelf icon.

TIP To open a library from the Desktop, double-click the library file icon. The extension for libraries is ".qxl". A library created in Mac OS X can't be opened in Windows, and vice versa.

TIP To close a library palette, click its close button. Don't use File > Close.

Picture paths

When a picture is added to a library, information about the path to the original picture file is stored with the library item. Similarly, when a picture is retrieved from a library, the picture's path information is stored with the project. For an image to print properly, the original picture file must be kept in the same location, with the same file name. If you move or rename the original picture file, you should update it in the library.

One way to update a library item is to relink the picture in the layout, select it with the Item tool, copy it (Cmd-C/Ctrl-C), click the library item to be replaced, paste (Cmd-V/choose Paste from the Edit menu on the library palette in Windows), then click OK in the alert dialog box.

To retrieve an item from a library:

1. Choose the Item or Content tool.

2. If the layout has multiple layers, choose a layer for the library item.

3. Drag an item from a library into a layout page (you can enlarge the palette or use the scroll arrows to display items that are out of view) **2**. Simple as that.

If a library contains a lot of items, it can become difficult to find the items you need. By labeling related library items, you can limit the number of items that are displayed at a given time. You can assign a different label to each item or assign the same label to multiple items.

To label a library item:

1. Double-click a library item.
2. Enter a name in the Label field **1**.
   or
   Choose an existing label, if there are any, from the Label menu **2**. You can retype the same label for various items, but it's easier to choose an existing label, and you'll be less likely to make a typing error.
3. Click OK. If you created a new label, it will appear on the menu at the top of the library palette.

To display items by label:

Choose a label category from the pop-up menu (Mac OS X) **3**/Labels menu (Windows) **4**. More than one label category can be displayed at a time.

Choose All to display all the items in the library, both labeled and unlabeled.

Choose Unlabeled to display only those items that don't have a label.

To hide items bearing the same label:

A check mark on the menu on a library palette means that that label category is displayed. Reselect a selected label to uncheck it.

To delete an item from a library:

1. Choose the Item or Content tool.
2. Click a library item.
3. In Mac OS X, choose Edit > Clear or press Delete. In Windows, choose Delete from the Edit menu on the library palette or press Ctrl-X (Cut).
4. Click OK. You can't undo the deletion!

Making arrangements

Arranging library items in a logical order on the palette makes it easier to locate them. Just drag a library item to a different spot on the palette (note the arrowheads as you do this).

1 *Type a new label in the* **Label** *field…*   **2** *…or choose an existing label from the menu.*

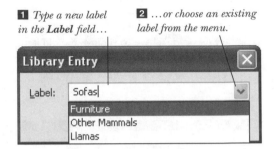

3 *In Mac OS X, when more than one label is chosen and the pop-up menu isn't open, it says* **Mixed Labels***.*

4 *The Labels menu (Windows) on a library palette shows a check mark next to each category that is currently displayed.*

Synchronize 20

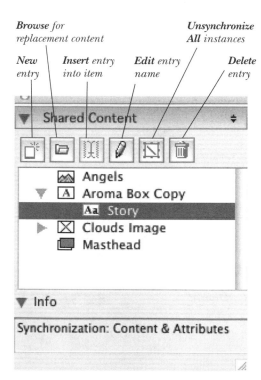

Browse for replacement content
Unsynchronize All instances

New entry
Insert entry into item
Edit entry name
Delete entry

1 *Shared content is listed in the upper portion of the palette. Click an item, then click the Info triangle to see a listing of what type of shared content is synchronized in that item.*

Synchronizing content

What is synchronized content?

If you have specific content that you need to use in different parts of a project, either within a layout or across several layouts, you can synchronize it so if it's modified in one place, the changes are automatically applied to the same content throughout the project. Synchronizing content helps you keep things such as mastheads, legal copy, or prices consistent throughout a project.

Synchronized content expands upon the concept of synchronized text, which was introduced in QuarkXPress 6. As the name implies, synchronized text applied only to text; now shared content can include text (with and without formatting), pictures, boxes, lines, and composition zones.

Synchronized content is kept in a virtual storage bin called the shared content library. The Shared Content palette is your window into the shared content library **1**. When you add an item to the Shared Content palette, the Shared Item Properties dialog box opens, allowing you to choose which attributes of that item are shared.

Here are the basics, in brief:

To create a shared content entry, you add an item to the Shared Content palette.

When you insert a shared content entry into a project, it's called an "instance."

When you edit any instance in a project, your changes are reflected in other instances of the same shared content, depending on which shared item properties you've chosen for that entry.

Share Content

Things that are eligible to become shared content include items (boxes, text paths, and lines) and contents (a picture; or all the text in a box, on a path, or in a table cell). You can also synchronize a composition zone, which is discussed in Chapter 23. You can't synchronize groups, entire tables, or anything on a master page.

To add an entry to the Shared Content palette:

1. Display the Shared Content palette (Window > Shared Content).

2. Choose the Item or Content tool.

3. Click the item you want to become shared content 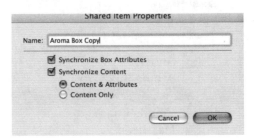.

4. Click New on the Shared Content palette.
   or
   Control-click/Right-click the item in your layout and choose Share.

5. The Shared Item Properties dialog box opens **2**. Enter a descriptive name in the Name field.

6. Specify how you want to synchronize the item. For lines and contentless boxes, it's easy—Synchronize Attributes is checked for you and dimmed so you can't uncheck it.

   Note: The settings chosen here can't be changed, so think carefully about how you want the selection to be synchronized. For text and pictures, you can check any of the following:

   Synchronize Box Attributes to keep all the box attributes (size, frame, background color, etc.) the same, except for the location of the item in the layout.

   Synchronize Content to synchronize the text or picture content and keep the words or picture exactly the same.

   If you check Synchronize Content, you can fine tune how it works by clicking Content & Attributes to preserve the

> **Real World Aromatherapy**
> Try our new scents!
> Aggravate—Causes irritation
> Worry-worry—Heightens anxiety
> Wanna—Instills envy
> Skunk—Breeds solitude

1 *Click an item that contains attributes and/or content that you want to use throughout the layout or project.*

2 *In the **Shared Item Properties** dialog box, type a name and specify which aspects of the item are to be synchronized.*

What's in synch?

To see a listing of which attributes of shared content are synchronized, click an item on the Shared Content palette, then click the **Info** triangle. For example, "Box Attributes and Content & Attributes" would indicate a fully synchronized item, meaning changes to the item and/or content will be reflected in all other instances of the same entry.

1 *Entries on the **Shared Content** palette have icons indicating the content type.*

attributes of the picture and/or text, or Content Only to keep the words or picture the same but allow the attributes of individual instances to be edited.

7. Click OK. The new entry will appear on the Shared Content palette **1**. Once you add this entry to a layout, any changes you make to it will be reflected in all the instances of the entry, depending on the chosen properties.

TIP When you synchronize text, all the text in the item is synchronized, so in some cases you may need to break up text into different boxes.

TIP Locked content remains locked, even if you add it as shared content. For example, if Item > Lock > Story is checked and you check Synchronize Content when you add a text box to the palette, all instances of that story will be locked when added to the layout. Similarly, if Item > Lock > Position is checked and you check Synchronize Box Attributes, all instances of the text box will also be locked in a layout. Changes to the locked/unlocked status of one instance of shared content will be reflected in the other instances.

TIP To rename an entry in the Shared Content palette, click it, then type a new name.

Add Entry, Rename Entry

Creating instances

The synchronization options selected when an entry is created determine how you create instances of that entry. If Synchronize Box Attributes or Synchronize Attributes is checked, you can drag the entire entry into a layout. If only Synchronize Content is checked, you have to add the entry to an existing box in the layout.

To insert a synchronized item into a layout:

1. Choose Window > Shared Content.

2. Select the Item tool or Content tool.

3. Click an entry in the palette whose Box Attributes (or simply Attributes) are synchronized (check the Info area to be sure) or look at the icon for the entry (picture box, text box, or line) **1**.

4. Drag the entry into the layout.

To insert a synchronized picture into a layout: NEW

1. Choose Window > Shared Content.

2. Select the Item tool or Content tool.

3. Click a picture entry in the palette.

4. Drag the picture to a picture box in the layout **2**. If the box already contains a picture, an alert warns you that the existing picture will be replaced.

TIP To replace a synchronized picture, click a picture icon in the palette, then click the Browse button. All instances of that picture will change.

To insert a synchronized story into a layout: NEW

1. Choose Window > Shared Content.

2. Select the Content tool and click in a text box.

3. Click a story entry in the palette.

4. Click the Insert button on the palette. If the box already contains text, an alert warns you that all that existing text will be replaced.

Contents vs. attributes

If you check only **Synchronize Content** (and not Synchronize Box Attributes), the text or picture will be listed as an individual entry in the palette with a story icon [Aa] or picture icon. You have to add a synchronized story to an existing text box, text path, or table cell, or add a synchronized picture to an existing picture box.

If the entry has both **Synchronize Box Attributes** and **Synchronize Content** checked, you can still create an instance of just the content in an entry: Click its triangle to reveal the content icon, then drag that content icon to a box, text path, or table cell.

1 *Dragging a synchronized item to a layout*

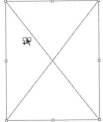

2 *Dragging a synchronized picture to a picture box*

Quick unsynchronization

If you copy or cut and paste synchronized text, the pasted text won't be synchronized.

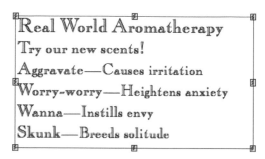

1 *When shared content is selected, lightning bolt icons display on its resize handles.*

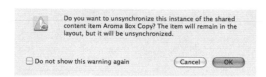

2 *This prompt appears if you **unsynchronize one** instance of shared content.*

3 *The **Unsynchronize All** button on the Shared Content palette*

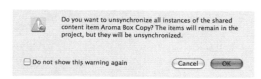

4 *This prompt will appear if you **unsynchronize all** the instances of a shared content entry.*

Unsynchronizing

You can unsynchronize one instance of shared content at a time or you can unsynchronized all the instances of a particular entry. All the former instances remain in the project, but the link to the Shared Content palette and any other former instances is broken. The entry remains in the Shared Content palette and can be added anew to a layout.

To unsynchronize one instance:

1. Select the Item tool or Content tool.

2. Click an instance of shared content. Tiny lightning bolts will appear on the item's resize handles, indicating the item is an instance **1**.

3. Choose Item > Unsynchronize.
or
Or Control-click/Right-click the item and choose Unsynchronize.

4. When the alert dialog box appears **2**, click OK.

To unsynchronize all instances of an entry:

1. Choose Window > Shared Content.

2. Click an entry whose current instances you want to unsynchronize.

3. Click the Unsynchronize All button **3**.
or
Control-click/Right-click the entry on the palette and choose Unsynchronize All.

4. When the alert dialog box appears **4**, click OK. This can be undone.

TIP The entry will remain on the palette, so you can still use it to add new instances to the layout.

If the Shared Content palette starts to fill up with entries that you no longer have any use for, it's time to weed some of them out. If you remove an entry from the Shared Content palette, any former instances of that entry will remain in the project, but they will no longer be synchronized with one another and can be edited independently of one another.

To delete an entry from the Shared Content palette:

1. Display the Shared Content palette (Window > Shared Content).

2. Click an entry to delete and click the Delete button 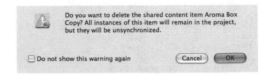.

   or

   Control-click/Right-click the entry on the palette and choose Delete.

3. When the alert dialog box appears 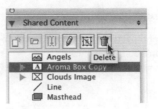, click OK. This can be undone.

TIP Deleting a layout that contains shared content has no effect on entries on the Shared Content palette or instances in other layouts.

1 *The* ***Delete*** *button*

2 *This prompt will appear if you* ***delete*** *an* ***entry*** *from the Shared Content palette.*

Delete Entry

Elaine's Book

Like libraries, book palettes have their own unique file icons and can be opened using File > Open.

Move Chapter Up

Add Chapter

Move Chapter Down

Print Chapter

Remove Chapter

Synchronize Book

...	Chapter	Pages	Status
M	qxp 7 vqs maste...	1	Modified
	:....:toc vqs 7.qxp	i*–iv*	Available
	01 Interface.qxp	1*–30*	Available
	:....:02 Startup.qxp	31–50	Modified
	03 Navigate+Und...	51–61	Available
	:....:04 Text.qxp	63–80	Modified

1 *A master file and several chapter files are displayed on this Book palette.*

Books, lists, and indexes

In this chapter we cover three features: books, lists, and indexing.

In QuarkXPress, a book is an umbrella file that's used for organizing and synchronizing multiple chapter files. A book can be any kind of publication that comprises more than one QuarkXPress file (e.g., magazine, newsletter, manual). Once individual book chapter files are united into a book, all of its style sheets, colors, H&Js, lists, and dashes & stripes are then derived from the file that you designate as the master, and page numbering flows continuously from one file to the next. In a workgroup situation, individual chapters of a book can be open and edited simultaneously on a network. If a book is edited at one station, any open copies of the same book on other stations will update automatically. Each book has its own book palette **1** and can contain up to 1,000 chapters.

A list is a compilation, from one or more projects, of text passages that have the same paragraph or character style sheet applied to them. A common use for this feature would be to construct a table of contents. Via the Lists palette, you can choose options, such as whether the list will be alphabetized and whether it will include page numbers.

And lastly, you can create an index by manually tagging individual entries in a layout and then assigning an indent level and other formats to each entry via the Index palette (yup, it's as time-consuming as it sounds!). You can generate a different index for each layout in a project or an index for an entire book.

Books

Creating books

Before creating a book, you need a master file. Specifications from this master will be applied to all the book chapters.

To create a master file:

Create a new file that contains only the master page(s), style sheets, colors, H&Js, lists, and dashes & stripes that you want all the chapter files to share. Insert the Current Page Number character (Cmd-3/Ctrl-3) into a text box on the master page. Save the file (you can include the word "master" in the title to help prevent confusion later).

or

Open an existing file, and use File > Save As to save a copy of it (use the word "master" in the name). Delete all the text and all the pages except the first page, then resave the file. As with a new file, make sure it contains only the master pages, style sheets, colors, H&Js, lists, and dashes & stripes that you want all the chapter files to share, and make sure it contains the Current Page Number command in a text box on the master page.

You can use File > Append to append style sheets, colors, lists, etc. from any other file to the master.

To create a book:

1. Choose File > New > Book.
2. Enter a name for the book, and choose a location in which to save it .
3. Click Create (Return/Enter).
4. In the top-left corner of the Book palette that opens, click the Add Chapter button.
5. Locate and click the name of the file that you want to serve as the master , then click Add (Return/Enter) 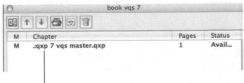. Now you can start adding chapters to the book (follow the instructions on the next page).

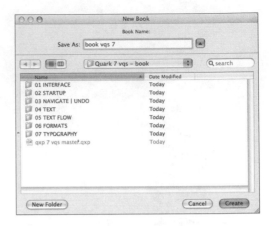

1 *Type a name for the book, then click* **Create.**

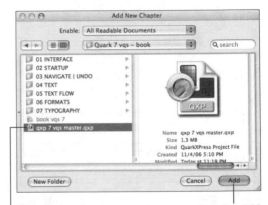

2 *Click the file that you want*   ...*then click* **Add.**
to serve as the **master**...

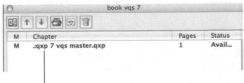

3 *The* **Master** *file name appears on the* **Book palette.**

Create a Book

To add chapters to a book:

1. Prepare the chapter files. You can use File > Export > Layout as Project to generate copies of the master file, or you can use existing files. Chapters in an individual book don't have to have the same page size.

2. Click the Add Chapter (leftmost) button 📖 on the Book palette, locate and click the name of a file that you want to add as a chapter in the book, then click Add (Return/Enter) **1**. Repeat this step for any other files that you want to add as chapters. The actual files don't have to be open.

    Note: If no chapter name is selected when you click the Add Chapter button, the new chapter will be added at the end of the list. If a chapter name is selected when you click the Add Chapter button, the new chapter will be added directly after the selected one.

Note: A project can be added to a book only if it contains one, and only one, print layout. If it contains more than one layout, make copies of the project using Save As, delete all the layouts but one in each copy, then add any of those separate files to the book. **NEW**

3. Click the Synchronize Book button **2**. 🔄

4. In the Synchronize list in the Synchronize Selected Chapters dialog box, click the items from the master chapter that you want to add to all the chapter files (click, then Shift-click to select consecutive items; or Cmd-click/Ctrl-click to select nonconsecutive items), then click the right arrow in the middle of the dialog box to add the selected items **3**. (Click the left arrow at any time to remove the currently selected items.)
    or
    Click Include All to include all the items in the currently displayed category.

(Continued on the following page)

1 *After **adding** chapters to the book...*

2 *...click the **Synchronize Book** button.*

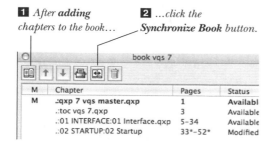

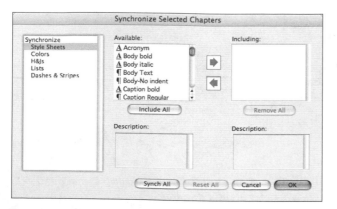

3 *Use the **Synchronize Selected Chapters** dialog box to specify which Style Sheets, Colors, H&Js, Lists, and Dashes & Stripes are to be added to all the chapter files.*

Add Chapters to a Book

TIP Remove All removes all the items in the current category from the Including window; Reset All eliminates your selections from all categories.

or

Click Synch All to synchronize everything from the master file to the chapter files.

5. Click OK, and answer any warning prompts. Page numbering will advance incrementally through the chapter files (unless any files contain section numbering; see page 344).

6. Close the Book palette by clicking the close button. All open book chapters will also close; you'll be prompted to save changes, if any were made.

TIP Once chapters have been added to a book, all you have to do is double-click a chapter name on the palette to open that chapter.

TIP A chapter file can be part of only one book at a time. To get around this, you can open the file and make a copy of it (being sure to change its name) using File > Save As. Then you can use the copy in a different book.

To change the chapter order:

On the Book palette, click a chapter name, then click the Move Chapter Up button ⬆ or Move Chapter Down button ⬇ **1**–**2**.

or

Drag a chapter name upward or downward to a new spot on the chapter list **3**.

To delete a chapter from a book:

1. On the Book palette, click the name of the chapter that you want to delete.

2. Click the Remove Chapter button.

3. Click OK.

No backing out

Book changes, such as adding or rearranging chapters, **can't be undone,** nor can the Revert to Saved command be used to restore a book to an earlier version.

Save edits to an individual chapter as you would any project.

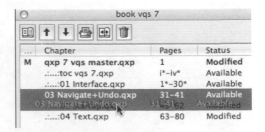

1 *Click the chapter you want to* ***move.***

2 *Clicking the* ***Move Chapter Down*** *button causes the selected chapter to move downward one slot.*

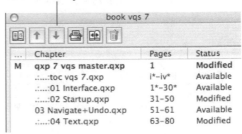

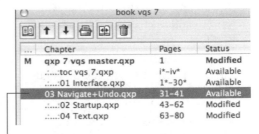

3 *You can also* ***restack*** *a chapter by dragging it upward or downward.*

Change Chapter Order; Delete Chapter

Out of sync?

You may add style sheets, colors, and so on to any individual chapter file. But bear in mind that those added elements won't appear in any other chapter files unless they're added to the master file and then the chapters are synchronized.

If you synchronize, any style sheet, color, etc. in an individual chapter file that doesn't have a double in the master file will be left alone. A style sheet, color, etc. that *does* have a matching name in the master file, but whose specifications don't match, will be updated in the chapter file to match the master file. A component that is present in the master file but not in a chapter file will be added to the chapter file.

1 The **Status** column on the Book palette tells you whether individual chapters are **Available,** already **Open,** have been **Modified** (edited), or are **Missing** (were moved).

Synchronizing optional

If no chapter is selected in the book palette, then all Available chapters will be included when you click the Synchronize All button. If there are chapters in your book whose specifications you don't want to change every time you synchronize, simply select only those chapters that you do want synchronize before pressing the button.

If you work with a book on a network, you'll need to look in the Status column on the Book palette to find out if someone else on the network has a chapter of that book open. On a network, chapters should always be opened and closed from the server.

Deciphering the Status column

Available **1** means that the chapter can be opened.

Open means that the chapter is open at your station.

[Other station name] means that the chapter is open at another station on the network.

Modified means that the chapter was opened and edited outside the book when the Book palette was closed. To update it, double-click the chapter name on the Book palette, then close the newly opened project window.

Missing means that the chapter was moved. To relink the chapter to the book, double-click its name on the palette, then locate and open the file.

To edit the master file:

1. Double-click the master file on the Book palette.
2. Create new style sheets, colors, H&Js, lists, and dashes & stripes in the master file, or use the File > Append command to add any of those elements from another file to the master file.
3. Make sure all the chapters in the book have a status of Available. If a chapter has a Modified status, double-click it, then close it.
4. Click the Synchronize Book button to add the new elements from the master file to all the book chapters.
5. Click OK.

Numbering pages in a book

There are two ways to number pages in a book, both of which we discuss below. With either method, for any numbering to show up on any layout pages, the Current Page Number character (Cmd-3/Ctrl-3) must be inserted into a text box on the master page of the master file.

One option is to let the page numbering occur automatically without doing anything. Chapters will have their pages numbered sequentially, and Book Chapter Start will be checked in the Page > Section dialog box for each one 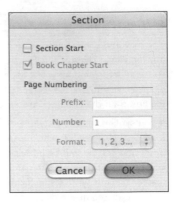.

A second option is to control the numbering yourself. On the Book palette, double-click the name of the chapter that is to begin a section, choose Page > Section, check Section Start 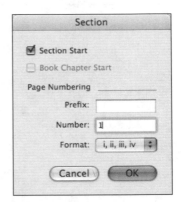, then enter a Number. Choose other options just as you would for a normal file. Section numbering will proceed through subsequent chapters up to the next section start, if there is one. You can make the first chapter (not the master) the beginning of the section, thus keeping the master outside the main flow of pages.

All book chapters adopt either the number format used in the first chapter file that's listed on the Book palette or any manual Section Start that occurs in any chapter that's listed above other chapters. Also, any master file counts as a page. To have chapter 1 start as page 1, set up a custom page number of 1 in the Section dialog box for that chapter.

1 *This is the default setting in the **Section** dialog box for a book.*

2 *To apply custom page numbering, click **Section Start**, then enter a starting page **Number**. If you want, you can also enter a **Prefix** and/or choose an alternative numbering **Format**.*

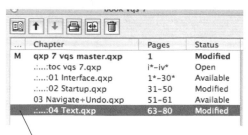

1 *To designate a different chapter file as the master, click it, then click in this blank area to the left of it.*

...	Chapter	Pages	Status
	qxp 7 vqs master.qxp	1	Modified
	.:...:toc vqs 7.qxp	i*–iv*	Open
	.:...:01 Interface.qxp	1*–30*	Available
	.:...:02 Startup.qxp	31–50	Modified
	03 Navigate+Undo.qxp	51–61	Available
M	.:...:04 Text.qxp	63–80	Modified

2 *Chapter 4 is now the **master** file.*

To print book chapters:

1. To print an individual chapter in a book, click its name on the Book palette. Only a chapter file with a status of Available or Open will print. The chapter doesn't have to be open.

   or

   To selectively print more than one chapter, Cmd-click/Ctrl-click individual chapter names, or click and then Shift-click to select consecutively listed chapters.

   or

   To print a whole book, make sure no chapter names are selected (click in the blank area below the chapter names), and make sure no chapters have a Missing or Modified status or are open at another station on the network.

2. Click the Print Chapters button. 🖨

3. Choose the desired Print settings (including a Print Style, if desired), then click Print.

To designate a different chapter as the master:

1. On the Book palette, click the name of the chapter that you want to become the new master **1**.

2. Click in the blank area to the left of the chapter name **2**.

Creating lists

The purpose of the Lists feature is to generate a table of contents or other list for a layout (or a book), with or without page reference numbers, and with or without alphabetization . It works by grabbing chapters names and numbers, section subheads, captions, sidebars, reference tables, etc. from a layout by searching for the style sheets that are assigned to paragraphs and characters.

For example, let's say you want all your text that has been assigned a subhead style to be gathered into a table of contents. First you use the Edit List dialog box to specify which style sheets are to be searched for. Then you decide how the list will be formatted. And finally, you use the Lists palette to preview and build the actual list.

To summarize, these are the basic steps you'll follow to create a list:

- Create a list definition by choosing which style sheets you want the program to search for throughout the layout or book, and by choosing format options.

- Preview the list in the scroll window on the Lists palette.

- Build the actual list in a text box in a layout.

To create and build a list definition for a project, follow the instructions starting on this page. To create and build a list for a book, follow the instructions on pages 350–351. The list definition you create draws only from the currently active layout when you preview and build it, but it can be reused for any other layouts in the same project or appended to other projects.

To create a list definition for a project:

1. Create separate style sheets for styling the list. And make sure your project's style sheets are consistent and are applied correctly to the categories of text that you want to appear in the table of contents.

allspice	cloves	paprika
basil	coriander	parsley
bay leaf	cumin	red pepper
caraway	dill	rosemary
cardamom	ginger	saffron
cayenne	lavender	sage
chervil	mace	savory
chives	mint	tarragon
cilantro	nutmeg	thyme
cinnamon	oregano	turmeric

1 A **list** can consist of anything from a simple alphabetized shopping list to a whole table of contents for a book.

2 Click **New.**

Create List Definition

1 *Enter a name.*

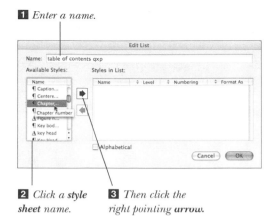

2 *Click a style* **3** *Then click the*
sheet name. *right pointing arrow.*

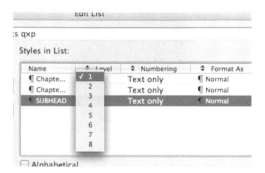

4 *For each style sheet category, choose an indent* **Level**,...

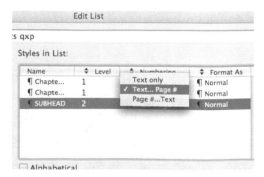

5 ...*choose a* **Numbering** *option,...*

2. If you're generating a table of contents from one project, open that project now.

3. Choose Edit > Lists, click New (**2**, previous page) then enter a Name for the list definition **1**.

4. On the Available Styles scroll list, click the style sheet name (text category) to be searched for in the project **2**, then click the right-pointing arrow to add that style sheet to the Styles in List window **3**. Or just double-click the style sheet name.

To add multiple style sheets at a time, click and then Shift-click to select a consecutive series, or Cmd-click/Ctrl-click to select multiple style sheet names individually, then click the right-pointing arrow. (Click the left-pointing arrow if you need to remove a style sheet from the Styles in List area.) You can select both paragraph and character style sheets for a list.

5. Click a style sheet in the Styles in List area and then, from the drop-down menus, choose the following:

The **Level** of indent text you want that style sheet content to have in the list (1, 2, 3, and so on) **4**. For example, you might assign level 1 to chapter names, the level 2 to headers, the level 3 to subheads, and so on.

A page **Numbering** style **5**. Choose Text...Page # if you want the page number to follow the text; choose Page #...Text if you want the page number to precede the text. Choose "Text only" if you don't want page numbers to appear at all.

Which style sheet (from the **Format As** menu) will be applied to that text

(Continued on the following page)

category 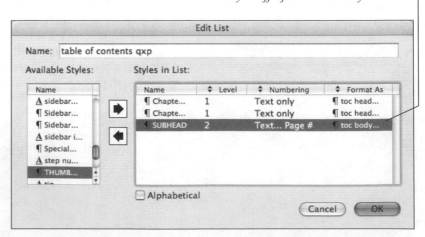. If you created a style sheet(s) specifically for the list, this is the time to choose it.

Do the same for the other style sheets.

6. *Optional:* Check Alphabetical to have items on the list appear in alphabetical order rather than the order in which they appear in the layout.

7. Click OK.

8. Click Save. Follow the instructions on the next page to build (generate) the list.

TIP In the Lists dialog box, click Duplicate to duplicate the currently selected list if you want to create a variation of it; click Delete to remove the currently selected list. To append a list from another project, follow the intructions for appending specifications on pages 49–50.

TIP The maximum number of style sheets that can be chosen for a list definition is 32. The maximum number of characters per paragraph that a list can contain is 256.

TIP For a list level that contains page number references, choose a style sheet with a right tab and a dot leader. The tab character will be inserted automatically.

1 *Choose a style sheet from the Format As menu. In our example, the Format As styles differ from the Name styles.*

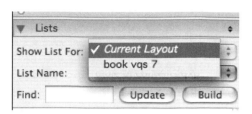

1 *From the **Show List For** menu in the Lists dialog box, choose **Current Layout**.*

2 *Choose an existing list from the **List Name** menu.*

3 *This **Lists** palette is displaying a layout's **table of contents**.*

Get there fast

If any project is open (even a chapter in a book) and you **double-click** a line of text on the Lists palette, the chapter that contains the text will open automatically and that text will be selected in the layout.

Once a list definition has been created and saved with your Levels, Numbering, and Format As (style sheet) choices, it's time to use the Lists palette to preview and build the actual list.

To preview and build a list for a layout:

1. Display the layout for which you want to build a list.

2. Make sure that Window > Lists is checked (Option-F11/Ctrl-F11).

3. Choose Show List For: Current Layout **1**.

4. From the List Name menu, choose the list that you want to build **2**. The list will preview in the scroll window on the palette **3**. If necessary, click Update.

5. Choose the Content tool, and in the same layout, click in an empty text box to create an insertion point. It can be either a new box or the first in a chain of linked text boxes.

   A list also can be appended to the end of a block of text. For example, you can write an introductory paragraph, and then have the list start after that paragraph.

6. Click Build on the Lists palette. The list will be built in the selected text box (or series of linked boxes), using your list definition, that is, the formatting options that were chosen in Edit > Lists.

TIP *Beware!* Don't delete any style sheets from a project that were used in a list. If you do, text that those style sheets were assigned to won't appear on the list when you build it.

TIP The stacking order of text boxes determines how entries will be listed, with the frontmost box on a page appearing first. If your chapter title box is stacked in front of the chapter number box, the chapter title will be listed first.

Note: Before executing these instructions, make sure the book's master file contains all the style sheets that are used in the book and a list definition has been created for that master. Also make sure that all the book chapters have a status of Available.

To create a list definition for a book:

1. Close all open files, open the book file (its Book palette will also open), and open the master file.

2. Choose Edit > Lists.

3. Create a new list definition (see pages 346–347).
   or
   Click Append, locate and open the file that contains the list definition you want to use, click the name, click the right-pointing arrow, click OK 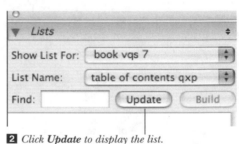, and finally, respond to any name conflicts.

4. Click Save, then save and close the master file.

5. On the Lists palette (Window > Lists or Option-F11/Ctrl-F11), make sure the book file is chosen in the Show List For menu.

6. Deselect all chapter names, then click the Synchronize Book button 📖 on the Book palette.

7. In the Synchronize Selected Chapters dialog box, click Lists, select the desired list definition name, click the right-pointing arrow to include that list definition, then click OK. (Click OK in any alert dialog boxes.)

8. Make sure the list definition chosen in the previous step appears on the List Name menu on the Lists palette, then click Update. The list that's generated from all the chapters will display on the palette 🔢–🔢. Note: If the list doesn't preview correctly, try opening the master file first, then click Update.

TIP If you renumber or rearrange pages in a book, you'll have to update and rebuild the list to make it current.

🔢 *Click the right-pointing arrow to **append** the list.*

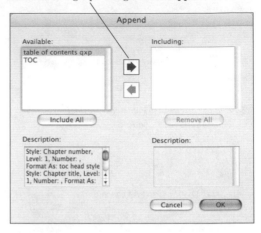

🔢 *Click **Update** to display the list.*

🔢 *The list previews on the **Lists** palette.*

*This is part of a **list** (table of contents) that was built from a book. This list is styled using style sheets that were created specifically for the list and assigned via the Format As menu in the Edit List dialog box.*

Perform the following steps after creating and updating a list definition for your book file (instructions on the previous page).

To build a list for a book file:

1. Create a new chapter for the book. One way to do this is by opening the master file, generating a copy of it using File > Save As, and stripping out the text from the new chapter. If it's going to be a table of contents and you want it to have its own numbering format, choose Page > Section, check Section Start, enter a Number, and choose a Format. And finally, make sure the file contains only one layout!

2. Add the new chapter to the book: Click the Add Chapter button 📖 on the Book palette, then locate and open the new chapter.

3. Click the Synchronize Book button 🔃 on the Book palette to copy the style sheets, colors, etc. from the master file to the new file, then click OK.

4. Click in a blank text box in the newly created chapter file.

5. On the Lists palette, choose Show List For [book name].

6. *Optional:* Turn on Auto Page Insertion in QuarkXPress (Edit, in Windows) > Preferences > Print Layout or Web Layout > General for the new chapter if you want overflow text from the list, if any, to flow into linked boxes on additional pages.

7. If the Build button is dimmed, click Update.

8. Click Build. The list will appear in the text box (or boxes).

Build List for Book

To revise a list:

1. Open the project and open the Lists palette (Option-F11/Ctrl-F11).

2. Choose a List Name.

3. For a nonbook file, double-click an entry; that text will become selected in the project window 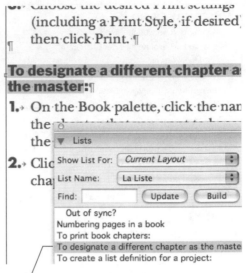. With any book chapter file open, if you double-click an entry from any chapter file, the chapter file will open and the text will become selected.

4. Make any modifications to the text in the layout. For example, to prevent a text passage from appearing on the list, apply any style sheet to it that isn't being searched for in the list.

5. Click Update on the Lists palette to update the list preview.

6. If you're going to rebuild the list in the same project, click in the text box that contains the list. Or if you're going to insert the rebuilt list and leave the old list unchanged, click exactly where you want the new one to appear. If the list is in a separate chapter of a book, open that chapter now.

7. Click Build.

8. Click Insert to build a new list and leave the old list unchanged .
   or
   Click Replace to replace the current list with the new list .

   You can't undo either operation.

TIP You can reformat a built list manually or apply different style sheets to it, but such changes will be lost if you rebuild the list using the Replace option.

TIP If the list on the palette is long and you want to quickly find a particular line, type the first word of the line in the Find field; a line will become selected after you start typing . You have to type enough of the entry to differentiate it from similar entries.

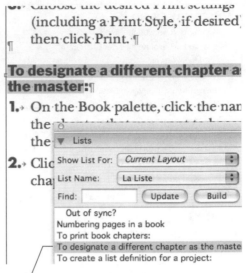

*For a nonbook file, **double-click** an entry on the Lists palette to view that entry in the project window.*

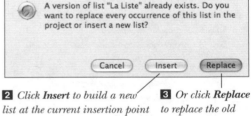

2 *Click **Insert** to build a new list at the current insertion point and leave the old list unchanged.*

3 *Or click **Replace** to replace the old list with the new list.*

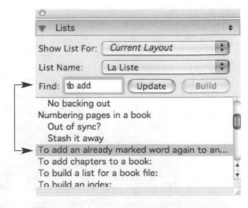

4 *An entry that was typed into the **Find** field on the Lists palette is found in the list.*

Revise List

A
anchor points, 2-3

I
Illustrator, 1-6; Adobe, 1; closed paths, 2; FreeHand,
1; Macintosh, 1; object-oriented, 1; Objects, 1;
precision tools, 5; Stroke, 3; tools, 2; vector
image, 1; Windows, 1

O
object-oriented, 1 vector, 3; versus raster, 4; paths, 5;
Pen tool, 5-7; printing, 8; resolution, 7

P
Pencil. See tool

1 *Portions of a built index in the **Run-in** format*

Indexing

Indexes are layout-specific, so you'll need
to build a different index for each layout in
a project. You can also build an index that
covers all the chapters in a book. Building
an index requires four main steps, in
roughly this order:

- Create the style sheets for the index
  itself, for letter headings, for the entries
  themselves, etc.

- Mark all the text that is to be referenced
  in the index.

- Build the index **1**–**2**.

- Look over the index, and edit it where
  necessary.

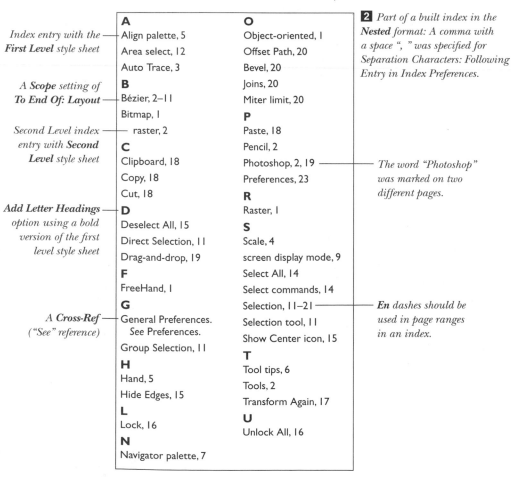

Index entry with the **First Level** *style sheet*

*A **Scope** setting of* **To End Of: Layout**

*Second Level index entry with **Second Level** style sheet*

Add Letter Headings *option using a bold version of the first level style sheet*

*A **Cross-Ref** ("See" reference)*

A
Align palette, 5
Area select, 12
Auto Trace, 3
B
Bézier, 2–11
Bitmap, 1
    raster, 2
C
Clipboard, 18
Copy, 18
Cut, 18
D
Deselect All, 15
Direct Selection, 11
Drag-and-drop, 19
F
FreeHand, 1
G
General Preferences.
    See Preferences.
Group Selection, 11
H
Hand, 5
Hide Edges, 15
L
Lock, 16
N
Navigator palette, 7

O
Object-oriented, 1
Offset Path, 20
Bevel, 20
Joins, 20
Miter limit, 20
P
Paste, 18
Pencil, 2
Photoshop, 2, 19
Preferences, 23
R
Raster, 1
S
Scale, 4
screen display mode, 9
Select All, 14
Select commands, 14
Selection, 11–21
Selection tool, 11
Show Center icon, 15
T
Tool tips, 6
Tools, 2
Transform Again, 17
U
Unlock All, 16

2 *Part of a built index in the* **Nested** *format: A comma with a space ", " was specified for Separation Characters: Following Entry in Index Preferences.*

The word "Photoshop" was marked on two different pages.

En dashes should be used in page ranges in an index.

Indexing

Use the Index palette to mark and format index references for individual text strings in a layout. This is a time-consuming process. After that you'll build the index itself in the same file or in a separate file.

To mark a layout for indexing:

1. Enable Quark's Index.xnt XTension, if it's not already enabled.

2. Display a layout to mark for indexing or create a new layout to be marked as you enter text.

3. If you're going to do any "see also " cross-referencing or if you want page number references to appear in a different style from the index entries, create the character style sheet(s) that you want to apply to those references.

   This is also a good time to create all the other style sheets that you want to use in the built index. An index can have either a nested or run-in format (see the illustrations on the previous page). You can edit the style sheets later.

   For a nested index, you'll need a style sheet for the First Level text passages as well as a style sheet for each subsequent indent level. In the Edit Style Sheet dialog box, you can use the Based On option for this, and apply progressively larger Left Indent values for the Second, Third, and Fourth Level styles.

   Also create a style sheet for letter headings if you're going to use them (A, B, C, and so on). Apply a Space Before value via Style > Formats, and choose a bolder font than the body text for that style sheet so it stands out.

4. Choose Window > Index.

5. In the layout, select a word or phrase that you want to include in the index 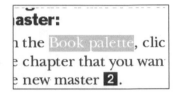. You'll be choosing settings for each individual entry separately.
   or
   Select any text in the layout that you want to create an entry for; it will

Building a nest

To create **nested** (indented) entries, follow the instructions on this page and the next two pages, with this additional step: Click in the Index palette scroll window to the left of an existing First Level entry to move the indent arrow to that entry, then choose Level: Second Level, Third Level, or Fourth Level. When you add the entry, it will appear below, and indented from, the chosen First Level entry.

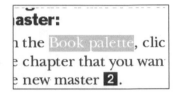

1 *Start by selecting a word or phrase in a layout that you want included in the index.*

2 *Text that's currently selected in the layout will display in the **Text** field on the Index palette.*

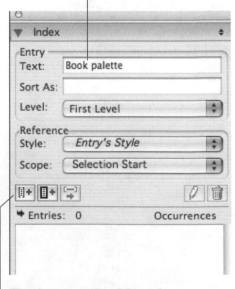

These buttons are, from left to right,
Add, Add All, *and* ***Find Next Entry.***

Mark Layout for Indexing

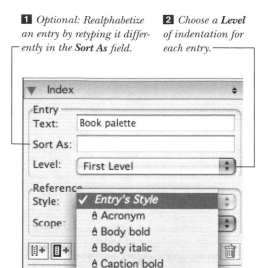

1 *Optional: Realphabetize an entry by retyping it differently in the **Sort As** field.*

2 *Choose a **Level** of indentation for each entry.*

3 *Choose a **character** style sheet for each entry.*

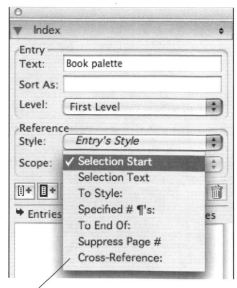

4 *Choose a **Scope** (range of pages) for each entry. For example, to index "Mark a layout for indexing," in this book, if we choose To Style and choose our subhead style, that topic will be listed on the relevant pages.*

display in the Text field on the Index palette (**2**, previous page). Change the text in this field if you want to create a broad category for the entry as opposed to having the item be indexed as written.

6. On the Index palette, review the text in the Text field, and change any capitalization or word endings, if desired.

7. *Optional:* In the Sort As field, enter a different method for alphabetizing **1**. For example, if you spell out a number in this field (e.g., "Seven-Up" instead of "7-Up"), that number will be sorted alphabetically in the index rather than be placed at the top of the index. The Sort As spelling won't affect the spelling of the entry in the layout.

8. Choose indent Level: First Level **2**.

9. *Optional:* From the Style menu **3**, choose a custom style to be assigned to any cross-reference words (see step 10) and page number(s) for this entry.

10. From the Scope menu, specify the range of pages to be referenced in the index for the current entry **4**:

Selection Start to specify the page on which the entry is located. If the entry spans more than one page, the page where the selection starts will be used.

Selection Text to specify the page(s) of a block of text.

To Style to specify the range from the selection start (or cursor position) to a style sheet you choose from the adjoining menu.

Specified # ¶'s to specify a range spanning the exact number of paragraphs that you enter in the adjoining field.

To End Of to specify either the end of the story or the end of the layout, whichever you choose from the menu. Choose this option for the title of any section that you want listed as a range of pages (e.g., "42–58").

(Continued on the following page)

Suppress Page # to suppress the page number. This is a good idea when you want to include a broad category, say "Preferences," that will have second-level items, such as "Application preferences" and "Layout preferences."

Cross-Reference to create a cross-reference for the current text. Choose "See," "See also," or "See herein" and enter the reference in the text field on the right.

11. Click the Add button **1**. The newly added entry will preview at the bottom of the palette and will be listed alphabetically in its chosen indent level. While the Index palette is open, an index marker (red brackets) will surround that passage in the layout **2**. When text is typed directly into the Text field on the palette, a square box appears in the layout at the location of the cursor.

12. Repeat steps 5–11 for all the remaining text in the layout that you want the index to include.

TIP If you double-click an index entry's page number on the palette, the text will become selected in the layout.

TIP To delete an entry, click it in the scroll window on the Index palette, click the Delete button on the palette, then click OK (you can't undo this!). No need to select the text in the layout; the brackets will be removed automatically.

---

delete a chapter from a bo

ʿOn the ⌐book palette⌐, click t̶
of the chapter that you wan⌐

ʿClick the Remove Chapter ⌐

2 *If you select a word or phrase in a layout with the Index palette open, left and right **index marker brackets** will surround that passage. The hollow square marks where text was entered directly into the **Text** field on the Index palette.*

Mark Layout for Indexing

Index palette shortcuts

Display palette/ select **Text** field	Cmd-Option-I/Ctrl-Alt-I
Click **Add** button	Cmd-Option-Shift-I/ Ctrl-Alt-Shift-I

Index palette buttons

■ To find, mark, and add all instances of the current text as an entry, using the current settings, click the Add All button.⊞➕

■ To zip through a story to review the entries you've marked, keep clicking the Find Next Entry button.⇥

■ Hold down Option/Alt to turn the Add button into Add Reversed, which creates an entry based on the last word in the currently selected text; do the same to turn Add All into Add All Reversed, which does what Add Reversed does for all occurrences of that phrase. Option/Alt also turns Find Next Entry into Find First Entry.

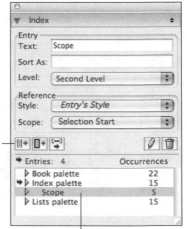

1 *Click the **Add** button to make the **Text** entry appear in the bottom part of the palette.*

*The "Scope" entry has been specified as a **Second Level** indent under the "Index palette" entry. Note the position of the indent arrow (which appeared when we clicked in the arrow column for "Index palette") and the indentation of the "Scope" entry in the scroll window.*

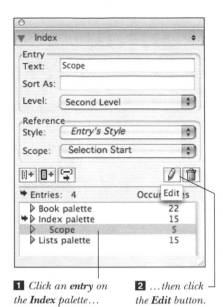

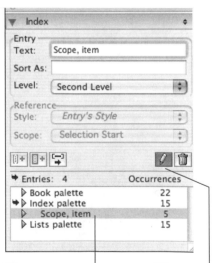

1 *Click an* **entry** *on the* **Index** *palette…*

2 *…then click the* **Edit** *button.*

4 *When you edit an entry in the* **Text** *field, it updates here.*

3 *The* **Edit** *button darkens when clicked.*

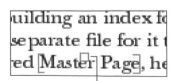

5 *The* **second** *index entry marker box appears when a word is indexed more than once.*

To edit an index entry:

1. Click an index entry in the scroll window on the Index palette **1**.
2. Click the Edit button **2**. ✐ The button will change shade **3**.
3. Edit the text in the Text field and/or the Sort As field **4**, change the Level value, then press Tab. The entry will update immediately.
   and/or
   Click the entry's reference (page number or cross-reference) in the scroll window (click the arrowhead/+ to reveal it, if necessary), then change the Reference: Style or Scope. The reference will update immediately.
4. Click any other entries, and edit them as needed.
5. Click the Edit button again when you're finished editing.

If you want to add an entry a second time, as a Second Level entry under a different First Level entry, you can't add it the same way. You'll need to follow these instructions instead.

To add an already marked word again to an index:

1. Click in the original marked word in the layout (don't select it).
2. Click in the Text field on the Index palette, then retype the entry.
3. Choose other Entry and Reference options.
4. To create a nested entry, click in the indent arrow (leftmost) column next to the entry below which you want the new entry to nest.
5. Click Add. A small hollow square will display inside the index marker brackets in the layout **5**.

To cross-reference an index entry:

1. Click in the text box in the layout that contains the indexed word.

2. Click the entry in the scroll window on the Index palette.

3. Choose Scope: Cross-Reference, choose menu, then type the cross-referenced word.

4. Click Add 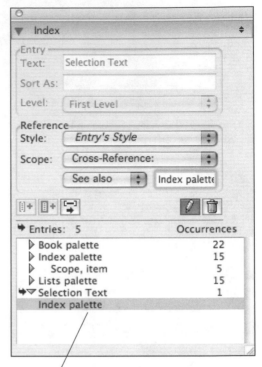. Click the arrowhead/+ next to the entry to preview. Click the arrowhead again to hide the entry.

Before building or rebuilding an index, you can use the Index pane of the Preferences dialog box to specify which punctuation marks will be used in the index.

To choose Index preferences:

1. Choose QuarkXPress (Edit, in Windows) > Preferences > Index.

2. *Optional:* To change the Index Marker Color (the brackets in marked text), click the color square, choose a new color, then click OK.

3. Change any or all of the settings in the Separation Characters fields **2**:

   Following Entry is the punctuation to follow each index entry (e.g., the comma in "Biscuit,").

   Between Page Numbers is the punctuation between nonconsecutive page numbers (as in "34, 77").

   Between Page Range is the punctuation used to define a range of pages (as in "24–102"). Use an en dash (Option-hyphen/Ctrl-Alt-Shift-hyphen).

   Before Cross-Reference is the punctuation that's used before a "See" cross-reference (as in "Biscuit, 20. *See also* Rolls"). (This character will replace the chosen "Following Entry" character, when necessary.)

   The **Cross-Reference Style** pop-up menu lists all the character style sheets in

1 A *"see also"* reference added to an index

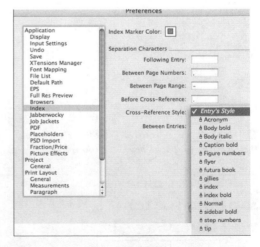

2 Choose **Index Preferences** before building or rebuilding an index.

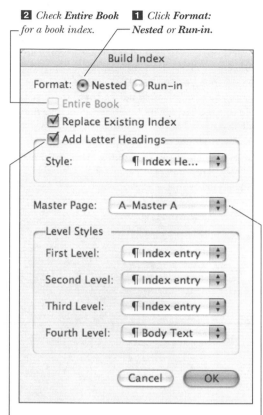

2 *Check **Entire Book*** *for a book index.* **1** *Click **Format:*** *Nested or Run-in.*

3 *Check **Add Letter Headings** to have each alphabetical group of index entries be separated by the appropriate alphabet letter.*

4 *Choose a **Master Page** format for the index.*

Keep track of Index Preferences

Unfortunately, changes made in the Index pane of the Preferences dialog box are saved with the application—not the individual layout or project—so they are not specific to an individual index. If you use different index punctuation for different publications or clients, you need to keep records of each collection of settings. Then be sure to check the preferences each time before building an index.

your project. Choose a style for the cross-referenced words, such as "See" or "See also."

Between Entries is the punctuation between entries in a run-in style index (as in "frog, 17; toad, 18") and the ending punctuation in paragraphs in a nested style index.

4. Click OK.

Follow these instructions to build the actual index after the layout or book project has been marked for indexing and the pagination is finalized.

Note: Before building an index, you can choose Index Preferences (previous page).

To build an index:

1. For a book, create a new chapter file to hold the index, and make it the last chapter. Or open a nonbook project to create an index for just that marked project.

2. Turn Auto Page Insertion on in Preferences > Print Layout > General.

3. *Optional:* If you haven't already done so, create style sheets for each level of indentation and for alphabet letter headings. For a book, do this in the master file and then Synchronize.

4. Choose Utilities > Build Index.

5. Choose Format: Nested to indent each progressive level in the index **1**.
or
Choose Format: Run-in to string the index entry levels together in paragraph form following the First Level entry. They will be separated by the Between Entries punctuation mark that you chose in Index Preferences.

6. *Do any of these optional steps:*
Check Entire Book to index an entire set of book files **2**.

(Continued on the following page)

Build an Index

Check Replace Existing Index to replace an existing, previously built index with the newly built index.

Check Add Letter Headings to separate each alphabetical group of index entries by the appropriate letter of the alphabet (**3**, previous page). Choose a Style sheet for the headings from the menu.

7. Choose a Master Page for the index (**4**, previous page). The master page you choose *must* contain an automatic text box for the index to flow into.

8. In the Level Styles area of the dialog box:

For the Nested format, choose a paragraph style sheet for each level of indent (First Level, Second Level, Third Level, and Fourth Level).
or
For the Run-in format, choose a First Level style sheet.

9. Click OK (see the illustrations on page 353). The index will be built and a new page will be added to the end of your layout. (You don't have to select a text box first.)

TIP After building an index, if you want to edit any of the style sheets that were assigned via the Level Styles area of the Build Index dialog box, use Edit > Style Sheets. This index, and any other index that uses those style sheets, will update to reflect your changes. These changes will also be applied if you rebuild the index.

Editing an index

Any manual changes you make to a built index will be lost if you rebuild the index. In general, the best strategy is to make content changes in the Index palette and then rebuild the index until you're completely satisfied with the results. Editing the built index is a mistake because the changes are not permanent and will not be reflected in future versions of the index. If you need to change the style of the index, however, simply edit the paragraph and character style sheets that you used to format it.

Preferences 22

Preferences shortcuts

Preferences dialog box	Cmd-Option-Shift-Y/ Ctrl-Alt-Shift-Y
Paragraph preferences	Cmd-Option-Y/Ctrl-Alt-Y
Tools preferences	Double-click item creation or Zoom tool

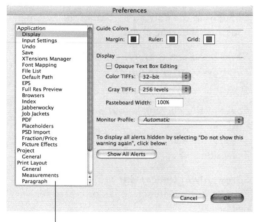

1 *Click an option in the scroll list on the left side of the* **Preferences** *dialog box to display that pane.*

Preferences that are covered in other chapters

Index	Chapter 21
Jabberwocky	Chapter 5
Output Styles	Chapter 24
Trapping	Chapter 24

For avenue.quark, Browsers, Placeholders, and XML Import preferences, see the QuarkXPress documentation resources.

Getting to the preferences

The Preferences dialog box

Preferences are the default values that automatically apply when a feature or a tool is used. For example, when the Line tool is used, a line is automatically drawn in a particular width; that width is one of its default settings. Other default settings for the Line tool include its color and style.

If you select project-level preferences when a project is open, the preferences affect only that project. Likewise, if you select layout-level preferences when a specific layout is active, the preferences affect only that layout. If no projects are open, however, project-level and layout-level preferences become defaults for all new projects and their layouts.

Other preferences, such as whether the XTensions Manager displays at startup, apply to the whole application, regardless of whether any projects are open when you choose them.

To open the main Preferences dialog box **1**, use any of these three methods:

- Choose QuarkXPress (Edit, in Windows) > Preferences.

- Press one of the keyboard shortcuts listed in the sidebar at left.

- Control-click/Right-click a blank area in a layout and choose Preferences.

Once you're in the Preferences dialog box, click an option in the scroll list at left to display a pane (a category) of preferences.

Other kinds of preferences and defaults

In addition to the preferences you can set via the Preferences dialog box, you can also specify other kinds of very useful defaults for the application. For example, any paragraph or character style sheet that's created or appended when no projects are open will appear on the Style Sheets palette of subsequently created projects. The same holds true for colors, H&Js, lists, dashes and stripes, and the default auxiliary dictionary. Normal, the default paragraph and character style sheets that automatically appear in every new project and in any text box to which type specifications have not yet been applied, can be edited for all future layouts when no projects are open. Don't overlook setting these kinds of defaults—they're enormous time-savers!

Tracking and kerning table settings, and hyphenation exceptions, are stored in individual projects and in the XPress Preferences file. (On Mac OS: [hard drive]/Users/[user name]/Library/Preferences/Quark/QuarkXPress 7.0. On Windows: C: > Documents and Settings\ [current user]\Application Data\Quark\ QuarkXPress 7.0). If, upon opening a file, the project settings don't match the XPress Preferences settings, an alert dialog box will appear. Click Use XPress Preferences (Cmd-./Esc) to apply the preferences resident on that computer, or click Keep Document Settings (Return/Enter) to leave the project as is (see the sidebar).

If you trash your XPress Preferences.prf file, the application will create a new one automatically, but in the process all your custom settings will be lost. For this reason, you should trash the Preferences file only if the application becomes corrupt or if you intentionally want to restore the program defaults for some reason. You can copy your Preferences file and stash the copy for safekeeping.

Inside XPress Preferences

Preferences and defaults are saved at various levels: in XPress Preferences, with projects, and with individual layouts. Knowing what preferences and defaults affect—for example, whether a change to a character preference affects the current layout or all the layouts in the project—is important and yet confusing. Here's a guide.

Saves in XPress Preferences and affects all projects immediately
- Application Preferences (such as Display and Input Settings)
- Default Project Preferences and Print/Web Layout Preferences (set with no projects open)
- PPD Manager and Profile Manager (Utilities menu); font replacement rules
- Output Styles, Color Setups, and all the other options in the bottom portion of the Edit menu such as Underline Styles

Saves in XPress Preferences and affects all projects after relaunch
XTensions Manager

Saves in the current layout and in XPress Preferences
Kerning Table Edit, Tracking Edit, Hyphenation Exceptions

Saves only in the current print layout
Print Layout Preferences; open or create auxiliary dictionary

Preferences in workgroups

If all the members of a workgroup are working one publication or similar publications, it's a good idea to use the same Preferences settings so you can ensure consistency in kerning, tracking, spelling, etc. You can copy the XPress Preferences file to the same location on different computers to enforce this type of consistency.

Choosing application preferences

Remember that changes to Application Preferences affect all projects—as soon as you make the changes.

Display pane 1

To choose the color for **Margin** or **Ruler** guides, or the **Grid,** click the appropriate square, then choose a color from the Color Picker. The Margin color is also used to represent the item boundary in the Runaround and Clipping dialog boxes; the Ruler color also represents the clipping path; and the Grid color also represents the runaround path.

With **Opaque Text Box Editing** on, if you click a text box with the Content tool, it will look opaque, making it easier to edit the text, whether or not the box actually has a background color. With this option off (the default), a text box will keep its current background color, whether it's a solid color, a blend, or None (transparent).

Choose a color depth for the screen preview that QuarkXPress creates for imported **Color TIFFs.** A picture's screen preview affects its redraw speed and the storage size of the QuarkXPress file. The 8-bit (256 possible colors) option produces a faster redraw speed and smaller file size, but with an inferior screen preview. Style > Contrast isn't available for a picture that has a 16-bit preview (thousands of possible colors) or 32-bit (Mac OS)/24-bit (Windows) preview (millions of possible colors).

Choose a color depth for the screen preview for imported **Gray** [grayscale] **TIFFs.**

The **Pasteboard Width** is the percentage of the total width of the layout that's allocated to the pasteboard. 100% is the default. (48 is the maximum total width.)

If you clicked "Do not show this warning again" in any alert dialog box, you can click **Show All Alerts** here to allow alert dialog boxes to redisplay.

The **Monitor Profile** menu lets you tell QuarkXPress what type of computer monitor you are using so it knows how to display color. The default setting, Automatic, matches the monitor profile selected on your system. If for some reason it is incorrect, or on the rare occasion that you want to simulate a different monitor, you can choose a different profile. If you acquire a new monitor and it provides a profile, drag that profile into the Profiles folder inside the QuarkXPress application folder (if the folder doesn't exist, create it). Then, choose that profile from this menu.

Windows only: The **Display DPI Value** is the monitor resolution. Read about this setting in the QuarkXPress documentation.

1 *The **Display** pane of QuarkXPress (Edit, in Windows) > Preferences > Application*

Input Settings pane 1

Move the **Scrolling** slider to choose a rate of speed for the scroll arrows and boxes on the project window.

With **Speed Scroll** on, on a slow machine, large pictures and blends will be greeked (display as solid gray) as you scroll and then redraw when you stop scrolling.

With **Live Scroll** on, the layout will redraw as you drag a scroll box on the project window. Turn this option off if you have a slow machine. Option-drag/Alt-drag a scroll box to temporarily turn Live Scroll on or off. The Page Grabber always produces a live scroll.

With **Smart Quotes** on, smart quotation marks are inserted automatically when the ' or " key is pressed (see page 130). Choose a Format (style) for the quotes. Professional typesetters always use Smart Quotes. Un-smart quotes look, well, un-smart.

Choose **Page Range Separators** for the symbols to be used in the Print dialog box to separate the page numbers you want to print. This is something you only need to worry about if your section page numbers include the default characters. For example, if you have pages such as "A-1," then you couldn't use a hyphen to separate a range of page numbers you want to print.

Mac OS X only: Choose which function you want the **Control Key** to have: Zoom in/out or access Contextual Menus (the default).

NEW Adjust the **Delay Before Live Refresh** value to control how long you need to pause before you can see an item as you drag it with the mouse. Enter the number of seconds (or fraction of a second) in the field that you want to pause before dragging (0.75–5 seconds).

With **Drag and Drop Text** on, you can select text and drag it to a new location within the same story (one or more linked text boxes or table cells). See page 70.

screen redraw shortcuts

Forced redraw	Cmd-Option-. (period)/Shift-Esc
Stop redraw	*Mac OS X:* Cmd-. (period)
	Mac OS X and Windows: Esc or perform another operation (e.g., select an item, choose another command)

If **Show Tool Tips** is checked and you rest the pointer on an interface element—such as a tool, icon, or palette button—its name will display. Knowing the names is also helpful for looking up information.

When **Maintain Picture Box Attributes** is **NEW** checked, Maintain Picture Attributes is automatically checked in File > Import Picture when you import a picture into a box that already contains a picture. This setting also controls whether attributes (such as offset and scale) are maintained when you paste pictures into boxes that already contain pictures.

If **Font Fallback** is checked and you im- **NEW** port or paste text containing special characters that are not available in the current font, QuarkXPress attempts to find the character in another active font and displays that character. When this is unchecked, QuarkXPress displays a box for missing characters. Uncheck this if you prefer to handle all font issues yourself.

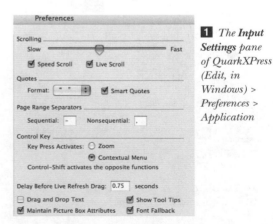

1 *The Input Settings pane of QuarkXPress (Edit, in Windows) > Preferences > Application*

Undo pane 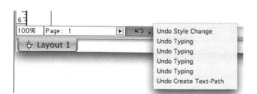 1

In Mac OS X, Cmd-Shift-Z is the default keyboard shortcut for Redo. To change this shortcut, choose Cmd-Z or Cmd-Y from the **Redo Key** menu. *Note:* If you choose Cmd-Z for Redo, you'll need to press Cmd-Option-Z when you want to reverse your steps back through the Undo history.

In Windows, Ctrl-Y is the default keyboard shortcut for Redo. To change this shortcut, choose Ctrl-Shift-Z or Ctrl-Z from the Redo Key menu. *Note:* If you choose Ctrl-Z for Redo, you'll need to press Ctrl-Alt-Z to reverse your steps back through the Undo history.

If you choose Cmd-Z/Ctrl-Z as your shortcut for Redo, you can then toggle back and forth between undoing and redoing the last edit.

In the **Maximum History Actions** field, you can specify the maximum number (1–30) of edits (actions) that can be stored in your Undo history. The default setting is 20. If the number of actions in a work session exceeds this maximum, the oldest action will be removed from the **Undo** menu.

1 *The **Undo** pane of QuarkXPress (Edit, in Windows) > Preferences > Application*

*The **Undo/Redo** menus in the lower-left corner of the project window*

Save pane (**1**, next page)

Auto Save and Auto Backup are like system or power failure insurance. With **Auto Save** enabled, modifications are saved in a temporary file at the interval specified in the "Every [ ] minutes" field. Five minutes is the default. There may be a short (but potentially annoying) interruption in processing while an Auto Save occurs. If a system or power failure occurs while you're modifying a layout and you restart and then reopen the project, a prompt will appear. Click OK to reopen the last auto-saved version. *Beware!* Auto Save can't retrieve a project that's never been saved!

To restore the last manually saved version of an open project, choose File > Revert to Saved. To restore the last auto-saved version of a project, hold down Option/Alt while choosing File > Revert to Saved.

Unlike Auto Save, which saves only modifications made to a project in a temporary file, **Auto Backup** creates a backup version of the entire project when the Save command is executed. Progressively higher numbers are appended to the backup names. To specify how many backup versions will be created before the oldest backup version is deleted, enter a number between 1 and 100 in the "Keep [ ] revisions" field.

Auto backups are saved in the current document (project) folder, unless you specify a different destination. Designating a different location for the backups can help prevent confusion. If you want to designate a different destination, click Other Folder and use the Browse button to specify a new location. To reset the destination as the current project folder at any time, click Project Folder.

(Continued on the following page)

Undo, Save Preferences

With **Auto Library Save** on, a library will be saved whenever an item is added to it. With Auto Library Save off, a library will be saved only when it's closed or when you quit/exit the application.

With **Save Layout Position** on, when a project is reopened, it will open to the same layout with the same zoom level, window size, and position onscreen that it had when it was last closed.

XTensions Manager pane 2

With **Show XTensions Manager at Startup: Always** on, the XTensions Manager will open automatically whenever the application is launched.

With **When: XTension Folder Changes** on instead, the XTensions Manager will open during launch only if you've added or removed an XTension or XTensions from your XTension folder since the application was last open.

With **When: Error Occurs While Loading XTensions** on, the XTensions Manager will open during a launch only if QuarkXPress encounters a problem while loading XTensions.

Font Mapping pane 3 NEW

The Font Mapping preferences control what happens when you open a project that uses a font that is not active in your system. Usually, the answer is to locate and activate the font. You can, however, save font replacement "rules" for all projects by choosing replacement fonts and clicking Save as Rule in the Missing Fonts dialog box.

For handling missing fonts without rules, check **Specify Default Replacement Font** and select a font from the menu. If you have rules in place to handle most missing fonts, check **Do Not Display Missing Fonts Dialog,** and then specify how to handle fonts without rules: **Display Missing Fonts Dialog** or **Replace Missing Fonts with Replacement Font** (specified in the menu above).

1 *The **Save** pane of QuarkXPress (Edit, in Windows) > Preferences > Application*

2 *The **XTensions Manager** pane of QuarkXPress (Edit, in Windows) > Preferences > Application*

3 *The **Font Mapping** pane of QuarkXPress (Edit, in Windows) > Preferences > Application*

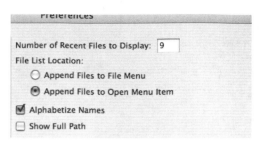

1 *The **File List** pane of QuarkXPress (Edit, in Windows) > Preferences > Application*

Preferences

Number of Recent Files to Display: 9
File List Location:
  ○ Append Files to File Menu
  ◉ Append Files to Open Menu Item
  ☑ Alphabetize Names
  ☐ Show Full Path

Preferences

☐ Use Default Path for Open _____
                              (Browse...)

☐ Use Default Path for Save/Save As _____
                              (Browse...)

☐ Use Default Path for Import Text _____
                              (Browse...)

☐ Use Default Path for Import Picture _____
                              (Browse...)

2 *The **Default Path** pane of QuarkXPress (Edit, in Windows) > Preferences > Application*

Preferences

Preview: [Embedded ▼]
Virtual Memory: [100] MB

3 *The **EPS** pane of QuarkXPress (Edit, in Windows) > Preferences > Application*

File List pane **1**

Enter the maximum **Number of Recent Files to Display** (recently opened and saved files), from 3–9, that can be listed on the File menu.

Click **Append Files to File Menu** to have file names be listed on the first level of the File menu, or click **Append Files to Open Menu Item** to have file names be listed on the File > Open submenu.

Check **Alphabetize Names** to have file names be listed in alphabetical order. With this option unchecked, names will appear in the order in which they were opened or saved.

Check **Show Full Path** to have a file's location (drive and folder) be listed next to its name on the File menu.

Default Path pane **2**

If you tend to navigate to the same folder each time you use the Open, Save/Save As, Import Text, or Import Picture command, it's worth your while to use Default Path preferences to designate a default path for those dialog boxes.

Click any or all of the four **Use Default Path for...** check boxes, and for each one you check, use the Browse button to specify a path.

TIP To disable a default path, uncheck that box in the Default Path preferences dialog box. The default path will still be listed, but it won't be active.

EPS pane **3** NEW

The **Preview** menu lets you specify what displays when you import a picture in EPS format. Choose Embedded to display the built-in preview (saved with a picture in Illustrator, for example) or Generate to have QuarkXPress create a new preview.

In Mac OS, you can increase the memory available for creating EPS files from QuarkXPress (File > Save Page as EPS) by increasing the **Virtual Memory** value.

File List, Default Path, EPS Preferences

Full Res Preview pane 1

High-resolution previews aren't stored in project files. Rather, they're stored in a folder called Preview Cache, located in the **QuarkXPress Preferences Folder**. To change it to a location with more space such as an external hard drive, click Other Folder and use the Browse button to specify a new location.

Enter the **Maximum Cache Folder Size** (200–4000 MB) for storage in the designated preview cache location.

With Display Full Resolution Preview for: **All Full Resolution Previews** chosen, if you apply View > Full Resolution Preview to pictures in a QuarkXPress project and then open the project on another computer, the application will have to generate new previews, which can take a while. If you click **Selected Full Resolution Previews** instead, QuarkXPress won't display (or generate) any high-resolution previews until or unless a picture is selected.

To turn off the display of high-resolution previews, check **Disable Full Resolution Previews on Open.** Then, if and when you're ready to see the high-resolution previews, you can turn them back on again by choosing View > Show Full Res Previews.

Job Jackets pane 2 NEW

When using the Job Jackets feature, you can test layouts to see if they comply with rules and output specifications—such as whether a layout should use spot colors. Under **Evaluate Layout,** check when you want the tests to be performed. For the average user, On Open or On Close would be adequate whereas a service bureau might want On Output.

To store Job Jackets in your system's Documents/My Documents folder, click Use Default Folder for Shared Job Jackets under **Job Jacket Location.** Otherwise, click Other Folder and use the Browse button to specify a new location.

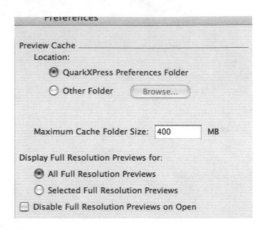

1 *The Full Res Preview pane of QuarkXPress (Edit, in Windows) > Preferences > Application*

2 *The Job Jackets pane of QuarkXPress (Edit, in Windows) > Preferences > Application*

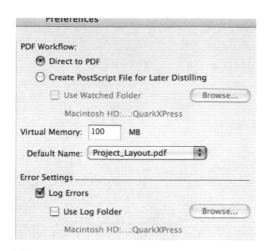

1 *The **PDF** pane of QuarkXPress (Edit, in Windows) > Preferences > Application*

(The PSD Import pane shown below)

Preferences

Preview Cache
  Location:
    ⦿ QuarkXPress Preferences Folder
    ○ Other Folder   Browse...

Maximum Cache Folder Size: 100   MB

    Clear Cache

2 *The **PSD Import** pane of QuarkXPress (Edit, in Windows) > Preferences > Application*

PDF pane **1**

If you choose File > Export > Layout as PDF to export a layout to PDF format and PDF Workflow: **Direct to PDF** is chosen as the Preferences setting, QuarkXPress will export the layout directly into the PDF format. If the setting is **Create PostScript File for Later Distilling** instead, when you choose the Layout as PDF command, QuarkXPress will create a PostScript export file that you can later convert to PDF using Adobe Acrobat Distiller.

If you check **Use Watched Folder** and then use the Browse button to designate a folder for exported PostScript files, Distiller will periodically check this folder and automatically distill any files saved to it.

NEW In Mac OS, you can increase the memory available for creating PDFs by increasing the value in the **Virtual Memory** field.

NEW To specify a default naming convention for exported PDF files, choose an option from the **Default Name** menu. If your projects don't include multiple layouts, we suggest choosing Project.PDF rather than the default shown (Project_Layout.pdf).

To create a log file describing any errors when exporting a PDF, check **Log Errors.** To store all the log files in one location, check Use Log Folder and use the Browse button to specify a location. Otherwise, log files are stored in the same place as the exported PDF.

PSD Import pane **2** **NEW**

Previews for import PSD (native Photoshop) files are stored in a folder called PSD Import Cache, located in the **QuarkXPress Preferences Folder**. To change to a location with more space such as an external hard drive, click Other Folder and use the Browse button to specify a new location.

Enter the **Maximum Cache Folder Size** (1–32,767 MB) for storage in the designated preview cache location.

Fraction/Price pane

Fraction/Price preferences control the proportions of fractions (e.g., ½, ¼) and prices (e.g., $24⁹⁹, $99.⁹⁹). To produce a fraction in QuarkXPress, type the normal characters (e.g., 1/4), then select them and choose Style > Type Style > Make Fraction. Or for a price, type and select the characters, then choose Style > Type Style > Make Price. When the preferences are changed, only subsequently created fractions and prices are affected.

For fractions, you can change the **VScale** (vertical scale) and **HScale** (horizontal scale) for the Numerator, Slash, or Denominator to make them chunkier or thinner, and you can enter a **Kern** value for the space between the numerals and the slash. With **Fraction Slash** unchecked, the program will insert a normal slash; with this option checked (we recommend checking it), a special slash that fits better around the numerals will be used instead.

For the Make Price command, check **Underline Cents** if you want the cents digits be underlined, as in $24⁹⁹. Whether or not you opt to have underlining, the cents will appear in the Superior style. Check **Delete Radix** to have a radix (decimal point or comma) appear in prices (as in $10.⁹⁹); or uncheck this option to produce prices without a radix (as in $10⁹⁹).

Picture Effects pane ▣ **NEW**

When you click the Save Preset or Load Preset button on the Picture Effects palette (Window menu), the location specified under **Picture Effects Presets Location** opens by default. The default location is the **QuarkXPress Preferences Folder** but you can change this to a more convenient location. Click **Other Folder** and use the Browse button to specify a location.

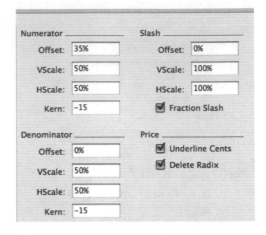

▣ *The **Fraction/Price** pane of QuarkXPress (Edit, in Windows) > Preferences > Application*

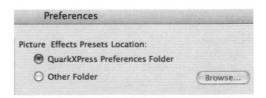

▣ *The **Picture Effects** pane of QuarkXPress (Edit, in Windows) > Preferences > Application*

Fraction/Price, Picture Effects Preferences

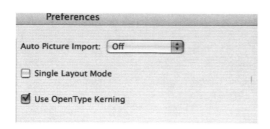

1 *The **General** pane of QuarkXPress (Edit, in Windows) > Preferences > Project*

2 *The **Single Layout Mode** option in the General pane of Project Preferences controls the default setting of the same check box in the **New Project dialog box** (File > New > Project).*

Choosing project preferences (NEW)

Changes to Project Preferences affect all the layouts in the active project. If no projects are open, the changes become the new default settings for all new projects.

General pane **1**

When you open a project, the **Auto Picture Import** options control whether pictures used in the project are updated if they were modified after the project was last closed. For example, if you edit a picture in Photoshop after importing it, QuarkXPress considers it to be "modified" and needs to update the picture's preview. Choose On to have pictures reimport automatically without a dialog box opening; choose Verify to have an alert dialog box appear if pictures were modified (see page 183); or choose Off to turn this feature off.

If you do not store multiple layouts in a project file, you can use the **Single Layout Mode**. This simplifies file naming because you need only one file name—not a project name and a layout name. If a project contains only one layout but is in multiple-layout mode, you can check Single Layout Mode to streamline its file name. Or, check Single Layout Mode when no projects are open, and Single Layout Mode will be checked automatically in the New Project dialog box for all future projects **2**.

OpenType fonts include default kerning values that you can automatically apply to all layouts by checking **Use OpenType Kerning.** The OpenType kerning values will override anything you specified for the font in Kerning Table Edit (Utilities menu), but you can apply additional kerning manually (Style > Kern).

Project Preferences: General

Choosing print layout preferences

Changes to Print Layout Preferences affect the active layout. If no projects are open, the changes become the new default settings for layouts in all new projects.

General pane **1**

Greek Text Below is the point size below which text will display as solid gray bars to help speed up screen redraw. Greeking is also affected by the current zoom level.

With **Greek Pictures** on, pictures display as gray boxes until you select them. This speeds screen redraw but is unnecessary if your computer is reasonably fast.

Set ruler **Guides** to display In Front of or Behind items on a page (see page 203).

The **Snap Distance** is the range in pixels within which an item (or table gridline) will snap to a guide if View > Snap to Guides is checked.

The **Master Page Items** options, Keep Changes and Delete Changes, affect whether modified master page items on layout pages are retained or deleted when master pages are applied or reapplied (see page 252).

Framing is added either to the Inside (the default) or Outside edges of a box. With Outside chosen, framing increases the dimensions of a box and changes its x/y location; with Inside chosen, those settings are unaffected. The Framing setting affects only subsequently created boxes.

In print layouts, with **Auto Page Insertion** on, pages will be added to a chain of automatic text boxes, when necessary, at the location of your choosing: End of Story, End of Section, or End of Document (see page 81). Choose Off to turn this feature off.

With **Auto Constrain** on, each newly created item (child) is constrained by the dimensions of an existing (parent) item.

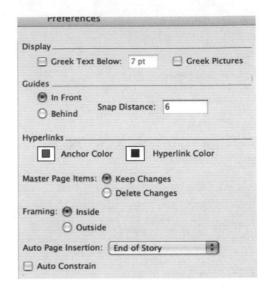

1 *The **General** pane of QuarkXPress (Edit, in Windows) > Preferences > Print Layout*

No constraints

The mysterious Auto Constrain feature is a holdover from previous versions of Quark-XPress—previous as in version 2. The only reason to work this way is if you really enjoyed it 20 years ago, or you are creating an extremely structured design with no overlapping elements. You can also turn on Constrain (Item menu) for a selected box.

1 *The Measurements pane of QuarkXPress (Edit, in Windows) > Preferences > Print Layout*

Abbreviations

Inches	**in** *or* **"**
Inches Decimal	**in** *or* **"** with a decimal
Picas	**p**
Points	**pt** *or* **p** followed by a number (as in "p6")
Millimeters	**mm**
Centimeters	**cm**
Ciceros	**c**
Agates	**ag**
quarter of a millimeter	**q** *(used in Japan)*
Pixels	**px*****

*In a print layout, pixels can't be chosen as the unit, but "px" can be used when entering values.

2 *The Paragraph pane of QuarkXPress (Edit, in Windows) > Preferences > Print Layout*

Measurements pane **1**

For Measurements, choose the default **Horizontal** and **Vertical** units separately: Inches, Inches Decimal, Picas, Points, Millimeters, Centimeters, Ciceros, or Agates (see page 29). These units are used for the Measurements palette, rulers, and dialog boxes—except for font size, leading, frame width, and line width, which always display in points, regardless of the current default unit.

72 points/inch is the current standard **Points/Inch** ratio in desktop publishing, so there's no need to change it. Ditto for **Ciceros/cm,** the ciceros-to-centimeter conversion ratio (2.197 is the default).

With **Item Coordinates: Page** chosen (the default setting), horizontal ruler increments start anew at zero on each page. With **Spread** chosen, horizontal ruler increments advance uninterrupted across any multipage spreads.

TIP You can also Control-click/Right-click the horizontal or vertical ruler in the project window, then choose a unit from the Measure submenu.

Paragraph pane **2**

With **Mode: Typesetting** chosen, leading is measured from baseline to baseline, as in traditional typesetting. In **Word Processing** mode, leading is measured from ascent to ascent. Most publishers stick with Typesetting mode.

Auto Leading is enabled when "auto" or "0" is entered in the Leading field on the Measurements palette or in the Formats dialog box. When Auto Leading is used, you may see variable spacing between lines within the same paragraph, because it calculates the leading separately for each line based on the point size of the largest character per line. An increment can be entered instead of "auto" or "0." If you enter "+2," for example, 2 points will be

(Continued on the following page)

Measurements, Paragraph Preferences

added to the point size of the text to arrive at the leading amount (thus, 10-point text would have 12-point leading). The Auto Leading setting affects both newly created and *existing* text.

If **Maintain Leading** is on and an item is positioned within a column of text, the first line of text that's forced below the obstructing item will snap to the nearest leading increment (allowing for the current Item Runaround value), thereby enabling text baselines to align across columns. With Maintain Leading off, text will be offset from the bottom of an obstructing item only by any existing Item Runaround value, making it difficult, but not impossible, to align text across columns.

By aligning text or items in a layout across columns using the nonprinting **Baseline Grid** 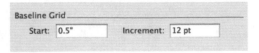, you can make pages look more symmetrical and uniform. To use this feature, specify an Increment that's equal to or a multiple of the current text leading. The Start value should match the vertical (*y*) position of the first baseline of the text.

The choices for **Hyphenation: Method** are, in order of appearance and quality from earlier versions of QuarkXPress to this version: Standard, Enhanced, and Expanded. Click a Language to access this menu.

Character pane 2

The **Superscript** Offset is the distance a superscript character is raised above the baseline, and it's measured as a percentage of the current point size. The **Subscript** Offset is the distance a character is lowered below the baseline. The **Superscript, Subscript, Small Caps,** and **Superior** VScale (height) and HScale (width) are calculated as a percentage of a normal uppercase letter.

TIP Increase the HScale for Small Caps (it looks better), or better yet, use an expert font with built-in small caps.

Baseline Grid

Start: 0.5"   Increment: 12 pt

1 *The **Baseline Grid** area in the **Paragraph** pane of QuarkXPress (Edit, in Windows) > Preferences > Print Layout*

Snapping text to the baseline grid

To use the baseline gridlines specified in Paragraph Preferences:

• Select the paragraphs and click the Lock to **NEW** Baseline Grid icon on the Paragraph tab of the Measurements palette or choose Style > Formats, then check Lock to Baseline Grid.

• To display the grid, check View > Baseline Grid.

Note: If Justified is chosen as the Vertical Alignment Type in Item > Modify > Text, only the first and last lines in a column will lock to the grid.

Preferences

Superscript
Offset: 33%
VScale: 60%
HScale: 60%

Subscript
Offset: 33%
VScale: 100%
HScale: 100%

Small Caps
VScale: 75%
HScale: 75%

Superior
VScale: 60%
HScale: 60%

Ligatures
Break Above: 1   ☐ Not "ffi" or "ffl"

☑ Auto Kern Above: 4 pt   ☑ Standard Em Space
Flex Space Width: 50%   ☑ Accents for All Caps

2 *The **Character** pane of QuarkXPress (Edit, in Windows) > Preferences > Print Layout*

> "By the time she had caught the flamingo and brought it back, the fight was over…" *Lewis Carroll*

1 *The "fl" and "fi" **ligatures** (boldface added for emphasis)*

2 *The **Ligatures** area in the **Character** pane of QuarkXPress (Edit, in Windows) > Preferences > Print Layout*

Applying ligatures to characters (NEW)

In QuarkXPress 7, the use of ligatures is no longer a layout-wide preference limited to Mac OS. You can now apply ligatures on both Mac OS and Windows to selected text via the Character tab of the Measurements palette or the Character Attributes dialog box (Style > Character). The character format works according to the Ligatures options in Character Preferences. For OpenType fonts, do not use the Ligatures character format—use the Standard Ligatures and Discretionary Ligatures options in the OpenType menu. Note that QuarkXPress does not "create" ligatures; it simply swaps in ligatures built into the font. Use the Glyphs palette (Window menu) see what, if any, ligatures are included in a font.

> Accent n.: a mark (as É, À, õ, ü) used in writing or printing to indicate a specific sound value, stress, or pitch.

3 *With **Accents for All Caps** on, accent marks can be inserted above uppercase characters.*

A **ligature** is a pair of serif characters (such as an "f" followed by an "l") that are joined into one character to prevent them from ungracefully knocking into each other (**1**). The hyphenation and check spelling features treat ligatures that are produced this way as normal characters. The **Break Above** value **2** is the amount of tracking or kerning in a line of type above which characters with Ligatures applied won't be joined as ligatures (for justified type, try 3 or 4). If **Not "ffi" or "ffl"** is checked, you will not get "fi" and "fl" ligatures for those letter combinations—unless the font includes actual ligatures for "ffi" and "ffl."

The **Auto Kern Above** value is the point size above which characters will be kerned automatically, based on each particular font's built-in kerning values as well as any user-defined QuarkXPress Tracking Edit or Kerning Table Edit values. Kerning is essential for professional-looking type. For OpenType fonts, use the Use Open-Type Kerning setting in the General pane of Project Preferences.

The increment used for tracking in QuarkXPress is 1/200 of an em space. With **Standard Em Space** off (the default setting), an em space equals the width of two zeros in the current font. With this option on, an em space equals the point size of the text.

The **Flex Space Width** (0–400%) is a percentage of an en space in the current font. To enter a flexible space or a nonbreaking flexible space in text, use the Utilities > Insert Character submenus. To make the flex space the same width as an em space, enter 200%.

Check **Accents for All Caps** to permit foreign-language accent marks on small caps or all caps text **3**. Note that they're acceptable in some languages and not others. To learn the keystrokes for producing foreign-language accent marks (such as é, ö, ã, à), see Appendix A.

Tools pane 1

To choose default settings for a tool, click its icon in the Tools pane or double-click the tool on the Tools palette. Click **Modify** to change the default settings for the currently selected tool icon(s). Among the many item creation tool settings you can change are the background color, Frame Width, and Runaround Type for any Picture Box tool or Text Box tool, the Text Inset for the Text Box tools, and the Width for the Line tool **2**. For the Zoom tool, you can specify Minimum and Maximum values 10–800%) and an Increment value (1–400%). For the Tables tool, you can specify defaults for table creation and formatting.

To set preferences for more than one tool at a time, first Cmd-click/Ctrl-click their icons individually. Or click one tool icon, then click **Similar Types** or **Similar Shapes** to change the default settings for related tools. Fewer Modify dialog box settings may be available when more than one tool icon is selected.

To restore the default *settings* for the currently selected tools, click **Use Default Prefs.** To restore the default *arrangement* of tools on the Tools palette and pop-out menus, click **Default Tool Palette.**

Layers pane 3

Choose whether newly created layers will be **Visible.** Invisible layers don't print. Choose whether to **Suppress Output** of all items on subsequently created layers.

TIP To control the printing of individual items on a layer instead of all the items on a layer, use the Suppress Output or Suppress Picture Output option in Item > Modify.

Choose whether you want new layers to be **Locked.** Check **Keep Runaround** to preserve the current Runaround settings for text on visible layers, even if the items the text is wrapping around are hidden.

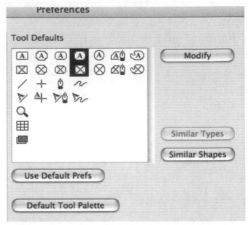

1 *The **Tools** pane of QuarkXPress (Edit, in Windows) > Preferences > Print Layout*

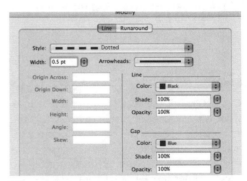

2 *A sample of defaults available for the Line tool*

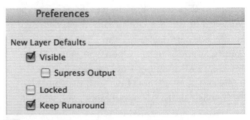

3 *The **Layers** pane of QuarkXPress (Edit, in Windows) > Preferences > Print Layout*

Setting layer defaults

Not sure what options to check in the Layers pane? We suggest you leave Visible checked—unless you enjoy playing tricks on yourself. Also, keep the Suppress Output and Locked options unchecked. The default setting for Keep Runaround is checked, and we leave it that way.

What does "!Error" mean?

The word **!Error** in the Status column for an XTension is a warning that QuarkXPress had a problem loading that XTension while launching.

Choose an XTensions set from the Set menu.

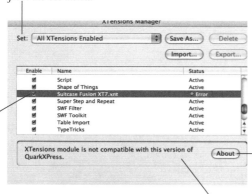

1 *Click in the **Enable** column in the **XTensions Manager** to enable or disable a Quark XTension, import/export filter, or third-party XTension.*

Read more information about the status of the currently selected XTension here.

*Click **About** (or double-click an XTension name) to learn more about an XTension, such as its own version number and whether it's optimized for the current version of QuarkXPress.*

XTensions Manager at startup

If you want the XTensions Manager to open automatically whenever the application is launched, go to QuarkXPress (Edit, in Windows) > Preferences > Application > XTensions Manager, then click **Show XTensions Manager at Startup: Always.** If either of the other two preference options are chosen, you can force the XTensions Manager to open as you launch QuarkXPress by holding down the Spacebar. Keep the Spacebar pressed until the Manager opens.

Managing XTensions

XTensions are add-ons to QuarkXPress that extend the program's capabilities. Some XTensions are included with the application, such as the filters for importing word processing files, whereas others are produced by third-party developers and must be purchased separately (see page 28).

Using the XTensions Manager, you can enable or disable program and/or third-party XTensions from within the application, as long as they're located either in the XTension folder or the XTension Disabled folder. To conserve memory, you should disable any XTensions that you're not using. You can also use this utility to save, export, import, or delete XTension sets, which are user-defined groups of XTensions that you want to use together.

To enable/disable XTensions or import/export filters:

1. Choose Utilities > XTensions Manager.

2. Click a check mark to disable an XTension, or click an empty check box/empty space in the Enable column to enable it **1**. Repeat for any other XTensions you want to turn on or off.
   or
   Choose an XTensions set from the Set menu (see the next page).

3. *Optional:* Click About or double-click an XTension name to display information about the currently selected XTension. Click in the info dialog box to return to the Manager.

4. Click OK. The XTensions Manager changes won't take effect until you quit/exit and relaunch QuarkXPress.

To help you organize XTensions and make it easier to turn them on and off (this XTension on, that XTension off, etc.), you can save your custom XTensions Manager settings as a set. You can also choose which set will be in effect when the application is launched. XTensions sets are saved in the XPress Preferences file. Whichever set is chosen from the Set menu when you quit/exit QuarkXPress will be in effect when the program is relaunched.

To create an XTensions set:

1. Choose Utilities > XTensions Manager.

2. Disable any XTensions that you don't want included in your set, and enable any XTensions that you do want included by clicking the box in the far left column.

3. Click Save As **1**.

4. Enter a name for the current set **2**.

5. Click Save. Your custom set will appear on the Set menu in the XTensions Manager **3**, and it will be enabled when the application is relaunched.

6. Click OK.

TIP To enable all the XTensions, choose Set: All XTensions Enabled. To disable them all, choose All XTensions Disabled from the same menu.

TIP To delete a user-defined set, choose it from the Set menu, then click Delete. This can't be undone!

To backup and share XTensions sets:

If you're a member of a workgroup, you can share XTensions sets by exporting and importing them. Click Export to export the currently active XTensions set. Other users can then use the Import button to access your set— provided they also own those XTensions. You can also use this method to backup your XTensions sets.

1 *Click* **Save As** *in the* **XTensions Manager** *to create a custom set.*

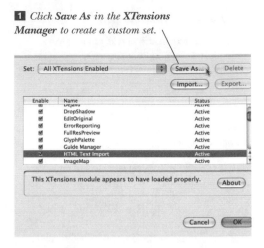

2 *Enter a* **name** *for the XTensions set.*

3 *The new set name appears on the* **Set** *menu.*

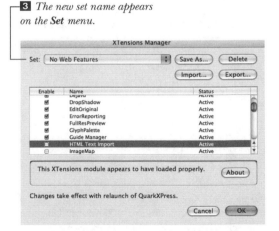

Workgroups 23

What's in a Job Jackets file?

QuarkXPress Job Jackets are JDF-based XML files that contain a variety of specifications, including:

- Project-level resources for colors, style sheets, output styles, and color management
- Layout-level resources such as page size and orientation, output specifications, and rules to check against (for example, no spot colors)
- Information about the job (such as the job number) and contact information

The information in Job Jackets is organized into "Job Tickets" for creating individual layouts.

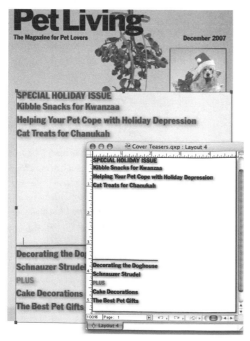

In this example, we created a Composition Zone for the magazine cover's teaser lines. We can send it to an editor for edits, and then update it in the layout.

Collaborating in QuarkXPress

You don't have to work in publishing long to discover two things. The first is that it's easy to create layouts that will not print, cost too much to print, print incorrectly, or don't meet design standards. The second thing you'll learn is that it's easy for content to become "trapped" inside a single file on one person's computer. When that lovingly crafted text or carefully positioned picture changes, those changes have to funnel back through that single person, whether or not he or she has the time or skill to deal with it.

These two things are significant problems, considering that the ability to print and revise are essential for publishing. To address these two issues, QuarkXPress 7 provides two new features: Job Jackets and Composition Zones. Both features are incredibly powerful and—in true Quark fashion, where great power comes with great complexity—they are insanely complicated. As a result, in this QuickStart format, we simply introduce you to these features in the way you are most likely to encounter them.

Job Jackets are XML files based on the industry-standard Job Definition Format (JDF). Job Jackets contain "Job Tickets," which in turn contain layout, color, style sheet, output, and other specifications for a particular job. By assigning a Job Ticket to a layout, you'll start off on the right foot and have fewer output headaches.

A Composition Zone is all or part of a layout that you can share with another QuarkXPress user and which updates dynamically.

(NEW) Working with Job Jackets

Due to the complexity of the interface and the specifications involved, it is unlikely that the average user will ever create a Job Jackets file. Rather, as the feature is intended, you're likely to receive a Job Jackets file containing a Job Ticket template, which initiates a layout based on settings in the Job Jackets file. You can also link a project to an existing Job Ticket template, and you can check layouts against Job Tickets to ensure that the job is following its rules and specifications (this is sort of a sophisticated preflighting process).

To create a project from a Job Ticket:

1. First, you will receive a Job Jackets file  from a print provider, production department, or other source. (Or, they may just tell you where to access the file on a server.)

2. Choose File > New > Project from Ticket.

3. Click Browse, and then locate, select, and open the Job Jackets file.

4. All the Job Tickets inside the Job Jackets file are listed ▨. If you have been given instructions to use a specific one, select it. Otherwise, click Default Job Ticket.

5. Click Select to create a new project containing a new layout based on the Job Ticket.

Note: Depending on what was specified in the Job Jackets file, the layout should be the right size and may contain the correct colors, style sheets, H&Js, and more for the layout ▨. The Job Jackets feature, however, does not block you from making changes in QuarkXPress—whether they are appropriate or not. That's the job of the File > Job Jackets > Evaluate Layout feature described on the next page.

▨ *A **Job Jackets** file looks like this. You can store it wherever you want for easy access.*

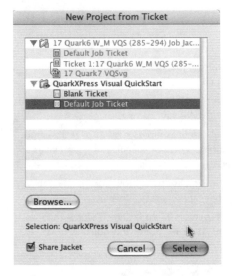

▨ *Choose **File > New > Project from Ticket,** then click Browse to locate a specific Job Jackets file. Click the Job Ticket you need, and then click Select.*

▨ *When you create a project from a Job Ticket, all the specifications you need can be built in. The Job Jackets feature is like a super template, not only providing what you need but helping you to stick to it.*

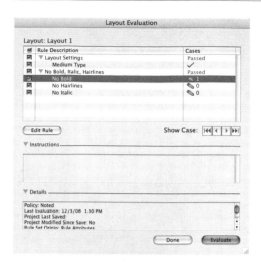

1 *Choose File > Job Jackets > Evaluate Layout and click* ***Evaluate*** *to confirm that your layout conforms to the specifications in the Job Ticket.*

2 *A rule for Text Characters might look something like this. In this case, we don't want Adobe Garamond sneaking into the layout instead of ITC Garamond, so we create a rule that* ***Font Name is not AGaramond.*** *In addition,* ***Font Size is not less than 10 pt*** *is set to ensure that point sizes remain at 10 pt or larger. To make sure no colors are applied to text, we set* ***Color is Black*** *as a rule, and then to prevent the Bold and Italic type styles from sneaking in (because they often cause production errors), we created rules for* ***Text Style is not Bold*** *and* ***Text Style is not Italic.*** *Rules are created with Job Jackets in Utilities> Job Jackets Manager, but can be edited via the Evaluate Layout dialog box.*

There's no safety valve in the Job Jackets feature to stop you from creating trouble. For example, you can add spot colors to a CMYK job or introduce new fonts to a layout even if the Job Ticket says otherwise. QuarkXPress does provide some protection, however, in the form of the Evaluate Layout command which evaluates your layout to see if it adheres to the specifications in the Job Ticket. Evaluate the layout and act on this feedback to ensure that the layout outputs as intended.

To evaluate a layout:

1. Display the layout you want to evaluate.

2. Choose File > Job Jackets > Evaluate Layout **1**.

3. If you want to skip any rules listed in the scroll list, uncheck them. You'll probably be checking against specifications provided to you, so you should leave them all checked **2**.

4. Click Evaluate.

5. A number in the Cases column indicates how many locations in the layout do not follow the rule. Click Show Case to see the page on which the rule is broken on. Your only option at this point, however, is to jot down what needs to be fixed—unfortunately, this isn't an automatic repair feature.

6. When you've finished reviewing broken rules, click Done. If you have multiple layouts in a project, be sure to evaluate each layout separately.

TIP If you would like QuarkXPress to evaluate your layouts automatically, you can use Preferences to specify when. Choose QuarkXPress (Edit, in Windows) > Preferences > Job Jackets. In the Evaluate Layout area, check On Open, On Save, On Output, and/or On Close. These are all unchecked by default, but at a minimum you should check On Output to be sure your layouts are evaluated for printing.

You can use the Link Project feature to retrofit legacy projects with Job Tickets.

To link a project to a Job Ticket:

1. Be sure you have the Job Jackets file you need—and you know where it is.

2. Open the project you want to link to a Job Ticket. There is no need to display a specific layout as the Job Jackets file will attach to the entire project.

3. Choose File > Job Jackets > Link Project.

4. In the Link Project dialog box **1**, click Browse to navigate to the Job Jackets file.

5. Select the Job Jackets file or one of its Job Tickets and click Open **2**.

6. Click Attach. When the alert displays, click OK.

TIP When you link a project to a new Job Jackets file, nothing is lost from the current project file, but any new style sheets, colors, H&Js, and other specifications will be added.

TIP As we said, the average user isn't likely to be involved in creating Job Jackets and/or Job Tickets. They are more likely to be the recipient and user of such files. To get a glimpse into the process, however, choose Utilities > Job Jackets Manager, then click the Advanced Button. This will give you an idea how complex the process is!

Link Project to Job Ticket

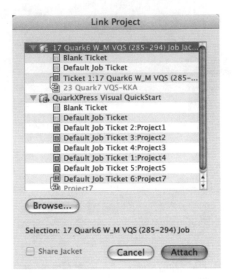

1 *Choose **File > Job Jackets > Link Project** to link a project to a Job Jackets file for the first time, to apply a different Job Jackets file, or to apply an updated version of the current Job Jackets file.*

2 *Select a Job Jackets file on the desktop to link to the active project.*

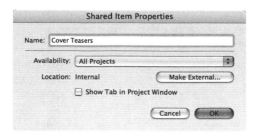

1 *The **Shared Item Properties** dialog box lets you name, share, and export a Composition Zone.*

Working with Composition Zones

Composition Zones provide a way to share pieces of a layout—even a single page—with members of a workgroup. You mark off an area as a Composition Zone, export it, and send it to another user. The other user works on this small version of a layout, sends it back to you, and you update it. You can work with Composition Zones in endless ways, including exporting an area of a page, selected items, or an entire layout. You can restrict Composition Zones to a single project or share them with multiple projects. And you can specify when changes to Composition Zones update.

To create a composition zone:

1. Choose the Composition Zones tool 🖥, then drag to specify a blank area on a page to be shared. Even if items are on the page, they won't become selected; you're simply defining an area.
   or
   If the items you want to share already exist, Shift-click to select the items or groups, then choose Item > Composition Zones > Create.

2. With the new Composition Zone selected, choose Item > Share. The Shared Item Properties dialog box appears **1**. Enter a descriptive name for the item in the Name field.

3. From the Availability menu, choose whether the Composition Zone is for This Project Only (for use with all the layouts in the project) or All Projects (for use with any layout in any project).

4. To be able to access the Composition Zone from the project window, check Show Tab in Project Window.

5. *Optional:* If you want to send the Composition Zone to another user (via e-mail, for example), click Make External and name the file. The Show Tab in Project Window checkbox disappears.

6. Click OK.

Create Composition Zone

To edit a Composition Zone:

1. If the Composition Zone is in the project you're working on, click it and choose Item > Composition Zones > Edit or click its tab in the project window (that is, if you created a tab in the Shared Item Properties dialog box).
or
If the Composition Zone is external and you received it from another user, use File > Open to open it.

2. The Composition Zone will open in its own project window like any other project . You can modify it, save, and close it like any other project file. If you are working on an external Composition Zone, be sure to send it back to the original designer if necessary.

To link to a Composition Zone:

1. If you create an external Composition Zone, other projects and layouts can link to and share its content. To link the active layout to a Composition Zone, choose File > Collaboration Setup.

2. Click the Linked Layouts tab, and then click Link Layout .

3. Navigate to the Composition Zone file you want to link to, then click Open.

4. Choose Window > Shared Content, then drag the Composition Zones into the layout.

To update a Composition Zone:

If you're working with an internal Composition Zone (one within the same project), it will update automatically each time you save changes to it. To control when it updates, use the Updates pane of the Collaboration Setup dialog box (File menu) 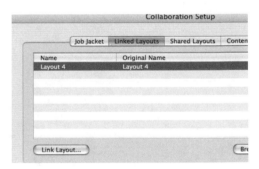.

If you're working with an external Composition Zone, you can update it in a layout via Utilities > Usage > Composition Zones. This works the same as updating a picture file via the Pictures pane of the Usage dialog box.

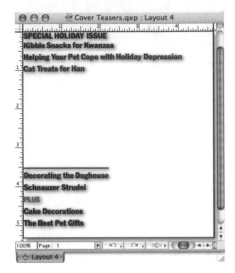

1 *When you open a* **Composition Zone** *to edit, it looks just like a standard QuarkXPress project.*

2 *To link a layout to an external Composition Zone and share its contents click* **Link Layout** *in the Linked Layouts pane of the Collaboraton Setup dialog box.*

3 *The* **Updates** *pane in the Collaboration Setup dialog box (File menu) lets you specify how often Composition Zones update in the layout.*

Printing files

To output a print layout:

1. Display the layout you want to print. You can print only one layout at a time.

2. Open the Print dialog box by choosing File > Print (Cmd-P/Ctrl-P).

3. Choose a printer from the Printer menu.

4. *Optional:* Choose a print style from the Print Style menu (see page 394). You can override the current print style settings temporarily by entering new settings via the panes in the Print dialog box. These changes won't affect the original print style. An asterisk will appear next to the print style name to show that a temporary change was made.

5. Enter the number of Copies of each page you want to print **1**. The default is 1.

6. To specify which pages to print, leave the default Pages setting on All, enter nonconsecutive page numbers divided by commas, or enter a range of numbers divided by a hyphen. (See "Absolute page numbers" on page 390.)

7. Choose an option from the Sequence menu to specify whether All, Odd, or Even pages print.

8. To change the size at which the layout prints, choose or enter a Scale value.

9. Check any of the following:

Collate to print full copies of the specified range of Pages instead of multiples of each page.

(Continued on the following page)

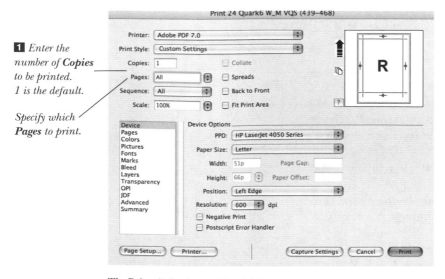

1 *Enter the number of **Copies** to be printed. 1 is the default.*

*Specify which **Pages** to print.*

*The **Print** dialog box in Mac OS X*

Spreads to print spreads horizontally on the same sheet of paper.

Back to Front to print pages in reverse order.

Fit Print Area to force the layout to fit on the paper.

10. Click any category in the scroll list on the left side to display related panes at the bottom of the Print dialog box. The controls will also vary depending on the Printer and PPD selected. You don't need to go through all the panes every time you print a file.

Use the **Device Options** pane to choose the correct Printer Description (PPD) , which automatically establishes the default Paper Size, Width, and Height. Depending on the PPD, you can change the Page Gap and Paper Offset. You can also change the Resolution, print a Negative Print, and turn on the PostScript Error Handler, which helps you identify printing problems.

Use the **Page Options** pane to change the Orientation of the pages on the paper, Include Blank Pages, print Thumbnails, specify Page Flip, and specify Page Tiling (for pages that are larger than the paper; see page 391).

Use the **Color Options** pane to choose a Mode (Composite or Separation) and a Setup (Grayscale, Composite RGB, Composite CMYK, Composite CMYK and Spot, or As Is) (see page 393); you can also choose custom output setups created by a color expert. For Halftones, choose Printer or Conventional (see the sidebar on this page and on page 393).

Use the **Picture Options** pane 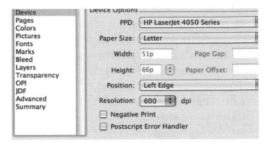 to change the Output type (Normal, Low Resolution, or Rough; see page 392), Data encoding, Overprint EPS/PDF Black, and Full Resolution TIFF Output setting.

The halftoning options

If you choose a process color from the **Halftone** menu in the Edit Color dialog box (Spot Color checked), the halftone Frequency, Angle, and Function options that are currently set for that process color (C, M, Y, or K) will be assigned to it. To view or change the current settings, choose File > Print, click the Colors option at left, then choose Halftones: Conventional. When you're all set to print the file, choose Mode: Separation. For more information, see page 393. Settings chosen in the Print dialog box override settings in the Edit Color dialog box.

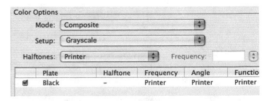

1 *The **Device Options** pane in the **Print** dialog box*

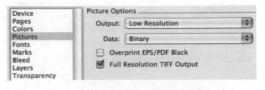

2 *Part of the **Color Options** pane in the **Print** dialog box*

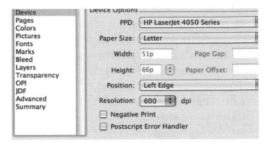

3 *The **Picture Options** pane in the **Print** dialog box*

1 *Part of the Font Options pane of the Print dialog box*

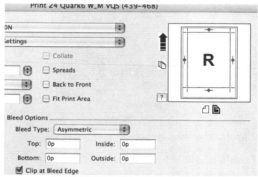

2 *The Registration Marks Options pane in the Print dialog box*

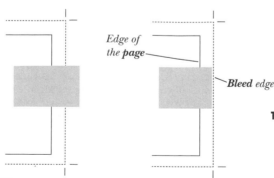

3 *The Bleed Options pane in the Print dialog box and the preview area (upper right) that allows you to preview your settings*

4 *With Page Items chosen, the whole item prints—as long as at least part of it is on the page.*

5 *With Asymmetric (or Symmetric) chosen and Clip at Bleed Edge checked, items print only up to the specified Amount (the bleed edge).*

When a PostScript printer is selected from the Printer menu, you can control which fonts download to the printer using the **Font Options** pane **1**. Leave Select All checked ; the only fonts you should prevent from downloading are 2-byte TrueType fonts resident on the printer (for Asian markets). If you are printing to a PostScript 2, version 2015, or PostScript level 3 or later output device, check Optimize Font Formats to speed up printing.

Use the **Registration Marks Options** pane (click Marks in the scroll list at left) **2** to add crop marks and registration marks to pages. Choose Centered or Off Center, and then use the Width and Length fields to specify the size of the crop marks. Use the Offset field to specify how far the marks are placed from the edge of the page.

Use the **Bleed Options** pane **3** to choose bleed options. From the Bleed Type menu, choose Page Items to allow any items that are at least partially on the page to print in their entirety. Asymmetric and Symmetric let you define the width of the bleed area. For Symmetric, enter one Amount value; for Asymmetric, enter Top, Bottom, Inside, and Outside values. With Clip at Bleed Edge unchecked, items that at least partially overlap the bleed area will print in their entirety, within the limits of the output device **4**; when it's unchecked, items won't print beyond the bleed area **5**.

TIP When working with marks and bleeds, it helps to consult the preview in the upper-right corner of the Print dialog box **3**. Icons indicate the type of device selected (cut sheet or roll fed) and the media feed direction. Point at the icons to view Tool Tips and click the question mark for a key to the colored guides on the preview.

(Continued on the following page)

Print Dialog Box

Use the **Layer Options** pane to turn printing temporarily on or off for individual layers (see page 392). If you're not sure what is on a layer, it might help to select it and view the Plates Used On Selected Layer area. Check Apply to Layout to apply the current print settings to the layers in the Layers palette.

NEW

If the layout contains objects that will be flattened on output (such as opacity, alpha channel masking, blends to None, line art TIFFs, or bitmap frames), you can choose settings in the **Transparency Options** pane . For the Transparency Flattening Resolution, enter a value in the field or choose an option from the menu. If you need to troubleshoot problems when printing transparencies, try checking Ignore Transparency Flattening to print opaque items. This can help narrow down a printing problem to a specific item.

Controls in the **OPI Options** pane 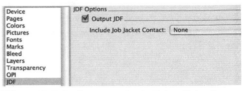 apply only if you're outputting to an OPI prepress system that's going to replace your pictures with high-resolution picture files stored on that OPI system. To get started, check OPI Active and then specify which pictures to exchange with the full-resolution versions by checking Include Images under TIFF Options and/or EPS Options. Both picture data and comments will be sent to output. For TIFF files, you also have the option to check Low Resolution and output the TIFF images used in the layout rather than the high-resolution versions.

NEW

If the project uses a Job Jacket (see Chapter 23), use the **JDF Options** pane 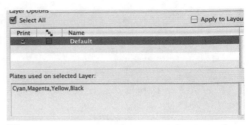 to specify how that information is handled. Check Output JDF to save the JDF file with the job. You can also choose whether to Include Job Jacket Contact information.

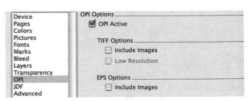

1 *The* **Layer Options** *pane in the* **Print** *dialog box*

2 *The* **Transparency Options** *pane in the* **Print** *dialog box*

3 *The* **OPI Options** *pane in the* **Print** *dialog box*

4 *The* **JDF Options** *pane in the* **Print** *dialog box*

Non-PostScript printers

For improved output when outputting high-resolution EPS pictures to non-PostScript printers (such as ink-jet printers), turn on Item > Preview Resolution > Full Resolution.

Low-res output

If you choose Low Resolution from the Output menu in File > Print > Options, all pictures in a layout, including those set to Full Resolution Preview, will print at a low resolution, regardless of what type of printer is being used.

Quick-and-dirty print

Once you've established your Print dialog box settings and you want to print an entire layout, press Cmd-P/Ctrl-P or Control-click/Right-click and choose **Print,** then press Return/Enter. Or to specify a range of pages, press Tab, type the starting page number, a hyphen, and the ending page number, then press Return/Enter.

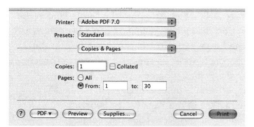

1 *Clicking Printer in the Print dialog box displays a Print dialog box that is specific to the selected printer (Mac OS X).*

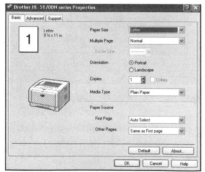

2 *Clicking Properties in the Print dialog box displays a Properties dialog box that is specific to the selected printer (Windows).*

Page Setup

In Mac OS X, clicking Page Setup in the Print dialog box opens the Page Setup dialog box for the System's device driver. Changes made in the Setup pane of the Print dialog box, such as the Reduce or Enlarge or Orientation settings, update automatically in the Page Setup dialog box, and vice versa. Exception: A change to the Paper Size in either dialog box won't update in the other dialog box.

Use the **Advanced Options** pane to choose the PostScript Level (2 or 3) used in embedded EPS and PDF files.

Use the **Summary** pane to review settings from all the panes to be sure they will work for the print job. **NEW**

11. Once you have reviewed all the settings and the preview, click Print.

Capture the settings

Click Capture Settings to save the current settings in the Print dialog box with the layout. This closes the Print dialog box without printing. To save the current settings as a print style, choose New Print Output Style from the Print Style menu.

Printer button: Mac OS X

Clicking the Printer button at the bottom of the QuarkXPress Print dialog box opens the Mac OS X Print dialog box **1**. The Printer menu at the top lets you change printers, and the Presets menu lets you choose from print styles you've saved at the system level. The menu in the middle lists options specific to the selected printer. In general, we suggest you choose printing options in the QuarkXPress Print dialog box to ensure proper output. You can, however, set options specific to your printer such as quality. To save new settings, click Print (this *won't* actually initiate printing).

Properties button: Windows

Clicking the Properties button in the QuarkXPress Print dialog box opens the printer's Properties dialog box **2**. Options in this dialog box will depend on which printer is currently selected.

Settings chosen in this dialog box override the current settings in the Print dialog box in QuarkXPress. Most settings, however, will update in the QuarkXPress Print dialog box (such as Copies and Orientation). The exception is Paper Size. When you're done choosing Properties settings, click OK to return to the QuarkXPress Print dialog box.

DeviceN

DeviceN composite color is a printing feature that allows a project containing colors of various types (e.g., a combination of CMYK colors, spot colors, blends, multi-inks, colorized TIFFs) to be output as a single composite print while preserving the file's color separation information. A print layout can be output as a composite or as separations, with no adjustments needed to the file. As an example, this dual output option would be useful for a project that is to be output to both PDF and to color separations for offset printing.

DeviceN can be chosen as a print option and when exporting to PDF and EPS. To specify DeviceN for print output, choose File > Print. In the Device pane, choose a PostScript composite color device from the PPD menu (only a PostScript level 3–compatible device can utilize DeviceN). In the Colors pane, choose Mode: Composite and Setup: Composite CMYK and Spot.

As Is

With the As Is composite color option chosen, an item in a print layout will output on a PostScript device using that item's original source color space. This option is helpful when you have, say, an RGB image from an RGB scanner or image-editing program that you want to print as an RGB color composite on a PostScript device. The final output device—not QuarkXPress—will color manage the output. As with DeviceN, As Is color can be chosen for print output (PostScript level 3 printers only), and for PDF and EPS export.

To specify As Is composite color for print output, choose File > Print. In the Device pane, choose a PostScript level 3–compatible device from the PPD menu. In the Colors pane, choose Setup: As Is.

If your layout contains section numbering, be sure to enter the page number accurately, including any prefix (as in "Page xii") in the Pages field in the Print dialog box. To print a page based on its position within the layout instead (its absolute page number), type a plus sign, then the number. To print the third and fourth pages in a layout, for example, you'd enter "+3-+4."

If your page numbers contain a hyphen (e.g., "Page A-8"), as specified in the Prefix field in the Section dialog box, you can't use a hyphen as a page range separator in the Pages field in the Print dialog box. To specify a different character for the Print dialog box, go to Preferences > Application > Input Settings and enter different characters in the Page Range Separators: Sequential and Nonsequential fields.

A better idea: Use an en dash for page numbers on your layout pages instead!

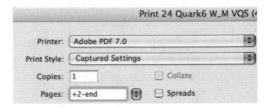

*The **Pages** field in the Print dialog box accepts absolute page numbers (preceded by a plus sign +) and the word "end." Here, QuarkXPress will print from the second page of the layout to the end of the layout, regardless of the numbers on the pages.*

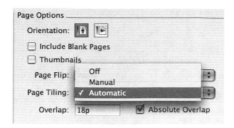

1 *The **Page Tiling** options are located in the Page Options pane of the Print dialog box.*

Get some help

Just to whet your appetite, here's an abbreviated list of output-related XTensions and their features. Be sure to check XTensions resellers such as The PowerXChange for updates as more XTensions become available for QuarkXPress 7.

BureauManager (CompuSense Ltd.) prepares files for an output service provider, generates a report and list of instructions, collects files, and searches for missing picture files.

Printools XT (Badia Software) previews printed pages, tiles oversized layouts, allows you to change print settings from a palette, prints individual items, produces document reports, and tracks revisions.

Quark Print Collection (a collection of XTensions formerly sold by a lowly apprentice production, inc., acquired by Quark in 2005) creates impositions in the print stream for both native QuarkXPress files and PDF files. Other XTensions let you create and place custom printer marks—including registration targets, color bars, and text slugs—on individual items or entire pages.

SpecTackler (GLUON, Inc.) marks each item on a page with a tag containing either text and paragraph specifications or picture data (e.g., scale, resolution, dimensions, name).

With automatic tiling, any layout whose page size is larger than the standard paper size can be printed in sections on multiple sheets of standard-size paper. Generally, you use tiling to print drafts of oversized documents, such as posters and the like. QuarkXPress automatically prints crop marks to be used as guides for trimming the page sections, as well as margin label codes notating the order for reassembling them into the larger whole.

To print using automatic tiling:

1. Display the layout you want to print, then choose File > Print (Cmd-P/ Ctrl-P).

2. Click Pages in the scroll list to display the Page Options pane.

3. Choose the appropriate Orientation icon. Portrait is a good choice for a tabloid page.

4. Choose Page Tiling: Automatic **1**.

5. Enter a number in the Overlap field. 3 (18p) is the default.

6. *Optional:* If you want your pages to be centered within the overall arrangement of tiles, *uncheck* Absolute Overlap.

7. Adjust any other print settings, then click the Preview pane to preview.

8. Click Print.

TIP To print an oversized layout on one standard size sheet of paper, check Fit Print Area at the top of the Print dialog box.

Automatic Tiling; XTensions

To suppress printing of a picture:

1. Choose Utilities > Usage.

2. Click the Pictures option in the scroll list at left.

3. In the Print column, uncheck any pictures you don't want to print 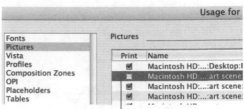. The picture won't print, but if a frame was applied to the box, it will print. (Click the blank box at any time to restore the check mark and turn printing back on.)

4. Click Done.

TIP You can also check Suppress Picture Output in Item > Modify > Picture.

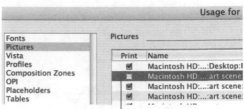

1 *To suppress the printing of a picture, remove its check mark in the **Print** column in Utilities > Usage > **Pictures.***

You can print a layout minus *all* pictures to speed up printing or to help you see the naked, "bare bones" composition.

To suppress printing of all pictures:

Choose File > Print. In the Pictures pane, choose Output: Rough 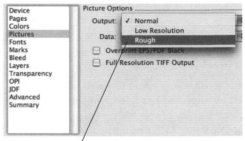. On the printout, an X will appear in each picture box and ornate frame styles won't print.

TIP Another way to hasten printing is to choose Output: Low Resolution. The low-resolution version of the picture that was saved automatically with the QuarkXPress file will print instead of the full-resolution version.

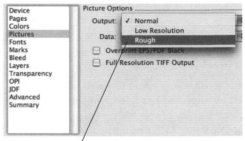

2 *Choose **Output: Rough** in File > Print > **Pictures.***

To suppress printing of an item:

To suppress printing of an entire item (box, text path, line, or table) from a print layout, including its contents, and including any frame applied to the item, select the item, go to Item > Modify > Box (or Line or Table)(Cmd-M/Ctrl-M), then check Suppress Output 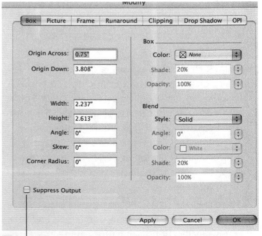.

To suppress printing of a layer:

Choose File > Print and then, in the Layers pane, click the check mark in the left column for any layer. You can also double-click a layer in the Layers palette (Window menu) and check Suppress Output. A non-printing layer is a good place to store notes and comments on pages.

3 *To prevent a picture (and frame, if any) from printing, check **Suppress Output** in Item > Modify > **Box.***

Suppress Output Options

You can modify halftones for composite output or separations. We'll discuss separations, but the process is similar for both. You may need to consult with your output service provider for the proper settings.

To modify halftone settings:

1. Choose File > Print, and then click Colors in the scroll list at left.

2. In the Color Options pane, choose Mode: Separation.

3. From the Setup menu, choose which plates to output: Process and Spot (all), Convert to Process, or In-RIP Separations (must be selected for a PostScript Level 3 device). You can also choose a custom output setup from a color expert.

4. Choose Halftones: Conventional.

5. Use the Print column to control which plates print (checked plates print).

6. Each spot color is assigned the screen values of one of the four process colors. Use the Halftone menu to apply screen values from another process color to the currently selected spot color.

Read all about it

To learn more about the complicated world of color separation, see one of the many useful reference books available, such as *Real World Color Management* by Bruce Fraser, Fred Bunting, and Chris Murphy (Peachpit Press).

7. According to instructions from your output provider, choose settings from the Frequency, Angle, and Function menus for each plate.

8. Choose other print settings, then click Print.

TIP If you choose Halftones: Printer for either composite or separation output, QuarkXPress sends no halftone information to the printer.

TIP To save yourself from repetitive setup work and ensure consistency, create a print output style that contains the desired halftoning options. Then you can choose that style from the Print Style menu in File > Print.

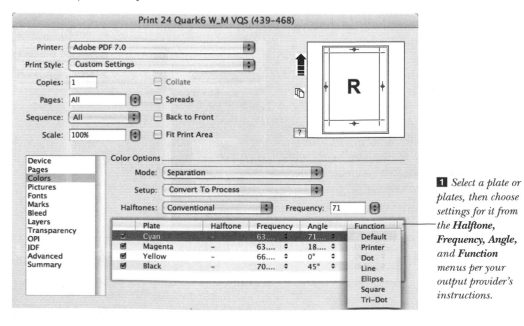

1 *Select a plate or plates, then choose settings for it from the* **Halftone, Frequency, Angle,** *and* **Function** *menus per your output provider's instructions.*

Modify Halftones

393

Output styles work like style sheets, except in this case they contain custom output settings for print, PPML, PDF, and EPS output. Using output styles not only saves you time but ensures consistency—so you can be sure the 50 or so settings you've chosen are the same each time you output a job.

Once you've created an output style for print, you can choose it from the Print Styles menu in the Print dialog box for *any* QuarkXPress print layout in any project, existing or future. You can temporarily override settings from the currently chosen print style simply by choosing new settings in the Print dialog box.

To create or edit a print output style:

1. Display a layout that uses the print settings you want to save as a style.

2. Choose File > Print.

3. Click the Summary option in the scroll list at left to make sure all the print options are set correctly, and then make any changes.

4. Choose New Print Output Style from the Print Style menu **1**. **NEW**

5. Enter a name for the style and then click OK.

6. Click Capture Settings (to save changes without printing) or Print. The new print style is available to all your projects.

TIP To create print styles from scratch (and to manage all your output styles), choose Edit > Output Styles **2**. Click the New button to display a menu and select the type of style to create: PDF, PPML, Print, or EPS. **NEW**

TIP You can modify the Default Print Output Style in Edit > Output Styles to better suit your needs.

sharing output styles

If you're in a workgroup, it's a good idea to share output styles for consistency. In addition, output providers may send you output styles to use to guarantee accuracy. The Output Styles dialog box lets you export a selected output style to a separate file, which you can backup or share. You can also import output styles you receive. By default, output styles are saved in the XPress Preferences file.

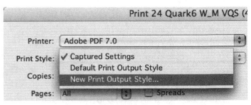

1 *Choose* **New Print Output Style** *from the Print Style menu in the Print dialog box to create an output style based on the current settings.*

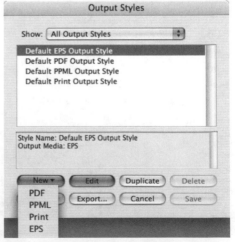

2 *Use Edit > Output Styles to manage all your output styles and to create them from scratch.*

Where your PPDs are

It's a good idea to leave the PPDs in the default location for your platform so they can be found and accessed by all your applications, including QuarkXPress. In Mac OS X, dozens of PPDs are installed in folders in Library/Printers/PPDs. QuarkXPress creates a PPD folder in the user's library: [User Name]/Library/Preferences/Quark/ QuarkXPress 7.0/PPD. QuarkXPress also looks in the root level Library folder.

In Windows, PPDs are stored in *systemroot*\ System32\Spool\Drivers\W32x86\3.

Changes made using the PPD Manager affect only QuarkXPress—not other applications.

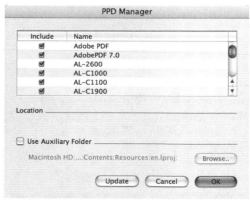

1 *Use the **PPD Manager** to load PPDs into QuarkXPress (or to exclude them from loading).*

What's a PPD?

A PPD, short for PostScript Printer Description, is a text file that contains information about a particular PostScript printer's parameters—how's that for alliteration?—such as its default resolution, usable paper and page sizes, and PostScript version number.

The PPD Manager (Utilities menu), which facilitates the loading of PPDs into Quark-XPress, is helpful in any setting where more than one kind of printer is used. It controls which of the System's PPDs (and thus printer names) are available in the PPD menu in the Device pane of the Print (File > Print) or Edit Print Style dialog box (Edit > Output Styles > New > Print).

Although an unlimited number of PPDs can be loaded at a time, you can restrict the ones that are loaded to just the printers you output to from QuarkXPress.

To use the PPD manager:

1. Choose Utilities > PPD Manager **1**.

2. Click a printer name.

3. In the Include column, click the check mark to exclude that printer or restore the check mark to include it.

4. Click OK. The PPD menus in Quark-XPress will update to reflect the new settings.

TIP If you add a new Printer Description file to your system, click Update in the PPD Manager dialog box. Any PPDs that you just added to the System or Library folder will also be added to the current PPD list (unless you checked Use Auxiliary Folder and selected a substitute folder).

Manage PPDs

Exporting files

Some print shops need a PostScript file of layouts for output. To do this, first prepare the layout according to the output provider's instructions—including confirming that no fonts or pictures are missing in the Usage dialog box (Utilities menu) and choosing all the prescribed settings in the Print dialog box. Also, be sure the proper Printer Description file for the final print output device is enabled via the PPD Manager (Utilities menu) so it's available in the Device pane of the Print dialog box.

To create a PostScript file in Mac OS X:

1. In the Mac OS Printer Setup Utility ([hard drive]/Applications/Utilities), confirm that a PostScript printer or a virtual PostScript printer is selected.

2. Display the layout you want to create a PostScript file of, then choose File > Print (Cmd-P).

3. Click Printer to display the printer driver's Print dialog box. If an alert displays, click OK to bypass it.

4. Choose a PostScript printer from the Printer menu and change any other options in the dialog box.

5. In Mac OS X 10.3 (Panther), check Save as File and choose Format: PostScript.
   or
   In Mac OS X 10.4 (Tiger), click the PDF button and choose Save PDF as PostScript from its menu .

6. Click Save, and then enter a name for the file and choose a location.

7. Click Save to return to the standard Print dialog box, and then click Print to save the layout as a PostScript file.

To create a PostScript file in Windows:

1. In Windows, choose Start > Settings > Printers > Add Printer.

2. In the Add Printer Wizard dialog box, click a Manufacturer in the scroll list at left, and then click a PostScript printer at right. You need to do this to map a printer to print to a file 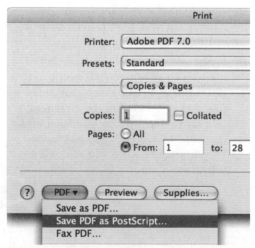. Use the Wizard to set up the printer as usual.

3. Choose File > Print.

4. From the Printer menu, choose the printer set up in the first step.

5. Click Print.

1 *The* **Save PDF as PostScript** *option in the Mac OS X 10.4 (Tiger) printer driver dialog box*

2 *Select a* **PostScript printer** *from the Printers list in the Add Printer Wizard dialog box.*

1 *The Export as PDF dialog box (File > Export > Layout as PDF)*

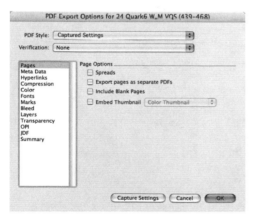

2 *For information about choosing PDF Export Options, see the QuarkXPress Help file.*

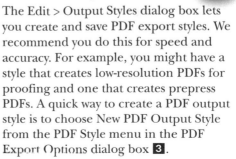

3 *You can create a PDF output style while setting options for PDF export (click Options in File > Export > Layout as PDF).*

Whether you need a PDF for proofing, onscreen viewing, or prepress, Quark-XPress makes it easy to produce one.

To save a layout as a PDF file:

1. Display the layout you want to save as a PDF, then choose File > Export > Layout as PDF.
or
Control-click/Right-click in a blank part of the layout and choose Export > Layout as PDF.

2. Enter a name, and choose a location for the file **1**. (Mac OS X users, keep the .pdf extension.)

3. At the bottom of the dialog box, enter a range of Pages to be exported.

4. *Optional:* Choose a PDF output style from the PDF Style menu. You can override these settings by clicking Options.

5. *Optional:* To change the export settings, click Options, then change settings in the various panes **2** and click OK. See the QuarkXPress Help file for information about these options.

6. Click Save. The PDF file will appear in the location you chose in step 2, above.

To set PDF preferences: NEW

To specify defaults for when PDFs are created, how the files are named, and whether a log file is created, choose QuarkXPress (Edit, in Windows) > Preferences > PDF. We change the Default Name for files from Project_Layout.pdf to Project.pdf.

To create a PDF output style: NEW

The Edit > Output Styles dialog box lets you create and save PDF export styles. We recommend you do this for speed and accuracy. For example, you might have a style that creates low-resolution PDFs for proofing and one that creates prepress PDFs. A quick way to create a PDF output style is to choose New PDF Output Style from the PDF Style menu in the PDF Export Options dialog box **3**.

Export PDF

The Save Page as EPS command converts a QuarkXPress page into a single picture. Reasons for using this feature include:

■ Your output provider or commercial printer requests an EPS file for color-separations.

■ You want to import a QuarkXPress page into another application, such as Adobe Photoshop or Adobe Illustrator.

■ You want to create a resizable page within a page (e.g., an advertisement or logo).

To save a page as an EPS file:

1. Display the layout that contains the page you want to save as an EPS file, then choose File > Save Page as EPS (Cmd-Option-Shift-S/Ctrl-Alt-Shift-S).

2. Change the file name in the Save As/File Name field **1** if desired and choose a location for the EPS file.

3. The page number that appears in the Page field will be saved as an EPS. The number of the currently displayed page appears here automatically, but you can enter a different number.

4. *Optional:* Choose an EPS output style from the EPS Style menu. You can override these settings by clicking Options.

5. *Optional:* To change the EPS settings, click Options in the primary Save Page as EPS dialog box, then change settings in the various panes and click OK **2**. See the QuarkXPress Help file for information about these options. Most of the controls are similar to those in the Print dialog box.

6. Click Save.

TIP EPS files can't be edited in Quark XPress, so be sure to save the original file from which it's generated so you'll be able to edit it or generate another EPS file from it later on!

1 *The primary Save Page as EPS dialog box (File > Save Page as EPS)*

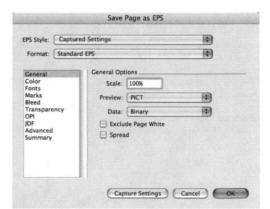

2 *The second Save Page as EPS dialog box, which displays when you click Options in the primary Save Page as EPS dialog box*

Save Page as EPS

Using a file saved as EPS

Save Page as EPS comes in handy if you have an ad or a logo that you created in QuarkXPress that you need to use in various sizes . To place an EPS into a layout, create a picture box and use File > Import Picture. As with any EPS file, in order to output it, the printer fonts must be available for any text it contains and the original files must be available for any pictures it contains.

To set EPS preferences: **NEW**

To increase the amount of virtual memory available for creating EPS files, choose QuarkXPress (Edit, in Windows) > Preferences > EPS. Increase the value in the Virtual Memory field. The Preview preference lets you choose whether to use the Embedded previews or Generate new previews when importing EPS pictures.

To create an EPS output style: **NEW**

The Edit > Output Styles dialog box lets you create and save EPS export styles. If you create EPS files often, particularly for different output methods, we recommend you do this.

1 *This logo was created in QuarkXPress, **saved as an EPS** file, and then imported into various-sized picture boxes.*

When you hand off a file to an output provider, you must supply the project and layout names, names of fonts and colors used in the project, and other data. You also must supply the original files for any pictures being used in the file, or they won't output properly. The Collect for Output command gathers copies of all the required elements together for you automatically, and also produces a report with information about the active layout. You can selectively choose whether the layout, linked pictures, color profiles, screen fonts, and printer fonts will be included in the output folder.

To collect for output:

1. Display the print layout you want to collect output for, then choose File > Collect for Output.

2. If the save alert appears, click Yes.

3. If any pictures can't be located or were modified after they were imported into the layout, an alert dialog box will appear. Click List Pictures, update the pictures, click OK, then respond to the next prompt by clicking Save.

4. In the Collect for Output dialog box, choose a location for the folder **1**. In Mac OS X, click New Folder, change the folder name, if desired, then click Create. In Windows, click the New Folder button, change the folder name, if desired, then double-click the folder icon to open it.

5. *Optional:* Change the report name in the Save As/File Name field.

Just the facts, ma'am

To have QuarkXPress produce a report only without gathering any files, check **Report Only** before clicking Save in the Collect for Output dialog box. If you hold down Option/Alt when you choose File > Collect for Output, Report Only will be checked automatically.

1 *The **Collect for Output** dialog box (File menu) in Mac OS X*

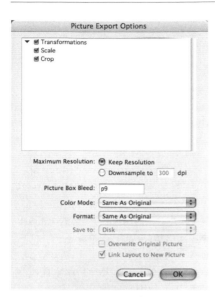

1 *The Picture Export Options dialog box displays if you check Render Picture Alterations in the Vista pane of the Collect for Output dialog box.*

Collect for Output report

The Collect for Output report contains a great deal of valuable information, including:

■ Total Pages

■ Page Width and Height

■ Required XTensions and Active XTensions

■ Fonts used

■ Graphics used, including Type, Page, Size, Box Angle, Picture Angle, Skew, XScale, YScale, and more

■ Paragraph Style Sheets

■ Character Style Sheets

■ H&Js

■ Colors and Trapping

■ Color Profiles

Basically, if anything happens to the layout at the output provider's office, they can go back to this report, find the original settings, and repair the layout.

6. Under Collect, check the file components you want QuarkXPress to place in the folder: Layout, Linked Pictures, and Color Profiles (ICC profiles). In Mac OS X, you also have Screen Fonts and Printer Fonts boxes; Windows has a Fonts box.

7. If you want to create new picture files that reflect alterations made in Quark-XPress and with the Picture Effects palette (Window menu), click the Vista tab and check Render Picture Alterations. The Picture Export Options dialog box displays so you can customize the exported pictures; make any changes and click OK. Quark-XPress will automatically collect (and reimport) the new picture files.

8. Click Save. If a dire warning prompt regarding collecting fonts appears, click OK if you're planning only to provide the fonts to your output provider or if you're collecting them for yourself. (In general, font licensing agreements don't allow you to simply share fonts with other users.)

A folder containing the current project, the components that you checked in the previous step, and a detailed report file, will be created.

After using the Collect for Output command, if you want to review the report, double-click the report text file in the folder you collected the files into. Take a look at the other files as well. Once you're satisfied that everything is there, you'll need to deliver the files to the service provider. You might burn a DVD, stuff the files and upload them to an FTP site, or use some other method as directed by the service provider.

Collect for Output

Imagesetting tips

An imagesetter is a device that produces high-resolution (1,250–3,540 dpi) paper or film output from electronic files. The paper or film output, in turn, is used by commercial printers to produce printing plates. *Note:* Some printers skip the intermediary film output step entirely and go directly to plate—so ask your printer! The following is a checklist of things to do to help your imagesetting run successfully:

■ Find out if your commercial printer can output your electronic files. Since they're intimately familiar with the printing press—its quirks and its requirements—they're often the best candidate for imagesetting.

■ If you're outputting the file with an output service provider, ask your commercial printer for specific advice regarding such settings as the lpi (lines per inch), emulsion up or down, and negative/positive. Tell your output service what output settings your commercial printer specified, and they'll enter the correct values in the Print dialog box when they output your file. Don't guess on this one. Also ask whether you should set trapping values (see pages 404–412) yourself or have the output service do the trapping on their high-end system. You can also ask your commercial printer to talk directly with your output service provider.

■ Make sure any pictures in the layout are saved at final printout size and at the appropriate resolution for the final output device, which means approximately 1.5 times the final lpi for a black-and-white or grayscale picture and 2 times the final lpi for a color picture. If a picture requires cropping, rotating, or scaling down, use the Vista tab in the Collect for Output dialog box (File menu) to generate new, modified files—they will output more quickly.

■ Use the File > Collect for Output command to collect your project and associated images and to produce a report file. If you don't supply your output service provider with the original picture files, the low-resolution versions will be used for printing (yech!). The report file lists important specifications that they need in order to output your file properly, such as the fonts used in the layout.

■ If your output service provider needs a PDF or PostScript file of your layout, ask them for specific instructions.

■ Be sure to supply the correct version of all the necessary fonts. For PostScript fonts, include both the screen and printer fonts, and don't forget to supply the fonts used in any imported EPS files.

■ Include printouts of your file with registration marks or send a PDF version of the file.

■ If your layout doesn't print or takes an inordinately long time to print on your laser printer, don't assume it will print quickly on an imagesetter. Large pictures, irregularly shaped picture boxes, and clipping paths are some of the many items that can cause a printing error. If you are using the same high-resolution picture more than once, but in very different sizes, import copies of the picture saved at those specific sizes.

■ To reduce the amount of information the imagesetter has to calculate, delete any extraneous items from the layout's pasteboard. To find out if there are any pictures on the pasteboard, choose Utilities > Usage, and click the Pictures tab. If you see the letters "PB" next to a picture name, it means that picture is on the pasteboard.

What's on your plate?

In standard four-color process printing, a layout is color-separated onto four plates, one each for cyan, yellow, magenta, and black. Other potential combinations include printing a spot color and black on two separate plates or printing a spot color and the four process colors (a total of five plates).

Hexachrome (high-fidelity) colors color-separate onto six process color plates, with the result being greater color fidelity due to the wider range of printable colors. An RGB picture can be color-separated using this method.

Printing a spot

Be sure to check **Spot Color** in the Edit Colors dialog box for any spot color that you want to color-separate onto a separate plate. To output a particular color, choose File > Print and then display the Color Options pane. Choose Mode: Separation and make sure the correct plate name is checked.

Spot colors, if they're saved in an Adobe Illustrator or Macromedia FreeHand file in the EPS format, will append to the Colors dialog box in the QuarkXPress layout and will also display in the plate scroll window in File > Print > Colors. Make sure the name that's assigned to any spot color being used in both QuarkXPress and Adobe Illustrator is exactly the same in each program; otherwise two plates will print instead of the desired single plate.

Color separation tips

- Always refer to a printed swatch book when choosing colors (e.g., a PANTONE swatch book). Computer screens only simulate printed colors, so you won't get reliable results by choosing colors based on how they appear onscreen.

- Don't change the shade percentage for a process color via the Colors palette or Item > Modify. Instead, mix a color that has the desired shade percentage built into it. It's perfectly okay to change the shade percentage for a spot color (e.g., PANTONE), though.

- If your layout contains continuous-tone pictures, such as scanned photographs or artwork produced in an image-editing program, ask your output service provider or commercial printer in which file format (e.g., TIFF, EPS) and in which image mode (e.g., CMYK, RGB) those pictures should be saved. You can use an image-editing program, such as Adobe Photoshop, to change a picture's file format, resolution, or image mode.

- Ask your output service provider whether to use QuarkXPress or an image-editing program to convert any color pictures from RGB to CMYK for separations. Pictures scanned into CMYK color mode don't require conversion.

- RGB spot colors from imported Illustrator EPS files will remain as RGB spot colors, and will be listed as such in the Colors dialog box.

- If your layout contains hand-drawn registration or crop marks, apply the Registration color to them to ensure that they appear on all the separation plates.

- For color work, order a color proof of the layout (e.g., Iris, Xerox DocuColor, Matchprint, or a high-end inkjet proof) so it can be inspected for color accuracy.

Trapping colors

Trapping is the deliberate overlapping of colors to help safeguard against gaps that may result on press due to the misalignment of plates, paper shifting, or paper stretching. In QuarkXPress, trapping is applied according to the way colors in each object interact with color(s) below it. Use the mini-glossary at right to familiarize yourself with trapping terminology.

Before exploring the circumstances in which trapping is necessary, we'll discuss a couple of circumstances in which trapping is unnecessary.

When not to apply trapping

Trapping is unnecessary when black type or a black item or frame is placed on top of a light background color. In this case, the black type will overprint (print on top of) the background color. You can specify a minimum percentage of black to control when and if overprinting will occur.

Trapping is also unnecessary if process colors and adjacent or overlapping colors contain a common color component (C, M, Y, or K). Let's say you have a red, which contains a percentage of magenta, that touches a blue area that also contains a small percentage of magenta. The two colors both contain magenta, so trapping is unnecessary.

When to apply trapping

Trapping is necessary when you print spot colors, print process colors that don't have a common color component, or print a light color on a dark background.

In QuarkXPress, trapping values are assigned to the foreground color. A light foreground color spreads into the background color by a specified amount, and a light background color chokes the foreground color. To produce a choke trap in QuarkXPress, the foreground color is assigned a negative trapping value.

(Continued on the following page)

Trapping mini-glossary

Overprint

The foreground object color prints on top of the background color, so the inks actually mix together. Overprint is used if black is the foreground object color or if inks are intentionally mixed to produce a third (overlap) color.

Knockout

To prevent inks from overprinting, the foreground item's color shape is cut out (knocked out) of the underlying background color on the background color plate. Although this eliminates the problem of ink mixing, it creates a potential problem of a gap between the edges of the foreground and background colors. Trapping closes this gap.

Spread

The spread method of trapping is used when colors knock out and the foreground color is lighter than the background color. The edge of the foreground color object is enlarged slightly to make the foreground color spread into the background color on press **1**.

Choke

The choke method of trapping is employed when the foreground color is darker than the background color. The edge of the foreground color object shrinks slightly as a result of overprinting. This is because the background color spreads into (chokes) the foreground color on press.

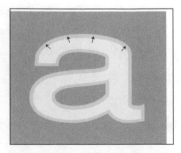

1 *In a **spread** trap, the foreground object color spreads into the background object color.*

Shut your trap!

If you feel queasy about setting traps in QuarkXPress, let your output service provider do it for you.

To turn off trapping, go to QuarkXPress (Edit, in Windows) > Preferences > Print Layout > Trapping, and click Trapping Method: Knockout All. Choose this option if you're producing a PostScript file for a high-end separation system. It's also appropriate for some color composite printers.

All of these objects (type and artwork) contain the process color magenta. Because they have this color in common, trapping is unnecessary.

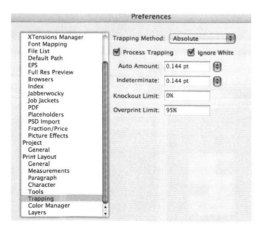

1 *Trapping preferences*

In QuarkXPress, trapping can be controlled using several features:

- On a **layout** basis using QuarkXPress (Edit, in Windows) > Preferences > Print Layout > **Trapping.**

- On an individual **color** basis using Edit > **Colors** (click Edit Trap).

- On an individual **item** basis using the **Show Trap Information** palette (Option-F12/Ctrl-F12).

The settings in Colors > Edit Trap override the settings in Trapping preferences. Trap Information palette settings override both the Edit > Colors > Edit Trap and the Trapping preferences settings.

To define automatic trap values and specify the defaults used by QuarkXPress for trapping object colors, you'll choose settings in the Trapping preferences dialog box.

To choose Trapping preferences for a whole layout:

1. Choose QuarkXPress (Edit, in Windows) > Preferences > Print Layout > Trapping **1**.

2. In the Trapping Method area choose Absolute to use the trapping value entered in the Auto Amount or Indeterminate field. The Auto Amount value is used if the foreground color is on top of a flat color. The Indeterminate value is used if the foreground color is on top of multiple shades or colors or over an imported picture. When the object color is darker, the background color chokes into the object color by the Auto Amount. When the foreground object color is lighter, the object color spreads into the background color by the Auto Amount.
   or
   Choose Proportional to use the trapping value entered in the Auto Amount field, multiplied by the difference in

(Continued on the following page)

Trapping Preferences

luminosity (lights and darks) between the foreground object color and the background color. The width of the trap will vary and be calculated by multiplying the Auto Amount value by the difference in luminosity between the object and background colors.
or
Choose Knockout All to turn trapping off for all objects. Objects will print with 0 trapping.

3. Check or uncheck Process Trapping. With Process Trapping on, each process component (cyan, magenta, yellow, and black) is spread or choked, depending on which one is darker—the foreground object or the background color. For example, if the cyan in the foreground object color is lighter than the cyan in the background color, the foreground object cyan is spread into the background cyan—but only on the cyan plate.

The trap width is equal to half the Auto Amount value when Absolute trapping is specified. When Proportional trapping is specified, the trap width will equal the Auto Amount value multiplied by the difference in luminosity values between the foreground object and background colors.

If Process Trapping is off, the same trapping value will be applied to all the process-color components, using the trapping settings for those colors as specified in the Trap Specifications dialog box (Colors > Edit Trap button).

4. Enter a trapping value in the Auto Amount field **1** or choose Overprint from the adjacent menu. Either the value entered or the Overprint setting will be used in the Trap Specifications dialog box (Edit > Colors > Edit Trap) and on the Trap Information palette whenever a field in either of these two locations is set to Auto Amount (+/–).

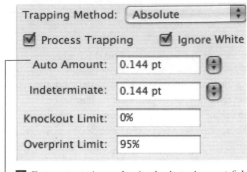

1 *Enter a trapping value in the **Auto Amount** field.*

Knockout Limit

If a color's gray value falls within the current Knockout Limit, that color knocks out the background color. The gray value is determined by subtracting a color's luminance value (as measured from its RGB components) from the number 1. This produces a percentage. The lighter the color, the lower the percentage. When the Knockout Limit is set to 10%, very light foreground colors knock out background colors, and medium light and darker foreground colors trap to the background color.

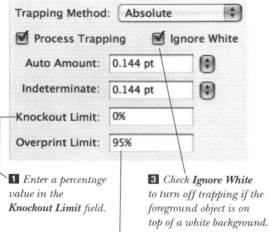

1 *Enter a percentage value in the* **Knockout Limit** *field.*

2 *Enter a percentage value in the* **Overprint Limit** *field.*

3 *Check* **Ignore White** *to turn off trapping if the foreground object is on top of a white background.*

5. Enter a trapping value in the Indeterminate field or choose Overprint from the menu. If a foreground object is over a background that consists of multiple shades or colors, or is over an imported picture, either the value you entered or the Overprint setting will be used.

6. Enter a Knockout Limit percentage **1** to set the gray (light and dark) value limit at which a foreground object color will knock out the background color (see the sidebar).

7. Enter an Overprint Limit value **2** for the shade percentage limit below which the foreground object color won't overprint the background color. For example, if the Overprint Limit is 92%, a foreground object that's 85% black won't overprint, even if that color or object is set to overprint via Edit > Colors > Edit Trap > Trap Specifications. The object will trap according to the Auto Amount value.

   An Overprint setting chosen on the Trap Information palette will cause the selected object to overprint regardless of the current trap settings or any Overprint Limit value entered in any other dialog box.

8. Leave Ignore White checked **3** to turn off trapping for any instance in which the foreground object is on top of background areas that contain white and other colors. This is the preferred situation, since the white area won't be considered when the trap is calculated for the other colors.

   With Ignore White unchecked, objects on a white background will overprint. If an object is set to spread over a background color, the Indeterminate value will be used for the spread.

9. Click OK to close the Preferences dialog box.

The Trap Specifications dialog box controls trapping on a color-by-color basis. The default settings for each color display in this dialog box and can be modified here.

Note: For these instructions, Absolute should be chosen as the Trapping Method in QuarkXPress (Edit, in Windows) > Preferences > Print Layout > Trapping.

To choose trapping values for a color (Trap Specifications):

1. Choose Edit > Colors (Shift-F12).

2. Click a color, then click Edit Trap .

3. The name of the foreground color you chose will appear in the title bar of the Trap Specifications dialog box. Click one of the remaining colors listed, any of which could potentially be a background color ■.

4. From the Trap menu ■, choose:

    Default to have QuarkXPress determine how colors will be trapped. With Default chosen, black always overprints.

    Overprint to have the foreground color overprint the selected background color when the foreground color shade is equal to or greater than the Overprint Limit value specified in QuarkXPress (Edit, in Windows) > Preferences > Print Layout > Trapping.

    Knockout to have the foreground color knock out the selected background color.

    Auto Amount (+) to use the auto spread value for the foreground color.

    Auto Amount (–) to use the auto choke value for the foreground color.

    Custom to enter a custom spread or choke (negative) value for the foreground color.

■ *Click a color, then click **Edit Trap**.*

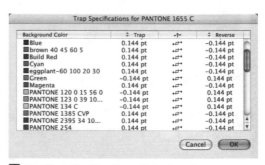

■ *The **Trap Specifications** dialog box opens.*

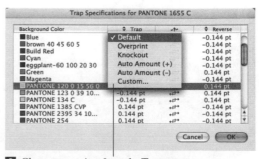

■ *Choose an option from the **Trap** menu.*

1 *Choose **Dependent Traps** or **Independent Traps** from the ↵?↵ menu.*

2 *Choose an option from the **Reverse** menu.*

TIP The Auto Amount and Overprint Limit settings were established in QuarkXPress (Edit, in Windows) > Preferences > Print Layout > Trapping.

5. From the second menu ↵?↵ ▼, choose Dependent Traps (the default) to create the reverse trap situation for the colors you chose in steps 2 and 3, based on the current setting in the Trap column. Or choose Independent Traps to create a unique trap setting in the Reverse column for these two colors **1**.

6. If Independent Traps is chosen in the second column, a different Trap setting for the selected background color can be chosen **2**. This Reverse Trap setting will be used when the selected color traps to the color named in the title bar of the dialog box. (If an option other than Default is chosen from the Reverse menu, an asterisk displays in the Reverse column.) The options are the same as in step 4.

Remember that when traps have a Dependent relationship, the Reverse column setting automatically derives from the current Trap column setting, and vice versa. Change either of these columns, and the other will change automatically. When traps have an independent relationship, unique settings can be set in these two columns.

7. Click OK, then click Save to close the Colors dialog box.

TIP Settings in the Trap Specifications dialog box override the settings in QuarkXPress (Edit, in Windows) > Preferences > Print Layout > Trapping.

TIP If a print layout is open when Edit > Colors is chosen, Edit Trap changes will apply only to the current layout. If no project is open, changes will apply to all subsequently created projects.

Trap Specifications

Note: Trap Information palette settings override the settings chosen in the Trapping preferences and Trap Specifications dialog boxes.

Note: For these instructions, Absolute should be chosen as the Trapping Method in QuarkXPress (Edit, in Windows) > Preferences > Print Layout > Trapping.

To choose trapping values for an object (Trap Information palette):

1. Choose Window > Trap Information to open the palette (Option-F12/Ctrl-F12) **1**.

2. Select the item to which you want to apply trapping.

3. Choose a new trap setting from any of the menus on the left side of the palette (the options will vary depending on the type of item chosen):

   Default to have the settings in Trapping preferences or Edit Trap be used to determine how colors will trap.

   Overprint to have the foreground item color overprint any background color.

   Knockout to have the foreground item color knock out any background color.

   Auto Amount (+) to have the auto spread value be used for the foreground color or **Auto Amount (–)** to have the auto choke value be used for the foreground color. The auto amount settings are established in QuarkXPress (Edit, in Windows) > Preferences > Print Layout > Trapping.

   Custom to enter a custom spread or choke value for the foreground color.

TIP Choosing Overprint from the palette will cause that item to overprint, regardless of the foreground or background color shade or the Overprint Limit value.

TIP To set trapping for text, select the text—the Text option on the palette will become available.

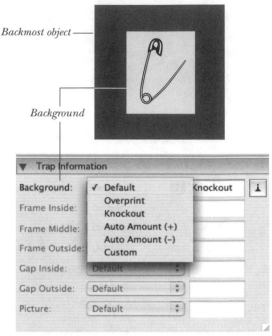

Backmost object

Background

1 *This is the **Trap Information** palette with a picture box selected. Here, the Background color of the picture box (20% Black) defaults to a spread trap of the Auto Amount over the darker color underneath.*

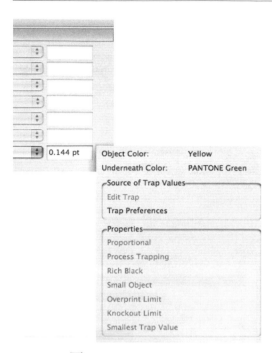

Object Color:	Yellow
Underneath Color:	PANTONE Green

┌─ Source of Trap Values ─
│ Edit Trap
│ Trap Preferences

┌─ Properties ─
│ Proportional
│ Process Trapping
│ Rich Black
│ Small Object
│ Overprint Limit
│ Knockout Limit
│ Smallest Trap Value

1 *Press the* ⬆ *icon on the Trap Information palette to display an explanation of the **Default Trap** setting.*

2 *In this example, the text only partially overlaps a background color.*

What follows are guidelines for common trapping situations that may occur.

Trapping type

When it comes to trapping, a text box is treated like a single foreground object. The text box color will trap to the background color based on the current trap settings. When a text box with a background of None is on top of a background color, QuarkXPress will trap the type, even if the type itself isn't overlapping the background color **1**. This can occur with type that appears inside a large text box.

To control how text traps, select the text and set it to Overprint or Knockout via the Trap Information palette. You can also select individual characters or words and apply a unique trap setting to them that's different from the remaining characters in the box. Any box that's layered on top of a text box will trap to the background color of the text box—not to the type **2**.

QuarkXPress regards type that's partially on top of a paragraph rule as trapping to an indeterminate background color. If the type is completely within the paragraph rule, the type is trapped based on the type color-to-rule color relationship as per the Edit > Colors trap settings. This relationship can be changed only via Edit > Colors > Edit Trap.

Trapping a frame

A frame is layered on top of the contents of the box the frame is attached to. Using the Trap Information palette, you can apply different trapping settings to the inside, middle, and outside parts of a single-line or multiline frame, and to the gaps in a dashed frame.

(Continued on the following page)

Trap Type, Frame

Trapping imported pictures

In QuarkXPress, a picture can't be spread or choked to a background color.

Trapping adjustments that are made to a vector (object-oriented) picture in a drawing program, such as Adobe Illustrator, will output successfully from QuarkXPress. The Trap Information palette provides no trapping controls for the picture itself. *Note:* Don't scale an imported vector picture that was created with built-in trapping, because such scaling will also resize the trapping areas in the picture.

You can use the Trap Information palette to specify that a raster (bitmap) picture knock out or overprint a background color. This is helpful if you're colorizing a grayscale TIFF picture in QuarkXPress. Click a picture, then choose Overprint or Knockout from the Picture menu on the Trap Information palette—whichever setting your commercial printer instructs you to choose.

A line art (black and white) picture to which you've applied a shade of black that's equal to or greater than the Overprint Limit in QuarkXPress will overprint any background color(s) it's positioned on top of. Use the Trap Information palette to set the picture to knock out, if desired.

Lines and boxes in QuarkXPress can knock out, overprint, or trap to pictures that are underneath them. Use the Trap Information palette to set the type of trap. Type can knock out, overprint, or spread to a picture underneath it.

Trapping bitmaps

You can apply trapping to some types of bitmap pictures via the Trap Information palette, including:

> Grayscale TIFF (8-bit)
> Black-and-white TIFF (1-bit)
> RGB TIFF
> CMYK TIFF
> Colorized grayscale TIFF

Trapping can't be applied to an EPS in QuarkXPress.

Special Characters **A**

In QuarkXPress 7, the easiest way to access special characters in any font is via the **Glyphs palette** (Window menu). Select a font, locate the character you want, and double-click it to insert it at the text insertion point. You can also enter some system-wide and QuarkXPress-specific special characters—including em dashes, non-breaking spaces, and automatic page number characters—using the **Utilities > Insert Character** submenu. **NEW**

TIP If you enter special characters often, however, it helps to remember the keyboard shortcuts provided here.

Zapf Dingbats: Mac OS X and Windows

Dingbat	Key Combo Mac/Win	ASCII
	space	32
✂	! (Shift-1)	33
✂	" (Shift-')	34
✂	# (Shift-3)	35
✂	$ (Shift-4)	36
☎	% (Shift-5)	37
✆	& (Shift-7)	38
✇	'	39
✈	((Shift-0)	40
✉	) (Shift-9)	41
☛	* (Shift-8)	42
☞	+ (Shift-=)	43
✌	,	44
✍	-	45
✎	.	46
✐	/	47
✏	0	48
✍	1	49
➡	2	50

Dingbat	Key Combo Mac/Win	ASCII
✓	3	51
✔	4	52
✕	5	53
✖	6	54
✗	7	55
✘	8	56
✚	9	57
✜	: (Shift-;)	58
✢	;	59
✣	< (Shift-,)	60
†	=	61
✞	> (Shift-.)	62
✠	? (Shift-/)	63
✡	@ (Shift-2)	64
✴	A	65
✦	B	66
✧	C	67
✶	D	68
✷	E	69

Zapf Dingbats

Dingbat	Key Combo Mac/Win	ASCII
✦	F	70
✧	G	71
★	H	72
☆	I	73
✪	J	74
☆	K	75
✩	L	76
✬	M	77
✩	N	78
✩	O	79
☆	P	80
✳	Q	81
✳	R	82
✳	S	83
✳	T	84
✴	U	85
✵	V	86
✷	W	87
✸	X	88
✹	Y	89
✺	Z	90
✳	[	91
✳	\	92
✳	]	93
✽	^ (Shift-6)	94
✿	_ (Shift--)	95
❀	`	96
❁	a	97
❂	b	98
✽	c	99
✾	d	100
✺	e	101

Dingbat	Key Combo Mac	Key Combo Win
✻	f	102
✼	g	103
❅	h	104
❆	i	105
❄	j	106
✳	k	107
●	l	108
○	m	109
■	n	110
❏	o	111
❐	p	112
❑	q	113
❒	r	114
▲	s	115
▼	t	116
◆	u	117
❖	v	118
◗	w	119
❘	x	120
❙	y	121
❚	z	122
❛	{	123
❜	|	124
❝	}	125
❞	~	126
❨	Opt-U Shift-A	Alt+0128
❩	Opt-Shift-A	Alt+0129
❪	Opt-Shift-C	Alt+0130
❫	Opt-E Shift-E	Alt+0131
❬	Opt-N Shift-N	Alt+0132
❭	Opt-U Shift-O	Alt+0133
❮	Opt-U Shift-U	Alt+0134

Dingbat	Key Combo Mac	Key Combo Win	Dingbat	Key Combo Mac	Key Combo Win
❭	Opt-E, A	Alt+0135	➎	Opt-B	Alt+0186
❬	Opt-`, A	Alt+0136	➏	Opt-9	Alt+0187
❭	Opt-I, A	Alt+0137	➐	Opt-0	Alt+0188
❴	Opt-U, A	Alt+0138	➑	Opt-Z	Alt+0189
❵	Opt-N, A	Alt+0139	➒	Opt-'	Alt+0190
❴	Opt-A	Alt+0140	➓	Opt-O	Alt+0191
❵	Opt-C	Alt+0141	①	Opt-Shift-/	Alt+0192
♣	Opt-Shift-8	Alt+0161	②	Opt-1	Alt+0193
❢	Opt-4	Alt+0162	③	Opt-L	Alt+0194
❣	Opt-3	Alt+0163	④	Opt-V	Alt+0195
♥	Opt-6	Alt+0164	⑤	Opt-F	Alt+0196
❧	Opt-8	Alt+0165	⑥	Opt-X	Alt+0197
❦	Opt-7	Alt+0166	⑦	Opt-J	Alt+0198
❧	Opt-S	Alt+0167	⑧	Opt-\	Alt+0199
♣	Opt-R	Alt+0168	⑨	Opt-Shift-\	Alt+0200
♦	Opt-G	Alt+0169	⑩	Opt-;	Alt+0201
♥	Opt-2	Alt+0170	❶	Opt-space	Alt+0202
♠	Opt-E	Alt+0171	❷	Opt-`, Shift-A	Alt+0203
①	Opt-U	Alt+0172	❸	Opt-N, Shift-A	Alt+0204
②	Opt-=	Alt+0173	❹	Opt-N, Shift-O	Alt+0205
③	Opt-Shift-'	Alt+0174	❺	Opt-Shift-Q	Alt+0206
④	Opt-Shift-O	Alt+0175	❻	Opt-Q	Alt+0207
⑤	Opt-5	Alt+0176	❼	Opt-hyphen	Alt+0208
⑥	Opt-Shift-=	Alt+0177	❽	Opt-Shift-hyphen	Alt+0209
⑦	Opt-,	Alt+0178	❾	Opt-[	Alt+0210
⑧	Opt-.	Alt+0179	❿	Opt-Shift-[	Alt+0211
⑨	Opt-Y	Alt+0180	→	Opt-]	Alt+0212
⑩	Opt-M	Alt+0181	→	Opt-Shift-]	Alt+0213
❶	Opt-D	Alt+0182	↔	Opt-/	Alt+0214
❷	Opt-W	Alt+0183	↕	Opt-Shift-V	Alt+0215
❸	Opt-Shift-P	Alt+0184	↘	Opt-u, Y	Alt+0216
❹	Opt-P	Alt+0185	→	Opt-U, Shift-Y	Alt+0217
			↗	Opt-Shift-1	Alt+0218

Zapf Dingbats

Dingbat	Key Combo Mac	Key Combo Win		Dingbat	Key Combo Mac	Key Combo Win
→	Opt-Shift-2	Alt+0219		⇨	Opt-`, Shift-I	Alt+0237
➜	Opt-Shift-3	Alt+0220		⇨	Opt-E, Shift-O	Alt+0238
→	Opt-Shift-4	Alt+0221		⇨	Opt-I, Shift-O	Alt+0239
→	Opt-Shift-5	Alt+0222		[not used]	Opt-Shift-K	Alt+0240
➠	Opt-Shift-6	Alt+0223		⇨	Opt-`, Shift-O	Alt+0241
➠	Opt-Shift-7	Alt+0224		⊃	Opt-E, Shift-U	Alt+0242
➡	Opt-Shift-9	Alt+0225		⯮	Opt-I, Shift-U	Alt+0243
➢	Opt-Shift-0	Alt+0226		➘	Opt-`, Shift-U	Alt+0244
➢	Opt-Shift-W	Alt+0227		➠	Opt-Shift-B	Alt+0245
➤	Opt-Shift-R	Alt+0228		➶	Opt-I, space	Alt+0246
➥	Opt-I, Shift-A	Alt+0229		➘	Opt-N, space	Alt+0247
➥	Opt-I, Shift-E	Alt+0230		➠	Opt-Shift-,	Alt+0248
➧	Opt-E, Shift-A	Alt+0231		➹	Opt-Shift-.	Alt+0249
➡	Opt-U, Shift-E	Alt+0232		➙	Opt-H	Alt+0250
⇨	Opt-`, Shift-E	Alt+0233		➤	Opt-K	Alt+0251
⇨	Opt-E, Shift-I	Alt+0234		➠	Opt-Shift-Z	Alt+0252
⇨	Opt-I, Shift-I	Alt+0235		➠	Opt-Shift-G	Alt+0253
⇨	Opt-U, Shift-I	Alt+0236		⇛	Opt-Shift-X	Alt+0254

Special Characters: Mac OS X *(not font specific)*

Character	Key Combo	ASCII Code		Character	Key Combo	ASCII Code
Ä	Opt-U, Shift-A	0128		â	Opt-i, A	0137
Å	Opt-Shift-A	0129		ä	Opt-U, A	0138
Ç	Opt-Shift-C	0130		ā	Opt-N, A	0139
É	Opt-E, Shift-E	0131		å	Opt-A	0140
Ñ	Opt-N, Shift-N	0132		ç	Opt-C	0141
Ö	Opt-U, Shift-O	0133		é	Opt-E, E	0142
Ü	Opt-U, Shift-U	0134		è	Opt-`, E	0143
á	Opt-E, A	0135		ê	Opt-I, E	0144
à	Opt-`, A	0136		ë	Opt-U, E	0145

Special Characters: Mac OS X

Character	Key Combo	ASCII Code
í	Opt-E, I	0146
ì	Opt-`, I	0147
î	Opt-I, I	0148
ï	Opt-U, I	0149
ñ	Opt-N, N	0150
ó	Opt-E, O	0151
ò	Opt-`, O	0152
ô	Opt-I, O	0153
ö	Opt-U, O	0154
õ	Opt-N, O	0155
ú	Opt-E, U	0156
ù	Opt-`, U	0157
û	Opt-I, U	0158
ü	Opt-U, U	0159
†	Opt-T	0160
°	Opt-Shift-8	0161
¢	Opt-4	0162
£	Opt-3	0163
§	Opt-6	0164
•	Opt-8	0165
¶	Opt-7	0166
ß	Opt-S	0167
®	Opt-R	0168
©	Opt-G	0169
™	Opt-2	0170
´	Opt-E, space	0171
¨	Opt-U, space	0172
≠	Opt-=	0173
Æ	Opt-Shift-'	0174
Ø	Opt-Shift-O	0175

Character	Key Combo	ASCII Code
∞	Opt-5	0176
±	Opt-Shift-=	0177
≤	Opt-,	0178
≥	Opt-.	0179
¥	Opt-Y	0180
µ	Opt-M	0181
∂	Opt-D	0182
Σ	Opt-W	0183
∏	Opt-Shift-P	0184
π	Opt-P	0185
∫	Opt-B	0186
ª	Opt-9	0187
º	Opt-0	0188
Ω	Opt-Z	0189
æ	Opt-'	0190
ø	Opt-O	0191
¿	Opt-Shift-/	0192
¡	Opt-1	0193
¬	Opt-L	0194
√	Opt-V	0195
ƒ	Opt-F	0196
≈	Opt-X	0197
∆	Opt-J	0198
«	Opt-\	0199
»	Opt-Shift-\	0200
…	Opt-;	0201
nonbreaking space	Opt-space	0202
À	Opt-`, Shift-A	0203
¯	Opt-N, Shift-A	0204
Õ	Opt-N, Shift-O	0205

Special Characters: Mac OS X

Character	Key Combo	ASCII Code	Character	Key Combo	ASCII Code
Œ	Opt-Shift-Q	0206	Á	Opt-E, Shift-A	0231
œ	Opt-Q	0207	Ë	Opt-U, Shift-E	0232
–	Opt-hyphen	0208	È	Opt-`, Shift-E	0233
—	Opt-Shift-hyphen	0209	Í	Opt-E, Shift-I	0234
"	Opt-[	0210	Î	Opt-I, Shift-I	0235
"	Opt-Shift-[	0211	Ï	Opt-U, Shift-I	0236
'	Opt-]	0212	Ì	Opt-`, Shift-I	0237
'	Opt-Shift-]	0213	Ó	Opt-E, Shift-O	0238
÷	Opt-/	0214	Ô	Opt-I, Shift-O	0239
◊	Opt-Shift-V	0215		Opt-Shift-K	0240
ÿ	Opt-u, Y	0216	Ò	Opt-`, Shift-O	0241
Ÿ	Opt-U, Shift-Y	0217	Ú	Opt-E, Shift-U	0242
⁄	Opt-Shift-1	0218	Û	Opt-I, Shift-U	0243
€	Opt-Shift-2	0219	Ù	Opt-`, Shift-U	0244
‹	Opt-Shift-3	0220	ı	Opt-Shift-B	0245
›	Opt-Shift-4	0221	ˆ	Opt-I, space	0246
ﬁ	Opt-Shift-5	0222	˜	Opt-N, space	0247
ﬂ	Opt-Shift-6	0223	¯	Opt-Shift-,	0248
‡	Opt-Shift-7	0224	˘	Opt-Shift-.	0249
·	Opt-Shift-9	0225	˙	Opt-H	0250
‚	Opt-Shift-0*	0226	°	Opt-K	0251
„	Opt-Shift-W	0227	¸	Opt-Shift-Z	0252
‰	Opt-Shift-R	0228	˝	Opt-Shift-G	0253
Â	Opt-I, Shift-A	0229	˛	Opt-Shift-X	0254
Ê	Opt-I, Shift-E	0230	ˇ	Opt-Shift-T	0255

Special Characters: Windows *(not font specific)*

Character	Key Combo (Alt+ANSI code)	Character	Key Combo (Alt+ANSI code)
€	Alt+0128	[*not used*]	Alt+0160
[*not used*]	Alt+0129	¡	Alt+0161
‚	Alt+0130	¢	Alt+0162
ƒ	Alt+0131	£	Alt+0163
„	Alt+0132	¤	Alt+0164
…	Alt+0133	¥	Alt+0165
†	Alt+0134	¦	Alt+0166
‡	Alt+0135	§	Alt+0167
ˆ	Alt+0136	¨	Alt+0168
‰	Alt+0137	©	Alt+0169
Š	Alt+0138	ª	Alt+0170
‹	Alt+0139	«	Alt+0171
Œ	Alt+0140	¬	Alt+0172
[*not used*]	Alt+0141		Alt+0173
Ž	Alt+0142	®	Alt+0174
[*not used*]	Alt+0143	¯	Alt+0175
[*not used*]	Alt+0144	°	Alt+0176
'	Alt+0145	±	Alt+0177
'	Alt+0146	²	Alt+0178
"	Alt+0147	³	Alt+0179
"	Alt+0148	´	Alt+0180
•	Alt+0149	µ	Alt+0181
–	Alt+0150	¶	Alt+0182
—	Alt+0151	·	Alt+0183
˜	Alt+0152	¸	Alt+0184
™	Alt+0153	¹	Alt+0185
š	Alt+0154	º	Alt+0186
›	Alt+0155	»	Alt+0187
œ	Alt+0156	¼	Alt+0188
[*not used*]	Alt+0157	½	Alt+0189
ž	Alt+0158	¾	Alt+0190
Ÿ	Alt+0159	¿	Alt+0191

Special Characters: Windows

Character	Key Combo (Alt+ANSI code)	Character	Key Combo (Alt+ANSI code)
À	Alt+0192	à	Alt+0224
Á	Alt+0193	á	Alt+0225
Â	Alt+0194	â	Alt+0226
Ã	Alt+0195	ã	Alt+0227
Ä	Alt+0196	ä	Alt+0228
Å	Alt+0197	å	Alt+0229
Æ	Alt+0198	æ	Alt+0230
Ç	Alt+0199	ç	Alt+0231
È	Alt+0200	è	Alt+0232
É	Alt+0201	é	Alt+0233
Ê	Alt+0202	ê	Alt+0234
Ë	Alt+0203	ë	Alt+0235
Ì	Alt+0204	ì	Alt+0236
Í	Alt+0205	í	Alt+0237
Î	Alt+0206	î	Alt+0238
Ï	Alt+0207	ï	Alt+0239
Ð	Alt+0208	ð	Alt+0240
Ñ	Alt+0209	ñ	Alt+0241
Ò	Alt+0210	ò	Alt+0242
Ó	Alt+0211	ó	Alt+0243
Ô	Alt+0212	ô	Alt+0244
Õ	Alt+0213	õ	Alt+0245
Ö	Alt+0214	ö	Alt+0246
×	Alt+0215	÷	Alt+0247
Ø	Alt+0216	ø	Alt+0248
Ù	Alt+0217	ù	Alt+0249
Ú	Alt+0218	ú	Alt+0250
Û	Alt+0219	û	Alt+0251
Ü	Alt+0220	ü	Alt+0252
Ý	Alt+0221	ý	Alt+0253
Þ	Alt+0222	þ	Alt+0254
ß	Alt+0223	ÿ	Alt+0255

Keyboard Shortcuts B

	Mac OS X	**Windows**
Show/hide palettes		
Tools	F8	F8
Measurements	F9	F9
Display Measurements palette and select first field (item selected)	Cmd-Option-M	Ctrl+Alt+M
Page Layout	F10	F4
Style Sheets	F11	F11
Colors	F12	F12
Find/Change	Cmd-F	Ctrl+F
Trap Information	Option-F12	Ctrl+F12
Lists	Option-F11	Ctrl+F11
Dialog boxes		
OK (or heavy bordered button)	Return *or* Enter	Enter
Display next pane	Cmd-Option-Tab	Ctrl+Tab
Display previous pane	Cmd-Option-Shift-Tab	Ctrl+Shift+Tab
Cancel	Cmd-. (period) *or* Esc	Esc
Apply *(Mac OS X only)*	Cmd-A	
Yes	Cmd-Y	Y
No	Cmd-N	N
Select field	Double-click	Double-click
Select consecutive items on list	Shift-click	Shift+click
Select nonconsecutive items on list	Cmd-click	Ctrl+click
Dialog boxes and palettes		
Select next field	Tab	Tab
Select previous field	Shift-Tab	Shift+Tab
Add	+	+
Subtract	–	–
Multiply	*	*
Divide	/	/
Revert to original values	Cmd-Z or F1	Ctrl+Shift+Z

	Mac OS X	Windows
Tools palette		
Select next tool	Cmd-Option-Tab	Ctrl+Alt+Tab
Select previous tool	Cmd-Option-Shift-Tab	Ctrl+Alt+Shift+Tab
Item tool/Content tool toggle	Shift-F8	Shift+F8
Turn Content tool into temporary Item tool	Cmd	Ctrl
Keep a tool selected	Option-click tool	Alt+click tool
Clipboard		
Cut	Cmd-X *or* F2	Ctrl+X
Copy	Cmd-C *or* F3	Ctrl+C
Paste	Cmd-V *or* F4	Ctrl+V
Paste in place	Cmd-Option-Shift-V	Ctrl+Alt+Shift+V
Whole project		
New Project dialog box	Cmd-N	Ctrl+N
New Library dialog box	Cmd-Option-N	Ctrl+Alt+N
Open dialog box	Cmd-O	Ctrl+O
Save	Cmd-S	Ctrl+S
Save As dialog box	Cmd-Option-S	Ctrl+Alt+S
Quit/Exit	Cmd-Q	Ctrl+Q *or* Alt+F4
Append	Cmd-Option-A	Ctrl+Alt+A
Revert to last Auto Save	Option-Revert to Saved	Alt+Revert to Saved
Close active project	Cmd-W	Ctrl+F4
Mac OS X only:		
Close all open QuarkXPress files	Cmd-Option-W *or* Option-click Close button	
Hide QuarkXPress	Cmd-H	
Hide Others [applications]	Cmd-Option-H	
Undo/Redo		
Undo	Cmd-Z *or* F1	Ctrl+Z
Redo*	Cmd-Shift-Z	Alt+Shift+Z

*Make sure your Preferences > Application > Undo > Redo Key setting is Cmd-Shift-Z/Ctrl-Shift-Z.

	Mac OS X	Windows
Display		
Fit in Window	Cmd-0 (zero) *or* Ctrl-click > Fit in Window	Ctrl+0 (zero) *or* Right-click > Fit in Window
Fit pasteboard in project window	Option-choose Fit in Window *or* Cmd-Option-0	Alt+choose Fit in Window *or* Ctrl+Alt+0 (zero)
Actual Size	Cmd-1 *or* Ctrl-click > Actual Size	Ctrl+1 *or* Right-click > Actual Size

	Mac OS X	**Windows**
Zoom in	Control-Shift-click* *or* drag *or* Cmd- + (plus)**	Ctrl+Space bar click *or* drag
Zoom out	Control-Option-click *or* Cmd- – (minus)**	Ctrl+Alt+Space bar click
Select view percent field	Control V	Ctrl+Alt+V
Thumbnails	Shift-F6 *or* enter "T" in View Percent field (press Return)	Shift F6 *or* enter "T" in View Percent field (press Enter)
Change to 200%, then toggle between 100% and 200%	Cmd-Option-click	Ctrl+Alt+click
Stop redraw	Cmd-. (period)	Esc
Force redraw	Cmd-Option-. (period)	Shift+Esc
Show/hide Baseline Grid	Option-F7	Ctrl+F7

If Control Key Activates: Zoom is chosen in Preferences > Input Settings, omit Shift
**For Cmd- + or Cmd- –, if Content tool is chosen, deselect all items first*

Rulers and guides

Show/hide Guides	F7	F7
Snap to Guides (toggle)	Shift-F7	Shift+F7
Show/hide Rulers	Cmd-R	Ctrl+R
Delete all horizontal ruler guides from page *(no pasteboard showing)*	Option-click horizontal ruler	Alt+click horizontal ruler
Delete all vertical ruler guides from page *(no pasteboard showing)*	Option-click vertical ruler	Alt+click vertical ruler

Project windows

Stack or tile/cascade or tile project windows	Shift-click project title bar and choose Stack or Tile	Window > Cascade, *or* Tile Horizontally, *or* Tile Vertically (no shortcut)
Maximize project window	Click zoom button	F3
Activate open project window *(Mac OS X only)*	Shift-click project window title bar and choose file name from pop-up menu	
Stack or tile/cascade or tile to Actual Size	(Hold Control) Window > Stack/Tile†	(Hold Ctrl+Alt) Window > Cascade/Tile
Stack or tile/cascade or tile to Fit in Window	(Hold Cmd) Window > Stack/Tile†	(Hold Ctrl) Window > Cascade/Tile
Stack or tile/cascade or tile to Thumbnails	(Hold Option) Window > Stack/Tile†	(Hold Alt) Window > Cascade/Tile

†Or add Shift to shortcut, click project window title bar, and choose command from pop-up menu

	Mac OS X	**Windows**
Navigate in a layout		
Go To Page dialog box	Cmd-J	Ctrl+J
Start of layout/story	Control A *or* Home	Ctrl+Home
End of layout/story	Control D *or* End	Ctrl+End
Up one screen	Control K *or* Page Up	Page Up
Down one screen	Control L *or* Page Down	Page Down
To first page	Control-Shift-A *or* Shift-Home	Ctrl+Page Up
To last page	Shift-End	Ctrl+Page Down
To previous page	Shift-Page Up	Shift+Page Up
To next page	Shift-Page Down	Shift+Page Down
To previous even or odd page	Option-Page Up	Alt+Page Up
To next even or odd page	Option-Page Down	Alt+Page Down
Page Grabber Hand (any tool except Zoom)	Option-drag	Alt+drag
Toggle master/layout page display	Shift-F10	Shift+F4
Display next master page	Option-F10	Ctrl+Shift+F4
Display previous master page	Option-Shift-F10	Ctrl+Shift+F3
Enable Live Scroll if off in Preferences > Input Settings, or disable if on	Option-drag scroll box	Alt+drag scroll box
Layout Properties dialog box	Cmd+Option+Shift+P	Ctrl+Alt+Shift+P
Items		
Modify dialog box	Cmd-M *or* double-click item with Item tool	Ctrl+M *or* double-click item with Item tool
Modify dialog box, Frame pane	Cmd-B	Ctrl+B
Modify dialog box, Drop Shadow pane	Cmd-Opt-Shift-D	Ctrl+Alt+Shift+D
Lock/Unlock Position	F6	F6
Delete item	Cmd-K	Ctrl+K
Constrain rotation to increment of 45° with Rotation tool	Shift while rotating	Shift while rotating
Move item (Content tool)	Cmd-drag	Ctrl+drag
Nudge item 1 point	Arrow keys	Arrow keys
Nudge item ¹⁄₁₀ point	Option-arrow keys	Alt+Arrow keys
Constrain movement to horizontal/vertical (Item tool)	Shift-drag	Shift+drag
Constrain movement to horizontal/vertical (Content tool)	Cmd-Shift-drag	Ctrl+Shift+drag

	Mac OS X	Windows
Multiple items		
Select All (Item tool)	Cmd-A	Ctrl+A
Select multiple items (Item tool)	Shift-click *or* marquee	Shift+click *or* marquee
Group	Cmd-G	Ctrl+G
Move item in a group (Content tool)	Cmd-drag	Ctrl+drag
Resize group proportionally	Cmd-Option-Shift drag handle	Ctrl+Alt-Shift+drag handle
Ungroup	Cmd-U	Ctrl+U
Duplicate	Cmd-D	Ctrl+D
Step and Repeat dialog box	Cmd-Option-R **NEW**	Ctrl+Alt+R **NEW**
Select behind other items	Cmd-Option-Shift-click	Ctrl+Alt+Shift+click
Bring to Front	F5	F5
Send to Back	Shift-F5	Shift+F5
Bring Forward one level	Option-Item menu > Bring Forward *or* Option-F5	Ctrl+F5
Send Backward one level	Option-Item menu > Send Backward *or* Option-Shift-F5	Ctrl+Shift+F5
Space/Align tab on Measurements palette (multiple items selected) **NEW**	Cmd-, (comma)	Ctrl+, (comma)
Apply last Space/Align command	Cmd-Option-/	Ctrl+Alt+/
Select text		
Show/Hide Invisibles	Cmd-I	Ctrl+I
One word (no punctuation mark)	Double-click	Double-click
One line	Triple-click	Triple-click
One paragraph	Click four times quickly	Click four times quickly
Entire story (Content tool)	Click five times quickly *or* Cmd-A	Click five times quickly *or* Ctrl+A

With cursor in text (keep pressing arrow to extend the selection):

Previous character	Shift-left arrow	Shift+left arrow
Next character	Shift-right arrow	Shift+right arrow
Previous line	Shift-up arrow	Shift+up arrow
Next line	Shift-down arrow	Shift+down arrow
Previous word	Cmd-Shift-left arrow	Ctrl+Shift+left arrow
Next word	Cmd-Shift-right arrow	Ctrl+Shift+right arrow

From the text insertion point to:

Start of paragraph	Cmd-Shift-up arrow	Ctrl+Shift+up arrow
End of paragraph	Cmd-Shift-down arrow	Ctrl+Shift+down arrow
Start of line	Cmd-Option-Shift-left arrow	Ctrl+Alt+Shift+left arrow *or* Shift+Home

Keyboard Shortcuts

	Mac OS X	**Windows**
End of line	Cmd-Option-Shift-right arrow	Ctrl+Alt+Shift+right arrow *or* Shift+End
Start of story	Cmd-Option-Shift-up arrow	Ctrl+Alt+Shift+up arrow *or* Ctrl+Shift+Home
End of story	Cmd-Option-Shift-down arrow	Ctrl+Alt+Shift+down arrow *or* Ctrl+Shift+End

Move the text insertion point

Character-by-character	Left and right arrows	Left and right arrows
Line-by-line	Up and down arrows	Up and down arrows
Word-by-word	Cmd-left and right arrows	Ctrl+left and right arrows
Paragraph-by-paragraph	Cmd-up and down arrows	Ctrl+up and down arrows
Start of line	Cmd-Option-left arrow	Ctrl+Alt+left arrow *or* Home
End of line	Cmd-Option-right arrow	Ctrl+Alt+right arrow *or* End
Start of story	Cmd-Option-up arrow	Ctrl+Alt+up arrow *or* Ctrl+Home
End of story	Cmd-Option-down arrow	Ctrl+Alt+down arrow Ctrl+End

Drag and drop text

Drag-move*	Drag	Drag
Drag-copy* (Drag and Drop Text on in Preferences > Input Settings	Shift-drag	Shift+drag

*Mac only: If Drag and Drop Text is off in Preferences > Input Settings, press Cmd-Control to move, or press Cmd-Control-Shift-drag to move a copy

Delete text

Previous character	Delete	Backspace
Next character	Shift-Delete *or* Del key	Delete or Shift+Backspace
Previous word	Cmd Delete	Ctrl+Backspace
Next word	Cmd-Shift-Delete	Ctrl+Delete *or* Ctrl+Shift+Backspace
Selected characters	Delete	Backspace

Resize text

Open Character Attributes dialog box, Size field selected	Cmd-Shift-\	Ctrl+Shift+\
Increase size to preset size	Cmd-Shift->	Ctrl+Shift+>
Increase size by 1 point	Cmd-Option-Shift->	Ctrl+Alt+Shift+>
Decrease size to preset size	Cmd-Shift-<	Ctrl+Shift+<
Decrease size by 1 point	Cmd-Option-Shift-<	Ctrl+Alt+Shift+<
Resize text and box*	Cmd-drag handle	Ctrl+drag handle

	Mac OS X	**Windows**
Resize text and box proportionally*	Cmd-Option-Shift-drag handle	Ctrl+Alt+Shift+drag handle

*Works on nonlinked text items only. For type on a path, turn off Item > Edit > Shape.

Text flow

Import Text dialog box (Content tool)	Cmd-E	Ctrl+E
Current page number (use on master page or layout page)	Cmd-3	Ctrl+3
Previous text box page number	Cmd-2	Ctrl+2
Next text box page number	Cmd-4	Ctrl+4
Next column	Enter	Keypad Enter
Next box	Shift-Enter	Shift+Keypad Enter
Save Text	Cmd-Option-E	Ctrl+Alt+E
Open Insert Pages dialog box	Option-drag master page into layout page area	Alt+drag master page into layout page area
Delete selected page icons on Page Layout palette, bypass prompt	Option-click Delete button	Alt+click Delete button
Apply master page	Select layout page icon(s), then Option-click master page icon	Select layout page icon(s), then Alt+click master page icon

Paragraph formats

Paragraph Attributes dialog box, Formats pane	Cmd-Shift-F	Ctrl+Shift+F
Paragraph Attributes dialog box, Leading field	Cmd-Shift-E	Ctrl+Shift+E
Paragraph Attributes dialog box, Tabs pane	Cmd-Shift-T	Ctrl+Shift+T
Paragraph Attributes dialog box, Rules pane	Cmd-Shift-N	Ctrl+Shift+N
Increase leading 1 point	Cmd-Shift-"	Ctrl+Shift+"
Decrease leading 1 point	Cmd-Shift-:	Ctrl+Shift+:
Increase leading $1/10$ point	Cmd-Option-Shift-"	Ctrl+Alt+Shift+"
Decrease leading $1/10$ point	Cmd-Option-Shift-:	Ctrl+Alt+Shift+:
Delete all tab stops	Option-click tabs ruler	Alt+click tabs ruler
Right indent tab	Option-Tab (in text box)	Shift+Tab
Display Suggested Hyphenation	Cmd-Option-Shift-H	Ctrl+Alt+Shift+H
Set button in Tabs pane in Paragraph Attributes dialog box	Cmd-S	Alt+S
Open H&Js dialog box	Cmd-Option-J *or* Option-Shift-F11	Ctrl+Alt+J *or* Ctrl+Shift+F11

	Mac OS X	Windows
Copy formats from one paragraph to another in the same story	Select paragraphs to be formatted, then Option-Shift-click in source paragraph	Select paragraphs to be formatted, then Alt+Shift+click in source paragraph

Fonts

	Mac OS X	Windows
Display Measurements palette and select font field (Classic tab) NEW	Cmd-Option-Shift-M	Ctrl+Alt+Shift+M
Display Measurements palette and insert cursor in font field (Classic tab)	Shift-F9	Shift+F9
Select next font	Select text, then Option-F9	Select text, then Ctrl+F9
Select previous font	Select text, then Option-Shift-F9	Select text, then Ctrl+Shift+F9
Insert one Zapf Dingbats character*	Cmd-Option-Z, then type character	Ctrl+Shift+Z, then type character
Insert one Symbol character	Cmd-Option-Q, then type character	Ctrl+Shift+Q, then type character

*For this keyboard shortcut to work, in Preferences > Application > Undo, the Redo Key setting must be Cmd-Shift-Z/Ctrl-Shift-Z.

Baseline shift

	Mac OS X	Windows
Baseline Shift-upward 1 point	Cmd-Option-Shift-+ (plus)	Ctrl+Alt+Shift+)
Baseline Shift-downward 1 point	Cmd-Option-Shift-– (minus)	Ctrl+Alt+Shift+(

Style text

	Mac OS X	Windows
Character Attributes dialog box	Cmd-Shift-D	Ctrl+Shift+D

Text style toggles:

	Mac OS X	Windows
Plain text	Cmd-Shift-P	Ctrl+Shift+P
Bold	Cmd-Shift-B	Ctrl+Shift+B
Italic	Cmd-Shift-I	Ctrl+Shift+I
Underline	Cmd-Shift-U	Ctrl+Shift+U
Word Underline	Cmd-Shift-W	Ctrl+Shift+W
Outline	Cmd-Shift-O	Ctrl+Shift+O
Shadow	Cmd-Shift-S	Ctrl+Shift+S
All Caps	Cmd-Shift-K	Ctrl+Shift+K
Small Caps	Cmd-Shift-H	Ctrl+Shift+H
Strike Thru	Cmd-Shift-/	Ctrl+Shift+/
Superscript	Cmd-Shift-+ (plus)	Ctrl+Shift+0 (zero)
Subscript	Cmd-Shift-– (minus)	Ctrl+Shift+9
Superior	Cmd-Shift-V	Ctrl+Shift+V

	Mac OS X	**Windows**
Horizontal alignment of text		
Left alignment	Cmd-Shift-L	Ctrl+Shift+L
Right alignment	Cmd-Shift-R	Ctrl+Shift+R
Center alignment	Cmd-Shift-C	Ctrl+Shift+C
Justified alignment	Cmd-Shift-J	Ctrl+Shift+J
Forced justify	Cmd-Option-Shift-J	Ctrl+Alt+Shift+J
Tracking and kerning		
Increase Kerning/Tracking 10 units	Cmd-Shift-]	Ctrl+Shift+]
Decrease Kerning/Tracking 10 units	Cmd-Shift-[	Ctrl+Shift+[
Increase Kerning/Tracking 1 unit	Cmd-Option-Shift-]	Ctrl+Alt+Shift+]
Decrease Kerning/Tracking 1 unit	Cmd-Option-Shift-[	Ctrl+Alt+Shift+[
Horizontal/vertical type scale		
Decrease scale 5%	Cmd-[	Ctrl+2
Increase scale 5%	Cmd-]	Ctrl+1
Decrease scale 1%	Cmd-Option-[	Ctrl+Alt+2
Increase scale 1%	Cmd-Option-]	Ctrl+Alt+1
Word space tracking		
Increase Word Space 10 units	Cmd-Shift-Control -]	Ctrl+Shift+2
Decrease Word Space 10 units	Cmd-Shift-Control -[	Ctrl+Shift+1
Increase Word Space 1 unit	Cmd-Option-Shift-Control -]	Ctrl+Alt+Shift+2
Decrease Word Space 1 unit	Cmd-Option-Shift-Control -[	Ctrl+Alt+Shift+1
Special text characters		
New paragraph	Return	Enter
New line	Shift-Return	Shift+Enter
Indent here	Cmd-\	Ctrl+\
Discretionary new line	Cmd-Return	Ctrl+Enter
Discretionary hyphen	Cmd-- (hyphen)	Ctrl+- (hyphen)
Nonbreaking standard hyphen	Cmd-=	Ctrl+=
Nonbreaking standard space	Cmd-Space bar *or* Cmd-5	Ctrl+5
Breaking en space	Option-Space bar	Ctrl+Shift+6
Nonbreaking en space	Cmd-Option-Space bar *or* Cmd-Option-5	Ctrl+Alt+Shift+6
Breaking flex space	Option-Shift-Space bar	Ctrl+Shift+5
Nonbreaking flex space	Cmd-Option-Shift-Space bar	Ctrl+Alt+Shift+5
Nonbreaking en dash	Option-- (hyphen)	Ctrl+Alt+Shift+- (hyphen)
Break at discretionary hyphen only	Cmd-- (hyphen) before first character in word	Ctrl+- (hyphen) before first character in word

	Mac OS X	**Windows**
Nonbreaking em dash	Cmd-Option-=	Ctrl+Alt+Shift+=
Breaking em dash	Option-Shift-– (hyphen)	Ctrl+Shift+=
Breaking punctuation space	Shift-Space bar	Shift+Space
Nonbreaking punctuation space	Cmd-Shift-Space bar	Ctrl+Shift+Space

For quotation marks, see page 130.

Resize tables

Resize table, rows, and columns (not content) proportionally	Option-Shift-drag	Alt+Shift+drag
Resize table, rows, columns, and content non-proportionally	Cmd-drag	Ctrl+drag
Resize table to a square; content doesn't resize	Shift-drag	Shift+drag
Resize table, rows, columns, and content proportionally	Cmd-Option-Shift-drag	Ctrl+Alt+Shift+drag
Resize table, rows, and columns (not content) non-proportionally	No modifier keys	

Jump between table cells *(non-linked cells only)*

Jump from one cell to the right or from the end of a row to the beginning of the next row	Control-Tab	Ctrl+Tab
Jump back to previous cell	Control-Shift-Tab	Ctrl+Shift+Tab
Jump one character at a time within a cell or from the end of one cell to the beginning of the next cell	Right arrow	Right arrow

Import a picture

Import Picture dialog box (Item or Content tool)	Cmd-E	Ctrl+E

Pictures and picture boxes or Béziers

Center picture in box	Cmd-Shift-M	Ctrl+Shift+M
Move picture in box 1 point	Arrow keys (Content tool)	Arrow keys (Content tool)
Move picture in box ¹⁄₁₀ point	Option-arrow keys (Content tool)	Alt+arrow keys (Content tool)
Fit picture to box	Cmd-Shift-F	Ctrl+Shift+F
Fit picture to box (maintain aspect ratio)	Cmd-Option-Shift-F	Ctrl+Alt+Shift+F
Enlarge picture in 5% increments	Cmd-Option-Shift->	Ctrl+Alt+Shift+>
Reduce picture in 5% increments	Cmd-Option-Shift-<	Ctrl+Alt+Shift+<
Constrain item or bounding box to square or circle	Shift-drag	Shift+drag
Resize box proportionally	Option-Shift-drag	Alt+Shift+drag

	Mac OS X	Windows
Resize picture and box (Item > Edit > Shape off for Béziers)	Cmd-drag	Ctrl+drag
Resize picture and box (constrain proportions of box, not picture)	Cmd-Shift-drag	Ctrl+Shift+drag
Resize picture and box (maintain aspect ratio)	Cmd-Option-Shift-drag	Ctrl+Alt+Shift+drag

Picture styling *(grayscale)*

Invert	Cmd-Shift- – (hyphen)	Ctrl+Shift+– (hyphen)
Halftone (grayscale, line art only)	Cmd-Shift-H	Ctrl+Shift+H

Runaround/clipping

Modify dialog box, Runaround pane	Cmd-T	Ctrl+T
Edit runaround path (Non-White Areasor Picture Bounds Type)	Option-F4	Ctrl+F10
Modify dialog box, Clipping pane	Cmd-Option-T	Ctrl+Alt+T
Edit clipping path	Option-Shift-F4	Ctrl+Shift+F10

Lines

Increase width to preset size	Cmd-Shift->	Ctrl+Shift+>
Increase width by 1 point	Cmd-Option-Shift->	Ctrl+Alt+Shift+>
Decrease width to preset size	Cmd-Shift-<	Ctrl+Shift+<
Decrease width by 1 point	Cmd-Option-Shift-<	Ctrl+Alt+Shift+<
Line Width field, Modify dialog box	Cmd-Shift-\	Ctrl+Shift+\
Constrain angle to increment of 45°	Shift-drag	Shift+drag
Constrain to current angle	Option-Shift-drag	Alt+Shift+drag

Bézier box or line (or clipping path)

Item > Edit > Shape toggle on/off	Shift-F4	F10
Add a point*	Option-click line segment	Alt+click line segment
Delete a point*	Option-click point	Alt+click point
Constrain movement of line, point, or handle to increment of 45°*	Shift-drag	Shift+drag
Temporarily suspend text reflow	Space bar	Space bar
Retract one curve handle	Option-click handle	Alt+click handle

With Edit > Shape checked

Retract both curve handles	Control-Shift-click point**	Ctrl+Shift+click point
Expose/create curve handle	Control-Shift-drag point**	Ctrl+Shift+drag point
Select all points in active item (combined items)	Cmd-Shift-A *or* triple-click point	Ctrl+Shift+A *or* triple-click point
Select all points in active item (single path)	Double-click point *or* Cmd-Shift-A	Ctrl+Shift+A *or* double-click point

	Mac OS X	**Windows**
Convert Bézier line to filled-center Bézier box	Option-Item menu > Shape > ◯	Alt+item menu > Shape > ◯

***If Zoom (instead of Contextual Menu) is the current Control Key Activates setting in Preferences > Application > Input Settings, omit the Shift key.*

As Bézier is being drawn

Move point or adjust handle	Cmd	Ctrl
Convert corner point to smooth point	Cmd-Option-Ctrl-drag from corner point	Ctrl+click, press Ctrl-F2, then drag from corner point
Convert smooth point to corner point	Cmd-Option-Ctrl-click smooth point	Ctrl+Alt+click smooth point
Retract one curve handle	Cmd-Option-click curve handle	Ctrl+Alt+click curve handle
Delete selected Bézier point while drawing shape	Delete	Backspace

Convert Bézier point

To a corner point	Option-F1	Ctrl+F1
To a smooth point	Option-F2	Ctrl+F2
To a symmetrical point	Option-F3	Ctrl+F3
Corner to smooth	Cmd-Option-Ctrl-drag from point	Ctrl+Shift+drag from point
Smooth to corner	Cmd-Option-Ctrl-click point	Ctrl+Alt+Shift+click point

Convert Bézier segment

Curved to a straight segment	Option-Shift-F1	Ctrl+Shift+F1
Straight to a curved segment	Option-Shift-F2	Ctrl+Shift+F2

Style sheets

Open Style Sheets dialog box	Shift-F11	Shift+F11
Open Edit Style Sheet dialog box	Cmd-click style sheet with Content tool	Ctrl+click style sheet with Content tool
Display Edit Style Sheet menu	Ctrl-click style sheet name	Right+click style sheet name
Apply No Style, then style sheet	Option-click style name on Style Sheets palette	Alt+click style name on Style Sheets palette

Note: If an F key is chosen as a Keyboard Equivalent for a style sheet, it will override that F key's default command.

Color

Open Colors dialog box	Cmd-click color on Colors palette *or* Shift-F12	Ctrl+click color on Color palette *or* Shift+F12
Apply color to multiple items via Colors palette	Select one item, then Cmd-drag swatch over each item	Select one item, then Ctrl+drag swatch over each item

	Mac OS X	**Windows**

Anchored boxes

| Text to box (anchor box and delete text) | Option-choose Style menu > Text to Box | Alt+choose Style menu > Text to Box |

Check spelling

Check Spelling > Word	Cmd-L	Ctrl+W
Check Spelling > Story	Cmd-Option-L	Ctrl+Alt+W
Check Spelling > Layout	Cmd-Option-Shift-L	Ctrl+Alt+Shift+W

In the Check Spelling dialog box:

Lookup	Cmd-L	Alt+L
Skip	Cmd-S	Alt+S
Add current suspect word to open auxiliary dictionary	Cmd-A	Alt+A
Add all suspect words to current auxiliary dictionary	Option-Shift-click Done button	Alt+Shift+click Close button

Find/Change

Find/Change palette	Cmd-F	Ctrl-F
Change Find Next button to Find First in Find/Change	Hold down Option	Hold down Alt
Close Find/Change palette	Cmd-Option-F	Ctrl+Alt+F
Wild card (Find what)	Cmd-?	Curl+?
Space	Space bar	Space bar
Tab	\t	\t *or* Ctrl+Tab
New paragraph	Cmd-Return *or* \p	Ctrl+Enter *or* \p
New line	Cmd-Shift-Return *or* \n	Ctrl+Shift+Enter *or* \n
New column	Cmd-Enter *or* \c	\c
New box	Cmd-Shift-Enter *or* \b	\b
Punctuation space	Cmd-. (period) *or* \.	Ctrl+. (period) *or* \.
Flex space	Cmd-Shift-F *or* \f	Ctrl+Shift+F *or* \f
Backslash	Cmd-\ *or* \\	Ctrl+\ *or* \\
Previous box page number character	Cmd-2 *or* \2	Ctrl+2 *or* \2
Current box page number character	Cmd-3 *or* \3	Ctrl+3 *or* \3
Next box page number character	Cmd-4 *or* \4	Ctrl+4 *or* \4
Utilities > Line Check command, jump to next instance	Cmd-;	Ctrl+;

Indexing

| Select Text field | Cmd-Option-I | Ctrl+Alt+I |
| Add selected entry | Cmd-Option-Shift-I | Ctrl+Alt+Shift+I |

	Mac OS X	**Windows**
Edit selected index entry *(Mac OS X only)*	Double-click	

Compare components

Compare two style sheets, colors, lists, H&Js, dashes & stripes, or print styles	Open dialog box from Edit menu, Cmd-click two components, then Option- click Append (Import button in Print Styles)	Open dialog box from Edit menu, Ctrl+click two components, then Alt+ click Append (Import button in Print Styles)

Web

Page Properties dialog box *(Web layouts only)*	Cmd-Option-Shift-A	Ctrl+Alt+Shift+A
New XML dialog box	Cmd-Shift-X	Ctrl+Shift+X

Preferences

Preferences dialog box, last displayed pane	Cmd-Option-Shift-Y	Ctrl+Alt+Shift+Y
Preferences dialog box, Paragraph pane	Cmd-Option-Y	Ctrl+Alt+Y
Preferences dialog box, Trapping pane	Option-Shift-F12	Ctrl+Shift+F12
Preferences dialog box, Tools pane	Double-click item creation *or* Zoom tool	Double-click item creation *or* Zoom tool

Output

Print	Cmd-P	Ctrl+P
Output Job dialog box	Cmd-Option-P	Ctrl+Alt+P
Save Page as EPS	Cmd-Option-Shift-S	Ctrl+Alt+Shift+S
Usage dialog box, Font Usage	F13	F2
Usage dialog box, Picture Usage *(Mac OS X only)*	Option-F13	

Index

Index

Index

Index

Register this Book!

Stop! Don't turn this page until you've registered this book at the Peachpit Press Web site! Benefits of registration include access to a chapter on "Web Layouts" in PDF form. Remember that this material is provided for your own personal use only. Please do not redistribute any of it.

To register, go to www.peachpit.com/ bookstore/register.asp. Enter the book's ISBN: 0321358279. You'll then be prompted to log in to peachpit.com or create an account if this is your first visit. After you register the book, a link to the supplemental content will be listed on your My Registered Books page. Come back to this page often for updated content!